Hebraic Literature

Translations from

THE TALMUD
MIDRASHIM and
KABBALA

TUDOR PUBLISHING CO.

NEW YORK

1936

SPECIAL INTRODUCTION

Among the absurd notions as to what the Talmud **was**, given credence in the Middle Ages, one was that it was a man! The mediæval priest or peasant was perhaps wiser than he knew. Almost, might we say, the Talmud was Man, for it is a record of the doings, the beliefs, the usages, the hopes, the sufferings, the patience, the humor, the mentality, and the morality of the Jewish people for half a millennium.

What is the Talmud? There is more than one answer. Ostensibly it is the *corpus juris* of the Jews from about the first century before the Christian era to about the fourth after it. But we shall see as we proceed that the Talmud was much more than this. The very word "Law" in Hebrew — "Torah" — means more than its translation would imply. The Jew interpreted his whole religion in terms of law. It is his name in fact, for the Bible's first five books — the Pentateuch. To explain what the Talmud is we must first explain the theory of its growth, more remarkable perhaps than the work itself. What was that theory? The Divine Law was revealed to Moses, not only through the Commands that were found written in the Bible, but also through all the later rules and regulations of post-exilic days. These additional laws it was presumed were handed down orally from Moses to Joshua, thence to the Prophets, and later still transmitted to the Scribes, and eventually to the Rabbis. The reason why the Rabbis ascribed to Moses the laws that they later evolved, was due to their intense reverence for Scripture, and their modest sense of their own authority and qualification. "If the men of old were giants then we are pigmies," said they. They felt and believed that all duty for the guidance of man was found in the Bible either directly or inferentially. Their motto was then, "Search the Scriptures," and they did search them with a literalness and a painstaking thoroughness never since repeated. Not a word, not a letter escaped them. Every redundancy of expression was freighted with meaning, every repetition was made to give birth to new truth. Some of the inferences were logical and natural, some artificial and far-fetched, but all ingenious. Sometimes the method was inductive and sometimes deductive. That is, occasionally a needed law was promulgated by the Jewish Sanhedrin, and then its authority sought in the Scripture, or the Scripture would be sought in the first instance to reveal new law.

So while the Jewish code, religious and civil, continued to grow during the era of the Restoration of the second Temple, to meet the more complex conditions of later times, still the theory was maintained that all was evolved from original Scripture and always transmitted, either written or oral, from Moses from Mount Sinai. It was not, however, till the year 219 after the Christian era that a compiled summary of the so-called oral law was made — perhaps compiled from earlier summaries — by Rabbi Jehudah Hanassi (the Prince), and the added work was called the Mishnah or Second Law. Mark the date. We have passed the period of the fall of Judea's nationality. And it was these very academies in which the Jewish tradition — the Jewish Law was studied, that kept alive the Jewish people as a religious community after they had ceased to be a nation. This Mishnah, divided into six *sedarim* or chapters, and subdivided into thirty-six treatises, became now in the academies of Palestine, and later in Babylonia, the text of further legal elaboration, with the theory of deduction from Scripture still maintained.

Although the life of denationalized Israel was much narrower and more circumscribed, with fewer outlets to their capacities, nevertheless the new laws deduced from the Mishnah code in the academies grew far larger than the original source, while the discussions which grew around each Halacha, as the final decision was termed, and which was usually transmitted with the decision, grew so voluminous that it became gradually impossible to retain the complex tradition in the memory — remarkable as the Oriental memory was and is. That fact, added to the growing persecutions from Israel's over-lords, and the consequent precarious fate of these precious traditions, made it necessary to write them down in spite of the prejudice against committing the oral law to writing at all. This work was undertaken by Rav Asche and his disciples, and was completed before the year 500. The Mishnah, together with the laws that later grew out of it, called also Gamara, or Commentary, from the Talmud. While the Palestinian school evolved a Gamara from the Mishnah which is called the "Palestinian Talmud," it was the tradition of the Babylonian academies, far vaster because they continued for so many more centuries, that is the Talmud *per se*, that great work of 2,947 folio leaves. Were we to continue the tradition further, we might show how often this vast legal compilation was the subject of further commentary, discussion and deduction by yet later scholars. But that takes us beyond our theme and is another story.

In forming an estimate of these laws, we must first remember that they belonged to the days when religion and state were one. So we shall find priestly laws mixed up with police laws, sanitary regulations side by side with regulations of sanctity, the injunctions teaching political economy and morality almost in the same line. It should rather then be compared to codes of law than to religious scriptures, though often there the comparison would be incomplete, since the religious atmosphere pervaded even the most secular circumstance of the life of the Jew. There was no secular. The meanest function in life must be brought in relation to the great Divine. This must be understood in studying the Talmud, this must be understood in studying the Jew. As law, it compares favorably with the Roman code — its contemporary in part. In the treatment of a criminal it is almost quixotically humane. It abhors the shedding of blood, and no man can be put to death on circumstantial evidence. Many of its injunctions are intensely minute and hair-splitting to the extreme of casuistry. Yet these elements are familiar in the interpretation of law, not only in the olden time, but in some measure even to-day. There are instances where Talmudic law is tenderer than the Biblical; for example, the *lex talionis* is softened into an equivalent.

Yet the legal does not form the whole of the Talmud, nor perhaps the part that would most interest the casual reader or the world at large. It is the dry, prosaic half. There is a poetic half, let us say a homiletic half, what we call Agada, as distinct from the legal portion called Halacha. The term Agada, "narrative," is wofully insufficient to describe the diverse material that falls under this head, for it comprehends all the discursive elements that come up in the legal discussions in the old Babylonian and Palestinian academies. These elements are occasionally biographical, — fragments of the lives of the great scholars, occasionally historical, — little bits of Israel's long tragedy, occasionally didactic, — facts, morals, life lessons taught by the way; occasionally anecdotic, stories told to relieve the monotony of discussion; not infrequently fanciful; bits of philosophy, old folk-lore, weird imaginings, quaint beliefs, superstitions and humor. They are presented haphazard, most irrelevantly introduced in between the complex discussions, breaking the thread that however is never lost, but always taken up again.

From this point of view the Talmud is a great maze and apparently the simplest roads lead off into strange, winding by-paths. It is hard to deduce any distinct system of ethics, any consistent philosophy, any coherent doctrine. Yet patience rewards the student here too, and from this confused medley of material, he can build the intellectual world of the early mediæval Jew. In the realm of doctrine we find that "original sin," "vicarious atonement," and "everlasting punishment," are denied. Man is made the author of his own salvation. Life beyond the grave is still progressive; the soul is pre-existent.

A suggestion of the wit and wisdom of the Talmud may be gathered from the following quotations: —

SPECIAL INTRODUCTION

A single light answers as well for a hundred men as for one.

The ass complains of cold even in July.

A myrtle in the desert remains a myrtle.

Teach thy tongue to say, "I do not know."

Hospitality is an expression of Divine worship.

Thy friend has a friend, and thy friend's friend has a friend; be discreet.

Attend no auctions if thou hast no money.

Rather flay a carcass, than be idly dependent on charity.

The place honors not the man, 'tis the man who gives honor to the place.

Drain not the waters of thy well while other people may desire them.

The rose grows among thorns.

Two pieces of coin in one bag make more noise than a hundred.

The rivalry of scholars advances science.

Truth is heavy, therefore few care to carry it.

He who is loved by man is loved by God.

Use thy noble vase to-day; to-morrow it may break.

The soldiers fight and the kings are heroes.

Commit a sin twice, it will seem a sin no longer.

The world is saved by the breath of the school children.

A miser is as wicked as an idolater.

Do not make woman weep, for God counts her tears.

The best preacher is the heart; the best teacher time; the best book the world; the best friend God.

The philosophy in the Talmud, rather than the philosophy of it, has been made the subject of separate treatment just as the whole of the Agada has been drawn out of the Talmud and published as a separate work.

What is the Talmud to the Jew to-day? It is literature rather than law. He no longer goes to the voluminous Talmud to find specific injunction for specific need. Search in that vast sea would be tedious and unfruitful. Its legal portion has long been codified in separate digests. Maimonides was the first to classify Talmudic law. Still later one Ascheri prepared a digest called the "Four Rows," in which the decisions of later Rabbis were incorporated.

But it was the famous Shulchan Aruch (a prepared table) written by Joseph Caro in the sixteenth century, that formed the most complete code of Talmudic law enlarged to date, and accepted as religious authority by the orthodox Jews to-day.

I have already referred to the literature that has grown out of the Talmud. The "Jewish Encyclopedia" treats every law recognized by nations from the Talmudic standpoint. This will give the world a complete Talmudic point of view. In speaking of it as literature, it lacks perhaps that beauty of form in its language which the stricter demand as literature *sine qua non*, and yet its language is unique. It is something more than terse, for many a word is a whole sentence. Written in Aramaic, it contains many words in the languages of the nations with whom Israel came in contact—Greek, Roman, Persian, and words from other tongues.

Like the Jew, the Talmud has had a history, almost as checkered as that of its creator. Like him it was singled out for persecution. Louis IX. burned twenty-four cart-loads of Talmuds in Paris. Its right of survival had often been wrested through church synods and councils. It has been banned, it has been excommunicated, it has been made the subject of popish bulls; but it was in the sixteenth century that the Benedictine Monks made a particular determined effort to destroy it. Fortunately they knew not the times. It was the age of Humanism, the forerunner of the Reformation, and the Talmud found its ablest defender in the great Christian humanist, John Reuchlin. He was the one first to tell his co-religionists, " Do not condemn the Talmud before you understand it. Burning is no argument. Instead of burning all Jewish literature, it were better to found chairs in the universities for its exposition." The cause of liberality and light gained the day, and the printing-press decided the perpetuation of the Talmud.

In the second stage of its persecution the censor figures. His Philistine pen passed ruthlessly over everything that seemed to hint at criticism of the Church ; but not content with expunging the heretical and the inferentially heretical, the censor at times went even so far as to erase sentiments particularly lofty, in order that the Talmud should not have the credit of expounding noble doctrine, nor the Jew the advantage of studying it.

But the latest stage of its persecution belongs to more modern days, when inquisitions were out of date and monkish claws were cut. The traducer would spitefully engage the services of some renegade Jew, to gather from the Talmud all portions and passages that might seem grotesque and ridiculous, so that the world might form an unfavorable impression of the Talmud and of the people who treasure it. This has been done with so much success that up till very recently the Gentile world, including the Christian clergy, knew of the Talmud only through these unfortunate perversions and caricatures. Imagine the citation of a chapter from *Leviticus* and one from *Chronicles*, of some vindictive passages in the *Psalms*, of a few skeptical bits in *Ecclesiastes* and *Job*, and one or two of the barbaric stories in *Judges*, to be offered to the world as a fair picture of the Bible, and you will understand the sort of treatment the Talmud has received from the world at large and the kind of estimate it has been given opportunity to form.

What is the value of the Talmud for the Jew? Certainly its greatest value was rendered in the Middle Ages, when literature was scant and copies of the few books in existence were rarer. When the Jew was shut out of the world's pleasure and the world's culture and barred up in Ghetto slums, then it was that the Talmud became his recreation and his consolation, feeding his mind and his faith. In this way it not only became in the Middle Ages a picture of the Jew, but largely formed his character. It made him a keen dialectician, tempered with a thoughtful and poetic touch. It fostered his patience and his humor and kept vivid his ideals. It linked him with the Orient, while living in the Occident and made him a bridge between the old and the new.

To the world at large it has great value archæologically. Here are preserved ancient laws, glint lights on past history, forgotten forms in the classic tongues, and pictures of old civilization. No one criticism can cover the whole work.

It is so many-sided. It includes so many different standards of worth and value. If we take it as a whole, it is good, it is bad and indifferent; it is trash and it is treasure; it is dust and it is diamonds; it is potsherd and it is pearls; and in the hands of impartial scholars, it is one of the great monuments of mental achievement, one of the world's wonders.

Maurice H. Harris

CONTENTS

THE TALMUD

THE TALMUD, THE MIDRASHIM, AND KABBALA

WHERE do we learn that the Shechinah rests even upon one who studies the law? In Exodus xx. 24, where it is written, "In all places where I record my name I will come unto thee, and I will bless thee."

Berachoth, fol. 6, col. 1.

One pang of remorse at a man's heart is of more avail than many stripes applied to him. (See Prov. xvii. 10.)

Ibid., fol. 7, col. 1.

"Here, O Israel, the Lord our God is one Lord!" (Deut. vi. 4.) Whosoever prolongs the utterance of the word one, shall have his days and years prolonged to him. So also *Zohar*, syn. tit. ii.

Ibid., fol. 13, col. 2.

Once, as the Rabbis tell us, the Roman Government issued a decree forbidding Israel to study the law. Whereupon Pappus, the son of Yehudah, one day found Rabbi Akiva teaching it openly to multitudes, whom he had gathered round him to hear it. "Akiva," said he, "art thou not afraid of the Government?" "List," was the reply, "and I will tell thee how it is by a parable. It is with me as with the fishes whom a fox, walking once by a river's side, saw darting distractedly to and fro in the stream; and, addressing, inquired, 'From what, pray, are ye fleeing?' 'From the nets,' they replied, 'which the children of men have set to ensnare us.' 'Why, then,' rejoined the fox, 'not try the dry land with me, where you and I can live together, as our fathers managed to do before us?' 'Surely,' exclaimed they, 'thou art not he of whom we have heard so much as the most cunning of animals, for herein thou art not wise, but foolish. For if we have cause to fear where it is natural for us to live, how much more reason have we to do so where we needs must die!'

(3)

Just so," continued Akiva, "is it with us who study the
law, in which (Deut. xxx. 20) it is written, 'He is thy
life and the length of thy days;' for if we suffer while
we study the law, how much more shall we if we neglect
it?" Not many days after, it is related, this Rabbi Akiva
was apprehended and thrown into prison. As it happened,
they led him out for execution just at the time when
"Hear, O Israel!" fell to be repeated, and as they tore his
flesh with currycombs, and as he was with long-drawn
breath sounding forth the word one, his soul departed from
him. Then came forth a voice from heaven which said,
"Blessed art thou, Rabbi Akiva, for thy soul and the word
one left thy body together." *Berachoth*, fol. 61, col. 2.

The badger, as it existed in the days of Moses, was an
animal of unique type, and the learned are not agreed
whether it was a wild one or a domestic. It had only one
horn on its forehead; and was assigned for the time to
Moses, who made a covering of its skin for the tabernacle;
after which it became extinct, having served the purpose of
its existence. Rabbi Yehudah says, "The ox, also, which
the first man, Adam, sacrificed, had but one horn on its
forehead." *Shabbath*, fol. 28, col. 2.

Once a Gentile came to Shamai, and said, "Proselytize
me, but on condition that thou teach me the whole law,
even the whole of it, while I stand upon one leg." Shamai
drove him off with the builder's rod which he held in his
hand. When he came to Hillel with the same challenge,
Hillel converted him by answering him on the spot, "That
which is hateful to thyself, do not do to thy neighbor.
This is the whole law, and the rest is its commentary."
(Tobit, iv. 15; Matt. vii. 12.) *Ibid.*, fol. 31, col. 1.

When Rabbi Shimon ben Yochai and his son, Rabbi Elazar, came out of their cave on a Friday afternoon, they
saw an old man hurrying along with two bunches of myrtle
in his hand. "What," said they, accosting him, "dost
thou want with these?" "To smell them in honor of the
Sabbath," was the reply. "Would not one bunch," they
remarked, "be enough for that purpose?" "Nay," the old
man replied; "one is in honor of 'Remember' ⎰Exod.

xxii. 28); and one in honor of 'Keep' (Deut. v. 8)."
Thereupon Rabbi Shimon remarked to his son, "Behold
how the commandments are regarded by Israel!"

Ibid., fol. 33, col. 2.

Not one single thing has God created in vain. He created the snail as a remedy for a blister; the fly for the
sting of a wasp; the gnat for the bite of a serpent; the
serpent itself for healing the itch (or the scab); and
the lizard (or the spider) for the sting of a scorpion.

Ibid., fol. 77. col. 2.

When a man is dangerously ill, the law grants dispensation, for it says, "You may break one Sabbath on his behalf, that he may be preserved to keep many Sabbaths."

Shabbath, fol. 151, col. 2.

Once when Rabbi Ishmael paid a visit to Rabbi Shimon,
he was offered a cup of wine, which he at once, without
being asked twice, accepted, and drained at one draught.
"Sir," said his host, "dost thou not know the proverb,
that he who drinks off a cup of wine at a draught is a
greedy one?" "Ah!" was the answer, "that fits not this
case; for thy cup is small, thy wine is sweet, and my
stomach is capacious." *P'sachim*, fol. 86, col. 2.

At the time when Nimrod the wicked had cast our
Father Abraham into the fiery furnace, Gabriel stood forth
in the presence of the Holy One — blessed be He! — and
said, "Lord of the universe, let me, I pray thee, go down
and cool the furnace, and deliver that righteous one from
it." Then the Holy One — blessed be He! — said unto
him, "I am One in my world and he is one in his world;
it is more becoming that He who is one should deliver
him who is one." But as God does not withhold His reward from any creature, He said to Gabriel, "For this thy
good intention, be thine the honor of rescuing three of his
descendants." At the time when Nebuchadnezzar the
wicked cast Hananiah, Mishael, and Azariah into the fiery
furnace, Yourkami, the prince of hail, arose before God and
said, "Lord of the universe, let me, I pray thee, go down
and cool the fiery furnace, and rescue these righteous men
from its fury." Whereupon Gabriel interposed, and said,

"God's power is not to be demonstrated thus, for thou art the prince of hail, and everybody knows that water quenches fire; but I, the prince of fire, will go down and cool the flame within and intensify it without (so as to consume the executioners), and thus will I perform a miracle within a miracle." Then the Holy One — blessed be He! — said to him, "Go down." Upon which Gabriel exclaimed, "Verily the truth of the Lord endureth forever!" (Ps. cxvii. 2.)   *P'sachim*, fol. 118, col. 1.

One peppercorn to-day is better than a basketful of pumpkins to-morrow.   *Chaggigah*, fol. 10, col. 1.

One day of a year is counted for a whole year.
                        Rosh Hashanah, fol. 2, col. 2.

If a king be crowned on the twenty-ninth of Adar (the last month of the sacred year), on the morrow — the first of Nissan — it is reckoned that he commences his second year, that being the new year's day for royal and ecclesiastical affairs.

For the sake of one righteous man the whole world is preserved in existence, as it is written (Prov. x. 25), "The righteous man is an everlasting foundation."
                        Yoma, fol. 38, col. 2.

Rabbi Meyer saith, "Great is repentance, because for the sake of one that truly repenteth the whole world is pardoned; as it is written (Hosea xiv. 4), 'I will heal their backsliding, I will love them freely, for mine anger is turned away from him.'" It is not said, "from them," but "from him."   *Ibid.*, fol. 86, col. 2.

He who observes one precept, in addition to those which, as originally laid upon him, he has discharged, shall receive favor from above, and is equal to him who has fulfilled the whole law.   *Kiddushin*, fol. 39, col. 2.

If any man vow a vow by only one of all the utensils of the altar, he has vowed by the corban, even although he did not mention the word in his oath. Rabbi Yehuda says, "He who swears by the word Jerusalem is as though he had said nothing."   *Nedarim*, fol. 10, col. 2.

Balaam was lame in one foot and blind in one eye.
   Soteh, fol. 10, col. 1, and *Sanhedrin*, fol. 105, col. 1.

One wins eternal life after a struggle of years; another finds it in one hour (see Luke xxiii. 43).

Avodah Zarah, fol. 17, col. 1.

This saying is applied by Rabbi the Holy to Rabbi Eliezar, the son of Durdia, a profligate who recommended himself to the favor of heaven by one prolonged act of determined penitence, placing his head between his knees and groaning and weeping till his soul departed from him, and his sin and misery along with it; for at the moment of death a voice from heaven came forth and said, "Rabbi Eliezar, the son of Durdia, is appointed to life everlasting." When Rabbi the Holy heard this, he wept, and said, "One wins eternal life after a struggle of years; another finds it in one hour." (Compare Luke xv. 11–32.)

Whosoever destroyeth one soul of Israel, Scripture counts it to him as though he had destroyed the whole world; and whoso preserveth one soul of Israel, Scripture counts it as though he had preserved the whole world.

Sanhedrin, fol. 37, col. 1.

The greatness of God is infinite; for while with one die man impresses many coins and all are exactly alike, the King of kings, the Holy One — blessed be He! — with one die impresses the same image (of Adam) on all men, and yet not one of them is like his neighbor. So that every one ought to say, "For myself is the world created."

Ibid., fol. 37, col. 1.

"He caused the lame to mount on the back of the blind, and judged them both as one." Antoninus said to the Rabbi, "Body and soul might each plead right of acquittal at the day of judgment." "How so?" he asked. "The body might plead that it was the soul that had sinned, and urge, saying, 'See, since the departure of the soul I have lain in the grave as still as a stone.' And the soul might plead, 'It was the body that sinned, for since the day I left it, I have flitted about in the air as innocent as a bird.'" To which the Rabbi replied and said, "Whereunto this thing is like, I will tell thee in a parable. It is like unto a king who had an orchard with some fine young fig trees planted in it. He set two gardeners to take care of them, of whom one was lame and the other blind. One day the lame one said to the blind

'I see some fine figs in the garden; come, take me on thy
shoulders, and we will pluck them and eat them.' By and
by the lord of the garden came, and missing the fruit from
the fig trees, began to make inquiry after them. The
lame one, to excuse himself, pleaded, 'I have no legs to
walk with;' and the blind one, to excuse himself, pleaded,
'I have no eyes to see with.' What did the lord of the
garden do? He caused the lame to mount upon the back
of the blind, and judged them both as one." So likewise
will God re-unite soul and body, and judge them both as
one together; as it is written (Ps. l. 4), "He shall call to
the heavens from above, and to the earth, that He may
judge His people." "He shall call to the heavens from
above," that alludes to the soul; "and to the earth, that
He may judge His people," that refers to the body.

Sanhedrin, fol. 91, cols. 1, 2.

Rabbi Yehudah, surnamed the Holy, the editor of the Mishnah, is the
personage here and elsewhere spoken of as the Rabbi by pre-eminence.
He was an intimate friend of the Roman Emperor Antoninus Pius.

One thing obtained with difficulty is far better than a
hundred things procured with ease.

Avoth d' Rab. Nathan, ch. 3.

In the name of Rav, Rabbi Yehoshua bar Abba says,
"Whoso buys a scroll of the law in the market seizes possession of another's meritorious act; but if he himself copies
out a scroll of the law, Scripture considers him as if he
had himself received it direct from Mount Sinai." "Nay,"
adds Rav Yehudah, in the name of Rav, "even if he has
amended one letter in it, Scripture considers him as if he
had written it out entirely." *Menachoth*, fol. 30, col. 1.

He who forgets one thing that he has learned breaks a
negative commandment; for it is written (Deut. iv. 9),
"Take heed to thyself . . . lest thou forget the things."

Menachoth, fol. 99, col. 2.

A proselyte who has taken it upon himself to observe
the law, but is suspected of neglecting one point, is to be
suspected of being guilty of neglecting the whole law, and
therefore regarded as an apostate Israelite, and to be punished accordingly.   *Bechoroth*, fol. 30, col. 2.

It is written (Gen. xxviii. 11), "And he took from the stones of the place;" and again it is written (ver. 18), "And he took the stone." Rabbi Isaac says this teaches that all these stones gathered themselves together into one place, as if each were eager that the saint should lay his head upon it. It happened, as the Rabbis tell us, that all the stones were swallowed up by one another, and thus merged into one stone. *Chullin*, fol. 91, col. 2.

Though the Midrash and two of the Targums, that of Jonathan and the Yerushalmi, tell the same fanciful story about these stones, Aben Ezra and R. Shemuel ben Meir among others adopt the opposite and common-sense interpretation which assigns to the word in Gen. xxviii. 11, no such occult meaning.

The psalms commencing "Blessed is the man" and "Why do the heathen rage" constitute but one psalm.
Berachoth, fol. 9, col. 2.

The former Chasidim used to sit still one hour, and then pray for one hour, and then again sit still for one hour.
Ibid., fol. 32, col. 2.

All the benedictions in the Temple used to conclude with the words "Blessed be the Lord God of Israel unto eternity;" but when the Sadducees, corrupting the faith, maintained that there was only one world, it was enacted that they should conclude with the words "from eternity unto eternity." *Berachoth*, fol. 54, col. 1.

The Sadducees (Zadokim), so called after Zadok their master, as is known, stood rigidly by the original Mosaic code, and set themselves determinedly against all traditional developments. To the Talmudists, therefore, they were especially obnoxious, and their bald, cold creed is looked upon by them with something like horror. It is thus the Talmud warns against them — "Believe not in thyself till the day of thy death, for, behold, Yochanan, after officiating in the High Priesthood for eighty years, became in the end a Sadducee." (*Berachoth*, fol. 29, col. 1.) In Derech Eretz Zuta, chap. i., a caution is given which might well provoke attention — "Learn or inquire nothing of the Sadducees, lest thou be drawn into hell."

Rabbi Yehudah tells us that Rav says a man should never absent himself from the lecture hall, not even for one hour; for the above Mishnah had been taught at college for many years, but the reason of it had never been made plain till the hour when Rabbi Chanina ben Akavia came and explained it.   *Shabbath*, fol. 83, col. 2.

The Mishnah alluded to is short and simple, viz, Where is it taught that a ship is clean to the touch? From Prov. xxx. 19, "The way of a ship in the midst of the sea" (*i. e.*, as the sea is clean to the touch, therefore a ship must also be clean to the touch).

It is indiscreet for one to sleep in a house as the sole occupant, for Lilith will seize hold of him.

Ibid., fol. 151, col. 2.

Lilith (the night-visiting one) is the name of a night spectre, said to have been Adam's first wife, but who, for her refractory conduct, was transformed into a demon endowed with power to injure and even destroy infants unprotected by the necessary amulet or charm.

"Thou hast acknowledged the Lord this day to be thy God; and the Lord hath acknowledged thee this day to be His peculiar people" (Deut. xxvi. 17, 18). The Holy One — blessed be He! — said unto Israel, "Ye have made Me a name in the world, as it is written (Deut. vi. 4), 'Hear, O Israel, the Lord our God is one Lord;' and so I will make you a name in the world, as it is said (1 Chron. xvii. 21), 'And what one nation in the earth is like Thy people Israel?'"   *Chaggigah*, fol. 3, col. 1.

Why are the words of the Law compared to fire? (Jer. xxiii. 29.) Because, as fire does not burn when there is but one piece of wood, so do the words of the Law not maintain the fire of life when meditated on by one alone (see, in confirmation, Matt. xviii. 20).

Taanith, fol. 7, col. 1.

"And Moses went up from the plains of Moab unto the mountain of Nebo" (Deut. xxxiv. 1). Tradition says there were twelve stairs, but that Moses surmounted them all in one step.   *Soteh*, fol. 13, col. 2.

Pieces of money given in charity should not be counted over by twos, but one by one. *Bava Bathra*, fol. 8, col. 2.

"Knowest thou the time when the wild goats of the rock bring forth?" (Job xxxix. 1.) The wild goat is cruel to her offspring. As soon as they are brought forth, she climbs with them to the steep cliffs, that they may fall headlong and die. But, said God to Job, to prevent this I provide an eagle to catch the kid upon its wings, and then carry and lay it before its cruel mother. Now, if that eagle should be too soon or too late by one second only, instant death to the kid could not be averted; but with Me one second is never changed for another. Shall Job be now changed by Me, therefore, into an enemy. (Comp. Job ix. 17, and xxxiv. 35.)   *Bava Bathra*, fol. 16, cols. 1, 2.

A generation can have one leader only, and not two.

Sanhedrin, fol. 8, col. 1.

"Like the hammer that breaketh the rock in pieces" (Jer. xxiii. 29). As a hammer divideth fire into many sparks, so one verse of Scripture has many meanings and many explanations.   *Ibid.*, fol. 34, col. 1.

In the Machser for Pentecost (p. 69) God is said to have "explained the law to His people, face to face, and on every point ninety-eight explanations are given."

Adam was created one without Eve. Why? That the Sadducees might not assert the plurality of powers in heaven.   *Ibid.*, fol. 37, col. 1.

As the Sadducees did not believe in a plurality of powers in heaven, but only the Christians, in the regard of the Jews, did so (by their profession of the doctrine of the Trinity), it is obvious that here, as well as often elsewhere, the latter and not the former are intended.

"And the frog came up and covered the land of Egypt" (Exod. viii. 1; A. V. viii. 6). "There was but one frog," said Rabbi Elazar, "and she so multiplied as to fill the whole land of Egypt." "Yes, indeed," said Rabbi Akiva, "there was, as you say, but one frog, but she herself was so large as to fill all the land of Egypt." Whereupon Rabbi Elazar ben Azariah said unto him, "Akiva, what business hast thou with Haggadah? Be off with thy legends, and get thee to the laws thou art familiar with about plagues and tents. Though thou sayest right in this matter, for there was only one frog, but she croaked so loud that the frogs came from everywhere else to her croaking."   *Sanhedrin*, fol. 67, col. 2.

Rabba, the grandson of Channa, said that he himself once saw a frog larger than any seen now, though not so large as the frog in

Egypt. It was as large as Acra, a village of some sixty houses. (*Bava Bathra*, fol. 73, col. 2.)

Apropos to the part the frog was conceived to play or symbolize in the Jewish conception of the mode and ministry of Divine judgment, we quote the following : — "We are told that Samuel once saw a frog carrying a scorpion on its back across a river, upon the opposite bank of which a man stood waiting ready to be stung. The sting proving fatal, so that the man died ; upon which Samuel exclaimed, 'Lord, they wait for Thy judgments this day : for all are Thy servants.' (Ps. cxix. 91.)" (*Nedarim*, fol. 41, col. 1.)

"According to the days of one king" (Isa. xxiii. 15). What king is this that is singled out as one? Thou must say this is the King Messiah, and no other.

Sanhedrin, fol. 99, col. 1.

Rabbi Levi contends that Manasseh has no portion in the world to come, while Rabbi Yehudah maintains that he has ; and each supports his conclusion in contradiction of the other, from one and the same Scripture text.

Ibid., fol. 102, col. 2.

The words, "Remember the Sabbath day," in Exod. xx. 8, and "Keep the Sabbath day," in Deut. v. 12, were uttered in one breath, as no man's mouth could utter them, and no man's ear could hear.   *Shevuoth*, fol. 20, col. 2.

The officer who inflicts flagellation on a criminal must smite with one hand only, but yet with all his force.

Maccoth, fol. 22, col. 2.

I would rather be called a fool all my days than sin one hour before God.   *Edioth*, chap. 5, mish. 6.

He who observes but one precept secures for himself an advocate, and he who commits one single sin procures for himself an accuser.   *Avoth*, chap. 4, mish. 15.

He who learns from another one chapter, one halachah, one verse, or one word or even a single letter, is bound to respect him.   *Ibid.*, chap. 6, mish. 3.

The above is one evidence, among many, of the high esteem in which learning and the office of a teacher are held among the Jews. Education is one of the virtues — of which the following, extracted from the Talmud, is a list — the interest of which the Jew considers he enjoys in this world, while the capital remains intact against the exigencies of the world to come. These are : — The honoring of father and mother, acts of benevolence. hospitality to strangers, visiting the sick, devotion in prayer, promotion of peace between man and man, and study in general, but the study of the law outweighs them all. (*Shabbath*, fol. 127, col. 1.) The study of the law, it is said, is of greater merit to rescue one from accidental death, than building the Temple, and greater than honoring father or mother. (*Meggillah*, fol. 16, col 2.)

"Repent one day before thy death." In relation to which Rabbi Eliezer was asked by his disciples, "How is a man to repent one day before his death, since he does not know on what day he shall die?" "So much the more reason is there," he replied, "that he should repent to-day, lest he die to-morrow; and repent to-morrow, lest he die the day after: and thus will all his days be penitential ones."

Avoth d'Rab. Nathan, chap. 15.

He who obliterates one letter from the written name of God, breaks a negative command, for it is said, "And destroy the names of them out of that place. Ye shall not do so unto the Lord your God" (Deut. xii. 3, 4).

Sophrim, chap. 5, hal. 6.

Rabbi Chanina could put on and off his shoes while standing on one leg only, though he was eighty years of age. *Chullin*, fol. 24, col. 2.

A priest who is blind in one eye should not be judge of the plague; for it is said (Lev. xiii. 12), "Wheresoever the priest (with both eyes) looketh."

Negaim, chap. 2, mish. 3.

The twig of a bunch without any grapes is clean; but if there remained one grape on it, it is unclean.

Okzin, chap. 1, mish. 5.

Not every man deserves to have two tables.

Berachoth, fol. 5, col. 2.

The meaning of this rather ambiguous sentence may either be, that all men are not able to succeed in more enterprises than one at a time; or that it is not given to every one to make the best both of the present world and of that which is to come.

Abba Benjamin used to say "There are two things about which I have all my life been much concerned: that my prayer should be offered in front of my bed, and that the position of my bed should be from north to south."

Ibid., fol. 5, col. 2.

There are several reasons which may be adduced to account for Abba Benjamin's anxiety, and they are all more or less connected with the important consequences which were supposed to depend upon determining his position with reference to the Shechinah, which rested in the east or the west.

Abba Benjamin felt anxious to have children, for "any man not having children is counted as dead," as it is written (Gen. xxx. 1), "Give me children, or else I die." (*Nedarin*, fol. 64, col. 2.)

With the Jew one great consideration of life is to have children, and more especially male children; because when a boy is born all rejoice over him, but over a girl they all mourn. When a boy comes into the world he brings peace with him, and a loaf of bread in his hand, but a girl brings nothing. (*Niddah*, fol. 31, col. 2.)

It is impossible for the world to be without males and females, but blessed is he whose children are boys, and hapless is he whose children are girls. (*Kiddushin*, fol. 82, col. 2.)

Whosoever does not leave a son to be heir, God will heap wrath upon him. (Scripture is quoted in proof of this, compare Numb. xxvii. 8 with Zeph. i. 15.) (*Bava Bathra*, fol. 116, col. 1.)

"There are two ways before me, one leading into Paradise, the other into Hell." When Yochanan, the son of Zachai, was sick unto death, his disciples came to visit him; and when he saw them he wept, upon which his disciples exclaimed, "Light of Israel! Pillar of the right! Mighty Hammer! why weepest thou?" He replied, "If I were going to be led into the presence of a king, who is but flesh and blood, to-day here and to-morrow in the grave, whose anger with me could not last forever, whose sentence against me, were it even unto death, could not endure forever, and whom perhaps I might pacify with words or bribe with money, yet for all that should I weep; but now that I am about to enter the presence of the King of kings, the Holy One—blessed be He forever and ever!— whose anger would be everlasting, whose sentence of death or imprisonment admits of no reprieve, and who is not to be pacified with words nor bribed with money, and in whose presence there are two roads before me, one leading into Paradise and the other into Hell, and should I not weep?" Then prayed they him, and said, "Rabbi, give us thy farewell blessing;" and he said unto them, "Oh that the fear of God may be as much upon you as the fear of man." *Berachoth*, fol. 28, col. 2.

Rabbi Ami says, " Knowledge is of great price, for it is placed between two divine names, as it is written (1 Sam. ii. 3), "A God of knowledge is the Lord," and therefore mercy is to be denied to him who has no knowledge ; for it is written (Isa. xxvii. 11), " It is a people of no understanding, therefore He that hath made them will not have mercy on them." *Berachoth*, fol. 33, col. 1.

Here we have a clear law, drawn from Scripture, forbidding, or at any rate denying, mercy to the ignorant. The words of Rabbi (the Holy) are a practical commentary on the text worth quoting, "Woe is unto me because I have given my morsel to an ignorant one." (*Bava Bathra*, fol. 8, col. 1.)

But who is the ignorant one from whom this mercy is to be withheld? Here the doctors disagree. He, says Rabbi Eliezer, who does not read the Shema, " Hear, O Israel," etc., both morning and evening. According to Rabbi Yehudah, he that does not put on phylacteries is an ignorant one. Rabbi Azai affirms that he who wears no fringes to his garment is an ignorant one, etc. Others again say he who even reads the Bible and the Mishna but does not serve the disciples of the wise, is an ignorant one. Rabbi Huna winds up with the words "the law is as the others have said," and so leaves the difficulty where he finds it. (*Berachoth*, fol. 47, col. 2.)

Of him " who transgresses the words of the wise, which he is commanded to obey," it is written, " He is guilty of death and has forfeited his life." (*Berachoth*, fol. 4, col. 2, and *Yevamoth*, fol. 20, col. 1.) Whoso, therefore, shows mercy to him contradicts the purpose and incurs the displeasure of God. It was in application of this principle, literally interpreted, that the wise should hold no parley with the ignorant, which led the Jews to condemn the contrary procedure of Jesus Christ.

It was this prohibition to show mercy to the ignorant, together with the solemn threatenings directed against those who neglected the study of the law, that worked such a wonderful revolution in Hezekiah's time ; for it is said that then "they searched from Dan to Beersheba, and did not find an ignorant one." (*Sanhedrin*, fol. 94, col. 2.)

When the Holy One — blessed be He ! — remembers that His children are in trouble among the nations of the world, He drops two tears into the great ocean, the noise of which startles the world from one end to the other, and causes the earth to quake. *Berachoth*, fol. 59, col. 1.

We read in the Talmud that a Gentile once came to Shamai and said, " How many laws have you?" Shamai replied, " We have two, the written law and the oral law."

To which the Gentile made answer, "When you speak of the written law, I believe you, but in your oral law I have no faith. Nevertheless, you may make me a proselyte on condition that you teach me the written law only." Upon this Shamai rated him sharply, and sent him away with indignant abuse. When, however, this Gentile came with the same object, and proposed the same terms to Hillel, the latter proceeded at once to proselytize him, and on the first day taught him Aleph, Beth, Gemel, Daleth. On the morrow Hillel reversed the order of these letters, upon which the proselyte remonstrated and said, "But thou didst not teach me so yesterday." "True," said Hillel, "but thou didst trust me in what I taught thee then; why, then, dost thou not trust me now in what I tell thee respecting the oral law?"

Shabbath, fol. 31, col. 1.

Every man as he goes on the eve of the Sabbath from the synagogue to his house is escorted by two angels, one of which is a good angel and the other an evil. When the man comes home and finds the lamps lit, the table spread, and the bed in order, the good angel says, "May the coming Sabbath be even as the present;" to which the evil angel (though with reluctance) is obliged to say, "Amen." But if all be in disorder, then the bad angel says, "May the coming Sabbath be even as the present," and the good angel is (with equal reluctance, obliged to say "Amen" to it. *Ibid.*, fol. 119, col. 2.

Two are better than three. Alas! for the one that goes and does not return again. *Shabbath*, fol. 152, col. 1.

As in the riddle of the Sphinx, the "two" here stands for youth with its two sufficient legs, and the "three" for old age, which requires a third support in a staff.

There were two things which God first thought of creating on the eve of the Sabbath, which, however, were not created till after the Sabbath had closed. The first was fire, which Adam by divine suggestion drew forth by striking together two stones; and the second, was the mule, produced by the crossing of two different animals.

P'sachim, fol. 54, col. 1.

"Every one has two portions, one in paradise and another in hell." Acheer asked Rabbi Meyer, "What meaneth this that is written (Eccl. vii. 14), 'God also has set the one over against the other'?" Rabbi Meyer replied, "There is nothing which God has created of which He has not also created the opposite. He who created mountains and hills created also seas and rivers." But said Acheer to Rabbi Meyer, "Thy master, Rabbi Akiva, did not say so, but spake in this way: He created the righteous and also the wicked; He created paradise and hell: every man has two portions, one portion in paradise, and the other in hell. The righteous, who has personal merit, carries both his own portion of good and that of his wicked neighbor away with him to paradise; the wicked, who is guilty and condemned, carries both his own portion of evil and also that of his righteous neighbor away with him to hell." When Rav Mesharshia asked what Scripture guarantee there was for this, this was the reply: "With regard to the righteous, it is written (Isa. lxi. 7), 'They shall rejoice in their portion, therefore in their land (beyond the grave) they shall possess the double.' Respecting the wicked it is written (Jer. xvii. 18), 'And destroy them with double destruction.'" *Chaggigah*, fol. 15, col. 1.

The question asked above by Acheer has been practically resolved by all wise men from the beginning of the world, but it is the boast of the Hegelians that it has for the first time been resolved philosophically by their master. Others had maintained that you could not think a thing but through its opposite; he first maintained it could not exist but through its opposite, that, in fact, the thing and its opposite must needs arise together, and that eternally, as complements of one unity: the white is not there without the black, nor the black without the white; the good is not there without the evil, nor the evil without the good.

Pride is unbecoming in women. There were two proud women, and their names were contemptible; the name of the one, Deborah, meaning wasp, and of the other, Huldah, weasel. Respecting the wasp it is written (Judges iv. 6), "And she sent and called Barak," whereas she ought to have gone to him. Concerning the weasel it is written (2 Kings xxii. 15), "Tell the man that sent you," whereas she should have said, "Tell the king." *Meggillah*, fol. 14, col. 2.

2

If speech is worth one sela (a small coin so called),
silence is worth two.   *Ibid.*, fol. 18, col. 1.

The Swiss motto, «Speech is worth silver, silence worth gold,» expresses a sentiment which finds great favor with the authors and
varied expression in the pages of the Talmud.

If silence be good for wise men, how much better must
it be for fools !   *P'sachim*, fol. 98, col. 2.

For every evil silence is the best remedy.
                          Meggillah, fol. 18, col. 1.

Silence is as good as confession.
                          Yevamoth, fol. 87, col. 1.

Silence in a Babylonian was a mark of his being of good
family.   *Kiddushin*, fol. 71, col. 2.

Simeon, the son of Gamliel, said, " I have been brought
up all my life among the wise, and I have never found
anything of more material benefit than silence."
                          Avoth, chap. 1.

Rabbi Akiva said, " Laughter and levity lead a man to
lewdness ; but tradition is a fence to the law, tithes are a
fence to riches, vows are a fence to abstinence, while the
fence of wisdom is silence."   *Ibid.*, chap. 3.

When they opened his brain, they found in it a gnat as
big as a swallow and weighing two selas.
                          Gittin, fol. 56, col. 2.

The context of the above states a tradition current among the Jews
in reference to Titus, the destroyer of Jerusalem. It is said that
when, after taking the city, he had shamefully violated and profaned
the Temple, he took the sacred vessels of the sanctuary, wrapped
them in the veil of the holy place, and sailed with them to Rome.
At sea a storm arose and threatened to sink the ship ; upon which he
was heard reflecting, "It seems the God of these Jews has no power
anywhere but at sea. Pharaoh He drowned, and Sisera He drowned,
and now He is about to drown me also. If He be mighty, let Him
go ashore and contend with me there." Then came a voice from
heaven and said, "O thou wicked one, son of a wicked man and
grandson of Esau the wicked, go ashore. I have a creature—an insignificant one in my world—go and fight with it."
This creature was a gnat, and is called insignificant because it must
receive and discharge what it eats by one aperture. Immediately,
therefore, he landed, when a gnat flew up his nostrils and made its
way to his brain, on which it fed for a period of seven years. One

day he happened to pass a blacksmith's forge, when the noise of the hammer soothed the gnawing at his brain. "Aha!" said Titus, "I have found a remedy at last;" and he ordered a blacksmith to hammer before him. To a Gentile for this he (for a time) paid four zuzim a day, but to a Jewish blacksmith he paid nothing, remarking to him, "It is payment enough to thee to see thy enemy suffering so painfully." For thirty days he felt relieved, but after, no amount of hammering in the least relieved him. As to what happened after his death, we have this testimony from Rabbi Phineas, the son of Aruba: "I myself was among the Roman magnates when an inquest was held upon the body of Titus, and on opening his brain they found therein a gnat as big as a swallow, weighing two selas." Others say it was as large as a pigeon a year old and weighed two litras. Abaii says, "We found its mouth was of copper and its claws of iron." Titus gave instructions that after his death his body should be burned, and the ashes thereof scattered over the surface of the seven seas, that the God of the Jews might not find him and bring him to judgment." (*Gittin*, fol. 56, col. 2.)

"The man with two wives, one young and the other old." Rav Ami and Rav Assi were in social converse with Rabbi Isaac Naphcha, when one of them said to him, "Tell us, sir, some pretty legend," and the other said, "Pray explain to us rather some nice point of law." When he began the legend he displeased the one, and when he proceeded to explain a point of law, he offended the other. Whereupon he took up this parable in illustration of the plight in which their obstinacy placed him. "I am like the man with the two wives, the one young and the other old. The young one plucked out all his gray hairs (that he might look young), and the old wife pulled out all his black hairs (that he might look old); and so between the one and the other he became bald. So is it with me between you. However, I've something nice for both of you. It is written (Exod. xxii. 6), 'If a fire break out and catch in thorns, so that the stacks of corn, or the standing corn, or the field be consumed therewith, he that kindled the fire shall surely make restoration.' The Holy One—blessed be He!—hath said, 'I must both judge myself and take upon myself to indemnify the evil of the conflagration I have caused, for I have kindled a fire in Zion,' as it is written (Lament. iv. 11), 'He hath kindled a fire in Zion, and hath devoured the foundations thereof.' I must therefore rebuild her with fire, as it is written (Zech. ii. 5), 'I will be unto her a wall of fire round about, and will be the glory in the midst of her.'"

Bava Kama, fol. 60, col. 2.

Rabbi Oshaia asked, "What is this that is written, (Zech. xi. 7), 'I took unto me two staves; the one I called Amiable and the other Destroyer'?" The staff called Amiable represents the disciples of the wise in the land of Israel, who were friendly one toward another in their debates about the law. The staff called Destroyer represents the disciples of the wise of Babylon, who in the like debates were fierce tempered and not friendly toward one another. What is the meaning of Babel or Babylon? Rabbi Yochanan says it means "confused in the Bible, confused in the Mishna, and confused in the Talmud." "He hath set me in dark places, as they that be dead of old" (Lam. iii. 6). Rabbi Jeremiah said by this we are to understand the Babylonian Talmud.

Sanhedrin, fol. 24, col. 1.

The Rabbis say these three hate their fellows — dogs, cocks, and conjurors; to which some add, among others, the disciples of the wise of Babylon. (*P'sachim,* fol. 113, col.2.)

On his return from Babylon to the land of Israel, Rabbi Zira fasted a hundred fasts, during which he prayed that he might be enabled to forget the Babylonian Talmud. (*Bava Metzia,* fol. 85, col. 1.)

Rabbi Yochanan and Rabbi Yonathan traveled one day together; they came to two roads, one of which led by the door of a place devoted to the worship of idols, and the other by a place of ill fame. Upon which one said to the other, "Let us go by the former, because our inclination to the evil that waylays us there is already extinguished." "Nay, rather," said the other, "let us go by the latter, and curb our desires; so shall we receive a reward in recompense." In this resolution they went on, and as they passed the place the women humbled themselves before them and withdrew ashamed into their chambers. Then Yochanan asked the other, "How didst thou know that this would occur to us?" He made answer, "From what is written (in Prov. ii. 2), 'Discretion (in the law) shall preserve thee.'"

Avodah Zarah, fol. 17, cols. 1, 2.

Given two dry firebrands and one piece of green wood, the dry will set fire to the green.

Sanhedrin, fol. 93, col. 1.

With two dogs they caught the lion.

Ibid., fol. 95, col. 1.

Both these proverbs express the same idea, that a minority, be it ever so strong, must give way to a majority.

"And the elders of Moab and the elders of Midian departed together" (Numb. xxii. 7). Midian and Moab were never friendly toward each other; they were like two dogs tending a flock, always at variance. When the wolf came upon the one, however, the other thought, "If I do not help my neighbor to-day, the wolf may come upon myself to-morrow;" therefore the two dogs leagued together and killed the wolf. Hence, says Rabbi Pappa, the popular saying, "The mouse and the cat are combined to make a feast on the fat of the unfortunate."

Ibid., fol. 105, col. 1.

Rabbi Yochanan, in the name of Yossi, the son of Zimra, asks, "What is this that is written (Ps. cxx. 3), 'What shall be given unto thee, or what shall be added unto thee, O thou false tongue'?" The Holy One — blessed be He! — said to the tongue, "All the members of the body are erect, thou only art recumbent; all other members are without, thou art within, and not only so, for I have surrounded thee with two walls, one of bone and the other of flesh. What shall be given to thee, or what shall be added unto thee, O thou false tongue?" Rabbi Yochanan, in the name of Yossi, says, "He who slanders is an atheist, for it is written (Ps. xii. 4), 'Who have said, With our tongues will we prevail; our lips are with us; who is lord over us?'" *Erchin*, fol. 15, col. 2.

Here are a few sayings from the Talmud on the abuse of the tongue.

He who slanders, he who receives slander, and he who bears false witness against his neighbor, deserve to be cast to the dogs. *P'sachim*, fol. 118, col. 1.

All animals will one day remonstrate with the serpent and say, "The lion treads upon his prey and devours it,

the wolf tears and eats it, but thou, what profit hast thou
in biting?" The serpent will reply (Eccl. viii. 11), "I am
no worse than a slanderer." *Taanith*, fol. 8, col. 1.

Adonijah was deprived of life for no other reason than
that he was given to quarreling. It is lawful to slander
one so evil disposed as he was. *Perek Hashalom.*

God will say to the prince of hell, "I from above and
thou from below shall judge and condemn the slanderer."
Erchin, fol. 15, col. 2.

The third tongue (*i. e.*, slander) hurts three parties: the
slanderer himself, the receiver of slander, and the person
slandered. *Ibid.*

Four classes do not receive the presence of the Shechinah: scorners, liars, flatterers, and slanderers.
Sanhedrin, fol. 103, col. 1.

Where are we told that when two sit together and study
the law the Shechinah is with them? In Mal. iii. 16,
where it is written, "They that feared the Lord spake
often one to another, and the Lord hearkened and heard
it." *Berachoth*, fol. 6, col. 1.

Why did Elijah employ two invocations, saying twice
over, "Hear me! hear me!" (1 Kings xviii. 37.) Elijah
first prayed before God, "O Lord, King of the universe,
hear me!" that He might send fire down from heaven and
consume all that was upon the altar; and again he prayed,
"Hear me!" that they might not imagine that the result
was a matter of sorcery; for it is said, 'Thou hast turned
their heart back again.'" *Berachoth*, fol. 9, col. 2.

The twofold invocation of Elijah, which betokens his intense earnestness, anagrammatically expressed, is echoed in the words of the
bystanders, "The Lord He is the God, the Lord He is the God."

"I dreamed," said Bar Kappara one day to Rabbi (the
Holy), "that I beheld two pigeons, and they flew away
from me." "Thy dream is this," replied Rabbi, "thou hast
had two wives, and art separated from them both without
a bill of divorcement." *Ibid.*, fol. 56, col. 2.

The Rabbis teach concerning the two kidneys in man,
that one counsels him to do good and the other to do evil;

and it appears that the former is situated on the right side and the latter on the left.   Hence it is written (Eccl. x. 2), "A wise man's heart is at his right hand, but a fool's heart is at his left."   *Ibid.*, fol. 61, col. 1.

For two sins the common people perish : they speak of the holy ark as a box and the synagogue as a resort for the ignorant vulgar.   *Shabbath*, fol. 32, col. 1.

On the self-same day when Jeroboam introduced the two golden calves, the one into Bethel and the other into Dan, a hut was erected in a part of Italy which was then subject to the Greeks.   *Ibid.*, fol. 56, col. 2.

In the context where the above tradition occurs, which, as is obvious, relates to the founding of Rome, we meet with another on the same subject as follows : — When Solomon married the daughter of Pharaoh, the Angel Gabriel thrust a reed into the sea, stirring up therewith the sand and mud from the bottom.   This, gradually collecting, first shaped itself into an island and then expanded so as to unite itself with the continent.   And thus was the land created for the erection of the hut which should one day swell into the proportion of a proud imperial city.

If Israel kept only two Sabbaths, according to the strict requirement of the law, they would be freed at once from their compelled dispersion ; for it is written (Isa. lvi. 4, 7), "Thus saith the Lord unto the eunuchs that keep my Sabbaths, Even them will I bring to my holy mountain."
                    Shabbath, fol. 118, col. 2.

Adam had two faces; for it is said (Ps. cxxxix. 5), "Thou hast made me behind and before."
                    Eiruvin, fol. 18, col. 1.

There is a notion among the Rabbis that Adam was possessed originally of a bisexual organization, and this conclusion they draw from Gen. i. 27, where it is said, "God created man in his own image; male-female created He them."   These two natures, it was thought, lay side by side ; according to some, the male on the right and the female on the left; according to others, back to back; while there were those who maintained that Adam was created with a tail, and that it was from this appendage Eve was fashioned. Other Jewish traditions tell us that Eve was made from "the thirteenth rib of the right side" (Targ. Jonath.), and that "she was not drawn out by the head, lest she should be vain ; nor by the eyes, lest she should be wanton ; nor from the mouth, lest she should be given to garrulity ; nor by the ears, lest she should be an eavesdropper ;

nor by the hands, lest she should be intermeddling; nor by the feet, lest she be a gadder; nor by the heart, for fear she should be jealous; but she was taken out from the side. Yet, in spite of all these precautions, she had all the faults so carefully provided against.»

If in time of national calamity a man withdraw himself from his kindred and refuse to share in their sorrow, his two guardian angels come and lay their hands upon his head and say, "This man has isolated himself from his country in the day of its need, let him not live to see and enjoy the day when God shall restore its prosperity." When the community is in trouble, let no man say, "I will go home and eat and drink, and say, Peace be unto thee, oh my soul!" (Luke xii. 19); for to him Scripture hath solemnly said (Isa. xxii. 13, 14), "Surely this iniquity shall not be purged from you till you die."

Taanith, fol. 11, col. 1.

An infant that has died under a month old is (to be) carried to the grave in the arms (not in a coffin), and buried by one woman and two men, but not by one man and two women. *Moed Katan*, fol. 24, col. 1.

Both Rashi and the Tosephoth allude to a case which justifies the rule given here, where a woman actually carried a living child in a coffin, in order to avoid the suspicion of an assignation she had made with a man, who set out to join her. But the Tosephoth, after noticing this version of Rashi, gives another more to the point. The story in the Tosephoth is to this effect: — A woman was once weeping and groaning over the grave of her husband, and not very far away was a man who was guarding the corpse of a person who had been crucified. In the moment of mourning an affection sprung up between the two, and in the engrossment of it the corpse which the man guarded was stolen. He was in great trepidation for fear of the king's command. The woman said, "Don't be afraid; exhume my husband, and hang him up instead." This was accordingly done. (See *Kiddushin*, fol. 80, col. 2.)

There were two date trees in the Valley of Hinnom from between which smoke ascended, and this is the gate of hell.

Succah, fol. 32, col. 2.

According to Jewish tradition, there are three gates to Gehinnom, one in the desert, one in the sea, and one in Jerusalem: In the desert, as it is written (Numb. xvi. 33), "They went down, and all that belonged to them, alive into hell." In the sea, as it is written (Jonah

ii. 2), "Out of the belly of hell have I called," etc. In Jerusalem, as it is written (Isa. xxxi. 9), "Thus saith the Lord, whose fire is in Zion, and His furnace in Jerusalem."

When two women are seen sitting on opposite sides of a cross road facing each other, it is to be presumed that they are up to witchcraft and contemplate mischief. What in that case must you do? Go by another road, if there is one, and if not, with a companion, should such turn up, passing the crones arm-in-arm with him; but should there be no other road and no other man, then walk straight on repeating the counter-charm, as you pass them —

"Agrath is to Asia gone,
And Blussia's killed in battle."

P'sachim, fol. 111, col. 2.

Agrath and Blussia are two Amazons well known to those familiar with Rabbinic demonology.

"If Mordecai, before whom thou hast began to fall, be of the seed of the Jews, expect not to prevail against him, but thou shalt fall" (Esth. vi. 13). Wherefore these two fallings? They told Haman, saying, "This nation is likened to the dust, and is also likened to the stars; when they are down, they are down even to the dust, but when they begin to rise, they rise to the stars."

Meggillah, fol. 16, col. 1.

If any two disciples of the wise, dwelling in the same city, have a difference respecting the Halachah, let them remember what Scripture denounces against them, "And also I gave them statutes that are not good, and judgments by which they shall not live" (Ezek. xx. 25).

Ibid., fol. 32, col. 1.

If a man espouse one of two sisters, and does not know which he has espoused, he must give both a bill of divorce. If two men espouse two sisters, and neither of them know which he has espoused, then each man must give two bills of divorce, one to each woman. *Yevamoth*, fol. 23, col. 2.

There is a time coming (*i. e.*, in the days of the Messiah), when a grain of wheat will be as large as the two kidneys of the great ox. *Kethuboth*, fol. 111, col. 1.

According to a recent discovery, which has been confirmed by subsequent observation and experiment, wheat is a development by cultivation of the tiny grain of the *Ægilops ovata*, a sort of grass; but we are indebted to Rabbinic lore for the curious information that before the Fall of man wheat grew upon a tree whose trunk looked like gold, its branches like silver, and its leaves like so many emeralds. The wheat ears themselves were as red as rubies, and each bore five sparkling grains as white as snow, as sweet as honey, and as fragrant as musk. At first the grains were as big as an ostrich's egg, but in the time of Enoch they diminished to the size of a goose's egg, and in Elijah's to that of a hen, while at the commencement of the common era, they shrank so small as not to be larger than grapes, according to a law the inverse of the order of nature. Rabbi Yehudah (*Sanhedrin*, fol. 70, col. 1) says that wheat was the forbidden fruit. Hence probably the degeneracy.

Of two that quarrel, the one that first gives in shows the nobler nature. *Ibid.*, fol. 71, col. 2.

He who sets aside a portion of his wealth for the relief of the poor will be delivered from the judgment of hell. Of this the parable of the two sheep that attempted to ford a river is an illustration; one was shorn of its wool and the other not; the former, therefore, managed to get over, but the latter, being heavy-laden, sank.

Gittin, fol. 7, col. 1.

Zoreah and Eshtaol (Josh. xv. 33) were two large mountains, but Samson tore them up and grated the one against the other. *Soteh*, fol. 9, col. 2.

The above tradition is founded on Judges xiii. 25, in which it is said of Samson, "And the spirit of God began to move him at times in the camp of Dan, between Zoreah and Eshtaol," in which the word "move," signifies also to "strike a stroke," "step a step," and "once." Founding on which last two meanings, Rabbi Yehudah says, "Samson strode in one stride from Zoreah to Eshtaol," a giant stride of two miles or more. Taking the word in the sense of "strike," or "producing a ringing sound," another Rabbi tells us that the hairs of Samson's head stood upright, tinkling one against another like bells, the jingle of which might be heard from Zoreah to Eshtaol. The version in the text takes the same word in the sense of to "strike together."

On the day when Isaac was weaned, Abraham made a great feast, to which he invited all the people of the land. Not all of those who came to enjoy the feast believed in the alleged occasion of its celebration, for some said contemptuously, "This old couple have adopted a foundling, and provided a feast to persuade us to believe that the child is their own offspring." What did Abraham do? He invited all the great men of the day, and Sarah invited their wives, who brought their infants, but not their nurses, along with them. On this occasion Sarah's breasts became like two fountains, for she supplied, of her own body, nourishment to all the children. Still some were unconvinced, and said, "Shall a child be born to one that is a hundred years old, and shall Sarah, who is ninety years old, bear?" (Gen. xvii. 17.) Whereupon, to silence this objection, Isaac's face was changed, so that it became the very picture of Abraham's; then one and all exclaimed, "Abraham begat Isaac." *Bara Metzia*, fol. 87, col. 1.

Rava relates the following in the name of Rabbi Yochanan:—"Two Jewish slaves were one day walking along, when their master, who was following, overheard the one saying to the other, 'There is a camel ahead of us, as I judge—for I have not seen—that is blind of one eye and laden with two skin-bottles, one of which contains wine and the other oil, while two drivers attend it, one of them an Israelite, and the other a Gentile.' 'You perverse men,' said their master, 'how can you fabricate such a story as that?' The slave answered, and gave this as his reason, 'The grass is cropped only on one side of the track, the wine, that must have dripped, has soaked into the earth on the right, and the oil has trickled down, and may be seen on the left; while one of the drivers turned aside from the track to ease himself, but the other has not even left the road for the purpose.' Upon this the master stepped on before them in order to verify the correctness of their inferences, and found the conclusion true in every particular. He then turned back, and . . . after complimenting the two slaves for their shrewdness, he at once gave them their liberty." *Sanhedrin*, fol. 104, col. 2.

When the disciples of Shamai and Hillel increased in Israel, contention increased along with them, so much so, that the one law became as two laws (and these contradictory). *Soteh*, fol. 47, col. 2.

If two parties deposit money with a third, one a single manah and the other two hundred, and both afterward appear and claim the larger sum, the depositary should give each depositor one manah only, and leave the rest undivided till the coming of Elijah.   *Bava Metzia*, fol. 37, col. 2.

"Till Elijah comes" is a phrase which is in use among the Jews to express postponement forever, like *ad Kalendas Græcas*. It is applied to questions that would take Elijah to settle, which, it is believed, he will not appear to do till doomsday.

"And I will make thy windows of agates" (Isa. liv. 12). Two of the angels in heaven, Gabriel and Michael, once disputed about this: one maintained that the stone should be an onyx, and the other asserted it should be a jasper; but the Holy One — blessed be He ! — said unto them, "Let it be as both say, which, in Hebrew, abbreviated, is an agate.   *Bava Bathra*, fol. 75, col. 1.

"The horseleech has two daughters, crying, Give ! give !" (Prov. xxx. 15.)   Mar Ukva says, "This has reference to the voice of two daughters crying out from torture in hell, because their voice is heard in this world crying, 'Give ! give !' — namely — heresy and officialism."
Avodah Zarah, fol. 17, col. 1.

Rashi says heresy here refers to the "heresy of James," or, in other words, Christianity.

Two cemeteries were provided by the judicial authorities, one for beheaded and strangled criminals, and the other for those that were stoned or burned.   When the flesh of these was consumed, they collected the bones and buried them in their own place, after which the relations came and saluted the judge and the witnesses, and said, "We owe you no grudge, for you passed a just judgment."
Sanhedrin, fol. 46, col. 1.

Alas ! for the loss which the world has sustained in the degradation of the helpful serpent.   If the serpent had not been degraded, every Israelite would have been attended by two of kindly disposition, one of which might have been sent to the north, and the other to the south, to bring for its owner precious corals and costly stones and pearls.
Sanhedrin, fol. 59, col. 2.

Here are two or three other sayings from the Talmud relative to the serpent.

Benjamin the son of Jacob, Amram the father of Moses, and Jesse the father of David all died, not because of their own sin (for they had none, says Rashi), but because of the (original) sin committed under the serpent's temptation. *Shabbath*, fol. 55, col. 2.

No man was ever injured by a serpent or scorpion in Jerusalem. *Yoma*, fol. 21, col. 1.

"And dust is the serpent's food" (Isa. lxv. 25). Rav Ammi says, "To the serpent no delicacy in the world has any other flavor than that of dust;" and Rav Assi says, "No delicacy in the world satisfies him like dust." *Ibid.*, fol. 75, col. 1.

Two negatives or two affirmatives are as good as an oath. *Shevuoth*, fol. 36, col. 1.

Like two pearls were the two drops of holy oil that were suspended from the two corners of the beard of Aaron. *Horayoth*, fol. 12, col. 1.

For two to sit together and have no discourse about the law, is to sit in the seat of the scornful; as it is said (Ps. i. 1), "And sitteth not in the seat of the scornful." *Avoth*, chap. iii.

When two are seated together at table, the younger shall not partake before the elder, otherwise the younger shall be justly accounted a glutton. *Derech Eretz*, chap. vii.

Philemo once asked Rabbi (the Holy), "If a man has two heads, on which is he to put the phylactery?" To which Rabbi replied, "Either get up and be off, or take an anathema; for thou art making fun of me." *Menachoth*, fol. 37, col. 1.

It is thus Rav Yoseph taught what is meant when it is written in Isaiah xii. 1, "I will praise Thee, O Lord, because Thou wast angry with me: Thine anger will depart and Thou wilt comfort me." "The text applies," he says, "to two men who were going abroad on a mercantile enterprise, one of whom, having had a thorn run into his foot, had to forego his intended journey, and began in consequence

to utter reproaches and blaspheme. Having afterward
learned that the ship in which his companion had sailed
had sunk to the bottom of the sea, he confessed his shortsightedness and praised God for His mercy."

Niddah, fol. 31, col. 1.

The night is divided into three watches, and at each watch
the Holy One — blessed be He ! — sits and roars like a
lion ; as it is written (Jer. xxv. 30), "The Lord will roar
from on high, . . . roaring, He will roar over his habitation." The marks by which this division of the night is
recognized are these : — In the first watch the ass brays ;
in the second the dog barks ; and in the third the babe is
at the breast and the wife converses with her husband.

Berachoth, fol. 3, col. 1.

The Rabbis have taught that there are three reasons why
a person should not enter a ruin : — 1. Because he may
be suspected of evil intent ; 2. Because the walls might
tumble upon him ; 3. And because of evil spirits that frequent such places.　　　　　*Ibid.*, fol. 3, col. 1.

He who three times a day repeats David's psalm of
praise (Ps. cxlv.) may be sure of an inheritance in the
world to come.　　　　　*Ibid.*, fol. 4, col. 2.

Three precious gifts were given to Israel, but none of
them without a special affliction : these three gifts were the
law, the land of Israel, and the world to come.

Ibid., fol. 5, col. 1.

These are also from the Talmud anent Israel and the Israelites.

All Israelites are princes.　　*Shabbath*, fol. 57, col. 1.

All Israelites are holy.　　　　*Ibid.*, fol. 86, col. 1.

Happy are ye, O Israel ! for every one of you, from the
least to the greatest, is a great philosopher. (*Eiruvin*, fol.
53, col. 1.) The Machzor for Pentecost says, Israelites are
as "full of meritorious works as a pomegranate is full of
pips."　　　　　See also *Chaggigah*, fol. 27, col. 1.

As it is impossible for the world to be without air, so
also is it impossible for the world to be without Israel.

Taanith, fol. 3, col. 2.

If the ox of an Israelite bruise the ox of a Gentile, the Israelite is exempt from paying damages; but should the ox of a Gentile bruise the ox of an Israelite, the Gentile is bound to recompense him in full.

Bava Kama, fol. 38, col. 1.

When an Israelite and a Gentile have a lawsuit before thee, if thou canst, acquit the former according to the laws of Israel, and tell the latter such is our law; if thou canst get him off in accordance with Gentile law, do so, and say to the plaintiff such is your law; but if he cannot be acquitted according to either law, then bring forward adroit pretexts and secure his acquittal. These are the words of the Rabbi Ishmael. Rabbi Akiva says, "No false pretext should be brought forward, because, if found out, the name of God would be blasphemed; but if there be no fear of that, then it may be adduced." *Ibid.*, fol. 113, col. 1.

If one find lost property in a locality where the majority are Israelites, he is bound to proclaim it; but he is not bound to do so if the majority be Gentiles.

Bava Metzia, fol. 24, col. 1.

(Prov. xiv. 34), "Almsgiving exalteth a nation, but benevolence is a sin to nations." "Almsgiving exalteth a nation," that is to say, the nation of Israel; as it is written (2 Sam. vii. 23), "And what one nation in the earth is like thy people, even like Israel?" but "benevolence" is a sin to nations, that is to say, for the Gentiles to exercise charity and benevolence is sin.

Bava Bathra, fol. 10, col. 2.

If a Gentile smite an Israelite, he is guilty of death; as it is written (Exod. ii. 12), "And he looked this way and that way, and when he saw there was no man, he slew the Egyptian." *Sanhedrin*, fol. 58, col. 2.

All Israelites have a portion in the world to come; as it is written (Isa. lx. 21), "And thy people are all righteous: they shall inherit the land." *Ibid.*, fol. 90, col. 1.

"And they shall fall one on account of another" (Lev. xxvi. 37),—one on account of the sins of another. This teaches us that all Israel are surety for one another.

Shevuoth, fol. 39, col. 1.

If one find a foundling in a locality where the majority are Gentiles, then the child is (to be reckoned) a Gentile; if the majority be Israelites, it is to be considered as an Israelite; and so also it is to be, providing the numbers are equal.   *Machsheerin*, chap. 2, Mish. 7.

"One generation passeth away, and another generation cometh, but the earth abideth forever" (Eccl. i. 4). One empire cometh and another passeth away, but Israel abideth forever.   *Perek Hashalom.*

The world was created only for Israel: none are called the children of God but Israel; none are beloved before God but Israel.   *Gerim*, chap. 1.

The Jew that has no wife abideth without joy, without a blessing, and without any good. Without joy, as it is written (Deut. xiv. 26), "And thou shalt reject, thou and thy household;" without blessing, as it is written (Ezek. xliv. 30), "That He may cause a blessing to rest on thy household;" without any good, for it is written (Gen. ii. 8), "It is not good that man should be alone."

          Yevamoth, fol. 62, col. 2.

The Jew that has no wife is not a man; for it is written (Gen. v. 2), "Male and female created He them and called their name man." To which Rabbi Eleazar adds, "So every one who has no landed property is no man; for it is written (Ps. cxv. 16), 'The heaven, even the heavens, are the Lord's, but the earth (the land, that is), hath He given to the children of man.'"

          Yevamoth, fol. 63, col. 1.

Three things did Moses ask of God: — 1. He asked that the Shechinah might rest upon Israel; 2. That the Shechinah might rest upon none but Israel; and 3. That God's ways might be made known unto him; and all these requests were granted.   *Berachoth*, fol. 7, col. 1.

What was the Shechinah? Was it the presence of a Divine person or only of a Divine power? The following quotations will show what is the teaching of the Talmud on the matter, and will be read with interest by the theologian, whether Jew or Christian.

Where do we learn that when ten persons pray together the Shechinah is with them? In Ps. lxxxii. 1, where it is written, "God standeth in the congregation of the mighty." And where do we 'learn that when two sit together and study the law the Shechinah is with them? In Mal. iii. 16, where it is written, "Then they that feared the Lord spake often one to another, and the Lord hearkened and heard it." (*Berachoth*, fol. 6, col. 1.)

Where do we learn that the Shechinah does strengthen the sick? In Ps. xli. 3, where it is written, "The Lord will strengthen him upon the bed of languishing." (*Shabbath*, fol. 12, col. 2.)

He who goes from the Synagogue to the lecture-room, and from the lecture-room back to the Synagogue, will become worthy to receive the presence of the Shechinah; as it is written (Ps. lxxxiv. 1), "They go from strength to strength; every one of them in Zion appeareth before God." (*Moed Katan*, fol. 29, col. 1.)

Rabbi Yossi says, "The Shechinah never came down here below, nor did Moses and Elijah ever ascend on high, because it is written (Ps. cxv. 16), 'The heaven, even the heavens, are the Lord's, but the earth hath he given to the children of men.'" (*Succah*, fol. 5, col. 1.)

Esther "stood in the inner court of the King's house" (Esth. v. 1). Rabbi Levi says, "When she reached the house of the images the Shechinah departed from her. Then she exclaimed, "My God! my God! why hast thou forsaken me?" (*Meggillah*, fol. 15, col. 2.)

"But ye that did cleave unto the Lord your God are alive every one of you this day" (Deut. iv. 4). Is it possible to cleave to the Shechinah? Is it not written (*ibid.*, verse 24), "For the Lord thy God is a consuming fire"? The reply is: — He that bestows his daughter in marriage on a disciple of the wise (that is, a Rabbi), or does business on behalf of the disciples of the wise, or maintains them from his property, Scripture accounts it as if he did cleave to the Shechinah. (*Kethuboth*, fol. 111, col. 25.)

He who is angry has no regard even for the Shechinah; as it is written (Ps. x. 4), "The wicked, when his anger rises, does not inquire after God; God is not in all his thoughts." (*Nedarim*, fol. 22, col. 2.)

He who visits the sick should not sit upon the bed, nor even upon a stool or a chair beside it, but he should wrap his mantle round him and sit upon the floor, because of the Shechinah which rests at the head of the bed of the invalid; as it is written (Ps. xli. 3), "The Lord will strengthen him upon the bed of languishing." (*Ibid.*, fol. 40, col. 1.)

When Israel went up out of the Red Sea, both the babe on its mother's lap and the suckling at the breast saw the Shechinah, and said, "This is my God, and I will prepare Him a habitation;" as it is written (Ps. viii. 2), "Out of the mouths of babes and sucklings thou hast ordained strength." (*Soteh*, fol. 30, col. 2.)

Where do we read that the Shechinah is present everywhere? In Zech. ii. 3, where it is written, "And behold the angel that talked with me went forth, and another angel went out to meet him." It is not said went out after him, but "went out to meet him." From this we know that the Shechinah is present everywhere. (*Bava Bathra*, fol. 25, col. 1.)

Rabbi Akiva says, "For three things I admire the Medes: — 1. When they carve meat, they do it on the table; 2. When they kiss, they only do so upon the hand; 3. And when they consult, they do so only in the field."

Berachoth, fol. 8, col. 2.

The stone which Og, king of Bashan, meant to throw upon Israel is the subject of a tradition delivered on Sinai. "The camp of Israel I see," he said, "extends three miles; I shall therefore go and root up a mountain three miles in extent and throw it upon them." So off he went, and finding such a mountain, raised it on his head, but the Holy One — blessed be He! — sent an army of ants against him, which so bored the mountain over his head that it slipped down upon his shoulders, from which he could not lift it, because his teeth, protruding, had riveted it upon him. This explains that which is written (Ps. iii. 7), "Thou hast broken the teeth of the ungodly;" where read not "Thou hast broken," but "Thou hast ramified," that is, "Thou hast caused to branch out." Moses being ten ells in height, seized an axe ten ells long, and springing up ten ells, struck a blow on Og's ankle and killed him.

Ibid., fol. 54, col. 2.

This same story is given with more than Talmudic exaggeration in the Targum of Jonathan ben Uzziel, while the author of the Book of Jasher (chap. lxv., verses 23, 24) makes the camp and the mountain forty miles in extent. The giant here figures in antediluvian tradition. He is said to have been saved at the Flood by laying hold of the ark, and being fed day by day through a hole in the side of the ark by Noah himself. A tradition which says the soles of his feet were forty miles long at once explains all the extraordinary feats ascribed to him.

Rav Yehudah used to say, "Three things shorten a man's days and years: — 1. Neglecting to read the law when it is given to him for that purpose; seeing it is written (Deut. xxx. 20), 'For He (who gave it) is thy life and the length of thy days.' 2. Omitting to repeat the customary benediction over a cup of blessing; for it is written (Gen. xii. 3), 'And I will bless them that bless thee.'

3. And the assumption of a Rabbinical air; for Rabbi Chama bar Chanena says, 'Joseph died before any of his brethren, because he domineered over them.'"

Berachoth, fol. 55, col. 1.

The first of these refers to the reading of the law in public worship, the second to a practice after meals when more than two adult Jews were present, and the third to the dictatorial air often assumed by the Rabbis.

Three things proceed by pre-eminence from God Himself:— Famine, plenty, and a wise ruler. Famine (2 Kings viii. 2): "The Lord hath called for a famine;" plenty (Ezek. xxxvi. 29): "I will call for corn and increase it;" a wise ruler; for it is written (Exod. xxxi. 2), "I have called by name Bezaleel." Rabbi Yitzchak says, "A ruler is not to be appointed unless the community be first consulted. God first consulted Moses, then Moses consulted the nation concerning the appointment of Bezaleel."

Ibid., fol. 55, col. 1.

Three dreams come to pass:— That which is dreamed in the morning; that which is also dreamed by one's neighbor; and a dream which is interpreted within a dream; to which some add, one that is dreamed by the same person twice; as it is written (Gen. xli. 32), "And for that the dream was doubled unto Pharaoh twice."

Ibid., fol. 55, col. 2.

Three things tranquilize the mind of man:— Melody, scenery, and sweet odor. Three things develop the mind of man:— A fine house, a handsome wife, and elegant furniture. *Ibid.*, fol. 57, col. 2.

The Rabbis have taught that there are three sorts of dropsy:— Thick, resulting from sin; bloated, in consequence of insufficient food; and thin, due to sorcery.

Shabbath, fol. 33, col. 1.

These three grow stronger as they grow older:— The fish, the serpent, and the pig. *Ibid.*, fol. 77, col. 2.

It were better to cut the hands off than to touch the eye, or the nose, or the mouth, or the ear, etc., with them without having first washed them. Unwashed hands may cause blindness, deafness, foulness of breath, or a polypus.

It is taught that Rabbi Nathan has said, "The evil spirit
Bath Chorin, which rests upon the hands at night, is very
strict; he will not depart till water is poured upon the
hands three times over."   *Ibid.*, fol. 109, col. 1.

The great importance of this ceremonial washing of the hands will
appear from the following anecdote, which we quote *verbatim* from
another part of the Talmud :— "It happened once, as the Rabbis
teach, that Rabbi Akiva was immured in a prison, and Yehoshua
Hagarsi was his attendant. One day the gaoler said to the latter as
he entered, 'What a lot of water thou hast brought to-day! Dost
thou need it to sap the walls of the prison?' So saying, he seized
the vessel and poured out half of the water. When Yehoshua brought
in what was left of the water to Rabbi Akiva, the latter, who was
weary of waiting, for he was faint and thirsty, reproachfully said to
him, 'Yehoshua, dost thou forget that I am old, and my very life
depends upon thee?' When the servant related what had happened,
the Rabbi asked for the water to wash his hands, 'Why, master,'
said Yehoshua, 'there's not enough for thee to drink, much less to
cleanse thy hands with.' To which the Rabbi replied, 'What am I
to do? They who neglect to wash their hands are judged worthy of
death; 'tis better that I should die by my own act from thirst than
act against the rules of my associates.' And accordingly it is
related that he abstained from tasting anything till they brought him
water to wash his hands." (*Eiruvin*, fol. 21, col. 2. See also *Maimonides, Hilc. Berach.*, vi. 19.)

From the context of the passage just quoted we cull the following,
which proves that the Talmud itself bases the precept concerning the
washing of hands on oral tradition and not on the written law :—
"Rav Yehudah ascribes this saying to Shemuel, that when Solomon
gave to the traditional rules that regulated the washing of hands and
other ceremonial rites the form and sanction of law, a Bath Kol came
forth and said (Prov. xxiii. 15), 'My son, if thy heart be wise, my
heart shall rejoice, even mine;' and again it said (Prov. xxvii, 11),
'My son, be wise, and make my heart glad, that I may answer him
that reproacheth me.'" (See Prov. xxx. 5, 6.)

There is a great deal in the Talmud about washing the hands, in addition to what is said in the treatise Yadaim, which is entirely devoted
to the subject. But this topic is subordinate to another, namely, the
alleged inferiority of the precepts of the Bible to the prescriptions of
the Rabbis, of which the punctilious rules regulative of hand washing
form only a small fraction. This is illustrated by an anecdote from the
Talmudic leaflet entitled Callah, respecting Rabbi Akiva, whose fame
extends from one end of the world to the other. (See *Yevamoth*, fol.
16, col. 2).

Once upon a time, as the Elders were sitting together, two lads
passed by them, one with his head covered and the other bareheaded.
Of the latter boy as he passed Rabbi Elazar said, "He is a Mamzer,"

and Rabbi Yehoshua, "He is a Ben Haniddah," but Rabbi Akiva contended, "He is both a Mamzer and a Ben Haniddah." Upon which the Elders said to Rabbi Akiva, "How darest thou be so bold as dispute the assertion of thy masters?" "Because I can substantiate what I say," was his answer. He then went to the mother of the lad, and found her selling pease in the market place. "Daughter," said he to her, "if thou wilt answer all that I ask of thee, I will ensure thee a portion in the life to come." She replied, "Let me have thy oath and I will do so." Then taking the oath with his lips but nullifying it in his heart, he asked her, "What sort of a son is thy lad?" She replied, "When I entered my bridal chamber I was a Niddah, and consequently my husband kept away from me." Thus it was found out that the boy was a Mamzer and a Ben Haniddah; upon which the sages exclaimed, "Great is Rabbi Akiva, for he has overcome his masters;" and as they congratulated him they said, "Blessed be the Lord God of Israel, who hath revealed His secret unto Akiva the son of Joseph." Thus did the Rabbi forswear himself, and thus did his companions compliment him on the success of his perjury; yet the Bible says, "Thou shalt not take the name of the Lord thy God in vain" (Exod. xx. 7), and "Keep thou far from a falsehood" (Exod. xxiii. 7).

Here is a companion picture from Yoma, fol. 84, col. 1.—"Rabbi Yochanan was suffering from scurvy, and he applied to a Gentile woman, who prepared a remedy for the fifth and then the sixth day of the week. 'But what shall I do to-morrow?' said he; 'I must not walk so far on the Sabbath.' 'Thou wilt not require any more,' she answered. 'But suppose I do,' he replied. 'Take an oath,' she answered, 'that thou wilt not reveal it, and I will tell thee how to compound the remedy.' This he did in the following words: 'By the God of Israel, I swear I will not divulge it.' Nevertheless, when he learned the secret, he went and revealed it. 'But was not that profaning the name of God?' asks one. 'No,' pleads another Rabbi, 'for, as he told her afterward, that what he meant was that he would not tell it to the God of Israel.' The remedy was yeast, water, oil, and salt."

The anecdote that follows is from Sanhedrin, fol. 97, col 1: —"In reference to the remark of Ravina, who said, 'I used to think that there was no truth in the world,' one of the Rabbis, Toviah (or Tavyoomah, as some say), would protest and say, 'If all the riches of the world were offered me, I would not tell a falsehood.' And he used to clench his protestation with the following apologue: 'I once went to a place called Kushta, where the people never swerve from the truth, and where (as a reward for their integrity) they do not die until old age; and there I married and settled down, and had two sons born unto me. One day as my wife was sitting and combing her hair, a woman who dwelt close by came to the door and asked to see her. Thinking that it was a breach of etiquette (that any one should see her at her toilet), I said she was not in. Soon after this my two children died, and the people came to inquire into the cause of their premature decease. When I told them of my evasive reply to the woman, they asked me to leave the town, lest by my misconduct I might involve the whole community in a like calamity, and death might be enticed to their place.»

Food remains for three days in the stomach of the dog, because God knew that his food would be scanty.

Shabbath, fol. 155, col. 1.

He who is born on the third day of the week will be rich and amorous. *Ibid.*, fol. 156, col. 1.

Rabbi Abba, in the name of Shemuel, says, " The schools of Shammai and Hillel were at variance three years, the one party contending and saying, 'The Halacha is according to us;' and the other, 'The Halacha is according to us.' Then came a voice from the Lord and said, 'Both these and those are the words of the living God, but yet the Halacha is according to the school of Hillel.' What was the merit of the school of Hillel that the Halacha should be pronounced to be according to it? Its disciples were gentle and forbearing, for while they stood by their own decisions, they also stated those maintained by the school of Shammai, and often even mentioned the tenets of the school of Shammai first and their own afterward. This teaches us that him who humbles himself, God will exalt; and him who exalts himself, God will abase. Whoso pursueth greatness, greatness will flee from him; and whoso fleeth from greatness, greatness will pursue him."

Eiruvin, fol. 13, col. 2.

There are three entrances to hell: — One in the desert, one in the sea, and one in Jerusalem.

Ibid., fol. 19, col. 1.

These three will never see hell: — He who is purified by poverty; he who is purged by a painful flux; and he who is harassed by importunate creditors; and some say, he also who is plagued with a termagant wife.

Eiruvin, fol. 41, col. 2.

Three effects are ascribed to Babylonian broth (which was made of moldy bread, sour milk, and salt): — It retards the action of the heart, it affects the eyesight, and emaciates the body. *P'sachim*, fol. 42, col. 1.

These three are not permitted to come between two men, nor is a man allowed to pass between any two of these three : — A dog, a palm tree, or a woman ; to which some add the pig, and others the serpent as well.

Ibid., fol. 111, col. 1.

One part of this regulation is rather hard and should surely be abolished ; that, viz, which ordains a woman shall not come between two men or a man pass between two women. The compiler of this Miscellany was once witness to a case which illustrates its inconvenience: it occurred at Tiberias. A pious young Jew who had to traverse a narrow road to pass from the lake to the town was kept standing for a very considerable time under a broiling sun, simply because two young women, to tease him, guarded the entrance, and dared him to pass between them. Of course he dared not accept the challenge, otherwise he would have incurred the penalty of death, according to the judgment of the Talmud ; for " Whosoever transgresses any of the words of the Scribes is guilty of death." (*Eiruvin*, fol. 21, col. 2.)

These three will inherit the world to come : — He who dwells in the land of Israel ; he who brings up his sons to the study of the law ; and he who repeats the ritual blessing over the appointed cup of wine at the close of the Sabbath. *P'sachim*, fol. 113, col. 1.

There are three whom the Holy One — blessed be He ! — Himself proclaims virtuous : — The unmarried man who lives in a city and does not sin ; the poor man who restores a lost thing which he has found to its owner ; and the rich man who pays the tithes of his increase unostentatiously. Rav Saphra was a bachelor, and he dwelt in a large city. A disciple of the wise once descanted upon the merits of a celibate life in the presence of Rava and this Rav Saphra, and the face of the latter beamed with delight. Remarking which, Rava said to him, "This does not refer to such a bachelor as thou art, but to such as Rabbi Chanena and Rabbi Oshaia." They were single men, who followed the trade of shoemakers, and dwelt in a street mostly occupied by *meretrices*, for whom they made shoes ; but when they fitted these on, they never raised their eyes to look at their faces. For this the women conceived such a respect for them, that when they swore, they swore by the life of the holy Rabbis of the land of Israel.

P'sachim, fol. 113, cols. 1, 2.

There are three whom the Holy One — blessed be He ! — abhorreth : He who says one thing but thinks another ; he who might bear witness in favor of his neighbor but refrains from doing so ; and he who, having seen his neighbor act disgracefully, goes and appears singly as a witness against him (thus only condemning, but not convicting, him, as the law requires two witnesses). As, for example, when Toviah transgressed and Zigud appeared against him singly before Rav Pappa, and Rav Pappa ordered this witness to receive forty stripes save one in return. "What !" said he, "Toviah has sinned, and should Zigud be flogged?" "Yes," replied the Rabbi, "for by testifying singly against him thou bringest him only into bad repute." (See Deut. xix. 15.)   *P'sachim*, fol. 113, col. 2.

"Toviah has sinned and Zigud is flogged," has long been a proverb among Jews.

There are three whose life is no life : — The sympathetic, the irascible, and the melancholy.
                        P'sachim, fol. 113, col. 2.

There are three which despise their fellows : — Dogs, cocks, and sorcerers. Some say strange women also, and some the disciples of the Babylonian Rabbis.   *Ibid.*

These three love their fellows : — Proselytes, slaves, and ravens.   *Ibid.*

These three are apt to strut : — Israel among the nations, the dog among animals, the cock among birds. Some say also the goat among small cattle, and some the caper shrub among trees.   *Ibid.*, fol. 25, col. 2.

There are three whose life is no life : — He who lives at another's table ; he whose wife domineers over him ; and he who suffers bodily affliction. Some say also he who has only a single shirt in his wardrobe. *Ibid.*, fol. 32, col. 2.

Three things are said respecting the finger-nails: — He who trims his nails and buries the parings is a pious man ; he who burns these is a righteous man ; but he who throws them away is a wicked man, for mischance might follow, should a female step over them. *Moed Katan*, fol. 18, col. 1.

The orthodox Jews in Poland are to this day careful to bury away or burn their nail parings.

Three classes appear on the day of judgment : — The perfectly righteous, who are at once written and sealed for eternal life ; the thoroughly bad, who are at once written and sealed for hell ; as it is written (Dan. xii. 2), " And many of them that sleep in the dust of the earth shall awake, some to everlasting life, and some to shame and everlasting contempt ; " and those in the intermediate state, who go down into hell, where they cry and howl for a time, whence they ascend again ; as it is written (Zech. xiii. 9), " And I will bring the third part through the fire, and will refine them as silver is refined, and will try them as gold is tried ; they shall call on my name, and I will hear them." It is of them Hannah said (1 Sam. ii. 6), " The Lord killeth and maketh alive ; He bringeth down to hell and bringeth up."

Rosh Hashanah, fol. 16, col. 2.

Our Rabbis have taught that there are three voices which can be heard from one end of the world to the other : — The sound emitted from the sphere of the sun ; the hum and din of the city of Rome ; and the voice of anguish uttered by the soul as it quits the body ; . . . but our Rabbis prayed that the soul might be spared this torture, and therefore the voice of its terrors has not since been heard. *Yoma*, fol. 20, col. 2.

In three particulars is benevolence superior to almsgiving : — Almsgiving is only the bestowment of money, but benevolence can be exercised by personal service as well. Alms can be given only to the poor, but benevolence can be shown no less to the rich. Alms are confined to the living, but benevolence may extend to both the dead and the living. *Succah*, fol. 49, col. 2.

Three marks characterize the nation of Israel : — They are compassionate, they are modest, and they are benevolent. Compassionate, as it is written (Deut. xiii. 18), " And show thee mercy, and have compassion upon thee, and multiply thee." Modest, as it is written (Exod. xx. 20), " That his fear may be before your faces." Benevolent, as it is written (Gen. xviii. 19), " For I know him," etc.

Yevamoth, fol. 79, col. 1.

Dates are good after meals in the morning and in the evening, but hurtful in the afternoon ; on the other hand, at noon they are most excellent, and an antidote to these three maladies : — Evil thought, constipation, and hemorrhoids. *Kethuboth*, fol. 10, col. 2.

Beware of these three things : — Do not sit too much, for it brings on hemorrhoids ; do not stand too much, for it is bad for the heart ; do not walk too much, for it is hurtful to the eyes. But sit a third, stand a third, and walk a third. *Ibid.*, fol. 111, col. 1.

He who holds his household in terror tempts to the commission of three sins : — Fornication, murder, and Sabbath breaking. *Gittin*, fol. 6, col. 2.

Three things weaken the strength of man : — Fear, travel, and sin. Fear, as it is written (Ps. xxxviii. 10), " My heart palpitates, my strength faileth me." Travel, as it is written (Ps. cii. 23), " He hath weakened my strength in the way." . . . Sin, as it is written (Ps. xxxi. 10), " My strength faileth me, because of my iniquity." *Ibid.*, fol. 70, col 2.

Abraham was three years old when he first learned to know his Creator ; as it is said (Gen. xxvi. 5), " Because Abraham obeyed my voice." *Nedarim*, fol. 32, col. 1.

The conclusion arrived at here is founded on interpreting the Hebrew letters of the word rendered "because" numerically, in which the value of the letters gives a total of one hundred and seventy-two ; so that the sense of the text is, "Abraham obeyed my voice" one hundred and seventy-two years. Now Abraham died when he was a hundred and seventy-five, therefore he must have been only three when he began to serve the Lord.

As Abraham plays so important a part both in the history and the imagination of the Jewish race, we may quote here a score or so of the Talmudic traditions regarding him. The traditions, as is like, contributed quite as much, if not more, to give character to his descendants as his actual personality and that spirit of faith which was the central fact in his history. Races and nations often draw more inspiration from what they fancy about their ancestry and early history than from what they know; their fables therefore are often more illuminative than the facts.

Abraham was Ethan the Ezrahite, who is mentioned in Ps. lxxxvii. 1. *Bava Bathra*, fol. 15, col. 1.

Abraham's mother was Amathlai, the daughter of Kar-
nebo.   *Bava Bathra*, fol. 91, col. 1.

Abraham was the head of a seminary for youth, and
kept both laws, the written and the oral.

Yoma, fol. 28, col. 2.

Abraham observed the whole ceremonial law, even before
it was given on Sinai.   *Kiddushin*, fol. 82, col. 1.

From the day Abraham was compelled to leave the idolatrous
worship and country of his fathers, it is reasonable to suppose that
his tent would become a rendezvous for his neighbors who shrunk
like himself from the abominations around them. There, from his
character, by which he recommended himself as the friend of God,
he might very naturally be looked upon as a religious teacher, and
men might gather together to learn from his lips or profit by his example. Hence, making due allowance for Eastern hyperbole, the
statement of the Book of Jasher (chap. xxvi. verse 36) is not unde-
serving of credit, where it is said that "Abraham brought all the
children of the land to the service of God, and he taught them the
ways of the Lord." The same remark applies to what is said in
Targ. Yerushalmi (Gen. xxi.), that Abraham' guests went not away
until "he had made them proselytes, and had taught them the way
everlasting." His son Isaac, says the Targ. of Ben Uzziel, went to
school at the "Beth Medrasha de Shem Rabba."

Though Abraham kept all the commandments, he was
not perfect till he was circumcised.

Nedarim, fol. 31, col. 2.

In whatever sense this may have been written, and whatever the interpretation that may be put upon it, there is one sense in which it is
absolutely and eternally true, and that is, that, in order to be perfect, a
man's life must be as pronounced on the negative side as the positive,
in its denials as in its affirmations, and that it is futile to attempt to
obey God unless one at the same time renounce all co-partnery with
the devil. Circumcision is the symbol of this renunciation, and it is
only as such it has any radical spiritual significance. Till he was circumcised, it is said, God did not speak to Abraham in Hebrew. Not
till then is sacredness of speech, any more than sacredness of life,
possible. Doubtless among the Jews circumcision was the symbol of
their separation from the ethnic religions; and hence the jealousy with
which their prophets looked upon any compromise with idolatry.
Hatred of that, utter and intense, was the one essential negative pole
of genuine Judaism, and circumcision was its sign and seal.

Abraham was the first of the proselytes.

Succah, fol. 49, col. 2.

Abraham it was that ordained the form of prayer for morning worship, which is extant to this very day.

Berachoth, fol. 26, col. 2.

As he himself was pious, so were his very camels, for they would not enter into a place where there were idols; as it is written (Gen. xxiv. 31), "I have prepared," *i. e.*, removed the idols from, "the house and room for the camels." *Avoth d' Rabbi Nathan*, chap. 8.

Abraham had a daughter, and her name was Bakol.

Ibid., fol. 16, col. 2.

Abraham was free from evil passion.

Bava Bathra, fol. 17, col. 1.

He was also free from the Angel of Death.

Ibid., fol. 17, col. 1.

He delivered to the children he had by Keturah a secret name, with which they learned to practice witchcraft and do the works of the devil. *Sanhedrin*, fol. 91, col. 1.

Though great, he personally waited on his guests, who had the appearance of Arabs and not of angels.

Kiddushin, fol. 32, col. 2.

Rabbi Yehudah says Abraham planted an ornamental garden with all kinds of choice fruits in it, and Rabbi Nehemiah says he erected an inn for travelers in order to make known the name of God to all who sojourned in it.

Soteh, fol. 10, col. 1.

Both the Targum of Ben Uzziel and the Yerushalmi say that Abraham planted a paradise at Beersheba for the entertainment and delectation of his guests; and in Jasher (chap. xxvii. verse 37) it is said that "Abraham formed a grove and planted a vineyard there, and had always ready in his tent meat and drink for those that passed through the land, so that they might satisfy themselves in his house."

He ranked as one of the seven shepherds of Israel (Micah v. 5). In this group David was the central figure, with Adam, Seth, and Methusaleh on his right hand, and Abraham, Jacob, and Moses on his left.

Succah, fol. 52, col. 2.

The coin of Jerusalem had the impress of David and Solomon on the one side, and the holy city of Jerusalem on the other. But the impress on the coin of our father

Abraham was an old man and an old woman on one side, and a young man and a damsel on the other.

Bava Kama, fol. 37, col. 2.

This, it is to be presumed, must be taken in some symbolical sense, for coins cannot be traced back to a date so early as this; and when Abraham purchased the cave to bury Sarah in from the sons of Heth, we read that he weighed to Ephron the silver.

Abraham pleaded with God on the behalf of Israel and said, "While there is a Temple they will get their sins atoned for, but when there shall be no Temple, what will become of them?" God, in answer to his prayer, assured him that He had prepared a prayer for them, by which, as often as they read it, He would be propitiated and would pardon all their sins. *Meggillah*, fol. 31, col. 2.

He was punished by his posterity being compelled to serve the Egyptians two hundred and ten years, because he had pressed the Rabbis under his tuition into military service in the expedition he had undertaken to recover Lot from those who had carried him off captive; for it is written (Gen. xiv. 14), "He armed his instructed." Samuel says Abraham was punished because he perversely distrusted the assurance of God; as it is written (Gen. xv. 8), "Whereby shall I know that I shall inherit it?"

Nedarim, fol. 31, col. 2.

Abraham was thrown into a fiery furnace by Nimrod, and God would not permit Gabriel to rescue him, but did so Himself; because God is One and Abraham was one, therefore it behooved the One to rescue the one.

P'sachim, fol. 118, col. 1.

The fire from which Abraham is here said to be delivered may simply refer to his deliverance by the hand of God from Ur of the Chaldees; Ur meaning "fire," and being the name of a place celebrated for fire worship. The Midrash (p. 20) says, "When the wicked Nimrod cast Abraham into the furnace, Gabriel said, 'Lord of the universe! permit me to deliver this holy one from the fire!' But the Lord made answer, 'I am the One Supreme in my world, and he is supreme in his; it is fitting therefore that the Supreme should rescue the supreme.'"

Abraham was a giant of giants; his height was as that of seventy-four men put together. His food, his drink, and

his strength were in the proportion of seventy-four men's
to one man's. He built an iron city for the abode of his
seventeen children by Keturah, the walls of which were so
lofty that the sun never penetrated them : he gave them a
bowl full of precious stones, the brilliancy of which supplied them with light in the absence of the sun.

Sophrim, chap. 21.

Abraham our father had a precious stone suspended from
his neck, and every sick person that gazed upon it was
immediately healed of his disease. But when Abraham died,
God hung up the stone on the sphere of the sun.

Bava Bathra, fol. 16, col. 2.

Till Abraham's time there was no such thing as a beard ;
but as many mistook Abraham for Isaac, and Isaac for
Abraham, they looked so exactly alike, Abraham prayed to
God for a beard to enable people to distinguish him from his
son, Isaac, and it was granted him ; as it is written (Gen.
xxiv. 1), " And to Abraham a beard came when he was
well stricken in age." *Sanhedrin*, fol. 107, col. 2.

Here the word which the translators of the English version render
" was old," is taken in another of its cognate meanings as a beard. The
Midrash is a trifle more modest in this legendary assertion. There
we read, " Before Abraham there was no special mark of old age," and
that for distinction's sake " the beard was made to turn gray."

When he died, all the chiefs of the nations of the world
stood in a line and exclaimed, " Alas for the world that has
lost its leader ! Alas for the ship that has lost its helms-
man ! " *Bava Bathra*, fol. 91, col. 2.

As Rabbi Banna went about to measure and to mark off
the outward and inward dimensions of the different caves,
when he came to the cave of Machpelah he found Eliezar,
Abraham's servant, at the entrance, and asked him, " What
is Abraham doing ? " The answer he received was, " He is
asleep in the arms of Sarah." *Ibid.*, fol. 58, col. 1.

Abraham being greater than Moses, for while the latter is only
called by God " My Servant " (Mal. iv. 4), the former is called " My
Friend " (Isa. xli. 8), we devote a little more space for a few more
extracts from other Jewish sources than the Talmud, in order to make
the picture they supply of Abraham's character a little more complete.

Rabbi Yochanan ben Nuri says : — "The Holy One — blessed be He ! — took Shem and separated him to be a priest to Himself, that he might serve before Him. He also caused His Shechinah to rest with him, and called his name Melchizedek, priest of the Most High and king of Salem. His brother Japheth even studied the law in his school, until Abraham came and also learned the law in the school of Shem, where God Himself instructed Abraham, so that all else he had learned from the lips of man was forgotten. Then came Abraham and prayed to God that His Shechinah might ever rest in the house of Shem, which also was promised to him ; as it is said (Ps. cx. 4), 'Thou art a priest forever after the order of Melchizedek.' "

Avodath Hakkodesh, part 3, chap. 20.

Wherever Jacob resided he studied the law as his fathers did. How is this, seeing the law had not yet been given, it is nevertheless written of Abraham (Gen. xxvi. 5), "And he kept my charge"? Whence then did Abraham learn the law? Rabbi Shimon says his reins (literally kidneys) were made like two water-jars, from which the law flowed forth. Where do we learn that it was so? From what is said in Ps. xvi. 7, "My reins also instruct me in the night season." *Bereshith Rabba*, chap. 95.

The masters of the Kabbalah, of blessed memory, say that Abraham's Rabbi, *i. e.*, teacher, was the angel Zadkiel.

Rabbi Menachem's comment on the Pent., Exod. iii. 5.

Adam's book, which contained celestial mysteries and holy wisdom, came down as an heirloom into the hands of Abraham, and he by means of it was able to see the glory of his Lord. *Zohar Parashah Bereshith.*

Abraham was the author of a treatise on the subject of different kinds of witchcraft and its unholy workings and fruits, as also of the Book of Creation, through holy names (by means of which, namely, anything could be created). *Nishmath Chayim*, chap. 29.

The whole world once believed that the souls of men were perishable, and that man had no pre-eminence above a beast, till Abraham came and preached the doctrine of immortality and transmigration. *Ibid.*, fol. 171, col. 1.

A good son delivers his father from the punishment of hell, for thus we find that Abraham our father delivered Terah, as it is said in Gen. xv. 15, "And thou shalt go to thy fathers in peace." This implies that God had communicated to him the tidings that his father had a portion in the world to come and was now "in peace" there.

Pesikta Zotarta, fol. 3, col. 2.

Before Abraham was circumcised God spake to him in the Chaldee language, that the angels should not understand it. (This is proved from Gen. xv. 1.)

Yalkut Chadash, fol. 117.

Rabbi Levi said Abraham sits at the gate of hell and does not permit any circumcised Israelite to enter. But if any appear who happen to have sinned unduly, these he (by an indescribable contrivance) causes to become uncircumcised and lets pass without scruple into the region of torment ; and this is what is said in Ps. lv. 20, "He hath put forth his hands against such as be at peace with him : he hath broken his covenant." *Yalkut Shimoni*, fol. 33, col. 2, sec. 18.

Abraham was circumcised on the Day of Atonement, and God looks that day annually on the blood of the covenant of our father Abraham's circumcision as atoning for all our iniquities, as it is said in Lev. xvi. 30, "For on that day shall he make an atonement for you, to cleanse you from all your sins." *Yalkut Chadash*, fol. 121, col. 1, sec. 3.

"And it came to pass that when Abram was come into Egypt" (Gen. xii. 14). And where was Sarah? He confined her in a chest, into which he locked her, lest any one should gaze on her beauty. When he came to the receipt of custom, he was summoned to open the chest, but declined, and offered payment of the duty. The officers said, "Thou carriest garments ;" and he offered duty for garments. "Nay, it is gold thou carriest ;" and he offered the impost laid on gold. Then they said, "It is costly silks, belike pearls, thou concealest ;" and he offered the custom on such articles. At length the Egyptian officers insisted, and he opened the box. And when he did so, all the land of Egypt was illumined by her beauty.

Bereshith Rabba, chap. 40.

The question may naturally be asked why Abraham hid his wife from the gaze of others first then and not before. The reply is to be deduced from the following double rendering of Gen. xii. 11 : — "Behold now I know that thou art a fair woman." As if to say, "Usually people lose their good looks on a long journey, but thou art as beautiful as ever." The second explanation is this : — Abraham was so piously modest that in all his life he never once looked a female in the face, his own wife not excepted. As he approached Egypt and was crossing some water, he saw in it the reflection of her face, and it was then that he exclaimed, "Behold now I know that thou art a fair woman." As the Egyptians are swarthy, Abraham at once perceived the magnitude of the danger, and hence his precaution to hide her beauty in a chest.

Zeenah Ureenah (1877 in Russia), fol. 28, col. 1.

When Abraham came to the cave of Machpelah to bury Sarah, Adam and Eve rose from their grave and protested against his committing her to the dust in that receptacle. "For," said they, "we are ever ashamed in the presence of the Holy One — blessed be He ! — on account of the sin which we committed, and now comest thou to add to our shame by the contrast therewith of the good works which ye two have done." On Abraham's assurance that he would intercede with God on their behalf that they should not bear the shame any longer, Adam immediately retired to his sepulchre, but Eve being still unwilling to do so, Abraham took her by the hand and led her back to the side of Adam ; and then he buried Sarah.

Yalkut Chadash, fol. 14, col. 3, sec. 68.

Abraham's father, Terah, was both an idolater, a manufacturer of idols, and a dealer in them. Once when Terah had some engagement elsewhere he left his son Abraham to attend to his business. When a customer came to purchase an idol, Abraham asked him, "How old art thou?" "Lo! so many years," was the ready reply. "What," exclaimed Abraham, "is it possible that a man of so many years should desire to worship a thing only a day old?" The customer, being ashamed of himself, went his way ;

and so did all other customers, who underwent a similar inquisition. Once an old woman brought a measure of fine flour and wished to present it as an offering to the gods. This so enraged Abraham that he took a staff and broke all the images, excepting the largest, into whose hands he fixed the staff. When his father came and questioned him about the destruction of the gods, he replied, "An old woman placed an offering of flour before them, which immediately set them all by the ears, for every one was hungrier than another, but the biggest god killed all the rest with this staff which thou now seest he still holds in his hands." Superstition, especially when combined with mercenary motives, knows neither reason nor human affection, therefore the father handed over his son Abraham to the inquisition of Nimrod, who threw him into the fiery furnace, as recorded elsewhere in this Miscellany. This is an historical fact, to the truth of which the whole orthodox Jewish world will bear testimony, and is solemnly recorded in *Shalsheleth Hakkabalah*, fol. 2. col. 1.

There are three graces: — The grace of a place in the eyes of its inhabitants; the grace of a woman in the eyes of her husband; the grace of a purchase in the eyes of the buyer. *Soteh*, fol. 47, col. 1.

A man should divide his capital into three parts, and invest one-third in land, employ one-third in merchandise, and reserve one-third in ready money.
Bava Metzia, fol. 42, col. 1.

All who go down to hell shall come up again, except these three : — He who commits adultery; he who shames another in public; and he who gives another a bad name.
Ibid., fol. 58, col. 2.

These three complain, but no one sympathizes with them : — He who lends money without witnesses; he who buys to himself a master; and he who is lorded over by his wife. *Ibid.*, fol. 75, col. 2.

There are three things on which the world stands : — The law, the temple service, and benevolence.
Avoth, chap. 1.

If three eat at one table and do not converse together on the law of the Lord, it is as if they ate from the sacrifices for the dead; but they, on the contrary, are as if they partook from a table of the Lord's own furnishing who, while they sit down to meat, season their talk with its holy precepts. *Avoth*, chap. 3.

There are three crowns:—The crown of the law, the crown of the priesthood, and the crown of royalty; but the crown of a good name surpasses them all.

Ibid., chap. 4.

He who possesses these three virtues is a disciple of Abraham our father, and he who possesses the three contrary vices is a son of Balaam the wicked. The disciples of our father Abraham have a kindly eye, a loyal spirit, and a lowly mind. The disciples of Balaam the wicked have an evil eye, a proud spirit, and a grasping soul.

Ibid., chap. 5.

Three things are said respecting the children of men:— He who gives alms brings a blessing on himself; he who lends does better; he who gives away half of what he hath to spare does best of all.

Avoth d'Rab. Nathan, chap. 41.

There are three classes of disciples, and among them three grades of worth:—He ranks first who asks and answers when asked; he who asks but does not answer ranks next; but he who neither asks nor answers ranks lowest of all. *Ibid.*

Over these three does God weep every day:—Over him who is able to study the law but neglects it; over him who studies it amid difficulties hard to overcome; and over the ruler who behaves arrogantly toward the community he should protect. *Chaggigah*, fol. 5, col. 2.

Rabbi Yochanan says there are three keys in the hands of the Holy One!—blessed be He!—which He never intrusts to the disposal of a messenger, and they are these: —(1.) The key of rain, (2.) the key of life, and (3.) the key of reviving the dead. The key of rain, for it is written (Deut. xxviii. 12), "The Lord shall open unto thee His good treasure, the heaven to give the rain unto thy

iand in season;" the key of life, as it is written (Gen.
xxx. 22), "God hearkened unto her, and opened her
womb;" the key of reviving the dead, for it is written
(Ezek. xxxvii. 13), "When I have opened your graves,
and brought you up out of your graves, and shall put my
spirit in you, and ye shall live," etc.

Taanith, fol. 2, cols. 1, 2.

A disciple of the wise who makes light of the washing of
hands is contemptible; but more contemptible is he who
begins to eat before his guest; more contemptible is that
guest who invites another guest; and still more contemptible
is he who begins to eat before a disciple of the wise; but
contemptible before all these three put together is that
guest which troubles another guest.

Derech Eretz Zuta, chap. viii.

A roll of the law which has two mistakes to a column
should be corrected; but if there be three, it should be
stowed away altogether.   *Menachoth*, fol. 29, col. 2.

The wolf, the lion, the bear, the leopard, the panther,
the elephant, and the sea-cat, each bear three years.   *Ibid.*

Rav Yehudah says, in the name of Rav, "The butcher is
bound to have three knives; one to slaughter with, one for
cutting up the carcass, and one to cut away the suet. Suet
being as unlawful for food as pork.

Chullin, fol. 8, col. 2.

Three classes of ministering angels raise a song of praise
every day. One class says, Holy! the second responds,
Holy! and the third continues, Holy is the Lord of hosts!
But in the presence of the Holy One — blessed be He! —
Israel is more beloved than the ministering angels; for
Israel reiterates the song every hour, while the ministering
angels repeat it only once a day, some say once a week, others
once a month, others once a year, others once in seven
years, others once in a jubilee, and others only once in
eternity. Again, Israel mentions The Name after two words,
as it is said (Deut. vi. 4), "Hear Israel, Yehovah," but
the ministering angels do not mention The Name till after
three, as it is written (Isa. vi. 3), "Holy! holy! holy!
Yehovah Zebaoth." Moreover, the ministering angels do

not take up the song above till Israel has started it below; for it is said (Job xxxviii. 7), "When the morning stars sang together, then all the sons of God shouted for joy."

Chullin, fol. 91, col. 2.

The Rabbis have taught, a man should not sell to his neighbor shoes made from the hide of a beast that has died of disease, as if of a beast that had been slaughtered in the shambles, for two reasons: first, because he imposes on him (for the skin of a beast that dies of itself is not so durable as the hide of a slaughtered animal); second, because there is danger (for the beast that died of itself might have been stung by a serpent, and the poison remaining in the leather might prove fatal to the wearer of shoes made of that leather). A man should not send his neighbor a barrel of wine with oil floating upon its surface; for it happened once that a man did so, and the recipient went and invited his friends to a feast, in the preparation of which oil was to form a chief ingredient; but when the guests assembled, it was found out that the cask contained wine, and not oil; and because the host had nothing else in preparation for a worthy feast, he went and committed suicide. Neither should guests give anything from what is set before them to the son or daughter of their host, unless the host himself give them leave to do so; for it once happened during a time of scarcity that a man invited three of his friends to dine, and he had nothing but three eggs to place before them. Meanwhile, as the guests were seated at the board, the son of the host came into the room, and first one of the guests gave him his share, and then the other two followed his example. Shortly afterward the host himself came in, and seeing the child with his mouth full and both hands, he knocked him down to the ground, so that he died on the instant. The mother, seeing this, went and threw herself headlong, from the housetop, and the father followed her example. Thus Rabbi Eliezar ben Yacob said, "There perished in this affair three souls of Israel."

Ibid., fol. 94, col. 1.

Once the Roman Government issued a decree that the Israelites should neither observe the Sabbath nor circumcise

their sons. Thereupon Reuben the son of Istrubli trimmed
his hair as a Gentile, and went among the Roman senators
and plied them with wise remonstrance. "If one," said he,
"has an enemy, does he wish him to be poor or rich?" "To
be poor," was the reply. "Then," he argued, "won't he be
poorer if you prohibit him from working on the Sabbath?"
"It is well said," observed the senators; and they at once
abolished their decree respecting the Sabbath. Again he
asked, "If one has an enemy, does he wish him to be
weak or strong?" "Why, weak, to be sure," was the
inevitable answer. "Then," said he, "let the Jews circumcise their children, then will they be weakened." "The
argument is good," said they, and the decree against cir-
cumsion was rescinded. Again he asked, "If one has an
enemy, does he wish him to increase or decrease?" "To
decrease, of course," said they. In response to his argument the decree against catamenia was accordingly abolished. When, however, they found out that he was a Jew,
they at once re-enacted the decrees they had canceled.
Upon this the question arose who should go to Rome and
appeal against these enactments. It was resolved that
Rabbi Shimon ben Yochai, who was reputed experienced in
miracles, should go, accompanied by Rabbi Elazar, the son
of Rabbi Yossi. . . . As they journeyed along, the
question was proposed to them, "Whence is it proved that
the blood of a reptile is unclean?" Rabbi Elazar replied
with a curl of the lip, and quoted Lev. ii. 29. "And these
shall be unclean unto you." Rabbi Shimon said unto him,
"By the curl of thy lip art thou recognizable as a disciple
of the wise! May the son never return to his father!"
for he was annoyed that he should presume to teach a
Halachah in his presence, and then and there he condemned
him to death. (See *Berachoth*, fol. 31, col. 2.) Thereupon
Ben Temalion (an evil sprite or imp) came, and greeting
him, said, "Do ye wish me to accompany you?" Rabbi
Shimon wept and said, "Alas! a maid-servant of my ancestor (Abraham) was assisted by three angels, and I have
not one to attend me! However, let a miracle be worked
for us anyhow." Then the evil spirit entered into the
Emperor's daughter, and when the Rabbi was called in to

cure the princess, he exorcised the spirit by saying, "Depart, Ben Temalion! Ben Temalion, depart!" and the evil spirit left her. By way of reward the Rabbis were bidden to ask whatsoever they pleased, and admitted into the imperial treasury that they might choose what seemed good to them. Espying there the edict against Israel, they chose it, and tore it to pieces. *Meyilah*, fol. 17, col. 1, 2.

At the time when the high priest enters to worship, three acolytes take hold of him, one by the right hand and another by the left, while the third lifts the gems attached to the train of his pontifical vestment.

Tamid, chap. 7; *Mishna*, 1.

"I once, when a grave-digger," says Abba Shaul, as the Rabbis relate, "chased a roe which had entered the shinbone of a dead man; and though I ran three miles after it, I could not overtake it, nor reach the end of the bone. When I returned, I was told that it was a bone of Og, king of Bashan." *Niddah*, fol. 24, col. 2.

The Rabbis have taught that during the first three months (of pregnancy) the child lies in the lower part (of the uterus); during the next three it occupies the middle part; and during the last three it is in the upper part; and that when the time of parturition comes, it turns over first, and this causes the birth-pains. We are also taught that the pains caused by a female child are greater than those caused by a male. Rabbi Elazar said, "What Scripture is there for this? 'When I was made in secret and curiously wrought, in the lowest parts of the earth' (Ps. cxxxix. 15). It is not said, 'I abode,' but, 'I was curiously wrought.' Why the difference? Why are the pains caused by a girl greater than those caused by a boy?"

Ibid., fol. 31, col. 1.

The Rabbis teach there are three that have a share in a man; God, and his father and mother. The father's part consists of all that is white in him — the bones, the veins, the nails, the brain, and the white of the eye. The mother's part consists of all that is red in him — the skin, the flesh, the hair, and the black part of the eye. God's part consists of the breath, the soul, the physiognomy, sight and hearing, speech, motive power, knowledge, understanding, and wisdom. And when the time comes that the man should depart from the world, God takes away His part, and leaves those which belong to the father and mother. Rav Pappa says, "This is the meaning of the proverb, 'Shake off the salt and throw the flesh to the dogs.'" *Niddah*, fol. 31. col. 1.

Rashi's explanatory note is this: "Shake off the salt from the flesh and it becomes fit only for dogs. The soul is the salt which preserves the body; when it departs, the body putrefies."

Four things require fortitude in the observance: — The law, good works, prayer, and social duties. Respecting the law and good works it is written (Josh. i. 7), "Be thou strong and firm, that thou mayest observe to do all the law;" in which the word "strong" refers to the law, and the word "firm" to good works. Of prayer it is written, "Wait on the Lord; be strong, and He shall make thine heart firm; wait, I say, upon the Lord" (Ps. xxvii. 14). In respect to social duties it is written (2 Sam. x. 2), "Be strong, and let us strengthen ourselves for our people, and for the cities of our God." *Berachoth*, fol. 32, col. 2.

There are four signs which tell tales: — Dropsy is a sign of sin; jaundice is a sign of hatred without a cause; poverty is a sign of pride; and quinsy is a sign of slander. *Shabbath*, fol. 33, col. 1.

"Unto Mamre, unto the city of Arbah," *i.e.*, four (Gen. xxxv. 27). Rabbi Isaac calls it the city of four couples, *i.e.*, Adam and Eve, Abraham and Sarah, Isaac and Rebekah, Jacob and Leah. These four couples being buried in Mamre, it was therefore called "the city of four." *Eiruvin*, fol. 53, col. 1.

The sun makes four quarterly circuits. In April, May, and June, *i.e.*, Nisan, Iyar, and Sivan, his circuit is between the mountains, in order to dissolve the snow; in July, August, and September, *i. e.*, Tamuz, Ab, and Ellul, his circuit is over the habitable parts of the earth, in order to ripen the fruits; in October, November, and December, *i. e.*, Tishri, Marcheshvan, and Kislev, his circuit is over the seas, to evaporate the waters; in January, February, and March, *i. e.*, Tebeth, Shebat, and Adar, his circuit is over the deserts, in order to protect the seed sown from being scorched. *P'sachim*, fol. 94, col. 2.

Four persons are intolerable : — A poor man who is proud, a rich man who is a liar, an old man who is incontinent, and a warden who behaves haughtily to a community for whom he has done nothing. To these some add him who has divorced his wife once or twice and married her again. *Ibid.*, fol. 113, col. 2.

Four things cancel the decrees of Heaven : — Alms, prayer, change of name, and reformation of conduct. Alms, as it is written (Prov. x. 2), "But alms (more correctly, righteousness) delivereth from death." Prayer as it is written (Ps. cvii. 6), "Then they cried unto the Lord in their trouble, and He delivered them out of their distresses." Change of name, as it is said (Gen. xvii. 15, 16), "As for Sarai thy wife, thou shalt not call her name Sarai, but Sarah shall be her name." And after this change of name it is written, "And I will bless her, and give thee a son of her." Reformation of conduct, as it is written (Jonah iii. 10), "And God saw their works," and "God repented of the evil," etc. Some say also change of residence has the effect of turning back the decree of Heaven (Gen. xii. 1), "And the Lord said unto Abram, Get thee out of thy country ;" and then it is said, "I will make of thee a great nation." *Rosh Hashanah*, fol. 16, col. 2.

Four things cause an eclipse of the sun : — When a chief magistrate dies and is not mourned over with the due lamentation ; when a betrothed damsel calls for help and no one comes to the rescue ; when the people commit the sin of Sodom and Gomorrah ; and when brother murders brother. *Succah*, fol. 29, col. 1.

Four things cause an eclipse among the luminaries of heaven : The writing of false documents ; the bearing false witness ; the breeding of small cattle, such as sheep and goats, in the land of Israel ; and the cutting down of fruit-trees. *Ibid.*, fol. 29, col. 1.

There are four things God repents of having created : — The Captivity, the Chaldeans, the Ishmaelites, and the evil passion in man. The Captivity, as it is written (Isa. lii. 5), "What have I here, saith the Lord, that my people are taken away for nought?" etc. The Chaldeans, as it is written (Isa. xxiii. 13), "Behold the land of the Chaldeans: this people was not." The Ishmaelites, as it is written (Job xii. 6), "The tents of robbers prosper, and they that provoke God are secure, into whose hand God bringeth abundance." The evil passion, as it is written (Micah iv. 6), "And whom I have caused to be evil."

Succah, fol. 52, col. 2.

There have been four beautiful women in the world: — Sarah, Abigail, Rahab, and Esther.

Meggillah, fol. 15, col. 1.

Tosephoth asks, "Why was not Eve numbered among these beauties, since even Sarah, in comparison with Eve, was an an ape compared to a man?" The reply is, "Only those born of woman are here enumerated."

In fol. 13, col. 1, of the same treatise from which the above is quoted, we are informed by Ben Azai that Esther was like the myrtle-tree, neither tall nor short statured, but middle-sized. Rabbi Yehoshua ben Korcha states that Esther's complexion was of a yellow or gold color.

One cup of wine is good for a woman, two are disgraceful, three demoralizing, and four brutalizing.

Kethuboth, fol. 65, col. 1.

He who traverses so much as four ells in the land of Israel is sure of everlasting life. *Ibid.*, fol. 111, col. 1.

To walk even four ells without bowing the head is an offense to Heaven; for it is written (Isa. vi. 3), "The whole earth is full of His glory."

Kiddushin, fol. 31, col. 1.

There are four who are accounted as dead: — The pauper, the leper, the blind man, and he who has no male children. *Nedarin*, fol. 64, col. 2.

Four things mark the characters of men: — He who says what is mine is mine, and what is thine is thine, is, according to some, a moderate man, but, according to others, a child of Sodom; he who says what is mine is thine, and what is thine is mine, is an ignorant man; he who says what is mine is thine and what is thy own is also thine, is a pious man ; he who says mine and thine are both my own, is a wicked man. *Avoth*, chap. 5, sec. 16.

There are four kinds of men, according to their degrees of passionateness : — He who is easily provoked and as readily pacified, and who loses more than he gains ; he whom it is difficult to rouse and as difficult to appease, and who gains more than he loses ; he who is not readily provoked, but easily pacified, who is a pious man ; he who is easily provoked and with difficulty appeased, who is a wicked man. *Ibid.*, chap. 5, sec. 19.

There are four classes of men who give alms, and they are thus distinguished : — He who is willing to give, but unwilling that others should do so, he has an evil eye toward others ; he who wishes others to give, but does not do so himself, he has an evil eye toward himself ; he who gives, and induces others to give, he is pious ; he who gives not, nor wishes others to give he is wicked.

Avoth, chap 5, sec. 19.

There are four marks by which one disciple differs from another : — One learns and does not teach, one teaches and does not learn, one learns and teaches, and one neither learns nor teaches. *Avoth d' Rab. Nathan*, chap. 29.

Four things, if kept in view and gravely pondered over, deter from sin : — That a man consider whence he cometh, whither he goeth, who the judge will be, and what the future will bring to pass. *Derech Eretz*, chap. 3.

What is the meaning of that which is written (Ps. lxxxvii 2), "The Lord loveth the gates of Zion more than all the dwellings of Jacob?" The answer is, The Lord loveth the gates that are marked with the Halachah more than the synagogues and the schools ; and this agrees with what Rabbi Cheeya bar Ami has said, in the name of Ulla, that since the destruction of the Temple nothing else has remained to God in His world but four ells of the Halachah. *Berachoth*, fol. 8, col. 1.

Whoso walks even four ells with a proud unbending gait is as though he spurned with his haughty head the feet of the Shechinah ; for it is written (Isa. vi. 3), "The whole earth is full of His glory." *Ibid.*, fol. 43, col. 2.

Four are in duty bound to return thanks to God : — They that have returned from a voyage at sea (Ps. cvii. 23, 24, 31); those who have traveled in the desert (verses 4–8); they who have recovered from a serious illness (verses 17–21); and those that are liberated from prison (verses 10–15).   *Berachoth*, fol. 54, col. 2.

If one does not walk, say four cubits, before falling asleep after a meal, that which he has eaten, being undigestible, causes foulness of breath.

Shabbath, fol. 41, col. 1.

Four have died in consequence of the seduction of the serpent : — Benjamin, the son of Jacob; Amram, the father of Moses; Jesse, the father of David; and Chileab, the son of David.   *Ibid.*, fol. 55, col. 2.

These four are reckoned to have died on account of original sin, and not solely because of actual transgression, which, says Rashi, they never committed.

The traveler who is overtaken with the approach of Sabbath-eve before he has completed his journey should hand over his purse to a Gentile to carry; and if there be no Gentile at hand, let him stow it away on his ass. As soon as the nearest halting-place is reached, those burdens which may be lifted on the Sabbath should then be removed, and then the cords should be slackened that the rest may slip off of its own accord. *Ibid.*, fol. 153, col. 1.

Here the Gemara very graciously appends a direction as to the disposal of the purse, in case the traveler should happen to be on foot and have no Gentile attendant. He may take care of it himself, provided he halt at every other step and deposit it on the ground, for at least a distance of four cubits.

A master is bound to rehearse a lesson to his pupil four times.   *Eiruvin*, fol. 54, col. 2.

Alas for the power which prepares a grave for its possessor, for there is not a prophet who hath not in his lifetime witnessed the decadence of four kings; as it is said (Isa. i. 1), "The vision of Isaiah . . . in the days of Uzziah, Jotham, Ahaz, and Hezekiah, kings of Judah" (see also Hosea i. 1).   *P'sachim*, fol. 87, col. 2.

Once Rav Pappa and Rav Hunnah partook together of a common meal, and as the latter ate only one morsel the former ate four. After this, when Rav Hunnah and Ravina ate together, the latter devoured eight portions to the other's one, upon which Rav Hunnah jocularly remarked, "A hundred (Rav) Pappas to one Ravina." *P'sachim*, fol. 89, col. 2.

No food may be eaten on Passover-eve from the time of the offering of the evening sacrifice (in order, *i. e.*, that abstinence may whet the appetite for the Matsoth). Even the poorest in Israel may not break his fast till the hour of reclining; nor is he to partake of less than four glasses of wine, even though he has been reduced so low as to subsist on the porridge doled out by public charity.

Ibid., fol. 99, col. 2.

There are four things the doing of which by man brings judgment upon his own head : — If he turn in between a wall and a date-palm; if he turn in between two date-palms; if he drink borrowed water; and if he step across spilt water, such even as his own wife may have thrown away. (All these doings, says Rashi, are bound to annoy the evil genii.) *Ibid.*, fol. 111, col. 1.

Four precepts did our holy Rabbi (Yehudah Hakadosh) urge upon his children : — Not to choose Shechentzia as a dwelling-place, for scoffers resided there; not to use the bed of a Syrian odalisque; not to shirk the payment of fiscal dues, lest the collector should confiscate all their property; not to face an ox when he came up (ruffled) from the cane-brake, for Satan sported betwixt his horns.

P'sachim, fol. 112, col. 2.

Whosoever prieth into the four things in the matter of the chariot in Ezekiel's vision — what is above, what is beneath, what is before, or what is behind — it were better for him if he had never been born.

Chaggigah, fol. 11, col. 2.

The work or matter of the chariot, the Rabbinic term for the Vision of Ezekiel, ranks among the Arcana Judaica, which are not to be told save to the initiated.

Four men entered Paradise — these are their names : — Ben Azai, Ben Zoma, Acher, and Rabbi Akiva. Rabbi

Akiva thus warned his companions: "When you come across pavements of pellucid marble, do not cry out 'Water! water!' for it is said (Ps. ci. 7), 'He that uttereth falsehood shall not dwell in my sight.'" Ben Azai looked and died; concerning him the Scripture says (Ps. cxvi. 15), "Precious in the sight of the Lord is the death of his saints." Ben Zoma looked and went out of his mind; of him the Scripture says (Prov. xxv. 16), "Hast thou found honey? eat only so much as is sufficient for thee, lest thou be filled therewith and vomit it." Acher cut the plants. Only Akiva departed in peace. *Chaggigah*, fol. 14, col. 2.

Rashi explains this by saying these men went up to heaven; but Maimonides much more rationally teaches that the Paradise or garden here is merely the retreat of profound philosophic meditation. These five intuitions were; — (1.) To know that there is a God; (2.) to ignore every other beside Him; (3.) to feel His unity; (4.) to love His person; and (5.) to stand in awe of His Majesty (see Yad Hachaz, chap. 4, sec. 19). Deep thought in these matters was spoken of by the Rabbis as *promenading in the garden.*

Four times a year is the world subject to an ordeal of judgment: — At Passover, which is decisive of the fruits of the field; at Pentecost, which is decisive of the fruits of the garden; at the feast of Tabernacles, which is decisive in respect of rain; on New Year's Day, when all who come into the world pass before the Lord like sheep, as it is said (Ps. xxxiii. 15), "Who formed their hearts together; who understandeth all their works."

Rosh Hashanah, fol. 16, col. 1.

There are four varieties of cedar: — Erez, Karthom, Etz-Shemen, and Berosh.   *Ibid.*, fol. 23, col. 1.

Ben Kamzar would not teach the art of writing, and yet it is related of him that he could, by taking four pens between his fingers, write off a word of four letters at one stroke.   *Yoma*, fol. 38, col. 2.

There are four kinds of quails: — Sichli, Kibli, Pisyoni, and the common quail. The first was of superior quality, and the last inferior.   *Ibid*, fol. 75, col. 2.

A man may obtain forgiveness after the third transgression, but if he repeat the offense a fourth time, he is not pardoned again; for it is said (Amos ii. 4), "For three transgressions of Judah, and for four, I will not turn away the punishment thereof;" and again (Job xxxiii. 29), "Lo! all these things doth God two or three times" (and so inferentially not four times) "with man to bring back his soul from the pit." *Yoma*, fol. 86, col. 2.

For four reasons does their property pass out of the hands of the avaricious: — Because they are backward in paying the wages of their hired servants; because they altogether neglect their welfare; because they shift the yoke from themselves and lay the burden upon their neighbors; and because of pride, which is of itself as bad as all the rest put together; whereas of the meek it is written (Ps. xxxvii. 11), "The meek shall inherit the earth." *Succah*, fol. 29, col. 2.

"And the Lord showed me four carpenters" (Zech. i, 20). Who are these four carpenters? Rav Chana bar Bizna says that Rabbi Shimon Chassida said they were Messiah the son of David, Messiah the son of Joseph, Elijah, and the Priest of Righteousness.
Ibid, fol. 52, col. 2.

No Synagogue is to be sold except on condition that there be power of re-purchase. These are the words of Rabbi Meir; but the sages say it may be sold unconditionly, except in these four particular cases: that it be not turned into a bath-house, a tannery, a wash-house, or a laundry. *Meggillah*, fol. 27, col. 2.

Rabbi Yochanan ben Zachai was once asked by his disciples how he had attained such length of days. "Never once," he said, "in my life have I acted irreverently within four cubits of a place where prayer is offered; never have I called a person by a wicked name; nor have I ever failed to sanctify the Sabbath over a cup of wine. Once my aged mother sold her head-dress to buy the consecration wine for me." *Ibid.*, fol. 27, col. 2.

When a sage is approaching, one should rise up before he gets within four ells' distance, and remain standing until he has gone as far past. When a chief magistrate is about to pass, one must rise as soon as he comes in sight,

and not resume the seat until he has passed four ells.
When a prince passes, one must stand up whenever he appears, and not sit down again until the prince himself is
seated ; for it is said (Exod. xxxiii, 8), " All the people
rose up, . . . and looked after Moses until he was gone
into the tabernacle." *Kiddushin*, fol. 33, col. 2.

When Nero came to the Holy Land, he tried his fortune
by belemnomancy thus : — He shot an arrow eastward, and
it fell upon Jerusalem ; he discharged his shafts towards the
four points of the compass, and every time they fell upon
Jerusalem. After this he met a Jewish boy, and said unto
him, " Repeat to me the text thou hast learned to-day."
The boy repeated, " I will lay my vengeance upon Edom
(*i. e.*, Rome) by the hand of my people Israel " (Ezek.
xxv. 14). Then said Nero, " The Holy One — blessed be
He ! — has determined to destroy His Temple and then
avenge Himself on the agent by whom its ruin is wrought."
Thereupon Nero fled and became a Jewish proselyte, and
Rabbi Meir is of his race. *Gittin*, fol. 56, col. 1.

They whose banquet is accompanied with four kinds of
instruments of music bring five calamities on the world ;
as it is said (Isa. v. 11–15), " Woe unto those that get up
early in the morning, that they may run after strong
drink ; and continue until late at night, till flushed with
wine. And the harp and psaltery, tambourine and flute,
and wine are at their carousals." *Soteh*, fol. 48, col. 1.

Let him carry the purse, and halt every time he accom-
plishes less than four cubits forward.

Shabbath, fol. 153, cols. 1, 2.

Rav Yitzchak here explains how the good Jew, belated on Sabbath-eve, may carry his purse himself, and so save his conscience.
The traveler is to halt at about every other step, and so measure off
the journey in four-cubit stages.

Though ever since the destruction of the Temple the
Sanhedrin has ceased to exist, the four kinds of capital
punishment have not failed to assert themselves. If a man
incurs the penalty of death by stoning, he is in the course
of Providence either punished by a fatal fall from a roof
or slain by some beast of prey ; if he has exposed himself

to the penalty of death by burning, it happens that he is either burned to death in the end or mortally stung by a serpent; if the penalty of the law is that he should be beheaded for his offense, he meets his death either from the Government officer or by the hand of an assassin; if the penalty be strangulation, he is sure to be drowned or suffocated. *Sanhedrin*, fol. 37, col. 2.

When a person is in a state of apprehension and cannot make out the cause of it (the star that presided at his birth and his genii know all about it), what should he do? Let him jump from where he is standing four cubits, or else let him repeat, "Hear, O Israel," etc. (Deut. vi. 4); or if the place be unfit for the repetition of Scripture, let him mutter to himself, "The goat at the butcher's is fatter than me." *Ibid.*, fol. 94, col. 1.

It is written in 2 Chron. xxxiii. 7, "A carved image;" and again it is written in verse 19, "Graven images." Rabbi Yochanan said, "At first he made the image with one face, but afterwards he made it with four — four, so that the Shechinah might see it from every point, and thus be exasperated." *Ibid.*, fol. 103, col. 2.

Moses uttered four judgments upon Israel, but four prophets revoked them: — (1.) First Moses said (Deut. xxxiii. 28), "Israel then shall dwell in safety alone;" then came Amos and set it aside (Amos vii. 5), "Cease, I beseech thee," etc.; and then it is written (verse 6), "This shall not be, saith the Lord." (2.) First Moses said (Deut. xxviii. 65), "Among these nations thou shalt find no ease;" then came Jeremiah and set this saying aside (Jer. xxxi. 2), "Even Israel, when I went to cause him to rest." (3.) First Moses said (Exod. xxxiv. 7), "Visiting the iniquities of the fathers upon the children;" then came Ezekiel and set this aside (Ezek. xviii. 4), "The soul that sinneth, it shall die." (4.) First Moses said (Lev. xxvi. 38), "And ye shall perish among the heathen;" then came Isaiah and reversed this (Isa. xxvii. 13), "And it shall come to pass in that day that the great trumpet shall be blown, and they shall come which were ready to perish." *Maccoth*, fol. 24, col. 1.

When Akavyah ben Mahalalel appeared to four halachahs contradicting the judgment of the wise on a certain important point of law, "Retract," they said, "and we will promote thee to be president of the tribunal." To which he replied, "I would rather be called a fool all the days of my life than be judged wicked for one hour before Him who is omnipresent." *Edioth*, chap. 5, mish. 6.

Let thy house be open wide toward the south, the east, the west, and the north, just as Job, who made four entrances to his house, in order that the poor might find entrance without trouble from whatever quarter they might come. *Avoth d' Rav. Nathan*, chap. 7.

Rabbah once saw a sea-monster on the day it was brought forth, and it was as large as Mount Tabor. And how large is Mount Tabor? Its neck was three miles long, and where it laid its head a mile and a half. Its dung choked up the Jordan, till, as Rashi says, its waters washed it away. *Bava Bathra*, fol. 73, col. 2.

Shemuel said, "We know remedies for all maladies except three:—That induced by unripe dates on an empty stomach; that induced by wearing a damp linen rope round one's loins; and that induced by falling asleep after meals without having first walked a distance of at least four cubits." *Bava Metzia*, fol. 113, col. 2.

The five times repeated "Bless the Lord, O my soul" (Ps. ciii. civ.), were said by David with reference both to God and the soul. As God fills the whole world, so does the soul fill the whole body; as God sees and is not seen, so the soul sees and is not seen; as God nourishes the whole world, so does the soul nourish the whole body; as God is pure, so also is the soul pure; as God dwelleth in secret, so does the soul dwell in secret. Therefore let him who possesses these five properties praise Him to whom these five attributes belong.

Berachoth, fol. 10, col. 1.

Five things have in them a sixtieth part of five other things:—Fire, honey, the Sabbath, sleep, and dreams. Fire is a sixtieth of hell, honey a sixtieth of manna, the Sabbath a sixtieth of the rest in the world to come, sleep the sixtieth of death, and a dream the sixtieth of prophecy.

Berachoth, fol. 57, col. 2.

There are five weak things that are a source of terror to the strong : — The mosquito is a terror to the lion, the gnat is a terror to the elephant, the ichneumon-fly is a terror to the scorpion, the flycatcher is a terror to the eagle, and the stickleback is a terror to the leviathan.

Shabbath, fol. 77, col. 2.

These five should be killed even on the Sabbath : — The fly of Egypt, the wasp of Nineveh, the scorpion of Hadabia, the serpent of the land of Israel, and the mad dog anywhere and everywhere. *Ibid.*, fol. 121, col. 2.

Five things did Canaan teach his children : — To love one another, to perpetrate robbery, to practice wantonness, to hate their masters, and not to speak the truth.

P'sachim, fol. 113, col. 2.

Five things were in the first Temple which were not in the second : — The ark and its cover, with the cherubim ; the fire ; the Shechinah ; the Holy Spirit ; and the Urim and Thummim. *Yoma*, fol. 21, col. 2.

Five things are said respecting the mad dog : — Its mouth gapes wide, it drops its saliva, its ears hang down, its tail is curled between its legs, and it slinks along the side of the road. Rav says that a dog's madness is caused by witches sporting with it. Samuel says it is because an evil spirit rests upon it. *Ibid.*, fol. 83, col. 2.

When a man has betrothed one of five women, and does not remember which of the five it is, while each of them claims the right of betrothment, then he is duty bound to give to each a bill of divorcement, and to distribute the dowry due to one among them all. This decision is according to Rabbi Tarphon, but Rabbi Akiva holds that he must not only divorce each, but give to each the legal dowry, otherwise he fails in his duty. *Yevamoth*, fol. 118, col. 2.

When a person having robbed one of five does not remember which of the five it was he had robbed, and each claims to have been the victim of the robbery, then he is to part the stolen property (or the value of it) among them all, and go his way. So says Rabbi Tarphon, but Rabbi Akiva argues that the defaulter does not in this way fully exonerate himself; he must restore to each and all the full value of the plunder.   *Yevamoth*, fol. 118, col. 2.

These things are said concerning garlic: — It nourishes, it glows inwardly, it brightens the complexion, and increases virility. Some say that it is a philtre for love, and that it exterminates jealousy.

Bava Kama, fol. 82, col. 1.

Five things cause forgetfulness : — Partaking of what has been gnawed by a mouse or a cat, eating bullock's heart, habitual use of olives, drinking water that has been washed in, and placing the feet one upon the other while bathing.

Horayoth, fol. 13, col. 2.

Five things restore the memory again: — Bread baked upon coals, soft-boiled eggs without salt, habitual use of olive oil, mulled wine, and plenty of salt.   *Ibid.*

He who does not cheer the bridegroom whose wedding breakfast he has enjoyed transgresses against the five voices (mentioned in Jer. xxxiii. 11) : — "The voice of joy, the voice of gladness, the voice of the bridegroom, and the voice of the bride, the voice of them that shall say ' Praise ye the Lord of Hosts.' "   *Berachoth*, fol. 6, col. 2.

Mount Sinai had five names : — (1.) Wilderness of Zin, because on it the Israelites were commanded to observe the law ; (2.) Wilderness of Kadesh, because on it the Israelites were consecrated to receive the law ; (3.) Wilderness of Kedemoth, because precedence was there given to Israel over all other nations ; (4.) Wilderness of Paran, because there the Israelites were fruitful and multiplied ; (5.) Wilderness of Sinai, because from it enmity came to be cherished to the Gentiles. It was denominated Horeb according to Rabbi Abhu, because from it came down destruction to the Gentiles.   *Shabbath*, fol. 89, cols. 1, 2.

Mar (the master) has said, " From dawn to the appearance of the sun is five miles." How is this proved ? It is written (Gen. xix. 15), " When the dawn arose the angels hurried Lot ; " and it is added (verse 25), " The sun was

risen upon the earth when Lot entered into Zoar." And
Rabbi Chanena said, "I myself have seen that place, and
the distance is five miles." *P'sachim*, fol. 93, col. 2.

He that cooks in milk the ischiadic sinew on an annual
festival is to be scourged five times forty stripes save one:
— For cooking the sinew, for eating the sinew, for cooking
flesh in milk, for eating flesh cooked in milk, and for
lighting the fire. *Baitza*, fol. 12, col. 1.

To this very day this sinew is extracted from the hind quarters of
all animals before it is allowable for a Jew to eat them. This operation, in popular parlance, is termed porging.

The mysteries of the law are not to be communicated
except to those who possess the faculties of these five in
combination : — "The captain of fifty, and the honorable
man, and the counselor, and the cunning artificer, and the
eloquent orator" (see Isa. iii. 3).

Chaggigah, fol. 13, col. 1.

"Captain of fifty." This should be read, not captain of
fifty, but captain of five, that is, such as knew how to
manage the five-fifths of the law (or Pentateuch).

Ibid., fol. 14, col. 1.

Five characteristics were ascribed to the fire upon the
altar : — It crouched there like a lion, it shone as the sun,
it was perceptible to the touch, it consumed liquids as
though they were dry materials, it caused no smoke.

Yoma, fol. 21, col. 2.

How is it that the word signifying "And I will be glorified," occurs in Hag. i. 8 without the letter which is the
symbol for five, though it is sounded as if that letter was
there? It indicates the absence of five things from the
second Temple which were to be found in the first. (1.)
The ark, *i. e.*, the mercy-seat of the cherubim; (2.) the
fire from heaven upon the altar; (3.) the visible presence;
(4.) the Holy Spirit (of prophecy, says Rashi); and (5.)
the Urim and Thummim. *Ibid.*

How then, it may be asked, if these five tokens of the Divine
presence and favor which rendered the first Temple so glorious were
wanting in the second could it be said (Hag. ii. 9), "The glory of
this latter house shall be greater than of the former"? It is a ques-

tion which it is natural to ask, and it should be ingenuously answered. Is it that these were tending to usurp the place of the spiritual, of which they were but the assurance and the symbol, and darken rather than reveal the eternal reality they adumbrated?

The Israelites relished any flavor they fancied in the manna except the flavor of these five things (mentioned in Num. xi. 59) : — "Cucumbers, melons, leeks, onions, and garlic."   *Yoma*, fol. 75, col. 1.

Five things happened to our forefathers on the 17th of Tammuz, and five on the 9th of Ab. On the 17th of Tammuz (1.) the tables of the covenant were broken; (2.) the daily sacrifice was done away with; (3.) the city walls were cleft asunder; (4.) Apostumes burned the roll of the law; (5.) and set up an idol in the temple. On the 9th of Ab (1.) the decree was uttered that our ancestors should not enter the land of Canaan; both the (2.) first and the (3.) second Temple were destroyed; (4.) Byther was subjugated and (5.) the city was plowed up.

Taanith, fol. 26, cols. 1, 2.

The Rabbis have taught where it is we learn that if one has five sons by five wives he is bound to redeem each and all of them. It is from what is taught in Exod. xxxiv. 20, where it is said, "All the first born of thy sons shalt thou redeem."   *Kiddushin*, fol. 29. col. 2.

If Israel had not sinned they would have had no other Scriptures than the five-fifths of the law (that is, the Pentateuch) and the book of Joshua, which last is indispensable, because therein is recorded how the land was distributed among the sons of Israel; but the remainder was added, "Because in much wisdom is much grief" (Eccles. i. 18).

Nedarim, fol. 22, col. 2.

"If a man steal an ox or a sheep and kill it or sell it, five oxen shall be given in restitution for one ox, and four sheep for one sheep" (Exod. xxii. 1). From this observe the value put upon work. For the loss of an ox, because it involves the loss of labor, the owner is recompensed with five oxen; but for the loss of a sheep, which does no work, he is only recompensed with four.

Bava Kama, fol. 79, col. 2.

"And Esau came from the field, and he was faint" (Gen. xxv. 29). Rabbi Yochanan said that wicked man committed on that day five transgressions: — He committed rape, committed murder, denied the being of God, denied the resurrection from the dead, and despised the birthright.

Bava Bathra, fol. 16, col. 2.

There are five celebrated idolatrous temples, and these are the names of them: — The Temple of Bel in Babylon, the Temple of Nebo in Chursi, the Temple of Thretha in Maphog, the Temple of Zeripha in Askelon, and the Temple of Nashra in Arabia. When Rabbi Dimmi came from Palestine to Babylon he said there were others, viz, the Temple of Yarid in Ainbechi, and that of Nadbacha in Accho.

Avodah Zarah, fol. 11, col. 2.

"And they also transgressed my covenant, which I have commanded them; and they also have taken of the accursed thing, and have also stolen, and dissembled also, and have also put it among their own stuff" (Josh. vii. 11). Rav Illaa says, in the name of Rav Yehudah ben Mispartha, the fivefold repetition of the particle also shows that Achan had trespassed against all the five books of Moses. The same Rabbi further adds that Achan had obliterated the sign of the covenant, for it is said in relation to him, "And they have also transgressed my covenant;" and with reference to circumcision, "He hath broken my covenant."

Sanhedrin, fol. 44, col. 1.

He who eats an ant is flogged five times with forty stripes save one.

Maccoth, fol. 16, col. 2.

Rabbi Akiva used to say there are five judgments on record each of twelve months' duration: — That of the deluge, that of Job, that of the Egyptians, that of Gog and Magog, and that of the wicked in hell. This last is said of those whose demerits outweigh their virtues, or those who have sinned against their bodies.

Edioth, chap. 2, mish. 10.

Five possessions hath the Holy One — blessed be He! — purchased for Himself in this world: — (1.) The law is one possession (Prov. viii. 22); (2.) Heaven and earth is one possession (Isa. lxvi. 1, Ps. civ. 24); (3.) Abraham is one possession (Gen. xiv. 9) ; (4.) Israel is one possession (Exod. xv. 16); (5.) the Temple is one possession, as it is said (Exod. xv. 17), "The sanctuary, O Lord, Thy hands have established." And it is also said (Ps. lxxviii. 54), "And He brought them to the border of His sanctuary, even to this mountain, which His right hand had purchased." *Avoth*, chap. 6.

Rabbi Akiva says he who marries a woman not suited to him violates five precepts : — (1.) Thou shalt not avenge ; (2.) thou shalt not bear a grudge ; (3.) thou shalt not hate thy brother in thy heart ; (4.) thou shalt love thy neighbor as thyself ; (5.) and that thy brother may live with thee. For if he hates her he wishes she were dead, and thus he diminishes the population.

Avoth d' Rab. Nathan, chap. 26.

Five have no forgiveness of sins : — (1.) He who keeps on sinning and repenting alternately ; (2.) he who sins in a sinless age ; (3.) he who sins on purpose to repent ; (4.) he who causes the name of God to be blasphemed. The fifth is not given in the Talmud. *Ibid.*, chap. 39.

He who has no fringes to his garment transgresses five positive commands (see Num. xv. 38. etc.; Deut. xxii. 12).

Menachoth, fol. 44, col. 1.

A learner who, after five years, sees no profit in studying, will never see it. Rabbi Yossi says, after three years, as it is written (Dan. i. 4, 5), "That they should be taught the literature and the language of the Chaldeans," so educating them in three years. *Chullin*, fol. 24, col. 1.

Any one who doeth any of these things sinneth against himself, and his blood is upon his own head : — He that (1.) eats garlic, onions, or eggs which were peeled the night before ; (2.) or drinks water drawn over night ; (3.) or sleeps all night in a burying-place ; (4.) or pares his nails and throws the cuttings into the public street.

Niddah, fol. 17, col. 1.

Rabbi Yossi said : — "Never once in all my life have the walls of my house seen the hem of my shirt ; and I have planted five cedars (sons are figuratively so termed, see Ps. xcii. 12) in Israel — namely, Rabbis Ishmael, Eliezar,

Chalafta, Artilas, and Menachem. Never once in my life
have I spoken of my wife by any other name than house,
and of my ox by any other name than field.

Shabbath, fol. 118, col. 2.

Six things are a disgrace to a disciple of the wise : — To
walk abroad perfumed, to walk alone by night, to wear old
clouted shoes, to talk with a woman in the street, to sit
at table with illiterate men, and to be late at the synagogue. Some add to these, walking with a proud step or
a haughty gait. *Berachoth*, fol. 43, col. 2.

A soft-boiled egg is better than six ounces of fine flour.
Ibid., fol. 44, col. 2.

Six things are a certain cure for sickness : — Cabbage,
beetroot, water distilled from dry moss, honey, the maw
and the matrix of an animal, and the edge of the liver.
Ibid.

These six things are good symptoms in an invalid : —
Sneezing, perspiration, evacuation, seminal emission, sleep,
and dreaming. *Ibid.*, fol. 57, col. 2.

Six things bear interest in this world and the capital re-
maineth in the world to come : — Hospitality to strangers,
visiting the sick, meditation in prayer, early attendance at
the school of instruction, the training of sons to the study
of the law, and judging charitably of one's neighbors.

Shabbath, fol. 127, col. 1.

There are six sorts of tears, three good and three bad :
— Those caused by smoke, or grief, or constipation are
bad ; and those caused by fragrant spices, laughter, and
aromatic herbs are good.

Ibid., fol. 151, col. 2 ; fol. 152, col. 1.

Six things are said respecting the illiterate : — No testimony is to be borne to them, none is to be accepted from
them ; no secret is to be disclosed to them ; they are not
to be appointed guardians over orphans, nor keepers of the
charity-box, and there should be no fellowship with them
when on a journey. Some say also no public notice is to be
given of their lost property. *P'sachim*, fol. 49, col. 2.

The expression here rendered "illiterate" means literally "people of the land," and was, there is reason to believe, originally applied to the primitive inhabitants of Canaan, traces of whom may still be found among the fellahin of Syria. They appear, like the aboriginal races in many countries of Christendom in relation to Christianity, to have remained generation after generation obdurately inaccessible to Jewish ideas, and so to have given name to the ignorant and untaught generally. This circumstance may account for the harshness of some of the quotations which are appended in reference to them.

He who aspires to be a fellow of the learned must not sell fruit, either green or dry, to an illiterate man, nor may he buy fresh fruit of him. He must not be the guest of an ignorant man, nor receive such an one as his guest.

Demai, chap. 2, mish. 2.

Our Rabbis teach, Let a man sell all that he has and marry the daughter of a learned man. If he cannot find the daughter of a learned man, let him marry the daughter of one of the great men of his day. If he does not find such a one, let him marry the daughter of one of the heads of the congregation, or, failing this, the daughter of a charity collector, or even the daughter of a schoolmaster; but let him not marry the daughter of an illiterate man, for the unlearned are an abomination, as also their wives and their daughters.　　*P'sachim*, fol. 49, col. 2.

It is said that Rabbi (the Holy) teaches that it is illegal for an unlearned man to eat animal food, for it is said (Lev. xi. 46), "This is the law of the beast and the fowl;" therefore he who studies the law may eat animal food, but he who does not study the law may not. Rabbi Eliezar said, "It is lawful to split open the nostrils of an unlearned man, even on the Day of Atonement which happens to fall on a Sabbath." To which his disciples responded, "Rabbi, say rather to slaughter him." He replied, "Nay, that would require the repetition of the usual benediction; but in tearing open his nostrils no benedictory formula is needed." Rabbi Eliezar has also said, "It is unlawful to travel with such a one, for it is said (Deut.

xxx. 30), 'For it is thy life and the length of thy days.'
The unlearned does not ensure his own life (since he has
no desire to study the law, which would prolong life), how
much less then will he regard the life of his neighbor?"
Rabbi Samuel, son of Nachman, says on behalf of Rabbi
Yochanan, that it is lawful to split open an unlearned man
like a fish. "Aye," adds Rabbi Samuel, "and that from
his back." *P'sachim*, fol. 49, col. 2.

Rav Yehudah says it is good to eat the pulp of a pump-
kin with beetroot as a remedy, also the essence of hemp
seed in Babylonian broth; but it is not lawful to mention
this in the presence of an illiterate man, because he might
derive a benefit from the knowledge not meant for him.
Nedarim, fol. 49, col. 1.

No contribution or heave-offering should be given to an
ignorant priest. *Sanhedrin*, fol. 90, col. 2.

No boor can be pious, nor an ignorant man a saint.
Avoth, chap. 2, mish. 6.

Sleep in the morning, wine at mid-day, the idle talk of
inexperienced youth, and attending the conventicles of the
ignorant drive a man out of the world.
Ibid., chap. 3, mish. 16.

Rabbi Jonathan says, "Where do we learn that no present is to be made to an ignorant priest?" In 2 Chron.
xxxi. 4, for there it is said Hezekiah "commanded that
all the people that dwelt in Jerusalem should give a portion to the priests and to the Levites, that they might be
strong in the law of the Lord." He who firmly lays hold
of the law has a claim to a portion, otherwise he has
none. *Chullin*, fol. 130, col. 2.

The aged, if ignorant, grow weaker in intellect the older
they become in years, for it is written (Job xii. 20), "He
removeth away the speech of the trusty, and taketh away
the understanding of the aged." But it is not so with them
that are old in the study of the law, for the older they
grow the more thoughtful they become, and the wiser, as
it is said (Job xii. 12), "With the ancient is wisdom, and
in length of days understanding." *Kinnin*, chap. 3.

The salutation of the ignorant should be responded to quietly, and with a reluctant nod of the head.

Taanith, fol. 14, col. 2.

No calamities ever befall the world except such as are brought on by the ignorant. *Bava Bathra*, fol. 8, col. 1.

Rav Hunna's widow once appeared before Rav Nachman as plaintiff in a lawsuit. "What shall I do?" he said. "If I rise before her (to honor her as the widow of a Rabbi), the defendant, who is an *amhaaretz*, will feel uneasy; and if I don't rise I shall break the rule which ordains that the wife of an associate is to be treated as an associate." So he said to his servant, "Loose a young goose over my head, then I'll get up."

Rav bar Sheravyah had a lawsuit with an *amhaaretz* before Rav Pappa, who bade him be seated, and also asked the other to sit down. When the officer of the court raised the *amhaaretz* with a kick, the magistrate did not request him to be seated again. *Shevuoth*, fol. 30, col. 2.

Six things are said respecting demons. In three particulars they are like angels, and in three they resemble men. They have wings like angels; like angels they fly from one end of the world to the other, and they know the future, as angels do, with this difference, that they learn by listening behind the veil what angels have revealed to them within. In three respects they resemble men. They eat and drink like men, they beget and increase like men, and like men they die. *Chaggigah*, fol. 16, col. 1.

The Talmud is particularly rich in demonology, and many are the forms which the evil principle assumes in its pages. We have no wish to drag these shapes to the light, and interrogate them as to the part they play in this intricate life. Enough now if we mention the circumstance of their existence, and introduce to the reader the story of Ashmedai, the king of the demons. The story is worth relating, both for its own sake and its historical significance.

In Ecclesiastes ii. 8, we read, "I gat me men singers and women singers, the delights of the sons of men, as musical instruments, and that of all sorts." These last seven words represent only two in the original Hebrew, *Shiddah-veshiddoth*. These two words in the original Hebrew translated by the last seven in this verse, have been a source of great perplexity to the critics, and their exact meaning is matter of debate to this hour. They in the West say they mean severally

carriages for lords and carriages for ladies, while we, says the Baby-
lonish Talmud, interpret them to signify male demons and female demons.
Whereupon, if this last is the correct rendering, the question arises, for
what purpose Solomon required them? The answer is to be found in
I Kings vi. 7, where it is written, "And the house, when it was in building,
was built of stone made ready before it was brought thither," etc.
For before the operation commenced Solomon asked the Rabbis,
"How shall I accomplish this without using tools of iron?" and they
remembering of an insect which had existed since the creation of the
world, whose powers were such as the hardest substances could not
resist, replied, "There is the Shameer, with which Moses cut the
precious stones of the Ephod." Solomon asked, "And where, pray, is
the Shameer to be found?" To which they made answer, "Let a
male demon and a female come, and do thou coerce them both;
mayhap they know and will reveal it to thee." He then conjured
into his presence a male and a female demon, and proceeded to torture them, but in vain, for said they, "We know not its whereabouts
and cannot tell; perhaps Ashmedai, the king of the demons, knows."
On being further interrogated as to where he in turn might be found,
they made this answer: "In yonder mount is his residence; there he
has dug a pit, and, after filling it with water, covered it over with a
stone, and sealed with his own seal. Daily he ascends to heaven and
studies in the school of wisdom there, then he comes down and
studies in the school of wisdom here; upon which he goes and ex-
amines the seal, then opens the pit, and after quenching his thirst,
covers it up again, re-seals it, and takes his departure."

Solomon thereupon sent Benaiah, the son of Jehoiada, provided
with a magic chain and ring, upon both of which the name of God
was engraved. He also provided him with a fleece of wool and sundry
skins with wine. Then Benaiah went and sank a pit below that of
Ashmedai, into which he drained off the water and plugged the duct
between with the fleece. Then he set to and dug another hole higher
up with a channel leading into the emptied pit of Ashmedia, by
means of which the pit was filled with the wine he had brought.
After leveling the ground so as not to rouse suspicion, he withdrew to
a tree close by, so as to watch the result and wait his opportunity.
After a while Ashmedai came, and examined the seal, when, seeing it
all right, he raised the stone, and to his surprise found wine in the
pit. For a time he stood muttering and saying, it is written, "Wine
is a mocker: strong drink is raging, and whosoever is deceived thereby
is not wise." And again, "Whoredom and wine and new wine take
away the heart." Therefore at first he was unwilling to drink, but
being thirsty, he could not long resist the temptation. He proceeded
to drink therefore, when, becoming intoxicated, he lay down to sleep.
Then Benaiah, came forth from his ambush, and stealthily approaching, fastened the chain round the sleeper's neck. Ashmedai, when he
awoke, began to fret and fume, and would have torn off the chain
that bound him, had not Benaiah warned him, saying, "The name of

thy Lord is upon thee." Having thus secured him, Benaiah proceeded to lead him away to his sovereign master. As they journeyed along they came to a palm-tree, against which Ashmedai rubbed himself, until he uprooted it and threw it down. When they drew near to a hut, the poor widow who inhabited it came out and entreated him not to rub himself against it, upon which, as he suddenly bent himself back, he snapt a bone of his body, and said, "This is that which is written (Prov. xxv. 15), 'And a gentle answer breaketh the bone.'" Descrying a blind man straying out of his way, he hailed him and directed him aright. He even did the same service to a man overcome with wine, who was in a similar predicament. At sight of a wedding party that passed rejoicing along, he wept; but he burst into uncontrollable laughter when he heard a man order at a shoemaker's stall a pair of shoes that would last seven years; and when he saw a magician at his work he broke forth into shrieks of scorn.

On arriving at the royal city, three days were allowed to pass before he was introduced to Solomon. On the first day he said, "Why does the king not invite me into his presence?" "He has drunk too much," was the answer, "and the wine has overpowered him." Upon which he lifted a brick and placed it upon the top of another. When this was communicated to Solomon, he replied "He meant by this, go and make him drunk again." On the day following he asked again, "Why does the king not invite me into his presence?" They replied, "He has eaten too much." On this he removed the brick again from the top of the other. When this was reported to the king, he interpreted it to mean, "Stint him in his food."

After the third day, he was introduced to the king; when measuring off four cubits upon the floor with the stick he held in his hand, he said to Solomon, "When thou diest, thou wilt not possess in this world (he referred to the grave) more than four cubits of earth. Meanwhile thou has conquered the world, yet thou wert not satisfied until thou hadst overcome me also." To this the king quietly replied, "I want nothing of thee, but I wish to build the Temple and have need of the *Shameer.*" To which Ashmedai at once answered, "The Shameer is not committed in charge to me, but to the Prince of the Sea, and he intrusts it to no one except to the great wild cock, and that upon an oath that he return it to him again." Whereupon Solomon asked, "And what does the wild cock do with the Shameer?" To which the demon replied, "He takes it to a barren rocky mountain, and by means of it he cleaves the mountain asunder, into the cleft of which, formed into a valley, he drops the seeds of various plants and trees, and thus the place becomes clothed with verdure and fit for habitation." This is the *Shameer* (Lev. xi. 19), Nagger Tura, which the Targum renders Mountain Splitter.

They therefore searched for the nest of the wild cock, which they found contained a young brood. This they covered with a glass, that the bird might see its young, but not be able to get at them. When accordingly the bird came and found his nest impenetrably glazed over, he went and fetched the Shameer. Just as he was about to apply it to the glass in order to cut it, Solomon's messenger gave a startling shout, and this so agitated the bird that he dropped the Shameer, and Solomon's messenger caught it up and made off with it. The cock thereupon went and strangled himself, because he was unable to keep the oath by which he had bound himself to return the Shameer.

Benaiah asked Ashmedai why, when he saw the blind man straying, he so promptly interfered to guide him? "Because," he replied, "it was proclaimed in heaven that that man was perfectly righteous, and that whosoever did him a good turn would earn a title to a place in the world of the future." "And when thou sawest the man overcome with wine wandering out of his way, why didst thou put him right again?" Ashmedai said, "Because it was made known in heaven that that man was thoroughly bad, and I have done him a good service that he might not lose all, but receive some good in the world that now is." "Well, and why didst thou weep when thou sawest the merry wedding-party pass?" "Because," said he, "the bridegroom was fated to die within thirty days and the bride must needs wait thirteen years for her husband's brother, who is now but an infant" (see Deut. xxv. 5-10). "Why didst thou laugh so when the man ordered a pair of shoes that would last him seven years?" Ashmedai replied, "Because the man himself was not sure of living seven days." "And why," asked Benaiah, "didst thou jeer when thou sawest the conjuror at his tricks?" "Because," said Ashmedai, "the man was at that very time sitting on a princely treasure, and he did not, with all his pretension, know that it was under him."

Having once acquired a power over Ashmedai, Solomon detained him till the building of the Temple was completed. One day after this, when they were alone, it is related that Solomon, adressing him, asked him, "What, pray, is your superiority over us, if it be true, as it is written (Num. xxiii. 22), 'He has the strength of a unicorn,' and the word 'strength,' as tradition alleges, means 'ministering angels,' and the word 'unicorn' means 'devils'?" Ashmedai replied, "Just take this chain from my neck, and give me thy signet-ring, and I'll soon show thee my superiority." No sooner did Solomon comply with this request, than Ashmedai, snatching him up, swallowed him; then stretching forth his wings — one touching the heaven and the other the earth — he vomited him out again to a distance of four hundred miles. It is with reference to this time that Solomon says (Eccl. i. 3; ii. 10), "What profit hath a man of all his labor which he taketh under the sun? This is my portion of all my labor." What does the word this mean? Upon this point Rav and Samuel are at variance, for the one says it means his staff, the other holds that it means his garment or water-jug; and that with one or other Solomon went about from door to door begging; and wherever he came he said (Eccl. i. 12), "I, the preacher, was king over Israel in Jerualem." When in his wanderings he came to the house of the Sanhedrin, the Rabbis reasoned and said, if he were mad he would

not keep repeating the same things over and over again; therefore
what does he mean? They therefore inquired of Benaiah, "Does the
king ask thee into his presence?" He replied, "No!" They then
sent to see whether the king visited the hareem. And the answer
to this was, "Yes, he comes." Then the Rabbis sent word back that
they should look at his feet, for the devil's feet are like those of a
cock. The reply was, "He comes to us in stockings." Upon this information the Rabbis escorted Solomon back to the palace, and
restored to him the chain and the ring, on both of which the name
of God was engraven. Arrayed with these, Solomon advanced straightway into the presence-chamber. Ashmedai sat at that moment on the
throne, but as soon as he saw Solomon enter, he took fright and
raising his wings, flew away, shrieking back into invisibility. In spite
of this, Solomon continued in great fear of him; and this explains
that which is written (Song of Songs, iii. 7, 8), "Behold the bed
which is Solomon's; threescore valiant men are about it, of the valiant of Israel; they all hold swords, being expert in war; every man
has his sword upon his thigh, because of fear in the night." (See
Gittin, fol. 68, cols. 1, 2.)

Ashmedai is the Asmodeus of the Book of Tobit, iii. 8, vi. 14, etc.
The Shameer is mentioned in Jer. xvii. 1; Ezek. iii. 9; Zech. vii. 12.
The Seventy in the former passage and the Vulgate passim take it
for the diamond.

Six things are said respecting the children of men, in
three of which they are like angels, and in three they are
like animals. They have intelligence like angels, they walk
erect like angels, and they converse in the holy tongue like
angels. They eat and drink like animals, they generate
and multiply like animals, and they relieve nature like animals.   *Chaggigah*, fol. 16, col. 1.

Six months did the Shechinah hesitate to depart from
the midst of Israel in the wilderness, in hopes that they
would repent. At last, when they persisted in impenitence,
the Shechinah said, "May their bones be blown;" as it is
written (Job xi. 20), "The eyes of the wicked shall fail,
they shall not escape, and their hopes shall be as the blowing out of the spirit."   *Rosh Hashanah*, fol. 31, col. 1.

Six names were given to Solomon:—Solomon, Jedidiah,
Koheleth, Son of Jakeh, Agur, and Lemuel.
                            Avoth d' Rab. Nathan, chap. 39.

Six years old was Dinah when she gave birth to Ase-
nath, whom she bore unto Shechem. *Sophrim*, chap. 21.

"And the Lord blessed Obed-edom and all his house-hold" (2 Sam. vi. 11). In what did the blessing consist? Rav Yehudah bar Zavidah says it consisted in this, that Hamoth, his wife, and her eight daughters-in-law gave birth each to six children at a time. (This is proved from 1 Chron. xxvi. 5, 8.) *Berachoth*, fol. 63, col. 2.

Six things were done by Hezekiah the king, but the sages praised him for three only : — (1.) He dragged the bones of his father Ahaz on a hurdle of ropes, for this they commended him ; (2.) he broke to pieces the brazen ser-pent, for this they commended him ; (3.) he hid the Book of Remedies, and for this too they praised him. For three they blamed him : — (1.) He stripped the doors of the Temple and sent the gold thereof to the King of Assyria ; (2.) he stopped up the upper aqueduct of Gihon ; (3.) he intercalated the month Nisan. *P'sachim*, fol. 56, col. 1.

The hiding of the Book of Remedies, harsh and inhuman as it might seem, was dictated by high moral considerations. It seemed right that the trangressor should feel the weight of his sin in the suffering that followed, and that the edge of judgment should not be dulled by a too easy access to anodyne applications. The reason for stopping the aqueduct of Gihon is given in 2 Chron. xxxii. 3, 4. The inhabitants of Jerusalem did the very same thing when the Crusaders besieged the city, A. D. 1099. Rashi tries to explain why this strata-gem was not commended ; the reason he gives is that Hezekiah ought to have trusted God, who had said (2 Kings xix. 34), "I will defend the city."

Six things are said of the horse : — It is wanton, it de-lights in the strife of war, it is high-spirited, it despises sleep, it eats much and it voids little. There are some that say it would fain kill its own master.

Ibid., fol. 113, col. 2.

The Rabbis have taught that there are six sorts of fire : — (1.) Fire that eats but drinks not, *i.e.*, common fire ; (2.) fire that drinks but does not eat, *i.e.*, a fever ; (3.) fire that eats and drinks, *i.e.*, Elijah, as it is written (1 Kings xviii. 38), "And licked up the water that was in the trench ; " (4.) fire that burns up moist things as soon as dry, *i.e.*, the fire on the altar ; (5.) fire that counteracts other fire, *i.e..* like that of Gabriel ; (6.) fire that consumes fire, for the Master has said (Sanhed., fol. 38, col. 2),

6

"God stretched out His finger among the angels and con‧ sumed them," *i.e.*, by His own essential fire.

Yoma, fol. 21, col. 2.

For six months David was afflicted with leprosy; for it is said (Ps. li. 7), "Purge me with hyssop, and I shall be clean; wash me, and I shall be whiter than snow." At that time the Shechinah departed from him; for it is said (Ps. li. 12), "Restore unto me the joy of Thy salvation;" and the Sanhedrin kept aloof from him, for it is said (Ps. cxix. 79), "Let those that fear thee turn unto me." That this ailment lasted six months is proved from I Kings ii. 11, where it is said, "And the days that David reigned over Israel were forty years; seven years he reigned in Hebron, and thirty-three years he reigned in Jerusalem;" whereas in 2 Sam. v. 5, it is said, "In Hebron he reigned over Judah seven years and six months." The reason why these six months are omitted in Kings is because during that period he was afflicted with leprosy.

Sanhedrin, fol. 107, col. 1.

The tables of stone were six ells long, six broad, and three thick.   *Nedarim*, fol. 38, col. 8.

It may help the reader to some idea of the strength of Moses if we work out arithmetically the size and probable weight of these stone slabs according to the Talmud. Taking the cubit or ell at its lowest estimate, that is eighteen inches, each slab, being nine feet long, nine feet wide, and four and a half feet thick, would weigh upward of twenty-eight tons, reckoning thirteen cubic feet to the ton,—the right estimate for such stone as is quarried from the Sinaitic cliff. The figures are $9 \times 9 \times \dfrac{9}{2} = \dfrac{729}{2} = 364.5 \times 173.5 = 63240.75 = 28$ tons, 4 cwt., 2 qrs., 16 lbs. avoirdupois.

The Rabbis have taught that these six things possess medicinal virtue:—Cabbage, lungwort, beetroot, water, and certain parts of the offal of animals, and some also say little fishes.   *Avodah Zarah*, fol. 29, col. 1.

Over six the Angel of Death had no dominion, and these were:—Abraham, Isaac, and Jacob, Moses, Aaron, and Miriam. Respecting the first three it is written, "in all" (Gen. xxiv. 1), "of all" (Gen. xxvii. 33) "all" (A. V. "enough," Gen. xxxiii. 11). Respecting the last three it

is written, "by the mouth of Jehovah" (see Num. xxxiii.
38, and Deut. xxxiv. 5). *Bava Bathra*, fol. 17, col. 1.

According to Jewish tradition, there are 903 kinds of death, as is
elicited by a Kabbalistic rule called gematria, from the word outlets
(Ps. lxviii. 20) ; the numeric value of the letters of which word is
903. Of these 903 kinds of death, the divine kiss is the easiest. God
puts His favorite children to sleep, the sleep of death, by kissing their
souls away. It was thus Abraham, Isaac, and Jacob fell asleep, as
may be inferred from the word all; that is to say, they had all the
honor God could confer upon them. Moses and Aaron fell asleep by
the divine kiss, for it is plainly stated to have been "by the mouth
of Jehovah." So also Miriam passed away, only the Scripture does
not say lest the scoffer should find fault. We are also informed
that quinsy is the hardest death of all. (See *Berachoth*, fol. 8, col. 1.)

"These six of barley gave he me." What does this mean ?
It cannot surely be understood of six barleycorns, for it
could not be the custom of Boaz to give a present of six
grains of barley. It must, therefore, have been six measures. But was it usual for a woman to carry such a load
as six measures would come to? What he intended by the
number six was to give her a hint that in process of time
six sons would proceed from her, each of which would be
blessed with six blessings ; and these were David, the Messiah, Daniel, Hananiah, Mishael, and Azariah. David, as
it is written (1 Sam. xvi. 8), (1.) "Cunning in playing,"
(2.) "and a mighty and valiant man," (3.) "a man of
war," (4.) "prudent in matters," (5.) "a comely person,"
(6.) and "the Lord is with him." The Messiah, for it is
written (Isa. xi. 2), "And the Spirit of the Lord shall rest
upon him," viz, (1.) "The spirit of wisdom and (2.)
understanding, (3.) the spirit of counsel and (4.) might,
(5.) the spirit of knowledge, and (6.) the fear of the Lord."
Daniel, Hananiah, Mishael, and Azariah, for regarding them
it is written (Dan. i. 4), (1.) "Young men in whom was
no blemish," (2.) "handsome in looks," (3.) "intelligent
in wisdom," (4.) "acquainted with knowledge," (5.) "and
understanding science, and such as (6.) had ability to stand
in the palace of the king," etc. But what is the meaning of
unblemished? Rav Chama ben Chanania says it means that
not even the scar of a lancet was upon them.

Sanhedrin, fol. 93, cols. 1, 2.

The words "not even the scar of a lancet was upon them," bespeak the prevalence of blood-letting in the East, and the absence of the scar of the lancet on the persons of Daniel and his companions is a testimony to their health of body and moral temperance and purity.

In Taanith (fol. 21, col. 2) mention is made of a certain phlebotomist—a noteworthy exception to the well-known rule (see Kiddushin, fol. 82, col. 2) that phlebotomists are to be regarded as morally depraved, and in the same class with goldsmiths, perfumers, hairdressers, etc.,—Abba Umna by name, who had a special mantle with slits in the sleeves for females, so that he could surgically operate upon them without seeing their naked arms, while he himself was covered over head and shoulders in a peculiar cloak, so that his own face could not by any chance be seen by them.

From Shabbath, fol. 156, col. 1, we learn that a person born under the influence of Maadim, *i. e.*, Mars, will in one way or another be a shedder of blood, such as a plebotomist, a butcher, a highwayman, etc., etc.

Six blasts of the horn were blown on Sabbath-eve. The first was to set free the laborers in the fields from their work; those that worked near the city waited for those that worked at a distance and all entered the place together. The second blast was to warn the citizens to suspend their employments and shut up their shops. At the third blast the women were to have ready the various dishes they had prepared for the Sabbath and to light the lamps in honor of the day. Then three more blasts were blown in succession, and the Sabbath commenced. *Shabbath*, fol. 35, col. 2.

He who passes seven nights in succession without dreaming deserves to be called wicked.

Berachoth, fol. 14, col. 1.

Gehinnorn has seven names:—Sheol (Jonah ii. 2), Avadon (Ps. lxxxviii. 11), Shachath (Ps. xvi. 2), Horrible pit (Ps. xl. 2), Miry clay (Ps. xl. 2), the Shadow of death (Ps. cvii. 14), the Subterranean land.

Eiruvin, fol. 19, col. 1.

A dog in a strange place does not bark for seven years.

Ibid., fol. 61, col. 1.

Seven things were formed before the creation of the world:—The Law, Repentance, Paradise, Gehenna, the Throne of Glory, the Temple, and the name of the Messiah. *P'sachim*, fol. 54, col. 1.

The Midrash Yalkut (p. 7) enumerates the same list almost word for word, and the Targum of Ben Uzziel develops the tradition still further, while the Targum Yerushalmi fixes the date of the origin of the seven prehistoric wonders at «two thousand years before the creation of the world.»

Seven things are hid from the knowledge of a man : — The day of death, the day of resurrection, the depth of judgment (*i. e.*, the future reward or punishment), what is in the heart of his fellow-man, what his reward will be, when the kingdom of David will be restored, and when the kingdom of Persia will fall.   *P'sachim*, fol. 54, col. 2.

Seven are excommunicated before heaven : — A Jew who has no wife, and even one who is married but has no male children ; and he that has sons but does not train them up to study the law; he who does not wear phylacteries on his forehead and upon his arm and fringes upon his garment, and has no mezuzah on his doorpost ; and he who goes barefooted.   *Ibid.*, fol. 113, col. 2.

There are seven skies : — Villon, Raakia, Shechakim, Zevul, Maaon, Maachon, and Aravoth.
                              Chaggigah, fol. 12, col. 2.

Seven days before the Day of Atonement they removed the high priest from his own residence to the chamber of the President, and appointed another priest as his deputy in case he should meet with such an accident as would incapacitate him from going through the service of the day. Rabbi Yehudah says they also had to betroth him to another woman lest his own wife should die meanwhile, for it is said, " And he shall make an atonement for himself and for his house," — his house, that is, his wife. In reference to this precautionary rule it was observed, there might then be no end to the matter (Rashi), should this woman die also.   *Yoma*, fol. 2, col. 1.

They associated with the high priest the senior elders of the Sanhedrin, who read over to him the *agenda* of the day, and then said to him, " My lord high priest, read thou for thyself; perhaps thou hast forgotten it, or maybe thou hast not learned it at all."   On the day before the Day of Atonement he was taken to the East Gate when they caused oxen, rams, and lambs to pass before him, that he might become well-versed and expert in his official duties. During the whole of the seven (preparatory) days neither victuals nor drink were withheld from him, but toward dusk on the eve of the Day of Atonement they did not allow him to eat much, for much food induces sleep. Then the elders of the Sanhedrin surrendered him to the elders of the priesthood, and these conducted him to the hall of the house of Abtinas, and there they swore him in ; and after bidding him good-bye, they went away. In administering the oath they said, " My lord high priest, we are ambassadors of the Sanhedrin ; thou art our ambassador and the ambassador of the Sanhedrin as well. We adjure thee, by Him who causes His name to dwell in this house, that thou alter not anything that we have told thee ! " Then they parted, both they and he weeping. He wept because they suspected he was a Sadducee, and they wept because the penalty for wrongly suspecting persons is scourging. If he was a learned man he preached (during the night) ; if not, learned men preached before him. If he was a ready reader, he read ; if not, others read to him. What were the books read over to him? Job, Ezra, and the Chronicles. Zechariah the son of Kevootal says, " I have often read before him the Book of Daniel." If he became drowsy, the juniors of the priestly order fillipped their middle fingers before him, and said, " My lord high priest, stand up and cool thy feet upon the pavement." Thus they kept him engaged till the time of slaughtering (the sacrifices). *Yoma*, fol. 18, cols. 1, 2 ; fol. 19, col. 2.

Sacerdos nascitur, non fit,—a priest is born, not made, we may truly say, just altering one word of a well-known proverb. His father was a priest, and so were his forefathers as far back as the time of Aaron ; his sons and his sons' sons after him will belong to the priestly order, and so the name was far too often only the badge for exclusive and hereditary privilege. This rule, that applies to the priests, holds good also with regard to the Levites. (*Berachoth*, fol. 29, col. 1.)

There was a town in the land of Israel called Gophnith, where there were eighty couples of brother priests who married eighty couples of sister priestesses in one night.

Berachoth, fol. 44. col. 1.

Flay a carcass and take thy fee, but say not it is humiliating because I am a priest, I am a great man.

P'sachim, fol. 113, col. 1.

Philo Judæus, De Sac. Honor. (p. 833), says, "The hides of the burnt-offerings proved a rich perquisite of the priesthood."

The number of high priests who officiated in succession during the 410 years of the continuance of the first Temple was only eighteen, but the number who held office during the 420 years of the second Temple amounted to more than three hundred, most of them having died within a year after their entrance upon the office. The reason assigned by the Talmud for the long lives of the former and the short lives of the latter is the text given in Prov. x. 27, "The fear of the Lord prolongeth days, but the years of the wicked shall be shortened." *Yoma*, fol. 9, col. 1.

Before a priest could be admitted into active service in the Temple he had to undergo bodily inspection at the hands of the syndicate of the Sanhedrin. If they found the least defect in his body, even a mole with hair upon it, he was ordered to dress in black and be dismissed ; but if he was perfectly free from blemish, he was arrayed in white, and at once introduced to his brother priests and official duties. *Ibid.*, fol. 19, col. 1.

The daughters of a male proselyte who has married the daughter of a female proselyte are eligible to marry priests.

Yevamoth, fol. 57, col. 1.

If thou seest an impudent priest, think not evil of him ; for it is said (Hosea iv. 4), "Thy people are as they that strive with the priest" (see chap. ii. p. 25, Note c.).

Kiddushin, fol. 70, col. 2.

So long as there is a diadem on the head of the priest, there is a crown on the head of every man. Remove the diadem from the head of the high priest and you take away the crown from the head of all the people. (This is a Talmudic comment on Ezek. xxi. 31 ; A. Ver., 26.)

Gittin, fol. 7, col. 1.

A king shaved his head every day, a high priest did the same once a week, and an ordinary priest once a month.

Sanhedrin, fol. 22, col. 2.

When a priest performs the service of the Temple in a state of defilement, his brother priests are not required to lead him before the tribunal, but the juniors of the priestly order are to drag him out into the hall and brain him with clubs. *Sanhedrin*, fol. 81, col. 2.

When kings were anointed, the holy oil was laid on the forehead in the form of a coronet, and when, says Rabbi Mansi bar Gadda, priests were anointed, the operation was performed in the shape of the Greek letter κ.

Horayoth, fol. 12, col. 1.

A learned man who is of illegitimate birth is preferable to an ignorant priest. *Ibid.*, fol. 13, col. 1.

A priest who makes no confession during service has no part in the priesthood. (He forfeits his emoluments.)

Menachoth, fol. 18, col. 2.

The bald-headed, the dwarfed, and the blear-eyed are ineligible for the priesthood. *Bechoroth*, fol. 43, col. 2.

Rav Chisda says, " The portions that fall to the priests are not to be eaten except roasted and that with mustard," because Scripture says (Num. xviii. 8), " by reason of the anointing," *i. e.*, by way of distinction, for only kings (who, of course, are anointed) eat roast meat with mustard.

Chullin, fol. 132, col. 2.

If a case of mistaken identity should occur between the child of a priestess and the child of her female slave, so that the one cannot be distinguished from the other, they both are to eat of the heave-offering and to receive one share from the threshing-floor. When grown up, each is to set the other free. *Gittin*, fol. 42, col. 2.

From the old clothes of the priests the wicks were made for the lamps in the Temple. *Shabbath*, fol. 21, col. 1.

Scripture authority is given in proof that the very garments possessed the faculty of making atonement for sin every whit as effectually as animal sacrifices. We are taught that the priest's shirt atones for murder, his drawers atone for whoredom, his mitre for pride, his girdle for evil thoughts, his breastplate for injustice. his ephod for idol-

atry; his overcoat atones for slander, and the golden plate
on his forehead atones for impudence.

Zevachim, fol. 88, col. 2.

All this and a great deal more on the subject may be found in the
Selichoth for Yom Kippur.

For seven years was the land of Israel strewn with
brimstone and salt.   *Yoma*, fol. 54, col. 1.

"Then shall we raise against him seven shepherds"
(Micah. v. 5). Who are these seven shepherds? David in
the middle; Adam, Seth, and Methuselah on his right
hand; Abraham, Jacob, and Moses on his left.

Succah, fol. 52, col. 2.

Who were the seven prophetesses? The answer is, Sarah,
Miriam, Deborah, Hannah, Abigail, Huldah, and Esther.

Meggillah, fol. 14, col. 2.

It is lawful to look into the face of a bride for seven
days after her marriage, in order to enhance the affection
with which she is regarded by her husband, and there is
no Halachah (or law) like this.

Kethuboth, fol. 17, col. 1.

The Rabbis are especially careful to caution their daughters to
guard against such habits as might lower them in the regard of their
husbands, lest they should lose aught of that purifying and elevating
power which they exercised as maidens. It is thus, for instance, Rav
Chisda counsels his daughters: "Be ye modest before your husbands
and do not even eat before them. Eat not vegetables or dates in the
evening, and touch not strong drink." (*Shabbath*, fol. 140, col. 2.)

Once upon a time a demon in the shape of a seven-
headed dragon came forth against Rav Acha and threatened
to harm him, but the Rabbi threw himself on his knees,
and every time he fell down to pray he knocked off one of
these heads, and thus eventually killed the dragon.

Kiddushin, fol. 29, col. 2.

On the seventh of the month Adar, Moses died, and on
that day the manna ceased to come down from heaven.

Ibid., fol. 38, col. 1.

The seventh of Adar is still, and has long been, kept sacred as the
day of the death of Moses our Rabbi — peace be with him! — and that
on the authority of T. B. Kiddushin (as quoted above), and Soteh,

fol. 10, col. 2; but Josephus (Book iv. chap. 8, sec. 49) most distinctly affirms that Moses died "on the first day of the month," and the Midrash on Esther may be quoted in corroboration of his statement. The probability is that the Talmud is right on this matter, but it is altogether wrong in connecting with this event the stoppage of the manna (see Josh. v. 10, 12).

Seven years did the nations of the world cultivate their vineyards with no other manure than the blood of Israel. Rabbi Chiya, the son of Abin, says that Rabbi Yehoshua, the son of Korcha, said, "An old man, an inhabitant of Jerusalem, related to me that Nebuzaradan, captain of the guard, killed in this valley 211 myriads (about 2,110,000), and in Jerusalem he slaughtered upon one stone 94 myriads (940,000), so that the blood flowed until it reached the blood of Zechariah, in order that that might be fulfilled which is said (Hosea iv. 2), 'And blood toucheth blood.' "

Gittin, fol. 57, col. 1.

The seventh of Adar, on which Moses died, was the same day of the same month on which he was born.

Soteh, fol. 10, col. 2.

A male hyæna after seven years becomes a bat; this after seven years, a vampire; this after other seven years, a nettle; this after seven years more, a thorn; and this again after seven years is turned into a demon. If a man does not devoutly bow during the repetition of the daily prayer which commences, "we reverently acknowledge," his spine after seven years becomes a serpent.

Bava Kama, fol. 16, col. 1.

It is related of Benjamin the righteous, who was keeper of the poor-box, that a woman came to him at a period of famine and solicited food. "By the worship of God," he replied, "there is nothing in the box." She then exclaimed, "O Rabbi, if thou dost not feed me I and my seven children must needs starve." Upon which he relieved her from his own private purse. In course of time he fell ill and was nigh unto death. Then the ministering angels interceded with the Holy One — blessed be He! — and said, "Lord of the Universe, Thou hast said he that preserveth one single soul of Israel alive is as if he had preserved the life of the whole world; and shall Benjamin the righteous, who preserved a poor woman and her seven children, die so prematurely?" Instantly the death-warrant which had gone forth was torn up, and twenty-two years were added to his life. *Bava Bathra*, fol. 11, col. 1.

Seven prophets have prophesied to the nations of the world, and these were Balaam and his father, Job, Eliphaz the Temanite, Bildad the Shuhite, Zophar the Naamathite, and Elihu the son of Barachel the Buzite.

Ibid., fol. 15. col. 2.

There are seven who are not consumed by the worm in the grave, and these are Abraham, Isaac, and Jacob, Moses, Aaron, and Miriam, and Benjamin the son of Jacob. *Ibid.*, fol. 17, col. 1.

Seven men form an unbroken series from the creation down to our own time. Methuselah saw Adam, Shem saw Methuselah, Jacob saw Shem, Amram saw Jacob, and Ahijah the Shilonite saw Amram, and Ahijah was seen by Elijah, who is alive to this day. *Ibid.*, fol. 121, col. 2.

Seven years' famine will not affect the artisan.

Sanhedrin, fol. 29, col. 1.

Seven years of pestilence will not cause a man to die before his time. *Ibid.*

"And it came to pass after seven days that the waters of the flood were upon the earth" (Gen. vii. 10). Why this delay of seven days? Rav says they were the days of mourning for Methuselah; and this teaches us that mourning for the righteous will defer a coming calamity. Another explanation is, that the Holy One — blessed be He ! — altered the course of nature during these seven days, so that the sun arose in the west and set in the east.

Ibid, fol. 108, col. 2.

The first step in transgression is evil thought, the second scoffing, the third pride, the fourth outrage, the fifth idleness, the sixth hatred, and the seventh an evil eye.

Derech Eretz Zuta, chap. 6.

Seven things cause affliction : — Slander, shedding of blood, perjury, adultery, pride, robbery, and envy.

Erchin, fol. 17, col. 2.

A ram has but one voice while alive but seven after he is dead. How so? His horns make two trumpets, his hip-bones two pipes, his skin can be extended into a drum, his larger intestines can yield strings for the lyre and the smaller chords for the harp.   *Kinnim*, chap. 3, mish. 6.

Rav Chisda said, The soul of a man mourns over him the first seven days after his decease; for it is said (Job xiv. 22), "And his soul shall mourn over him."

Shabbath, fol. 152, col. 2.

The Rabbis have taught that a man should not drink water on Wednesdays and Saturdays after night-fall, for if he does, his blood, because of risk, will be upon his own head. What risk? That from an evil spirit who on these evenings prowls abroad. But if the man be thirsty, what is he to do? Let him repeat over the water the seven voices ascribed to the Lord by David in Psalm xxix. 3–9, "The voice of the Lord is upon the waters," etc.

P'sachim, fol. 112, col. 1.

Seven precepts did Rabbi Akiva give to his son Rabbi Yehoshua: — (1.) My son, teach not in the highest place of the city; (2.) Dwell not in a city where the leading men are disciples of the wise; (3.) Enter not suddenly into thine own house, and of course not into thy neighbor's; (4.) Do not go about without shoes; (5.) Rise early and eat in summer time because of the heat, and in winter time because of the cold; (6.) Make thy Sabbath as a week-day rather than depend for support on other people; (7.) Strive to keep on close friendly terms with the man whom fortune favors (lit. on whom the present hour smiles). Rav Pappa adds, "This does not refer to buying or selling, but to partnership."   *Ibid.*

How is it proved that mourning should be kept up for seven days? It is written (Amos viii. 10), "I will turn your feasts into mourning," and these in many cases lasted seven days.   *Moed Katon*, fol 20, col. 1.

Rav Chisda said there are seven kinds of gold: — Gold, good gold, the gold of Ophir, purified gold, beaten gold, shut-up gold, and gold of Parvain.

Yoma, fol. 44, col. 2.

The shut-up gold (1 Kings vi. 12) was of the purest and rarest quality, so that when it appeared in the market for sale, all shops in the locality were "shut up," for there could be no sale of any other gold before that. All gold-dealers "shut up" their shops in order to be present on so rare an occasion ; and hence the name of this kind of gold — "shut-up gold."

Each day of the Feast of Tabernacles they walked round the altar once, and said, "O Lord, save us, we beseech Thee ! O Lord, prosper us, we beseech Thee !" But on the last day they encompassed it seven times. On their departure they said, "Beauty belongeth to thee, O altar ! Beauty belongeth to thee, O altar !"

Succah, fol. 45, col. 1.

It deserves to be noted here for the information of some of our readers that the words translated above, Save now, or Save, we beseech thee, are the original of our word Hosanna. The 25th and 26th verses of Psalm cxviii., which begin with this expression, were repeated at the Feast of Tabernacles ; and hence the bundles of palm and willow branches (carried on this occasion), the prayers, and the festival itself, were so named, *i. e.* Hosanna.

The Tempter is known by seven distinctive epithets : — (1.) The Holy One — blessed be He ! — calls him evil ; as it is said, "For the imagination of man's heart is evil." (2.) Moses calls him uncircumcised ; as it is said (Deut. x. 16), "Circumcise therefore the uncircumcised foreskin of your heart." (3.) David calls him unclean ; as it is said (Ps. li. 10), "Create in me a clean heart, O God !" Consequently there must be an unclean one. (4.) Solomon calls him enemy ; as it is said (Prov. xxv. 21, 22), "If thine enemy hunger, give him bread to eat ; if he be thirsty, give him water to drink ; for thus thou shalt heap coals of fire upon his head, and the Lord shall reward thee" (*i. e.*, oppose him with the law. The word rendered bread, is metaphorically taken for the law, Prov. ix. 5, so that give him water to drink means also the law, Isa. lv. 1 — Rashi. And the Lord reward thee, read not reward, but cause him to make peace with thee, not to war against thee.) (5.) Isaiah calls him stumbling-block ; as it is said (Isa. lvii. 14), "Cast ye up, cast ye up, prepare the way, take up the stumbling-block out of the way of my people." (6.) Ezekiel calls him stone ; as it is said

(Ezek. xxxvi. 26), "I will take away the heart of stone out of your flesh and I will give you a heart of flesh." (7.) Joel calls him the hidden one; as it is said (Joel ii. 20), "I will remove far from you the hidden one," *i. e.*, the tempter who remains hidden in the heart of man; "and I will drive him into a land barren and desolate," *i. e.*, where the children of men do not usually dwell; "with his face toward the former sea," *i. e.*, with his eyes set upon the first Temple, which he destroyed, slaying the disciples of the wise that were in it; "and his hinder part toward the latter sea," *i. e.*, with his eyes set on the second Temple, which he destroyed, also slaying the disciples of the wise that were in it. *Succah*, fol. 52, col. 1.

Once a Jewish mother with her seven sons suffered martyrdom at the hands of the Emperor. The sons, when ordered by the latter to do homage to the idols of the Empire, declined, and justified their disobedience by quoting each a simple text from the sacred Scriptures. When the seventh was brought forth, it is related that Cæsar, for appearance' sake, offered to spare him if only he would stoop and pick up a ring from the ground which had been dropped on purpose. "Alas for thee, O Cæsar!" answered the boy; "if thou art so zealous for thine honor, how much more zealous ought we to be for the honor of the Holy One — blessed be He!" On his being led away to the place of execution, the mother craved and obtained leave to give him a farewell kiss. "Go, my child," said she, "and say to Abraham, Thou didst build an altar for the sacrifice of one son, but I have erected altars for seven sons." She then turned away and threw herself down headlong from the roof and expired, when the echo of a voice was heard exclaiming (Ps. cxiii. 9), "The joyful mother of children" (or, the mother of the children rejoiceth). *Gittin*, fol. 57, col. 2.

The story of this martyrdom is narrated at much greater length in the Books of Maccabees (Book iii. chap. 7, Book iv. chaps. 8–18). In a Latin version the names are given, that of the mother Solomona, and her sons respectively Maccabeus, Aber, Machir, Judas, Achaz, Areth, while the hero of our Talmudic reference, the seventh and last, is styled Jacob. Josephus, Ant., Book xii. chap. 6, sec. 4, may also be referred to for further and varying details.

The land of Israel was not destroyed till the seven courts of judgment had fallen into idolatry, and these are they: — Jeroboam, the son of Nebat; Baasha, the son of Ahijah; Ahab, the son of Omri; Jehu, the son of Nimshi; Pekah, the son of Remaliah; Menahem, the son of Gadi; and Hoshea, the son of Elah; as it is written (Jer. xv. 9), "She that hath borne seven languisheth: she hath given up the ghost; her sun is gone down while it is yet day; she hath been ashamed and confounded."

Gittin, fol. 88, col. 1.

"He stood and measured the earth; he beheld and freed the Gentiles (A. V., he drove asunder the nations, Hab. iii. 6); he beheld that the seven precepts which the children of Noah accepted were not observed; he stood up and set their property free for the service of Israel."

Bava Kama, fol. 38, col. 1.

This is one of the weightier expositions met with from time to time in the Talmud, in which one recognizes a more than ordinarily deep and earnest feeling on the part of the commentator. The interpreter expresses himself as a man instinct with the exclusive Hebrew spirit, and as such claims his title to the whole inheritance. It is a claim abstractly defensible, and the just assertion of it is the basis of all rights over others. The only question here is whether the Jew alone is invested with the privilege. There can be little doubt that the principle on which he claims enfeoffment in the estate is a sound one, that the earth belongs in no case to the sons of Belial, only to the sons of God.

Seven things distinguish an ill-bred man and seven a wise man: — The wise man (1.) does not talk before his superior in wisdom and years; (2.) he does not interrupt another when speaking; (3.) he is not hasty to make reply; (4.) his questions are to the point, and his answers are according to the Halachah; (5.) his subjects of discourse are orderly arranged, the first subject first and the last last; (6.) if he has not heard of a thing, he says, I have not heard it; and (7.) he confesseth the truth. The characteristics of the ill-bred man are just the contrary of these.

Avoth, chap. 5, mish. 10.

If a man does not work during the six days of the week, he may be obliged to work all the seven.

Avoth d' Rab. Nathan, chap. 11.

Seven have no portion in the world to come : — A notary, a schoolmaster, the best of physicians, a judge who dispenses justice in his own native town, a wizard, a congregational reader (or law-officer), and a butcher.

Avoth d Rab. Nathan, chap. 37.

Seven attributes avail before the Throne of Glory, and these are : — Wisdom, righteousness, judgment, grace, mercy, truth, and peace. *Ibid.*, chap. 36.

There are seven points in which a righteous man excels another : — (1.) The wife of the one is more comely than the other's ; (2.) so are the children of the one as compared with those of the other ; (3.) if the two partake of one dish, each enjoys the taste according to his doings ; (4.) if the two dye in one vat, by one the article is dyed properly, by the other not ; (5, etc.) the one excels the other in wisdom, in understanding, in knowledge, and stature, as it is said (Prov. xii. 26), "The righteous is more excellent than his neighbor." *Ibid.*, chap. 37.

Seven patriarchs were covenant-makers : — Abraham, Isaac, and Jacob, Moses, Aaron, Phinehas, and David.

Derech Eretz Zuta, chap. 1.

Seven liquids are comprehended under the generic term drink (Lev. xi. 34) : — Dew, water, wine, oil, blood, milk, and honey. *Machshirin*, chap. 6, mish 6.

For tertian fever take seven small grapes from seven different vines ; seven threads from seven different pieces of cloth ; seven nails from seven different bridges ; seven handfuls of ashes from seven different fireplaces ; seven bits of pitch from seven ships, one piece from each ; seven scrapings of dust from as many separate doorways ; seven cummin seeds ; seven hairs from the lower jaw of a dog and tie them upon the throat with a paprus fibre.

Shabbath, fol. 66, col. 2.

The Rabbis teach that the precept relating to the lighting of a candle at the Feast of Dedication applies to a whole household, but that those who are particular light a candle for each individual member, and those that are extremely particular light up eight candles on the first day, seven on the second, decreasing the number by one each

day. This is according to the school of Shammai ; but the
school of Hillel say that he should light up one on the first
day, two on the second, increasing the number by one each
of the eight days of the fast. . . . What is the origin
of the feast of Dedication ?   On the twenty-fifth day of Kislev
(about December), the eight days of the Dedication commence, during which term no funeral oration is to be made,
nor public fast to be decreed.   When the Gentiles (Greeks)
entered the second Temple, it was thought they had defiled
all the holy oil they found in it ; but when the Hasmoneans prevailed and conquered them, they sought and found
still one jar of oil stamped with the seal of the High Priest,
and therefore undefiled.   Though the oil it contained would
only have sufficed for one day, a miracle was performed, so
that the oil lasted to the end of the week (during which
time more oil was provided and consecrated for the future
service of the Temple).   On the anniversary of this occasion the Feast of Dedication was instituted.

Shabbath, fol. 21, col. 2.

The Feast of Dedication is annually celebrated by all Jews everywhere, to commemorate the purifying of the Temple and the restoration of its worship after its desecration by Antiochus Epiphanes, of
which an account may be found in 1 Maccabees iv. 52-59. It is very
probable that some of our Christmas festivities are only adaptations of
the observances of this Jewish feast in symbolism of Christian ideas.
During the eight days of the festival they light up wax candles or oil
lamps, according to the rubric of the school of Hillel. Previous to the
lighting, the following benedictions are pronounced :—

"Blessed art Thou, O Lord, our God! King of the universe, who
hath sanctified us with Thy commandment, and commanded us to
light the light of Dedication."

"Blessed art Thou, O Lord, our God! King of the universe, who
wrought miracles for our fathers in those days and in this season !"

"Blessed art Thou, O Lord, Our God! King of the universe, who hath
preserved us alive, sustained us, and brought us to enjoy this season."

After the lighting, the following form is repeated : — "These lights
we light to praise Thee for the miracles, wonders, salvation, and vic-
tories which Thou didst perform for our fathers in those days and in
this season by the hands of Thy holy priests. Wherefore by command these lights are holy all the eight days of the Dedication,
neither are we permitted to make any other use of them, but to view
them, that we may return thanks to Thy name for Thy miracles, wonderful works, and salvation."

7

Another commemorative formula is repeated six or seven times a day during this festival; viz, during morning and evening prayers and after each meal.

Rabbi Yoshua ben Levi has said a man should never utter an indecent word, for the Scripture (Gen. vii. 6) uses eight letters more rather than make use of a word which, without them, would be indecent.

P'sachim, fol. 3, col. 1.

In the passage referred to, the words "that are not clean" are used instead of "unclean"; but see verse 2; there another word for not is used, which brings down the excess to five letters.

When the doors of the Temple were opened the creaking of the hinges was heard at the distance of eight Sabbath days' journeys. *Yoma*, fol. 39, col. 2.

It may be proper to remark that the journey is about nine furlongs, or a mile and one-eighth, so that the distance alluded to is nearly ten miles.

The eight princes alluded to in Micah (v. 5) are Jesse, Saul, Samuel, Amos, Zephaniah, Zedekiah, the Messiah, and Elijah. *Succah*, fol. 52, col. 2.

It is related of Rabbi Shimon, the son of Gamaliel, that at the rejoicing during the festival of the drawing of water on the Feast of Tabernacles, he threw eight flaming torches, one after the other in quick succession, into the air, and caught them again as they descended without suffering one to touch another. He also (in fulfillment of Ps. cii. 14) stooped and kissed the stone floor, supporting himself upon his two thumbs only,—a feat which no one else could perform. And this is what is termed stooping properly. *Ibid.*, fol. 53, col. 1.

Levi once in the presence of Rabbi (the Holy) conjured with eight knives. Samuel in the presence of Shavur the king (of Persia, Sapor 1, 240–273) performed the same feat with eight cups of wine. Abaii in the presence of Rava did likewise with eight eggs; some say with four only.

Ibid.

Eight prophets, who were priests as well, were descended from Rahab the harlot, and these are they:—Neraiah, Baruch, Seraiah, Maaseiah, Jeremiah, Hilkiah, Hanameel,

and Shallum.   Rabbi Yehudah says Huldah the prophetess
was one of the grandchildren of Rahab.

Meggillah, fol. 14, col. 2.

The last eight verses of the Law (Torah) were written
by Joshua.   *Bava Bathra,* fol. 14, col. 1.

There is a touching story in this very same tract, fol. 15, col. 1,
which is repeated in Menachoth, fol. 30, col. 1, and noticed by
Rashi in his commentary, to the effect that Moses himself wrote the
verses which record his own death at the dictation of the Almighty.
The account literally rendered is, "The Holy One—blessed be He!
—spake, and Moses wrote in tears."

There are eight sects of Pharisees, viz, these:—(1.)
The shoulder Pharisee, *i. e.,* he who, as it were, shoulders
his good works to be seen of men.   (2.) The time-gaining
Pharisee, he who says, "Wait a while; let me first perform
this or that good work."   (3.) The compounding Pharisee,
i. e., he who says, "May my few sins be deducted from
my many virtues, and thus atoned for" (or the blood-
letting Pharisee, *i. e.,* he who for fear lest he should look
by chance on a woman shuts his eyes and wounds his
face).   (4.) The Pharisee who so bends his back, stooping
with his head toward the ground, that he wears the appearance of an inverted mortar.   (5.) The Pharisee who
proudly says, "Remains there a virtue which I ought to
perform and have not?"   (6.) The Pharisee who is so out
of love for the reward which he hopes to earn by his observances.   (7.) The Pharisee who is so from fear lest he
should expose himself to punishment.   (8.) The Pharisee
who is born so.   *Avoth d'Rab. Nathan,* chap. 37.

Both Talmuds as a rule enumerate only seven sorts of Pharisees
(T. Yerush, Berachoth, fol. 13, Soteh, fol. 20, T. Babli, fol. 22, col.
2, and elsewhere); but Rabbi Nathan, as above, adds a new species
to the genus. The freehand sketches of Pharisees given in the Talmud are the reverse of complimentary.   In the words of the late E.
Deutsch, who was a Talmudist of no mean repute, "The Talmud in-
veighs even more bitterly and caustically than the New Testament
against what it calls 'the plague of Pharisaism,' 'the dyed ones.'
'who do evil deeds like Zimri, and require a goodly reward like
Phinehas,' 'they who preach beautifully, but do not act beautifully.'
Parodying their exaggerated logical arrangements, their scrupulous
divisions and subdivisions, the Talmud distinguishes seven classes

of Pharisees, one of whom only is worthy of that name. The real and only Pharisee is he 'who does the will of his Father which is in heaven because he loves Him.'"

He who neglects to wear phylacteries transgresseth eight commandments.   *Menachoth*, fol. 44, col. 1.

The following extract states the occasion when the wearing of phylacteries was prescribed as an equivalent that would be accepted instead of the observance of the law :—
" Rabbi Eliezer said the Israelites complained before God one day, 'We are anxious to be occupied day and night in the law, but we have not the necessary leisure.' Then the Holy One — blessed be He ! — said to them, 'Perform the commandment of the phylacteries, and I will count it as if you were occupied day and night in the law.'" (*Yalhut Shimeoni.*) Phylacteries, fringes, and Mezuzah, these three preserve one from sin ; as it is said (Eccl. iv. 2), " A threefold cord is not quickly broken ; " as also in Ps. xxxiv. 7, " The angel of the Lord encampeth about them that fear Him, and delivereth them."   *Ibid.*, fol. 43, col. 2.

The harp in the time of the Messiah will have eight strings ; as it is written (Ps. xii. 1), " The chief musician upon eight," etc.   *Eirchin*, fol. 13, col. 2.

On the ninth day of the month Ab (about August) both the first Temple and the second were destroyed.
                Rosh Hashanah, fol. 18, col. 2.

In 2 Kings xxv. 8, the seventh of Ab is the date given for the first of these events, whereas Jeremiah (lii. 12) mentions the tenth as the fatal day. Josephus (Wars of the Jews, Book vi. chap. 4, sec. 15) coincides with the latter.

On the ninth of Ab one must abstain from eating and drinking, and anointing one's self, and wearing shoes, and matrimonial intercourse. He may not read the Bible, the Talmud, the Midrash, the Halachoth, or the Haggadoth, excepting such portions as he is not in the habit of reading, such he may then read. The Lamentations, Job, and the hard words of Jeremiah should engage his study. Children should not go to school on this day, because it is said (Ps. xix. 8), " The statutes of the Lord are right, rejoicing the heart."   *Taanith*, fol. 30, col. 1.

Nowadays, on the date referred to, Jews do not wear their tallith and phylacteries at morning prayer; by this act laying aside the outward signs of their covenant with God; but, contrary to custom, they put them on in the evening, when the fast is nearly over.

He who does any work on the ninth of Ab will never see even a sign of blessing. The sages say, whoso does any work on that day and does not lament over Jerusalem will never see her joy; for it is said (Isa. lxvi. 10), " Rejoice ye with Jerusalem, and be glad with her; rejoice for joy, all ye that mourn for her."

Taanith, fol. 30, col. 2.

If there be nine shops all selling the meat of animals which have been legally butchered, and one selling the meat of animals which have not, and if a person who has bought meat does not know at which of these shops he bought it, he is not entitled to the benefit of the doubt; the meat he has purchased is prohibited.

Kethuboth, fol. 15, col. 1.

A woman prefers one measure of frivolity to nine measures of Pharisaic sanctimoniousness. *Soteh*, fol. 20, col. 1.

The Talmud has much to say, and does say a great deal, about women. And although what it says tends rather to discountenance than to promote their development, it is not insensible to what they might become under refinement of culture, and occasionally enforces the duty of attending to their higher education. In proof of both positions we appeal to the following quotations : —

In the Mishna, from which the above quotation is taken, we are told that Ben Azai (the son of impudence) says, a man is bound to instruct his daughter in the law, although Rabbi Eliezer, who always assumes an oracular air, and boasts that the Halachah is always according to his decision (*Bava Metzia*, fol. 59, col. 2), insists, on the other hand, that he who instructs his daughter in the law must be considered as training her into habits of frivolity ; and the saying above ascribes to the sex such a power of frivolity as connects itself evidently with the foregone conclusion that they are by nature incapable of being developed into any solidity of worth or character. The Gemara,

Tosephoth, and Rashi as well all support Rabbi Eliezer in laying a veto on female education, for fear lest, with the acquisition of knowledge, women might become cunning, and do things on the sly which ought not to be done by them. Literally the saying is: — For from it (*i. e.,* the acquisition of knowledge) she comes to understand cunning, and does things on the quiet.

Soteh, fol. 21, col. 2, Rashi.

Another good reason for neglecting female education those who take the Talmud as an authority find in these words: women are light-minded, *i. e.,* of shallow natural endowment, on which any serious discipline would be thrown away. *Kiddushin*, fol. 80, col. 2.

Another argument to the same effect is, that there is no distinct command in the law of Moses inculcating the duty; for in Deut. xi. 19 it is merely said, " And ye shall teach them to your children," a command which, as it passes refracted through the Rabbinic medium, becomes your sons, but not your daughters. *Ibid.*, fol. 29, col. 2.

As the immediately preceding command, so interpreted, cannot be carried out by any one not favored with male children, the well-known Talmudic dictum acquires force and point, " Blessed is the man whose children are sons, but luckless is he whose children are daughters."

Bava Bathra, fol. 16, col. 2.

A man prefers one measure obtained by his own earning to nine measures collected by the exertion of his neighbor.

Bava Metzia, fol. 38, col. 1.

Nine have entered alive into paradise, and these are they: — Enoch, the son of Jared; Elijah; the Messiah; Eliezer, the servant of Abraham; Hiram, king of Tyre; Ebed Melech, the Ethiopian; Jabez, the son of Rabbi Yehuda the prince; Bathia, the daughter of Pharaoh; and Sarah, the daughter of Asher. Some say also Rabbi Yoshua, the son of Levi. *Derech Eretz Zuta*, chap. 1.

As the last-mentioned personage, Rabbi Yoshua, entered paradise «not by the door," but some "other way," it may be interesting to not a few to know how he succeeded, and here accordingly we append the story of the feat. As Rabbi Yoshua's earthly career drew to a close, the angel of death was instructed to wait upon him, and at the same time show all respect for his wishes. The Rabbi, remarking the courteous demeanor of his visitant, requested him, before he despatched him, to favor him with a glimpse of the place he was to occupy in paradise above, and meantime commit to him his sword, as a gage that he would grant his petition and not take advantage of him on the journey. This request being granted and the sword delivered up, the Rabbi and his attendant took the road, pacing along till they halted together just outside the gates of the celestial city. Here the angel assisted the Rabbi to climb the wall, and proceeded to point out the place he would occupy some day in the future, when deftly throwing himself over, he left the angel standing outside and holding him fast by the skirt of his garment. When pressed to return, he swore he would not go back, protesting that, as he had never sought to be relieved of the obligation of his oath on earth, he would not be cajoled or coerced into an act of perjury within the precincts of heaven. He declined at first to give up the sword of the angel, and would have stood to his point but for the echo of a voice which peremptorily ordered its immediate restoration. (See *Kethuboth*, fol. 77, col. 2.)

Where is it taught that when ten join together in prayer the Shechinah is with them? In Ps. lxxxii. 1, where it is said, "God standeth in the congregation of the mighty."

Berachoth, fol. 6, col. 1.

According to Rabbinic law, it takes at least ten men to constitute a legally convened congregation. Nearly a thousand pounds were expended every year by the synagogues of the metropolis to hire (minyan) men to make up the congregational number, and thus ensure the due observance of this regulation.

When the Holy One — blessed be He! — enters the synagogue, and does not find ten men present, His anger is immediately stirred; as it is said (Isa. 1. 2), "Wherefore, when I came, was there no man? When I called, there was none to answer?" *Ibid.*, fol. 6, col. 2.

The passion of anger here ascribed to God is by not a few regarded as an attribute wholly alien to the proper nature of the Deity. Such, however, is evidently not the judgment of the Talmudists. Nor is this surprising when we see elsewhere how boldly they conceive and how freely they speak of the Divine Majesty. The Rabbis are not in general a shamefaced generation, and are all too prone to deal familiarly with the most sacred realities. The excerpts which follow amply justify this judgment.

God is represented as roaring like a lion, etc., etc.
Berachoth, fol. 3, col. 1. See chap. iii. No. 1, *supra*.
God is said to wear phylacteries. *Berachoth*, fol. 6, col. 1.

This is referred to in the morning service for Yom Kippur, where it is said He showed "the knot of the phylacteries to the meek one" (*i. e.*, Moses).

He is said to pray; for it is written (Isa. lvi. 7), "Them will I bring to my holy mountain, and make them joyful in the house of my prayer." It is thus He prays: "May it please me that my mercy may overcome my anger, that all my attributes may be invested with compassion, and that I may deal with my children in the attribute of kindness, and that out of regard to them I may pass by judgment."

Ibid., fol. 7, col. 1.

He is a respecter of persons; as it is written (Num. vi. 26), "The Lord lift up His countenance upon thee."

Ibid., fol. 20, col. 2.

When accused by Elijah of having turned Israel's heart back again (1 Kings xviii. 37), He confesseth the evil He had done (Micah iv. 6). *Ibid.*, fol. 31, col. 2.

God, when charged by Moses as being the cause of Israel's idolatry, confesseth the justice of that accusation by saying (Num. xiv. 20), "I have pardoned according to thy word." *Ibid.*, fol. 32, col. 1.

He drops two tears into the ocean, and this causes the earth to quake. *Ibid.*, fol. 59, col. 1.

He is represented as a hairdresser; for it is said He plaited Eve's hair (and some have actually enumerated the braids as 700). *Eiruvin*, fol. 18, col. 1.

In a Hagada (see Sanhedrin, fol. 95, col. 2), God is conceived as acting the barber to Sennacherib, a sort of parody on Isaiah vii. 20.

He is said to have created the evil as well as the good passions in man. *Berachoth*, fol. 61, col. 1.

God weeps every day. *Chaggigah*, fol. 3, col. 2.

He dresses Himself in a veil and shows Moses the Jewish Liturgy, saying unto him, "When the Israelites sin against me, let them copy this example, and I will pardon their sins.»   *Rosh Hashanah*, fol. 17, col. 2.

God is said to have regretted creating certain things.
                                                        Succah, fol. 52, col. 2.

God is represented as irrigating the land of Israel, but leaving the rest of the earth to be watered by an angel.
                                                        Taanith, fol. 10, col. 1.

It is said that He will make a dance for the righteous, and as He places Himself in the centre, they will point at Him with their fingers, and say (Isa. xxv. 9), "Behold, this is our God; we have waited for him; . . . we will be glad and rejoice in His salvation."
                                                        Ibid., fol. 31, col. 1.

God is said to have prevaricated in making peace between Abraham and Sarah, which is not so surprising; for while one Rabbi teaches that prevarication is under certain circumstances allowable, another asserts it absolutely as a duty; for it is written (1 Sam. xvi. 2), "And Samuel said, How can I go? if Saul hear it, he will kill me. And the Lord said, Take a heifer with thee, and say, I am come to sacrifice unto the Lord."   *Yevamoth*, fol. 65, col. 2.

This teaching may be easily matched by parallels from heathen literature, but we have room only for two or three examples:—Maximus Tyrius says, "There is nothing (essentially) decorous in truth, yea, truth is sometimes hurtful and lying profitable." Darius is represented by Herodotus (Book iii., p. 191) as saying, "When telling falsehood is profitable, let it be told." Menander says, "A lie is better than an annoying truth."

God utters a curse against those who remain single after they are twenty years of age; and those who marry at sixteen please him, and those who do so at fourteen still more.
                                                        Kiddushin, fol. 29, col. 2.

Elijah binds and God flogs the man who marries an unsuitable wife.   *Ibid.*, fol. 70, col. 1.

God acknowledges His weakness in argument, "My children have vanquished me! my children have vanquished me!" He exclaims. "They have defeated me in argument."
                                                        Bava Metzia, fol. 59, col. 2.

God's decision was controverted by the Academy in heaven, and the matter in debate was finally settled by a Rabbi, who had to be summoned from earth to heaven expressly to adjudicate in the case.

Bava Metzia, fol. 86, col. 1.

The classical student will recognize in this a parallel to the Greek myth in which the Olympian divinities refer their debate in the matter of the apple of discord to the judgment of Paris. May there not in both fables lie a dim forefeeling of the time when Justice shall transfer her seat from the skies, so that whatever her ministers bind on earth may be bound in heaven?

God will bear testimony before all the nations of the earth that His people Israel have kept the whole of the law. *Avodah Zarah*, fol. 3, col. 1.

God is occupied for twelve hours every day in study, at work, or at play. *Ibid.*, fol. 3, col. 2.

God does not act without first consulting the assembly above; as it is said (Dan. iv. 17), "This matter is by the decree of the watchers and the demand of the word of the Holy One," etc. *Sanhedrin*, fol. 38, col. 2.

God Himself is described as exacting an atonement for His own miscreations; as, for instance, His diminishing the size of the moon. *Shevuoth*, fol. 9, col. 1.

The general height of the Levites was ten ells.

Shabbath, fol. 92, col. 1.

Ten things cause hemorrhoids:—Eating cane leaves, the foliage and tendrils of the vine, the palate of cattle, the backbones of fish, half-cooked salt fish, wine lees, etc.

Berachoth, fol. 55, col. 1.

Ten things provoke a desperate relapse in a convalescent:—Eating beef, fat meat, broiled meat, fowl, or roasted eggs, shaving, eating cress, taking milk or cheese, or indulging in a bath. Some say also eating walnuts, others say eating cucumbers, which are as dangerous to the body as swords. *Ibid.*, fol. 57, col. 2.

Ten curses were pronounced against Eve:—The words "greatly multiply," "thy sorrow" (alluding to rearing a family), "thy conception," "in sorrow shalt thou bring forth," "thy desire shall be to thy husband," "he shall rule over thee," express six of these. The remainder are: —She should be wrapped up like a mourner (that is, she should not appear in public without having her head covered); she was restricted to one husband, though he might have more wives than one, and was to be kept within doors like a prisoner. *Eiruvin*, fol. 100, col. 2.

Ten things were created during the twilight of the first Sabbath-eve. These were: —The well that followed Israel in the wilderness, the manna, the rainbow, the letters of the alphabet, the stylus, the tables of the law, the grave of Moses, the cave in which Moses and Elijah stood, the opening of the mouth of Balaam's ass, the opening of the earth to swallow the wicked (Korah and his clique). Rav Nechemiah said, in his father's name, also fire and the mule. Rav Yosheyah, in his father's name, added also the ram which Abraham offered up instead of Isaac, and the Shameer. Rav Yehudah says the tongs also, etc.

P'sachim, fol. 54, col. 1.

To the ten things said to have been created on Sabbath-eve some add the rod of Aaron that budded and bloomed, and others malignant demons and the garments of Adam.

Ibid.

Rav Yehuda said, in the name of Rav, ten things were created on the first day: —Heaven and earth, chaos and confusion, light and darkness, wind and water, the measure of day and the measure of night. "Heaven and earth," for it is written, "In the beginning God made the heavens and the earth." "Chaos and confusion," for it is written, "And the earth was chaos and confusion." "Light and darkness," for it is written, "And darkness was upon the face of the abyss." "Wind and water," for it is written, "The wind of God hovered over the face of the waters." "The measure of day and the measure of night," for it is written, "Morning and evening were one day." *Chaggigah*, fol. 12, col. 1.

Ten facts witness to the presence of a supernatural power in the Temple: —No premature birth was ever caused by the odor of the sacrifices; the carcasses never became putrid; no fly was ever to be seen in the slaughter-houses; the high-priest was never defiled on the day of atonement; no defect was ever found in the wave-sheaf, the two wave-loaves, or the shewbread; however closely crowded the people were, every one had room enough for prostration; no serpent or scorpion ever stung a person in Jerusalem; and no one had ever to pass the night without sleeping-accommodation in the city.

Yoma, fol. 21, col. 1.

Tradition teaches that Rabbi Yossi said : — The She-chinah has never descended below, nor did Moses and Elijah ever ascend on high; for it is said (Ps. cxv. 16), "The heavens, even the heavens, are the Lords; but the earth hath he given to the children of men." True, it is written, he admitted (Exod. xix. 20), "And the Lord came down upon Mount Sinai ; " but that, he remarked, was ten handbreadths above the summit. And true, too, is it written (Zech. xiv. 4), "And His feet shall stand in that day upon the Mount of Olives ; " but that, too, he added, is ten handbreadths above it. And so, in like manner, Moses and Elijah halted ten handbreadths from heaven.

Succah, fol. 5, col. 1.

What entitles a place to rank as a large town? When there are in it ten unemployed men. Should there be fewer than that number, it is to be looked upon as a village.

Meggillah, fol. 3, col. 2.

In places where there are not ten Batlanim, men of leisure, that is, men always free to be present at every synagogue service, a minyan (number) has to be hired for the purpose. The notion that ten constitutes a congregation is based on the authority of Num. xiv, 27, "How long shall I bear with this congregation?" As the term "congregation" here refers to the ten spies who brought the evil report, it is concluded forsooth that ten men, and never less, is the orthodox minimum for a congregation.

Ten lights, said he, could not extinguish one ; how shall one extinguish ten? *Ibid.*, fol. 16, col. 2.

These words are said to have been spoken by Joseph to his brethren, who, after the death of their father Jacob, feared lest Joseph should revenge himself upon them (Gen. l. 21). The Midrash and the Targums as usual furnish much additional information.

Rav Assi said : — Nowadays, if a Gentile should betroth a Jewess, there is reason for regarding the betrothal as not therefore invalid, for he may be a descendant of the ten tribes, and so one of the seed of Israel.

Yevamoth, fol. 16, col. 2.

Rabbi Yochanan said : — If, after the death of her husband, a woman should remain unmarried for ten years and then marry again, she will have no children. Rav Nachman added : — Provided she have not thought of marrying all the while ; but if she had thought of marrying again, in that case she will have children. Rava once said to Rav Chisda's daughter (who bore children to Rava, though she did not marry him until ten years after her first husband's death), " The Rabbis have their doubts about you." She replied, " I had always set my heart upon thee." A woman once said to Rav Yoseph, " I waited ten years before I married again, and then I had children." " Daughter," said he, " do not bring the words of the wise into discredit. It is thou, not they, that are mistaken." Then the woman confessed that she had been a transgressor.

Ibid., fol. 34, col. 2.

The Rabbis teach that if a man live with a wife ten years without issue he should divorce her and give her the prescribed marriage portion, as he may not be deemed worthy to be built up by her (that is, to have children by her).

Ibid., fol. 64, col. 2.

As a set-off we append here a romantic story paraphrased from the Midrash Shir Hashirim. A certain Israelite of Sidon, having lived many years with his wife without being blessed with offspring, made up his mind to give her a bill of divorcement. They went accordingly together to Rabbi Shimon ben Yochai, that legal effect might be given to the act of separation. Upon presenting themselves before him, the Rabbi addressed them in these fatherly accents : — " My children," said he, " your divorce must not take place in pettishness or anger, lest people should surmise something guilty or disgraceful as the motive for the action. Let your parting, therefore, be like your meeting, friendly and cheerful. Go home, make a feast, and invite your friends to share it with you ; and then to-morrow return and I will ratify the divorce you seek for." Acting upon this advice, they went home, got ready a feast, invited their friends, and made merry together. " My dear," said the husband at length to his wife, " we have lived for many a long year lovingly together, and now that

we are about to be separated, it is not because there is any ill-will
between us, but simply because we are not blessed with a family. In
proof that my love is unchanged, and that I wish thee all good, I
give thee leave to choose whatever thou likest best in the house and
carry it away with thee." The wife with true womanly wit promptly
replied, "Well and good, my dear!" The evening thereafter glided
pleasantly by, the wine-cup went round freely and without stint, and
all passed off well, till first the guests one by one, and then the
master of the house himself, fell asleep, and lay buried in unconscious-
ness. The lady, who had planned this result, and only waited its *dé-
nouement*, immediately summoned her confidential handmaids and had
her lord and master gently borne away as he was to the house of her
father. On the following morning, as the stupor wore off, he awoke,
rubbing his eyes with astonishment. "Where am I?" he cried. "Be
easy, husband dear," responded the wife in his presence. "I have
only done as thou allowedst me. Dost thou remember permitting me
last night, in the hearing of our guests, to take away from our house
whatever best pleased me? There was nothing there I cared for so
much as thyself; thou art all in all to me, so I brought thee with
me here. Where I am there shalt thou be; let nothing but death
part us." The two thereupon went back to Rabbi Shimon as appointed, and reported their change of purpose, and that they had made
up their minds to remain united. So the Rabbi prayed for them to the
Lord, who couples and setteth the single in families. He then spoke
his blessing over the wife, who became thenceforth as a fruitful vine,
and honored her husband with children and children's children.

A parallel to this, illustrative of wifely devotion, is recorded in the
early history of Germany. In the year 1141, during the civil war in
Germany between the Guelphs and the Ghibellines, it happened that
the Emperor Conrad besieged the Guelph Count of Bavaria in the
Castle of Weinsberg. After a long and obstinate defense the garrison
was obliged at length to surrender, when the Emperor, annoyed that
they had held out so long and defied him, vowed that he would destroy the place with fire and put all to the sword except the women,
whom he gallantly promised to let go free and pass out unmolested.
The Guelph Countess, when she heard of this, begged as a further
favor that the women might be allowed to bear forth as much of
their valuables as they could severally manage to carry. The Emperor
having pledged his word and honor that he would grant this request,
on the morrow at daybreak, as the castle gates opened, he saw to his
amazement the women file out one by one, every married woman
carrying her husband with her young ones upon her back, and the
others each the friend or relation nearest and dearest to her. At sight
of this, the Emperor was tenderly moved, and could not help according to the action the homage of his admiration. The result was
that not only was life and liberty extended to the Guelphs, but the
place itself was spared and restored in perpetuity to its heroic de-
fenders. The Count and his Countess were henceforth treated by the

Emperor with honor and affection, and the town itself was for long after popularly known by the name of Weibertreue, *i. e.*, the abode of womanly fidelity.

Benedictory condolences are recited by ten men, not reckoning the mourners; but nuptial blessings are recited by ten men, including the bridegroom.

Kethuboth, fol. 8. col. 2.

The Mishnic Rabbis have ordained that ten cups of wine be drunk in the house by the funeral party; three before supper, to whet the appetite; three during supper, to aid digestion; and four after the meal, at the recitation of the four benedictions. Afterward four complimentary cups were added, one in honor of the precentors, one in honor of the municipal authorities, another in remembrance of the Temple, and the fourth in the memory of Rabbon Gamliel. Drunkenness so often ensued on these occasions that the number had to be curtailed to the original ten cups. The toast to the memory of Rabbon Gamliel was to commemorate his endeavors to reduce the extravagant expenses at burials, and the consequent abandonment of the dead by poor relations. He left orders that his own remains should be buried in a linen shroud, and since then, says Rav Pappa, corpses are buried in canvas shrouds about a zouz in value. *Ibid.*, fol. 8, col. 2.

At the age of ten years a child should begin to study the Mishna. *Ibid.*, fol. 50, col. 1.

Rabbi the Holy, when dying, lifted up his ten fingers toward heaven and said:— "Lord of the Universe, it is open and well-known unto Thee that with these ten fingers I have labored without ceasing in the law, and never sought after any worldly profit with even so much as my little finger; may it therefore please Thee that there may be peace in my rest!" A voice from heaven immediately responded (Isa. lvii. 2), "He shall enter peace: they shall rest in their beds." *Ibid.*, fol. 104, col. 2.

Ten measures of wisdom came down to the world; the land of Israel received nine and the rest of the world but one only. Ten measures of beauty came down to the world; Jerusalem monopolized nine and the rest of the

world had only one. Ten measures of riches came down to
the world ; Rome laid hold of nine and left the rest of the
world but one for a portion. Ten measures of poverty
came down to the world ; nine fell to the lot of Babylon
and one to the rest of the world. Ten measures of pride
came down to the world ; Elam appropriated nine and to
the rest of the world but one remained over. Ten measures
of bravery came to the world ; Persia took nine, leaving
but one for the rest of the world. Ten measures of vermin
came to the world ; nine fell to the Medes and one to the
rest of the world. Ten measures of sorcery came down to
the world ; Egypt received nine and one was shared by the
rest of the world. Ten measures of plagues came into the
world ; nine measures were alloted to the swine and the
rest of the world had the other. Ten measures of fornication came into the world ; nine of these belong to the
Arabs and to the rest of the world the other. Ten measures of impudence found its way into the world ; Mishan
appropriated nine, leaving one to the rest of the world.
Ten measures of talk came into the world ; women claimed
nine, leaving the tenth to the rest of the world. Ten
measures of early rising came into the world ; they of
Ethiopia received nine and the rest of the world one only.
Ten measures of sleep came to the world ; the servants
took nine of them, leaving one measure to the rest of the
world.   *Kiddushin*, fol. 49, col. 2.

Ten different sorts of people went up from Babylon :—
(1.) Priests, (2.) Levites, (3.) Israelites, (4.) Disqualified
Cohanim, (5.) Freedmen, (6.) Illegitimate, (7.) Nethinim,
(8.) Unaffiliated ones, and (10.) Foundlings.
                              Ibid., fol. 63, col. 1.

Ten characteristics mark the phlebotomist :— He walks
sideling along ; he is proud ; he stoops awhile before seat-
ing himself ; he has an envious and evil eye ; he is a
gourmand, but he defecates little at a time ; he is suspected
of incontinence, robbery, and murder.
                              Ibid., fol. 82, col. 1.

Rabbi Chanena ben Agil asked Rabbi Cheya ben Abba,
"Why does the word, 'signifying that it may be well

with thee' not occur in the first copy of the ten commandments (Exod. xx.) as it does in the second?"
(Deut. v.) He replied, "Before thou askest me such a
question, first tell me whether the word occurs in Deuteronomy or not? for I don't know if it does." The required
answer was given by another Rabbi, "The omission of the
word in the first publication of the ten commandments is
due to the foresight of what was to befall the first tables,
for if the word good had been in the tables, and broken
withal, then goodness would have ceased to bless the sons
of Israel."   *Bava Kama*, fol. 55, col. 1.

The Tosephoth in Bava Bathra (fol. 113, col. 1) ingenuously admits that the Rabbis were occasionally ignorant of the letter of
Scripture. The above quotation may be taken as a sample of several
in corroboration.

The Rabbis have taught that when pestilence is abroad
no one should walk along the middle of the road, for
there the angel of death would be sure to cross him.
Neither when there is pestilence in a town should a person
go to the synagogue alone, because there, provided no
children are taught there, and ten men are not met to
pray there, the angel of death hides his weapons. The
Rabbis have also taught that (like the Banshee of Ireland),
the howling of dogs indicates the approach of the angel of
death, whereas when they sport it is a sign that Elijah
the prophet is at hand, unless one of them happen to be a
female, for it is her presence among them, and not any
super-natural instinct, that is to be understood as the cause
of the demonstration.   *Ibid.*, fol. 60, col. 2.

Ten constitutions were founded by Ezra: — The reading
of a portion of Scripture during the afternoon prayers on
the Sabbath-day, and during morning prayers on the
second and fifth days of the week (a rule that is to this
day observed in orthodox places of worship), and this for
the reason that three days should not pass by without such
an exercise; to hold courts for the due administration of
justice on the second and fifth days of the week, when
the country people came to hear the public reading of the
Scriptures; to wash their garments, etc., on the fifth day,

and to prepare for the coming Sabbath; to eat garlic on the sixth day of the week, as this vegetable has the property of promoting secretions (see Exod. xxi. 10); that the wife should be up betimes and bake the bread, so as to have some ready in case any one should come begging; that the women should wear a girdle round the waist for decency sake; that they should comb their hair before bathing; that peddlers should hawk their perfumes about the streets in order that women should supply themselves with such things as will attract and please their husbands; and that certain unfortunates (see Lev. xv.) should bathe themselves before they came to the public reading of the law.   *Bava Kama*, fol. 82, col. 1.

Ten things are said about Jerusalem:— (1.) No mortgaged house was eventually alienated from its original owner (which was the case elsewhere in Jewry). (2.) Jerusalem never had occasion to behead a heifer by way of expiation for an unproved murder (see Deut. xxi. 1–9). (3.) She never could be regarded as a repudiated city (Deut. xiii. 12, etc.). (4.) No appearance of plagues in any house at Jerusalem rendered the house unclean, because the words of Lev. xiv. 34, are "your possession," an expression which could not apply to Jerusalem, as it had never been portioned among the ten tribes. (5.) Projecting cornices and balconies were not to be built in the city. (6.) Limekilns were not to be erected there. (7.) No refuse heaps were allowed in any quarter. (8.) No orchards or gardens were permitted, excepting certain flower-gardens, which had been there from the times of the earlier prophets. (9.) No cocks were reared in Jerusalem. (10.) No corpse ever remained over night within its walls; the funeral had to take place on the day of the decease.

                              Ibid., fol. 82, col. 2.

In the Book of Psalms David included those which were composed by ten elders:—Adam (Ps. cxxxix.); Melchizedek (Ps. cx.); Abraham (Ps. lxxxix.); Moses (Ps. xc.); the others alluded to were by Heman, Jeduthun, Asaph, and the three sons of Korah.

                              Bava Bathra, fol. 14, col. 2.

A man once overheard his wife telling her daughter that, though she had ten sons, only one of them could fairly claim her husband as his father. After the father's death it was found that he had bequeathed all his property to one son, but that the testament did not mention his name. The question therefore, arose, which of the ten was intended? So they came one and all to Rabbi Benaah and asked him to arbitrate between them. "Go," said he to them, "and beat at your father's grave, until he rises to tell you to which of you it was that he left the property." All except one did so; and he, because by so doing he showed most respect for his father's memory, was presumed to be the one on whom the father had fixed his affections; he accordingly was supposed to be the one intended, and the others were therefore excluded from the patrimony. The disappointed ones went straight to the government and de-nounced the Rabbi. "Here is a man," said they, "who arbitrarily deprives people of their rights, without proof or witnesses." The consequence was that the Rabbi was sent to prison, but he gave the authorities such evidence of his shrewdness and sense of justice, that he was soon restored to freedom. *Bava Bathra*, fol. 58, col. 1.

Till ten generations have passed speak thou not con-temptuously of the Gentiles in the hearing of a proselyte.
Sanhedrin, fol. 94, col. 1.

The ten tribes will never be restored, for it is said (Deut. xxiii. 28), "God cast them into another land, as it is this day." As this day passes away without return, so also they have passed away never more to return. So says Rabbi Akiva, but Rabbi Eleazar says, "'As it is this day' implies that, as the day darkens and lightens up again, so the ten tribes now in darkness shall in the future be re-stored to light." The Rabbis have thus taught that the ten tribes will have no portion in the world to come; for it is said (Deut. xxix. 28), "And the Lord rooted them out of their land in anger, and in wrath, and in great indigna-tion." "And he rooted them out of their land," that is, from this world, "and cast them into another land," that is, the world to come. So says Rabbi Akiva. Rabbi Shimon ben

Yehuda says, "If their designs continue as they are at this day, they will not return, but if they repent they will return." Rabbi (the Holy) says, "They will enter the world to come, for it is said (Isa. xxvii. 13), 'And it shall come to pass in that day that the great trumpet shall be blown, and they shall come which were ready to perish.'"

Sanhedrin, fol. 110, col. 2.

Ten things are detrimental to study : — Going under the halter of a camel, and still more passing under its body ; walking between two camels or between two women ; to be one of two men that a woman passes between ; to go where the atmosphere is tainted by a corpse ; to pass under a bridge beneath which no water has flowed for forty days ; to eat with a ladle that has been used for culinary purposes ; to drink water that runs through a cemetery. It is also dangerous to look at the face of a corpse, and some say also to read inscriptions on tombstones.

Horayoth, fol. 13, col. 2.

Ten strong things were created in the world (of which the one that comes after is stronger than that which preceded). A mountain is strong, but iron can hew it in pieces ; the fire weakens the iron ; the water quenches the fire ; the clouds carry off the water ; the wind disperses the clouds ; the living body resists the wind ; fear enervates the body ; wine abolishes fear ; sleep overcomes wine, and death is stronger than all together ; yet it is written (Prov. x. 2), "And alms delivereth from death" (the original word has two meanings, righteousness and alms).

Bava Bathra, fol. 10, col. 1.

With the utterance of ten words was the world created.

Avoth, chap. 5, mish. 1.

There were ten generations from Adam to Noah, to show how great is God's long-suffering, for each of these went on provoking Him more and more, till His forbearance relenting, He brought the flood upon them.

Ibid., mish. 2.

There were ten generations from Noah to Abraham, to show that God is long-suffering, since all those succeeding generations provoked Him, until Abraham came, and he received the reward that belonged to all of them.

Avoth, mish. 3.

The greatest sinner is uniformly presumed throughout the Talmud to have a certain amount of merit, and therefore a corresponding title to reward (see chap. 2, No. 10 = Ps. xxxvii. 35-37). Much of this last is enjoyed by the wicked themselves in the present world, and the surplus is often transferred to the credit of the righteous in the world to come (see "Genesis," page 482, No. 173 = Matt. xiii. 12).

Abraham our father was tested ten times ; in every case he stood firm ; which shows how great the love of our father Abraham was.   *Ibid.,* mish. 4.

Ten miracles were wrought for our forefathers in Egypt, and ten at the Red Sea. Ten plagues did the Holy One — blessed be He ! — inflict on the Egyptians in Egypt, and ten at the sea. Ten times did our ancestors tempt God in the wilderness, as it is said (Num. xiv. 22), "And have tempted me now these ten times, and have not hearkened to my voice."   *Ibid.,* mish. 5, 6, 7.

Ten times did God test our forefathers, and they were not so much as once found to be perfect.

Avoth d'Rab. Nathan, chap. 34.

Ten times the Shechinah came down unto the world : — At the garden of Eden (Gen. iii. 8) ; at the time of the Tower (Gen. xi. 5) ; at Sodom (Gen. xviii. 21) ; in Egypt Exod. iii. 8) ; at the Red Sea (Ps. xviii. 9) ; on Mount Sinai (Exod. xix. 20) ; into the Temple (Ezek. xliv. 2) ; in the pillar of cloud (Num. xi. 25). It will descend in the days of Gog and Magog, for it is said (Zech. xiv. 4), "And His feet shall stand in that day upon the Mount of Olives" (the tenth is omitted in the original).   *Ibid.*

The Shechinah made ten gradual ascents in passing from place to place : — From the cover of the ark to the cherub (2 Sam. xxii. 11) ; thence to the threshold of the house (Ezek. ix. 3) ; thence to the cherubim (Ezek. x. 18) ; thence to the roof of the Temple (Prov. xxi. 9) ; thence to the wall of the court (Amos vii. 7) ; thence to the altar (Amos ix. 1) ; thence to the city (Micah vi. 9) ; thence to the mount (Ezek. xi. 23) ; thence to the wilderness (Prov. xxi. 9); whence the Shechinah went up, as it is said (Hosea v. 15), "I will go and return to my place." *Avoth d' Rab. Nathan*, chap. 34.

Ten different terms are employed to express the title of prophet:—Ambassador, Faithful, Servant, Messenger, Seer, Watchman, Seer of Vision, Dreamer, Prophet, Man of God. *Ibid.*

Ten distinct designations are applied to the Holy Spirit:—Proverb, Interpretation, Dark, Saying, Oracle, Utterance, Decree, Burden, Prophecy, Vision. *Ibid.*

Ten are designated by the term Life or Living:—God, the law, Israel, the righteous, the garden of Eden, the tree of life, the land of Israel, Jerusalem, benevolence, the sages; and water also is described as life, as it is said (Zech. xiv. 8), "And it shall be in that day that living water shall go out from Jerusalem." *Ibid.*

If there are ten beds piled upon one another, and if beneath the lowermost there be any tissue woven of linen and wool (Lev. xix. 19), it is unlawful to lie down upon them. *Tamid*, fol. 27, col. 2.

Alexander of Macedon proposed ten queries to the elders of the south:—"Which are more remote from each other, the heavens from the earth or the east from the west?" They answered, "The east is more remote from the west, for when the sun is either in the east or in the west, any one can gaze upon him; but when the sun is in the zenith or heaven, none can gaze at him, he is so much nearer." The Mishnaic Rabbis, on the other hand, say they are equidistant; for it is written (Ps. ciii. 11, 12), "As the heavens are from the earth, . . . so is the east removed from the west." Alexander then asked, "Were the heavens created first or was the earth?" "The heavens," they replied, "for it is said, 'In the beginning God created the heavens and the earth.'" He then asked, "Was light created first or was darkness?" They replied, "This is an unanswerable question." They should have answered darkness was created first, for it is said, "And the earth was without form and void, and darkness was upon the face of the deep," and after this, "And God said, Let there be light, and there was light." *Tamid.*, fol. 31, col. 2.

There are ten degrees of holiness, and the land of Israel is holy above all other lands.

Kelim, chap. 1, mish. 6.

There are ten places which, though Gentile habitations, are not considered unclean : — (1.) Arab tents ; (2.) A watchman's hut ; (3.) The top of a tower ; (4.) A fruit-store ; (5.) A summer-house ; (6.) A gatekeeper's lodge ; (7.) An uncovered courtyard ; (8.) A bath-house ; (9.) An armory ; (10.) A military camp. *Oholoth*, chap. 18, mish. 10.

"An Ammonite or Moabite shall not enter the congregation of the Lord, even to the tenth generation," etc. (Deut. xxiii. 4). One day Yehuda, an Ammonite prophet, came into the academy and asked, "May I enter the congregation (if I marry a Jewess) ? " Rabban Gamliel said unto him, "Thou art not at liberty to do so ; " but Rabbi Joshua interposed and maintained, "He is at liberty to do so." Then Rabban Gamliel appealed to Scripture, which saith, "An Ammonite or Moabite shall not enter into the congregation of the Lord, even to the tenth generation." To this Rabbi Joshua retorted and asked, "Are then these nations still in their own native places ? Did not Sennacherib, the king of Assyria, transplant the nations ? as it is said (Isa. x. 13), 'I have removed the bounds of the people, and have robbed their treasures, and have put down the valor of the inhabitants.' " Rabban Gamliel replied, "Scripture saith (Jer. xlix. 6), 'Afterward I will bring again the captivity of the children of Ammon,' and so," he argued, "they must have already returned." Rabbi Joshua then promptly rejoined, "Scripture saith (Jer. xxx. 3), 'I will bring again the captivity of my people Israel and Judah,' and these have not returned yet." And on this reasoning the proselyte was permitted to enter the congregation. *Yadayim*, chap. 4, mish. 4.

Go and learn from the tariff of donkey-drivers, ten miles for one zouz, eleven for two zouzim.

Chaggigah, fol. 9, col. 2.

When Israel went up to Jerusalem to attend the festivals, they had to stand in the Temple court closely crowded together, yet when prostrated there was a wide space between each of them (Rashi says about four ells), so that they could not hear each other's confession, which might have caused them to blush. They had, however, when prostrated, to extend eleven ells behind the Holy of Holies. *Yoma*, fol. 21, col. 1,

In the days of Joel, the son of Pethuel, there was a great dearth, because (as is said in Joel i. 4) "That which the palmerworm hath left hath the locust eaten," etc. That year the month of Adar (about March) passed away and no rain came. When some rain fell, during the following month, the prophet said unto Israel, "Go ye forth and sow." They replied, "Shall he who has but a measure or two of wheat or barley eat and live or sow it and die?" Still the prophet urged, "Go forth and sow." Then they obeyed the prophet, and in eleven days the seed had grown and ripened; and it is with reference to that generation that it is said (Ps. cxxvi. 5), "They that sow in tears shall reap in joy." *Taanith*, fol. 5, col. 1.

What is a female in her minority? One who is between eleven years and one day, and twelve years and one day. When younger or older than these ages she is to be treated in the usual manner. *Yevamoth*, fol. 100, col. 2.

Whoever gives a prutah to a poor man has six blessings bestowed upon him, and he that speaks a kind word to him realizes eleven blessings in himself (see Isa. lviii. 7, 8). *Bava Bathra*, fol. 9, col. 2.

On the next page of the same tract it is said, "For one prutah given as alms to a poor man one is made partaker of the beatific vision." (See also Midrash Tillim on Ps. xvii. 15.)

The prutah was the smallest coin then current. It is estimated to have been equal to about one-twentieth of an English penny. In some quarters of Poland the Jews have small thin bits of brass, with the Hebrew word prutah impressed upon them, for the uses in charity on the part of those among them that cannot afford to give a kreutzer to a poor man. The poor, when they have collected a number of these, change them into larger coin at the almoner's appointed by the congregation. Thus even the poor are enabled to give alms to the poor. (See my "Genesis," p. 277, No. 31.)

Rabbi Yochanan said eleven sorts of spices were mentioned to Moses on Sinai. Rav Hunna asked, "What
Scripture text proves this?" (Exod. xxx. 34), "Take
unto thee sweet spices" (the plural implying two), "stacte,
myrrh, and galbanum" (these three thus making up five),
"sweet spices" (the repetition doubling the five into ten),
"with pure frankincense" (which makes up eleven).

Kerithoth, fol. 6, col. 2.

"Zion said, The Lord hath forsaken and forgotten me"
(Isa. xlix. 14). The community of Israel once pleaded
thus with the Holy One—blessed be He!—"Even a man
who marries a second wife still bears in mind the services
of the first, but Thou, Lord, hast forgotten me." The
Holy One — blessed be He ! — replied, "Daughter, I have
created twelve constellations in the firmament, and for each
constellation I have created thirty armies, and for each
army thirty legions, each legion containing thirty divisions,
each division thirty cohorts, each cohort having thirty
camps, and in each camp hang suspended 365,000 myriads
of stars, as many thousands of myriads as there are days
in the year; all these have I created for thy sake, and yet
thou sayest, 'Thou hast forsaken and forgotten me!' Can
a woman forget her sucking-child, that she should not have
compassion on the son of her womb? Yea, they may forget, yet will I not forget thee."

Berachoth, fol. 32, col. 2.

No deceased person is forgotten from the heart (of his
relatives that survive him) till after twelve months, for it
is said (Ps. xxxi. 12), "I am forgotten as a dead man
out of mind; I am like a lost vessel" (which, as Rashi
explains, is like all lost property, not thought of as lost
for twelve months, for not till then is proclamation for it
given up). *Ibid.*, fol. 58, col. 2.

Rabbi Yehudah, Rabbi Yossi, and Rabbi Shimon (ben
Yochai) were sitting together, and Yehudah ben Gerim
(the son, says Rashi, of proselyte parents) beside them.
In the course of conversation Rabbi Yehudah remarked,
"How beautiful and serviceable are the works of these
Romans! They have established markets, spanned rivers

by bridges, and erected baths." To this remark Rabbi
Yossi kept silent, but Rabbi Shimon replied, "Yea, indeed;
but all these they have done to benefit themselves. The
markets they have opened to feed licentiousness, they have
erected baths for their own pleasure, and the bridges they
have raised for collecting tolls." Yehudah ben Gerim thereupon went direct and informed against them, and the report having reached the Emperor's ears, an edict was
immediately issued that Rabbi Yehudah should be pro-
moted, Rabbi Yossi banished to Sepphoris, and Rabbi
Shimon taken and executed. Rabbi Shimon and his son,
however, managed to secret themselves in a college, where
they were purveyed to by the Rabbi's wife, who brought
them daily bread and water. One day mistrust seized the
Rabbi, and he said to his son, "Women are light-minded;
the Romans may tease her and then she will betray us."
So they stole away and hid themselves in a cave. Here
the Lord interposed by a miracle, and created a carob-tree
bearing fruit all the year round for their support, and
opened a perennial spring for their refreshment. To save
their clothes they laid them aside except at prayers, and
to protect their naked bodies from exposure they would at
other times sit up to their necks in sand, absorbed in
study. After they had passed twelve years thus in the
cave, Elijah was sent to inform them that the Emperor
was dead, and his decree powerless to touch them. On
leaving the cave, they noticed some people plowing and
sowing, when one of them exclaimed, "These folk
neglect eternal things and trouble themselves with the
things that are temporal." As they fixed their eyes upon
the place, fire came and burnt it up. Then a Bath Kol
was heard exclaiming, "What! are ye come forth to
destroy the world I have made? Get back to your cave
and hide you." Thither accordingly they returned, and
after they had stopped there twelve months longer, they
remonstrated, pleading that even the judgment of the
wicked in Gehenna lasted no longer than twelve months;
upon which a Bath Kol was again heard from heaven,
which said, "Come ye forth from your cave." Then they
arose and obeyed it.   *Shabbath*, fol. 33, col. 2.

Rabbi Yehoshua ben Levi said that at every utterance which proceeded from the mouth of the Holy One — blessed be He! — on Mount Sinai, Israel receded twelve miles, being conducted gently back by the ministering angels; for it is said (Ps. lxviii. 12), "The angels of hosts kept moving." *Shabbath*, fol. 88, col. 2.

A Sadducee once said to Rabbi Abhu, "Ye say that the souls of the righteous are treasured up under the throne of glory; how then had the Witch of Endor power to bring up the prophet Samuel by necromancy?" The Rabbi replied, "Because that occurred within twelve months after his death; for we are taught that during twelve months after death the body is preserved and the soul soars up and down, but that after twelve months the body is destroyed and the soul goes up never to return."

Ibid., fol. 152, col. 2.

Clever answers to puzzling questions like the above, are of frequent occurrence in the Talmud; and we select here a few out of the many specimens of Rabbinical ready wit and repartee.

Turnus Rufus once said to Rabbi Akiva, "If your God is a friend to the poor, why doesn't he feed them?" To which he promptly replied, "That we by maintaining them may escape the condemnation of Gehenna." "On the contrary," said the Emperor, "the very fact of your maintaining the poor will condemn you to Gehenna. I will tell thee by a parable whereto this is like, It is as if a king of our own flesh and blood should imprison a servant who has offended him, and command that neither food nor drink should be given him, and as if one of his subjects in spite of him should go and supply him with both. When the king hears of it will he not be angry with that man? And ye are called servants, as it is said (Lev. xxv. 55), 'For unto me the children of Israel are servants.'" To this Rabbi Akiva replied, "And I too will tell thee a parable whereunto the thing is like. It is like a king of our own flesh and blood who, being angry with his son, imprisons him, and orders that neither food nor drink be given him, but one goes and gives him both to eat and drink. When

the king hears of it will he not handsomely reward that
man? And we are sons, as it is written (Deut. xiv. 1),
'Ye are the sons of the Lord your God.'" "True," the
Emperor replied, "ye are both sons and servants; sons
when ye do the will of God; servants when ye do not;
and now ye are not doing the will of God."

Bava Bathra, fol. 10, col. 1.

Certain philosophers once asked the elders at Rome, "If
your God has no pleasure in idolatry, why does He not destroy the objects of it?" "And so He would," was the
reply, "if only such objects were worshiped as the world
does not stand in need of; but you idolators will worship
the sun and moon, the stars and the constellations. Should
He destroy the world because of the fools there are in it?
No! The world goes on as it has done all the same, but
they who abuse it will have to answer for their conduct.
On your philosophy, when one steals a measure of wheat
and sows it in his field it should by rights produce no
crop; nevertheless the world goes on as if no wrong had
been done, and they who abuse it will one day smart for
it."   *Avoda Zarah*, fol. 54, col. 2.

Antoninus Cæsar asked Rabbi (the Holy), "Why does
the sun rise in the east and set in the west?" "Thou
wouldst have asked," answered the Rabbi, "the same question if the order had been reversed." "What I mean," remarked Antoninus, "is this, is there any special reason why
he sets in the west?" "Yes," replied Rabbi, "to salute his
Creator (who is in the east), for it is said (Neh. ix. 6),
'And the host of heaven worship Thee.'"

Sanhedrin, fol. 91, col. 2.

Cæsar once said to Rabbi Tanchum, "Come, now, let us
be one people." "Very well," said Rabbi Tanchum, "only
we, being circumcised, cannot possibly become like you; if,
however, ye become circumcised we shall be alike in that
regard anyhow, and so be as one people." The Emperor
said, "Thou hast reasonably answered, but the Roman law
is, that he who nonpulses his ruler and puts him to silence
shall be cast to the lions." The word was no sooner uttered than the Rabbi was thrown into the den, but the

lions stood aloof and did not even touch him. A Sadducee, who looked on, remarked, "The lions do not devour him because they are not hungry," but, when at the royal command, the Sadducee himself was thrown in, he had scarcely reached the lions before they fell upon him and began to tear his flesh and devour him.   *Sanhedrin*, fol. 39, col. 1.

A certain Sadducee asked Rabbi Abhu, "Since your God is a priest, as it is written (Exod. xxv. 2), 'That they bring Me an offering,' in what did He bathe Himself after He was polluted by the burial (Num. xix. 11, 18) of the dead body of Moses? It could not be in the water, for it is written (Isa. xl. 12), 'Who has measured the waters in the hollow of His hand?' which therefore are insufficient for Him to bathe in." The Rabbi replied, "He bathed in fire, as it is written (Isa. lxvi. 15), 'For behold the Lord will come with fire.' "   *Ibid.*

Turnus Rufus asked this question also of Rabbi Akiva, "Why is the Sabbath distinguished from other days?" Rabbi Akiva replied, "Why art thou distinguished from other men?" The answer was, "Because it hath pleased my Master thus to honor me." And so retorted Akiva, "It hath pleased God to honor His Sabbath." "But what I mean," replied the other, "was how dost thou know that it is the Sabbath-day?" The reply was, "The river Sambatyon proves it; the necromancer proves it; the grave of thy father proves it, for the smoke thereof rises not on the Sabbath."   *Ibid.*, fol. 65, col. 2.

See Bereshith Rabba, fol. 4, with reference to what is here said about Turnus Rufus and his father's grave. The proof from the necromancer lies in the allegation that his art was unsuccessful if practiced on the Sabbath-day. The Sambatyon, Rashi says, is a pebbly river which rushes along all the days of the week except the Sabbath, on which it is perfectly still and quiet. In the Machsor for Pentecost (D. Levi's ed. p. 81), it is styled "the incomprehensible river," and a footnote thereto informs us that "This refers to the river said to rest on the Sabbath from throwing up stones, etc., which it does not cease to do all the rest of the week." (See Sanhedrin, fol. 65, col. 2; Yalkut on Isaiah, fol. 3, 1; Pesikta Tanchuma. See also Shalsheleth Hakabbala and Yuchsin.)

Those Israelites and Gentiles who have transgressed with their bodies (the former by neglecting to wear phylacteries,

and the latter by indulging in sensuous pleasures), shall go
down into Gehenna, and there be punished for twelve
months, after which period their bodies will be destroyed
and their soul consumed, and a wind shall scatter their
ashes under the soles of the feet of the righteous ; as it is
said (Mal. iv. 3), " And ye shall tread down the wicked ;
for they shall be as ashes under the soles of your feet."
But the Minim, the informers, and the Epicureans, they
who deny the law and the resurrection of the dead, they
who separate themselves from the manners of the congregation, they who have been a terror in the land of the living, and they who have sinned and have led the multitude
astray, as did Jeroboam the son of Nebat and his companions,— these shall go down into Gehenna, and there be
judged for generations upon generations, as it is said (Isa.
lxvi. 24), " And they shall go forth and look upon the
carcasses of the men that have transgressed against me,"
etc. Gehenna itself shall be consumed but they shall not
be burned up in the destruction ; as it is said (Ps. xlix.
14 ; Heb. xv.), " And their figures shall consume hell from
being a dwelling."　　　　　*Rosh Hashanah*, fol. 17, col. 1.

Once when Israel went up by pilgrimages to one of the
three annual feasts at Jerusalem (see Exod. xxxiv. 23, 24),
it so happened that there was no water to drink. Nicodemon ben Gorion therefore hired of a friendly neighbor
twelve huge reservoirs of water promising to have them
replenished against a given time, or failing this to forfeit
twelve talents of silver. The appointed day came and still
the drought continued, and therewith the scarcity of water ;
upon which the creditor appeared and demanded payment
of the forfeit. The answer of Nicodemon to the demand
was, " There's time yet ; the day is not over." The other
chuckled to himself, inwardly remarking, " There's no
chance now ; there's been no rain all the season," and off
he went to enjoy his bath. But Nicodemon sorrowful at
heart, wended his way to the Temple. After putting on
his prayer scarf, as he prayed, he pleaded, " Lord of the
Universe ! Thou knowest that I have not entered into this
obligation for my own sake, but for Thy glory and for the

benefit of Thy people." While he yet prayed the clouds gathered overhead, the rain fell in torrents, and the reservoirs were filled to overflowing. On going out of the house of prayer he was met by the exacting creditor, who still urged that the money was due to him, as he said, the rain came after sunset. But in answer to prayer the clouds immediately dispersed, and the sun shone out as brightly as ever. *Taanith*, fol. 19. col. 2.

Nicodemon ben Gorion of the above story is by some considered to be the Nicodemus of St. John's Gospel, iii. 1–10 ; vii. 50 ; xix. 30.

Would that my husband were here and could listen to me ; I should permit him to stay away another twelve years. *Kethuboth*, fol. 63. col. 1.

Hereto hangs a tale stranger than fiction, yet founded on fact. Rabbi Akiva was once a poor shepherd in the employ of Calba Shevua, one of the richest men in all Jerusalem. While engaged in that lowly occupation his master's only daughter fell in love with him, and the two carried on a clandestine courtship for some time together. Her father, hearing of it, threatened to disinherit her, to turn her out of doors and disown her altogether, if she did not break off her engagement. How could she connect herself with one who was the base-born son of a proselyte, a reputed descendant of Sisera and Jael, an ignorant fellow that could neither read nor write, and a man old enough to be her father? Rachel — for that was her name — determined to be true to her lover, and to brave the consequences by marrying him and exchanging the mansion of her father for the hovel of her husband. After a short spell of married life she prevailed upon her husband to leave her for a while in order to join a certain college in a distant land, where she felt sure that his talents would be recognized and his genius fostered into development worthy of it. As he sauntered along by himself he began to harbor misgivings in his mind as to the wisdom of the step, and more than once thought of returning. But when musing one day at a resting-place a waterfall arrested his attention, and he remarked how the water, by its continual dropping, was wearing away the solid rock. All at once, with the tact for which he was afterward so noted, he applied the lesson it yielded to himself. " So may the law," he reasoned, " work its way into my hard and stony heart ; " and he felt encouraged and pursued his journey. Under the tuition of Rabbi Eliezer, the son of Hyrcanus, and Rabbi Yehoshua, the son of Chananiah, his native ability soon began to appear, his name became known to fame, and he rose step by step until he ranked as a professor in the very college which he had entered as a poor student. After some twelve years of hard study and diligent service in the law he returned to Jerusalem, accompanied by a large number of disciples. On nearing the dwelling of his devoted wife he caught the sound of voices in eager conversation. He paused awhile and listened at the door, and overheard a gossiping neighbor blaming Rachel for her *mésalliance*, and twitting her with marrying a man who could run away and leave her as a widow for a dozen of years or more on the crazy pretext of going to college. He listened in eager curiosity, wondering what the reply would be. To his surprise, he heard his self-sacrificing wife exclaim, "Would that my husband were here and could listen to me ; I should permit, nay, urge him to stay other twelve years, if it would benefit him." Strange to say Akiva taking the hint from his wife, turned away and left Jerusalem without ever seeing her. He went abroad again for a time, and then returned for good ; this time, so the story says, with twice twelve thousand disciples. Well-nigh all Jerusalem turned out to do him honor, every one striving to be foremost to welcome him. Calba Shevua, who for many a long year had repented of his hasty resolution, which cost him at once his daughter and his happiness, went to Akiva to ask his opinion about annnulling this vow. Akiva replied by making himself known as his quondam servant and rejected son-in-law. As we may suppose, the two were at once reconciled, and Calba Shevua looked upon himself as favored of Heaven above all the fathers in Israel.

The Rabbis say that at first they used to communicate the Divine name of twelve letters to every one. But when the Antinomians began to abound, the knowledge of this name was imparted only to the more discreet of the priestly order, and they repeated it hastily while the other priests pronounced the benediction of the people. (What the name was, says Rashi, is not known.) Rabbi Tarphon, the story goes on to say, once listened to the high priest, and overheard him hurriedly pronouncing this name of twelve letters while the other priests were blessing the people.

Kiddushin, fol. 71, col. 1.

Twelve hours there are in the day : — The first three, the Holy One — blessed be He ! — employs in studying the law ; the next three He sits and judges the whole world ; the third three He spends in feeding all the world ; during the last three hours He sports with the leviathan ; as it is said (Ps. civ. 26), "This leviathan Thou hast created to play with it." *Avodah Zarah*, fol. 3, col. 2.

Rabbi Yochanan bar Chanena said : — The day consists of twelve hours. During the first hour Adam's dust was

collected from all parts of the world ; during the second it was
made into a lump ; during the third his limbs were formed ;
during the fourth his body was animated ; during the fifth
he stood upon his legs ; during the sixth he gave names to
the animals ; during the seventh he associated with Eve ;
during the eighth Cain and a twin sister were born (Abel
and his twin sister were born after the Fall, says the Tosephoth) ; during the ninth Adam was ordered not to eat of
the forbidden tree ; during the tenth he fell ; during the
eleventh he was judged ; and during the twelfth he was
ejected from paradise ; as it is said (Ps. xlix. 13, A. V.
12), "Man (Adam) abode not one night in his dignity."

Sanhedrin, fol. 38, col. 2.

Rabbi Akiva used to say : — Of five judgments, some
have lasted twelve months, others will do so ; — those of
the deluge, of Job, of the Egyptians, of Gog and Magog,
and of the wicked in Gehenna. *Edioth*, chap. 2, mish. 10.

Plagues come upon those that are proud, as was the case
with Uzziah (2 Chron. xxvi. 16), "But when he was
strong (proud), his heart was lifted up to destruction."
When the leprosy rose up in his forehead, the Temple was
cleft asunder twelve miles either way.

Avoth d' Rab. Nathan, chap. 9.

This hyperbole is evidently a mere fiction joined on to a truth for
the purpose of frightening the proud into humility. The end sancti-
fieth the means, as we well know from other instances recorded in
the Talmud.

Those who mourn for deceased relatives are prohibited
from entering a tavern for thirty days, but those who
mourn for either father or mother must not do so for
twelve months. *Semachoth*, chap. 9.

A creature that has no bones in his body does not live
more than twelve months. *Chullin*, fol. 58, col. 1.

The Alexandrians asked Rabbi Joshua twelve questions ;
three related to matters of wisdom, three to matters of
legend, three were frivolous, and three were of a worldly
nature — viz, how to grow wise, how to become rich, and
how to ensure a family of boys. *Niddah*, fol. 69, col. 2.

9

There was once a man named Joseph, who was renowned for honoring the Sabbath-day. He had a rich neighbor, a Gentile, whose property a certain fortune-teller had said would eventually revert to Joseph the Sabbatarian. To frustrate this prediction the Gentile disposed of his property, and with the proceeds of the sale he purchased a rare and costly jewel which he fixed to his turban. On crossing a bridge a gust of wind blew his turban into the river and a fish swallowed it. This fish being caught, was brought on a Friday to market, and, as luck would have it, it was bought by Joseph in honor of the coming Sabbath. When the fish was cut up the jewel was found, and this Joseph sold for thirteen purses of gold denarii. When his neighbor met him, he acknowledged that he who despised the Sabbath the Lord of the Sabbath would be sure to punish.

Shabbath, fol. 119, col. 1.

This story cannot fail to remind those who are conversant with Herodotus or Schiller of the legend of King Polycrates, which dates back five or six centuries before the present era. Polycrates, the king of Samos, was one of the most fortunate of men, and everything he took in hand was fabled to prosper. This unbroken series of successes caused disquietude to his friends, who saw in the circumstance foreboding of some dire disaster; till Amasis, king of Egypt, one of the number advised him to spurn the favor of fortune by throwing away what he valued dearest. The most valuable thing he possessed was an emerald signet-ring, and this accordingly he resolved to sacrifice. So, manning a galley, he rowed out to the sea, and threw the ring away into the waste of the waters. Some five or six days after this, a fisherman came to the palace and made the king a present of a very fine fish that he had caught. This the servants proceeded to open, when, to their surprise, they came upon a ring, which on examination proved to be the very ring which had been cast away by the king their master. (See Herodotus, book iii.)

Among the many legends that have clustered round the memory of Solomon, there is one which reads very much like an adaptation of this classic story. The version the Talmud gives of this story is quoted in another part of this Miscellany (chap. vi. No. 8, note), but in Emek Hammelech, fol. 14, col. 4, we have the legend in another form, with much amplitude and variety of detail, of which we can give here only an outline. When the building of the Temple was finished, the king of the demons begged Solomon to set him free from his service, and promised in return to teach him a secret he would be sure to value. Having cajoled Solomon out of possession of his signet-ring, he first flung the ring into the sea, where it was swallowed by a fish, and then taking up Solomon himself, he cast him into a foreign land some four hundred miles away, where for three weary long years he wandered up and down like a vagrant, begging his bread from door to door. In the course of his rambles he came to Mash Kemim, and was so fortunate as to be appointed head cook at the palace of the king of Ammon (Ana Hanun, see 1 Kings xii. 24; LXX.). While employed in this office, Naama, the king's daughter (see 1 Kings xiv. 21, 31, and 2 Chron. xii. 13), fell in love with him, and, determining to marry him, eloped with him for refuge to a distant land. One day as Naama was preparing a fish for dinner, she found in it a ring, and this turned out to be the very ring which the king of the demons had flung into the sea, and the loss of which had bewitched the king out of his power and dominion. In the recovery of the ring the king both recovered himself and the throne of his father David.

The occurrence of a fish and a ring on the arms of the city of Glasgow memorializes a legend in which we find the same singular combination of circumstances. A certain queen of the district one day gave her paramour a golden ring which the king her husband had committed to her charge as a keepsake. By some means or other the king got to know of the whereabouts of the ring, and cleverly contriving to secure possession of it, threw it into the sea. He then went straight to the queen and demanded to know where it was and what she had done with it. The queen in her distress repaired to St. Kentigern, and both made full confession of her guilt and her anxiety about the recovery of the ring, that she might regain the lost favor of her husband. The saint set off at once to the Clyde, and there caught a salmon and the identical ring in the mouth of it. This he handed over to the queen, who returned it to her lord with such expressions of penitence that the restoration of it became the bond and pledge between them of a higher and holier wedlock.

There were thirteen horn-shaped collecting-boxes, and thirteen tables, and thirteen devotional bowings in the Temple service. Those who belonged to the houses of Rabbi Gamliel and of Rabbi Chananiah, the president of the priests, bowed fourteen times. This extra act of bowing was directed to the quarter of the wood store, in consequence of a tradition they inherited from their ancestors that the Ark of the Covenant was hidden in that locality. The origin of the tradition was this: — A priest, being once engaged near the wood store, and observing that part of the plaster differed from the rest, went to tell his companions, but died before he had time to relate his discovery. Thus it became known for certain that the Ark was hidden there.

Shekalim, chap. 3, hal. 1.

It is more than probable that the Chananiah, mentioned above, is the person alluded to in the Acts, chap. xxiii. 2, as "the high priest Ananias." For the tradition about the Ark. see also 2 Macc. ii. 4, 5.

There were thirteen horn-shaped collecting-boxes in the Temple, and upon them were inscribed new shekels, old shekels, turtle-dove offerings, young-pigeon offerings, fire-wood, contributions for Galbanus, gold for the mercy-seat; and six boxes were inscribed for voluntary contributions. New shekels were for the current year, old shekels were for the past one.   *Yoma*, fol. 55, col. 2.

Once on account of long-continued drought Rabbi Eliezer proclaimed thirteen public fasts, but no rain came. At the termination of the last fast, just as the congregation was leaving the synagogue, he cried aloud, "Have you then prepared graves for yourselves?" Upon this all the people burst into bitter cries, and rain came down directly.

Taanith, fol. 25, col. 2.

A boy at thirteen years of age is bound to observe the usual fasts in full, *i. e.*, throughout the whole day. A girl is bound to do so when only twelve. Rashi gives this as the reason: — A boy is supposed to be weaker than a girl on account of the enervating effect of much study.

Kethuboth, fol. 5, col. 1.

A poor man once came to Rava and begged for a meal. "On what dost thou usually dine?" asked Rava. "On stuffed fowl and old wine," was the reply. "What!" said Rava, "art thou not concerned about being so burdensome to the community?" He replied, "I eat nothing belonging to them, only what the Lord provides;" as we are taught (Ps. cxlv. 15), 'The eyes of all wait upon Thee, and Thou givest them their meat in his season.' It is not said in their season, for so we learn that God provides for each individual in his season of need." While they were thus talking, in came Rava's sister, who had not been to see him for thirteen years, and she brought him as a present a stuffed fowl and some old wine also. Rava marveled at the coincidence, and turning to his poor visitor said, "I beg thy pardon, friend; rise, I pray thee, and eat."

Ibid., fol. 57, col. 2.

So great is circumcision that thirteen covenants were made concerning it. Tosafoth says that covenant is written thirteen times in the chapter of circumcision.

Nedarim, fol. 31, col. 2.

Rabbi (the Holy) says sufferings are to be borne with resignation. He himself bore them submissively for thirteen years; for six he suffered from lithiasis, and for seven years from stomatitis (or, as some say, six years from the former and seven from the latter). His groans were heard three miles off. *Bava Metzia*, fol. 85, col. 1.

The Rabbis have taught thirteen things respecting breakfast (morning-morsel) : — It counteracts the effects of heat, cold or draught; it protects from malignant demons; it makes wise the simple by keeping the mind in a healthy condition; it enables a man to come off clear from a judicial inquiry; it qualifies him both to learn and to teach the law; it makes him eagerly listened to, to have a retentive memory, etc. *Ibid.*, fol. 107, col. 2.

The land of Israel is in the future to be divided among thirteen tribes, and not, as at first, among twelve.

Bava Bathra, fol. 122, col. 1.

Rabbi Abhu once complimented Rav Saphra before the Minim by singling him out in their hearing as a man distinguished by his learning, and this led them to exempt him from tribute for thirteen years. It so happened that these Minim once posed Saphra about that which is written in Amos iii. 2, "You only have I known of all the families of the earth; therefore I will punish you for all your iniquities." "Ye say you are God's friends, but when one has a friend does he pour out his wrath upon him?" To this Rav Saphra make no reply. They then put a rope round his neck and tormented him. When he was in this sorry plight, Rabbi Abhu came up and inquired why they tormented him thus. To this they made answer, "Didst thou not tell us that he was a very learned man, and he does not even know how to explain a text of Scripture?" "Yes, I did so say," replied Rabbi Abhu; "he is an adept in the Talmud only, but not in the Scriptures." "Thou knowest the Scriptures;" they replied, "and why ought he not to

know them as well?" "I have daily intercourse with you,"
said the Rabbi, "and therefore I am obliged to study the
Scriptures, but he, having no intercourse with you, has no
need to trouble himself, and does not at all care about them."

Avodah Zarah, fol. 4, col. 1.

In order to understand aright the grounds on which Rabbi Abhu
would fain excuse Rav Saphra for not caring at all about the Scriptures, certain passages from both Talmuds should be read, which, in
the usual metaphorical style of the Rabbis, set forth the respective
merits of Scripture and Tradition. The three times three in Sophrim
(chap. 15), in which the Scripture is compared to water, the Mishna
to wine, and the Gemara to mulled wine, and that in which the Scripture is likened to salt, the Mishna to pepper, and the Gemara to
spice, and so on, are too well known to need more than passing mention; but far less familiar and much more explicit is the exposition
of Zech. viii. 10, as given in T. B. Chaggigah, fol. 10, col. 1, where,
commenting on the Scripture text, "Neither, was there any peace to
him that went out or came in," Rav expressly says, "He who leaves
a matter of Halachah for a matter of Scripture shall never more have
peace;" to which Shemuel adds, "Aye, and he also who leaves the
Talmud for the Mishna;" Rabbi Yochanan chiming in with "even
from Talmud to Talmud;" as if to say, "And he who turns from the
Babli to the Yerushalmi, even he shall have no peace." If we refer to
the Mishna (chap. 1, hal. 7) of Berachoth in the last-named Talmud,
we read there that Rabbi Tarphon, bent, while on a journey, on reading the Shema according to the school of Shammai, ran the risk of
falling into the hands of certain banditti whom he had not noticed
near him. "It would have served you right," remarked one, "because you did not follow the rule of Hillel." In the Gemara to this
passage Rabbi Yochanan says, "The words of the scribes are more
highly valued than the words of the law, for, as Rabbi Yuda remarks,
'If Rabbi Tarphon had not read the Shema at all he would only
have broken a positive command,' but since he transgressed the rule
of Hillel he was guilty of death, for it is written, 'He who breaks
down a hedge (the Rabbinic hedge to the law, of course), a serpent
shall bite him'" (Eccles. x. 8). Then Rabbi Chanina, the son of
Rabbi Ana, in the name of Rabbi Tanchum, the son of Rabbi Cheyah,
says, "The words of the elders are more important than the words of
the prophets." A prophet and an elder, whom do they resemble?
They are like two ambassadors sent by a king to a province. About
the one he sends word saying, "If he does not present credentials
with my signature and seal, trust him not;" whereas the other is
accredited without any such token; for in regard to the prophet it is
written (Deut. xiii. 2), "He giveth thee a sign or token;" while in
reference to the elders it is written (Deut. xvii. 11), "According to
the decision which they may say unto thee shalt thou do; thou shalt

not depart from the sentence which they may tell thee, to the right or to the left." Rashi's comment on this text is worth notice : "Even when they tell thee that right is left and left is right." In a word, a wise man (*i. e.*, a Rabbi) is better than a prophet. (*Bava Bathra*, fol. 12, col. 1.)

Oved, the Galilean, has expounded that there are thirteen *vavs* (*i. e.*, the letter *vav* occurs thirteen times) in connection with wine. *Vav* in Syriac means woe.

Sanhedrin, fol. 70, col. 1.

The Rabbis have a curious Haggada respecting the origin of the culture of the vine. Once while Noah was hard at work breaking up the fallow ground for a vineyard, Satan drew near and inquired what he was doing. On ascertaining that the patriarch was about to cultivate the grape, which he valued both for its fruit and its juice, he at once volunteered to assist him at his task, and began to manure the soil with the blood of a lamb, a lion, a pig, and a monkey. "Now," said he, when his work was done, "of those who taste the juice of the grape, some will become meek and gentle as the lamb, some bold and fearless as the lion, some foul and beastly as the pig, and others frolicsome and lively as the monkey." This quaint story may be found more fully detailed in the Midrash Tanchuma (see Noah) and the Yalkut on Genesis. The Mohammedan legend is somewhat similar. It relates how Satan on the like occasion used the blood of a peacock, of an ape, of a lion, and of a pig, and it deduces from the abuse of the vine the curse that fell on the children of Ham, and ascribes the color of the purple grape to the dark hue which thenceforth tinctured all the fruit of their land as well as their own complexions.

At thirteen years of age, a boy becomes bound to observe the (613) precepts of the law. *Avoth*, chap. 5.

Rabbi Ishmael says the law is to be expounded according to thirteen logical rules. *Chullin*, fol. 63, col. 1.

The thirteen rules of Rabbi Ishmael above referred to are not to be found together in any part of the Talmud, but they are collected for repetition in the Liturgy, and are as follows : —

1. Inference is valid from minor to major.
2. From similar phraseology.
3. From the gist or main point of one text to that of other passages.
4. Of general and particular.
5. Of particular and general.
6. From a general, or a particular and a general, the ruling both of the former and the latter is to be according to the middle term, *i. e.*, the one which is particularized.

7. From a general text that requires a particular instance, and *vice versâ*.

8. When a particular rule is laid down for something which has already been included in a general law, the rule is to apply to all.

9. When a general rule has an exception, the exception mitigates and does not aggravate the rule.

10. When a general rule has an exception not according therewith, the exception both mitigates and aggravates.

11. When an exception to a general rule is made to substantiate extraneous matter, that matter cannot be classed under the said general rule, unless the Scripture expressly says so.

12. The ruling is to be according to the context, or to the general drift of the argument.

13. When two texts are contradictory, a third is to be sought that reconciles them.

Rabbi Akiva was forty years of age when he began to study, and after thirteen years of study he began publicly to teach.   *Avoth d' Rab. Nathan.*

Thirteen treasurers and seven directors were appointed to serve in the Temple. (More there might be, never less.)
                    Tamid, fol. 27, col. 1.

Thirteen points of law regulate the decisions that require to be made relative to the carcass of a clean bird.
                    Taharoth, chap. 1, mish. 1.

A man must partake of fourteen meals in the booth during the Feast of Tabernacles.   *Succah*, fol. 27, col. 1.

Traditional chronology records that the Israelites killed the Paschal lamb on the fourteenth day of Nisan, the month on which they came out of Egypt. They came out on the fifteenth ; that day was a Friday.
                    Shabbath, fol. 88, col. 1.

The fifteen steps were according to the number of the Songs of Degrees in the Psalms. It is related that whosoever has not seen the joy at the annual ceremony of the water-drawing, has not seen rejoicing in his life. At the conclusion of the first part of the Feast of Tabernacles, the Priests and Levites descended into the women's ante-court, where they made great preparations (such as erecting temporary double galleries, the uppermost for women, and those under for men). There were golden candelabra there, each having four golden bowls on the top, four ladders reaching to them, and four of the young priests with cruses of oil ready to supply them, each cruse holding one hundred and twenty logs of oil. The lamp-wicks were made of the worn-out drawers and girdles of the priests. There was not a court in all Jerusalem that was not lit up by the illumination of the "water-drawing." Holy men, and men of dignity, with flaming torches in their hands, danced before the people, rehearsing songs and singing praises. The Levites, with harps, lutes, cymbals, trumpets, and innumerable musical instruments, were stationed on the fifteen steps which led from the ante-court of Israel to the women's court; the Levites stood upon the steps and played and sang. Two priests stood at the upper gate which led from the ante-court for Israel to that for the women, each provided with a trumpet, and as soon as the cock crew they blew one simple blast, then a compound or fragmentary one, and then a modulated or shouting blast. This was the preconcerted signal for the drawing of the water. As soon as they reached the tenth step, they blew again three blasts as before. When they came to the ante-court for women, they blew another three blasts, and after that they continued blowing till they came to the east gate. When they arrived at the east gate, they turned their faces westward (*i. e.*, toward the Temple), and said, "Our fathers, who were in this place, turned their backs toward the Temple of the Lord, and their faces toward the East, for they worshiped the sun in the East; but we turn our eyes to God!" Rabbi Yehudah says, "These words were repeated, echoing, 'We are for God, and unto God are our eyes directed!'" *Succah*, fol. 51, col. 1, 2.

Rabbon Shimon ben Gamliel has said there were no such gala-days for Israel as the fifteenth of Ab and the Day of Atonement, when the young maidens of Jerusalem used to resort to the vineyard all robed in white garments, that were required to be borrowed, lest those should feel humiliated who had none of their own. There they danced gleefully, calling to the lookers-on and saying, "Young men, have a care; the choice you now make may have consequences." *Taanith*, fol. 26, col. 2.

Rabbi Elazar the Great said, "From the fifteenth of Ab the influence of the sun declines, and from that day they leave off cutting wood for the altar fire, because it could not be properly dried (and green wood might harbor vermin, which would make it unfit for use)."

Taanith, fol. 31, col. 1.

He who eats turnips to beef, and sleeps out in the open air during the night of the fourteenth and fifteenth days of the months of summer (that is, when the moon is full), will most likely bring on an ague fever.

Gittin, fol. 70, col. 1.

A lad should, at the age of fifteen, begin to apply himself to the Gemara.   *Avoth*, chap. 5.

"So I bought her to me for fifteen" (Hosea iii. 2), that is, on the fifteenth day of Nisan, when Israel was redeemed from the bondage of Egypt. "Silver;" this refers to the righteous. "An homer and a half-homer;" these equal forty-five measures, and are the forty-five righteous men for whose sake the world is preserved. I don't know whether there are thirty here (that is, in Babylon), and fifteen in the land of Israel, or *vice versâ;* as it is said (Zech. xi. 13), "I took the thirty pieces of silver and cast them to the potter in the house of the Lord." It stands to reason that there are thirty in the land of Israel, and, therefore, fifteen here. Abaii says that the greater part are to be found under the gable end of the synagogue. Rav Yehudah says the reference is to the thirty righteous men always found among the nations of the world for whose sake they are preserved (but see No. 103 *infra*). Ulla says it refers to the thirty precepts received by the nations of the world, of which, however, they keep three only; *i. e.*, they do not enter into formal marriage-contracts with men; they do not expose for sale the bodies of such animals as have died from natural causes; and they have regard for the law.   *Chullin*, fol. 92, col. 1.

Rabbi Cheyah bar Abba says, "I once visited a householder at Ludkia, and they placed before him a golden table so loaded with silver plate, basins, cups, bottles and glasses, besides all sorts of dishes, delicacies, and spices, that it took sixteen men to carry it. When they set the table in its place they said (Ps. xxiv. 1), 'The earth is the Lord's and the fullness thereof,' and upon removing it, they said (Ps. cxv. 16), 'The heaven, even the heavens, are the Lord's, but the earth hath He given to the children of men.' I said, 'Son, how hast thou come to deserve all this?' 'I was,' replied he, 'a butcher by trade, and I always set apart for the Sabbath the best of the cattle.' 'How happy art thou,' I remarked (adds Rabbi Cheyah), 'to have merited such a reward, and blessed be God who has thus rewarded thee.' "

Shabbath, fol. 119, col. 1.

Rash Lakish said, " I have seen the flow of milk and honey at Tzipori ; it was sixteen miles by sixteen miles."

Meggillah, fol. 6, col. 1.

Rashi explains the above as follows:—The goats fed upon figs from which honey distilled, and this mingled with the milk which dropped from the goats as they walked along. On the spot arose a lake which covered an area of sixteen miles square. (See also Kethuboth, fol. 111, col. 2.)

A cedar tree once fell down in our place, the trunk of which was so wide that sixteen wagons were drawn abreast upon it. *Bechoroth*, fol. 57, col. 2.

Who can estimate the loss the world sustains in its ignorance of the trees of the Talmud? What a sapling in comparison with this giant cedar of Lebanon must the far-famed Mammoth tree have been which was lately cut down in California, and was the largest known to the present generation !

Rabbi Yochanan plaintively records, " I remember the time when a young man and a young woman sixteen or seventeen years of age could walk together in the streets and no harm came of it." *Bava Bathra*, fol. 91, col. 2.

On the deposition of Rabbon Gamliel, Rabbi Eleazar ben Azariah was chosen as his successor to the presidential chair of the academy. On being told of his elevation, he consulted with his wife as to whether or not he should accept the appointment. " What if they should depose thee also?" asked his wife. He replied, " Use the precious bowl while thou hast it, even if it be broken the next." But she rejoined, "Thou art only eighteen years old, and how canst thou at such an age expect folks to venerate thee?" By a miracle eighteen of his locks turned suddenly gray, so that he could say, "I am as one of seventy."

Berachoth, fol. 27, col. 2.

The Rabbis have taught that Shimon Happikoli had arranged the eighteen benedictions before Rabbon Gamliel at Javneh. Rabbon Gamliel appealed to the sages, "Is there not a man who knows how to compose an imprecation against the Sadducees?" Then Samuel the Little stood up and extemporized it.   *Ibid.*, fol. 28, col. 2.

The "imprecation against the Sadducees" stands twelfth among the collects of the Shemoneh Esreh. It is popularly known as "Velama-leshinim" from its opening words, and is given thus in modern Ashkenazi liturgies:—"Oh, let the slanderers have no hope, all the wicked be annihilated speedily, and all the tyrants be cut off, hurled down and reduced speedily; humble Thou them quickly in our days. Blessed art Thou, O Lord, who destroyest enemies and humblest tyrants." There has been much misconception with regard to this collect against heretics. There is every reason to believe it was composed without any reference whatever to the Christians. One point of interest, however, in connection with it is worth relating here. Some have sought to identify the author of it, Samuel the Little, with the Apostle Paul, grounded the conclusion on his original Hebrew name, Saul. They take Paulus as equal to *pusillus*, which means "very little" or "the less," and answers to the word *Hakaton*, a term of similar import. Samuel, however, died a good Jew (see Semachoth, chap. 8), and Rabbon Gamliel Hazaken and Rabbi Eleazar ben Azariah pronounced a funeral oration at his burial. "His key and his diary were placed on his coffin, because he had no son to succeed him." (See also Sanhedrin, fol. 11, col. 1.)

Eighteen denunciations did Isaiah make against the people of Israel, and he recovered not his equanimity until he was able to add, "The child shall behave himself proudly against the ancient, and the base against the honorable" (Isa. iii. 5).   *Chaggigah*, fol. 14, col. 1.

The Rabbis have related that there was once a family in Jerusalem the members of which died off regularly at eighteen years of age. Rabbi Yochanan ben Zacchai shrewdly guessed that they were descendants of Eli, regarding whom it is said (1 Sam. ii. 25), "And all the increase of thine house shall die in the flower of their age;"

and he accordingly advised them to devote themselves to
the study of the law, as the certain and only means of
neutralizing the curse. They acted upon the advice of the
Rabbi; their lives were in consequence prolonged; and
they thenceforth went by the name of their spiritual father.

Rosh Hashanah, fol. 18, col. 1.

Eighteen handbreadths was the height of the golden
candlestick.   *Menachoth*, fol. 28, col. 2.

If a man remain unmarried after the age of twenty, his
life is a constant transgression. The Holy One — blessed
be He! — waits until that period to see if one enters the
matrimonial state, and curses his bones if he remain single.

Kiddushin, fol. 29, col. 2.

A woman marrying under twenty years of age will bear
till she is sixty; if she marries at twenty she will bear
until she is forty; if she marries at forty she will not
have any family.   *Bava Bathra*, fol. 119, col. 2.

At twenty pursue the study of the law.

Avoth, chap. 5.

Rabbi Yehudah says the early Pietists used to suffer
some twenty days before death from diarrhœa, the effect of
which was to purge and purify them for the world to
come; for it is said, "As the fining pot for silver, and the
furnace for gold, so is a man to his praise" (Prov. xxvii.
21).   *Semachoth*, chap. 3, mish. 10.

It may not be out of place to append two or three parallel passages here by way of illustration : — "Bodily suffering purges away
sin" (*Berachoth*, fol. 5, col. 1). "He who suffers will not see hell"
(*Eiruvin*, fol. 41, col. 2). "To die of diarrhœa is an augury for
good, for most of the righteous die of that ailment" (*Kethuboth*, fol.
103, col. 2, and elsewhere).

The bathing season at (the hot baths of) Dimsis lasted
twenty-one days.   *Shabbath*, fol. 147, col. 2.

A fowl hatches in twenty-one days, and the almond tree
ripens its fruit in twenty-one days.

Bechoroth, fol. 8, col. 1.

Rabbi Levi says the realization of a good dream may be
hopefully expected for twenty-two years; for it is written
(Gen. xxxvii. 2), "These are the generations of Jacob,

Joseph being seventeen years old when he had the dreams."
And it is written also (Gen. xli. 46), "And Joseph was
thirty years old when he stood before Pharaoh," etc. From
seventeen to thirty are thirteen, to which add the seven
years of plenty and the two years of famine, which make
the sum total of twenty-two. *Berachoth*, fol. 55, col. 2.

In the pages which precede and follow the above quotation there is
much that is interesting on the subject of dreams and their interpretation, and one is strongly tempted to append selections, but we refrain in
order to make room for a prayer which occurs in the morning service
for the various festivals, and is given in the preceding context :—
"Sovereign of the Universe! I am thine, and my dreams are thine.
I have dreamed a dream, but know not what it portendeth. May it
be acceptable in Thy presence, O Lord my God, and the God of my
fathers, that all my dreams concerning myself and concerning all
Israel may be for my good. Whether I have dreamt concerning myself, or whether I have dreamt concerning others, or whether others
have dreamt concerning me, if they be good, strengthen and fortify
them, that they may be accomplished in me, as were the dreams of
the righteous Joseph ; and if they require cure, heal them as Thou
didst Hezekiah, king of Judah, from his sickness ; as Miriam the prophetess from her leprosy, and Naaman from his leprosy; as the bitter waters
of Marah by the hands of our legislator Moses, and those of Jericho
by the hands of Elisha. And as Thou wast pleased to turn the curse
of Balaam, the son of Beor, to a blessing, be pleased to convert all
my dreams concerning me and all Israel to a good end. Oh, guard
me ; let me be acceptable to Thee, and grant me life. Amen."*

Rabbi Levi said, "Come and see how unlike the character of the Holy One — blessed be He ! — is to that of those
who inherit the flesh and blood of humanity. God blessed
Israel with twenty-two benedictions and cursed them with
eight curses (Lev. xxvi. 3–13, xv. 43). But Moses, our
Rabbi, blessed them with eight benedictions and cursed
them with twenty-two imprecations" (see Deut. xxviii.
1–4, xv. 68). *Bava Bathra*, fol. 59, col. 1.

Once as they were journeying to Chesib (in Palestine),
some of Rabbi Akiva's disciples were overtaken by a band
of robbers, who demanded to know where they were going
to. "We are going to Acco," was the reply ; but on
arriving at Chesib, they went no farther. The robbers

*The translation of this prayer is borrowed from the Jewish
liturgy.

then asked them who they were? "Disciples of Rabbi Akiva," they replied. Upon hearing this the robbers exclaimed, "Blessed surely is Rabbi Akiva and his disciples too, for no man can ever do them any harm." Once as Rabbi Menasi was traveling to Thurtha (in Babylonia), some thieves surprised him on the road and asked him where he was bound for. "For Pumbeditha," was the reply; but upon reaching Thurtha, he stayed and went no farther. The highwaymen, thus balked, retorted, "Thou art the disciple of Yehuda the deceiver!" "Oh, you know my master, do you?" said the Rabbi. "Then in the name of God be every one of you anathematized." For twenty-two years thereafter they carried on their nefarious trade, but all their attempts at violence ended only in disappointment. Then all save one of them came to the Rabbi and craved his pardon, which was immediately granted. The one who did not come to confess his guilt and obtain absolution was a weaver, and he was eventually devoured by a lion. Hence the proverbs, "If a weaver does not humble himself, he shortens his life;" and, "Come and see the difference there is between the thieves of Babylon and the banditti of the land of Israel."

Avodah Zarah, fol. 26, col. 1.

Rabbi Eliezer ben Hyrcanus was twenty-two years of age when, contrary to the wishes of his father, he went to Rabbon Yochanan ben Zaccai purposing to devote himself to the study of the law. By the time he arrived at Rabbon Yochanan's he had been without food four-and-twenty hours, and yet, though repeatedly asked whether he had had anything to eat, refused to confess he was hungry. His father having come to know where he was, went one day to the place on purpose to disinherit him before the assembled Rabbis. It so happened that Rabbon Yochanan was at that time lecturing before some of the great men of Jerusalem, and when he saw the father enter, he pressed Rabbi Eliezer to deliver an exposition. So racy and cogent were his observations that Rabbon Yochanan rose and styled him his own Rabbi, and thanked him in the name of the rest for the instruction he had afforded them. Then the father of Rabbi Eliezer said,

"Rabbis, I came here for the purpose of disinheriting my son, but now I declare him sole heir of all I have, to the exclusion of his brothers." *Avoth d' Rab. Nathan*, chap. 6.

The father of Eliezer acts more magnanimously by his son than does the father of St. Francis. Like the Rabbi, as Mr. Ruskin relates in his "Mornings in Florence," St. Francis, one of whose three great virtues was obedience, "begins his spiritual life by quarreling with his father. He 'commercially invests' some of his father's goods in charity. His father objects to that investment, on which St. Francis runs away, taking what he can find about the house along with him. His father follows to claim his property, but finds it is all gone already, and that St. Francis has made friends with the Bishop of Assisi. His father flies into an indecent passion, and declares he will disinherit him; on which St. Francis, then and there, takes all his clothes off, throws them frantically in his father's face, and says he has nothing more to do with clothes or father."

Not the same strict scrutiny is required in money matters as in cases of capital punishment; for it is said (Lev. xxiv. 23), "Ye shall have one manner of law." What distinction is there made between them? With regard to money matters three judges are deemed sufficient, while in cases of capital offense twenty-three are required, etc.

Sanhedrin, fol. 32, col. 1.

Rabbi, Yehoshua ben Levi said, "In twenty-four cases doth the tribunal excommunicate for the honor of a Rabbi, and all are explained in our Mishna." Rabbi Elazer interposed and asked, "Where are they?" The reply was, "Go and seek, and thou shalt find." He went accordingly and sought, but found only three — the case of the man who lightly esteems the washing of hands; of him who whispers evil behind the bier of a disciple of the wise; and of him who behaves haughtily toward the Most High.

Berachoth, fol. 19, col. 1.

There are three degrees of excommunication, *i. e.*, separation, exclusion, and execration. That mentioned in the above extract is of the lowest degree, and lasts never less than thirty days. The second degree of excommunication is a prolongation of the first by thirty days more. The third or highest degree lasts for an indefinite time. See Moed Katon, fol. 17, col. 1; Shevuoth, fol. 36, col. 1; and consult Index II. appended.

A certain matron once said to Rabbi Yehuda ben Elaei, "Thy face is like that of one who breeds pigs and lends money on usury." He replied, " These offices are forbidden me by the rules of my religion, but between my residence and the academy there are twenty-four latrinæ ; these I regularly visit as I need." *Berachoth*, fol. 55, col. 1.

The Rabbi meant to say that paying attention to the regular action of his excretory organs was the secret of his healthy looks, and to imply that a disordered stomach is the root of most diseases,— a physiological opinion well worthy of regard by us moderns.

Rav Birim says that the venerable Rav Benaah once went to all the interpreters of dreams in Jerusalem, twenty-four in number. Every one of them gave a different interpretation, and each was fulfilled ; which substantiates the saying that it is the interpretation and not the dream that comes true. *Ibid.*, fol. 55, col. 2.

Twenty-four fasts were observed by the men of the Great Synagogue, in order that the writers of the books, phylacteries, and Mezuzahs might not grow rich, lest in becoming rich they might be tempted not to write any more.
P'sachim, fol. 50, col. 2.

When Solomon was desirous of conveying the Ark into the Temple, the doors shut themselves of their own accord against him. Here cited twenty-four psalms, yet they opened not. In vain he cried, " Lift up your heads, O ye gates " (Ps. xxiv. 9). But when he prayed, " O Lord God, turn not Thy face away from Thine anointed ; remember the mercies of David, Thy servant " (2 Chron. vi. 42), then the gates flew open at once. Then the enemies of David turned black in the face, for all knew by this that God had pardoned David's transgression with Bathshehcba.
Moed Katon, fol. 9, col. 1.

In the Midrash Rabbah (Devarim, chap. 15) the same story is told, with this additional circumstance among others, that a sacred respect was paid to the gates when the Temple was sacked at the time of the Captivity. When the glorious vessels and furniture of the Temple were being carried away into Babylon, the gates, which were so zealous for the glory of God, were buried on the spot (see Lam. ii. 9), there to await the restoration of Israel. This romantic episode is alluded to in the closing service for the Day of Atonement.

There are twenty-four species of unclean birds, but the clean birds are innumerable. *Chullin*, fol. 63, col. 2.

10

In twenty-four places priests are called Levites, and this is one of them (Ezek. xliv. 15), "But the priests, the Levites, the sons of Zadok."   *Tamid*, fol. 27, col. 1.

There are twenty-four extremities of members in the human body which do not suffer defilement in the case of diseased flesh (see Lev. xiii. 10, 24). The tip-ends of the fingers and toes, the edges of the ears, the tip of the nose, etc.   *Negaim*, chap. 6, mish. 7.

Twenty-five children is the highest number there should be in a class for elementary instruction. There should be an assistant appointed, if there be forty in number ; and if fifty, there should be two competent teachers. Rava says, "If there be two teachers in a place, one teaching the children more than the other, the one that teaches less is not to be dismissed, because if so, the other is liable to lapse into negligence also." Rav Deimi of Nehardaa, on the other hand, thinks the dismissal of the former will make the latter all the more eager to teach more, both out of fear lest he also be dismissed, and out of gratitude that he has been preferred to the other. Mar says, "The emulation of the scribes (or teachers) increaseth wisdom." Rava also says, "When there are two teachers, one teaching much but superficially, and one teaching thoroughly but not so much, the former is to be preferred, for the children will, in the long run, improve most by learning much." Rav Deimi of Nehardaa, however, thinks the latter is to be preferred, for a mistake or an error once learned is difficult to unlearn ; as it is written in 1 Kings xi. 16, "For six months did Joab remain there with all Israel, until he cut off every male in Edom." When David asked Joab why he killed only the males and not the females, he replied, "Because it is written in Deut. xxv. 19, 'Thou shalt blot out the male portion of Amalek.'" "But," said David, "we read 'the remembrance of Amalek.'" To this Joab replied, "My teacher taught me to read zachar and not zeichar," *i. e.*, male, and not remembrance. The teacher of Joab was sent for ; and being found guilty of having taught his pupil in a superficial manner, he was condemned to be beheaded. The poor teacher pleaded in vain for his life, for the king's judgment was based on Scripture (Jer. xlviii. 10), "Cursed be he that doeth the work of the Lord deceitfully, and cursed be he that keepeth back his sword from blood." *Bava Bathra*, fol. 21, col. 1.

The Romans faithfully observed their compact with Israel for twenty-six years. After that time they began to oppress them. *Avoda Zarah*, fol. 8, col. 2.

The Rabbis have taught that a small salt fish will cause death if partaken of after seven, seventeen, or twenty-seven days; some say after twenty-three days. This is said with reference to half-cooked fish, but when properly cooked there is no harm in it. Neither does any harm result from eating half-cooked fish, if strong drink be taken after it.
Berachoth, fol. 44, col. 2.

On the twenty-eigth day of Adar there came good news to the Jews. The Roman Government had passed a decree ordaining that they should neither study the law, nor circumcise their children, nor observe the Sabbath-days. Yehudah ben Shamua and his associates went to consult a certain matron, whom all the magnates of Rome were in the habit of visiting. She advised them to come at night and raise a loud outcry against the decree they complained of. They did so, and cried, "O heavens! are we not your brethren? are we not the children of one mother?" (Alluding to Rebekah, the mother of Jacob and Esau.) "Wherein are we worse than all other nations and tongues, that you should oppress us with such harsh decrees?" Thereupon the decrees were revoked; to commemorate which the Jews established a festival. *Rosh Hashanah*, fol. 19, col. 1.

The renewal of the moon comes round in not less than twenty-nine days and a half and forty minutes.
Ibid., fol. 25, col. 1.

Rav Mari reports that Rabbi Yochanan had said, "He who indulges in the practice of eating lentils once in thirty days keeps away quinsy, but they are not good to be eaten regularly because by them the breath is corrupted." He used also to say that mustard eaten once in thirty days drives away sickness, but if taken every day the action of the heart is apt to be affected. *Berachoth*, fol. 40, col. 1.

He who eates unripe dates and does not wash his hands will for thirty day be in constant fear, without knowing why, of something untoward happening.

P'sachim, fol. 111, col. 2.

The Rabbis have taught that the lighter kind of excommunication is not to last less than thirty days, and censure not less than seven. The latter is inferred from what is said in Num. xii. 14, "If her father had but spit in her face, should she not be ashamed seven days?"

Moed Katon, fol. 16, col. 1.

If we meet a friend during any of the thirty days of his mourning for a deceased relative, we must condole with him but not salute him; but after that time he may be saluted but not condoled with. If a man (because he has no family) re-marries within thirty days of the death of his wife, he should not be condoled with at home (lest it might hurt the feelings of his new partner); but if met with out of doors, he should be addressed in an undertone of voice, accompanied with a slight inclination of the head.

Ibid., fol. 21, col. 2.

During the thirty days of mourning for deceased friends or relatives, the bereaved should not trim their hair; but if they have lost their parents, they are not to attend to such matters until their friends force tham to do so.

Ibid., fol. 22, col. 2.

"And Haman told them of the glory of his riches and the multitude of his children" (Esth. v. 11). And how many children were there? Rav said thirty; ten had died, ten were hanged, and ten went about begging from door to door. The Rabbis say, "Those that went about begging from door to door were seventy; for it is written (1 Sam. ii. 5), 'They that were full have hired themselves for bread.'"

Meggillah, fol. 15, col. 2.

When Rabbi Chanena bar Pappa was about to die, the Angel of Death was told to go and render him some friendly service. He accordingly went and made himself known to him. The Rabbi requested him to leave him for thirty days, until he had repeated what he had been learning; for it is said, "Blessed is he who comes here with his studies in his hand." He accordingly left, and at the expiration of thirty days returned to him. The Rabbi then asked to be shown his place in Paradise, and the Angel of Death consented to show him while life was still in him. Then said the Rabbi, "Lend me thy sword, lest thou surprise me on the road and cheat me of my expectation." To this the Angel of Death said, "Dost thou mean to serve me as thy friend Rabbi Yoshua did?" and he declined to intrust the sword to the Rabbi. *Kethuboth*, fol. 77, col. 2.

If a man says to a woman, "Thou art betrothed to me after thirty days," and in the interim another comes and betroths her, she is the second suitor's.

Kiddushin, fol. 58, col. 2.

If one finds a scroll, he may peruse it once in thirty days, but he must not teach out of it, nor may another join him in reading it; if he does not know how to read, he must unroll it. If a garment be found, it should be shaken and spread out once in thirty days, for its own sake (to preserve it), but not for display. Silver and copper articles should be used to take care of them, but not for the sake of ornament. Gold and glass vessels he should not meddle with — till the coming of Elijah.

Bava Metzia, fol. 29, col. 2.

Rabbi Zira so inured his body (to endurance) that the fire of Gehenna had no power over it. Every thirty days he experimented on himself, ascending a fiery furnace, and finally sitting down in the midst of it without being affected by the fire. One day, however, as the Rabbis fixed their eyes upon him, his hips became singed, and from that day onward he was noted in Jewry as the little man with the singed hips. *Ibid.*, fol. 85, col. 1.

An Arab once said to Rabbah bar bar Channah, "Come and I will show thee the place where Korah and his accomplices were swallowed up." "There," says the Rabbi, "I observed smoke coming out from two cracks in the ground. Into one of these he inserted some wool tied on to the end of his spear, and when he drew it out again it was scorched. Then he bade me listen. I did so, and as I listened heard them groan out, 'Moses and his law are true, but we are liars.' The Arab then told me that they come round to this place once in every thirty days, being stirred about in the hell-surge like meat in the boiling caldron." *Bava Bathra*, fol. 74, col. 1.

Rabbi Yochanan, in expounding Isa. liv. 12, said, "The Holy One — blessed be He! — will bring precious stones and pearls, each measuring thirty cubits by thirty, and polishing them down to twenty cubits by ten, will place them in the gates of Jerusalem." A certain disciple contemptuously observed, "No one has ever yet seen a precious stone as large as a small bird's egg, and is it likely that such immense ones as these have any existence?" He happened one day after this to go forth on a voyage, and there in the sea he saw the angels quarrying precious stones and pearls like those his Rabbi had told him of, and upon inquiry he learned that they were intended for the gates of Jerusalem. On his return he went straight to Rabbi Yochanan and told him what he had seen and heard.

"Raca!" said the latter, "hadst thou not seen them thou wouldst have kept on deriding the words of the wise!" Then fixing his gaze intently upon him, he with the glance of his eye reduced to a heap of bones the carcass of his body. *Ibid.*, fol. 75, col. 1.

He who lends unconditionally a sum of money to his neighbor is not entitled to demand it back within thirty days thereafter. *Maccoth*, fol. 3, col. 2.

If a man has lost a relative, he is forbidden to engage in business until thirty days after the death. In the case of the decease of a father or a mother, he is not to resume work until his friends rebuke him and urge him to return.

Semachoth, chap. 9.

It is unlawful for one to enter a banqueting-house for thirty days after the death of a relative; but he must refrain from so doing for twelve months after the demise of either father or mother, unless on the behest of some higher requirement of piety. *Ibid.*

But I know not whether there are thirty righteous men here and fifteen in the land of Israel, or *vice versâ*.

Chullin, fol. 92, col. 1.

Thirty days in a year are equivalent to a whole year.
Niddah, fol. 44, col. 2.

"Moses, thou didst say unto me, 'What is Thy name?'
And now thou dost say, 'Neither hast Thou delivered Thy
people at all.' Now shalt thou see what I will do to Pharaoh (Exod. v. 23, vi. 1), but not what I am about to do
to the thirty-one kings." *Sanhedrin*, fol. 111, col. 1.

When Rav Deimi arrived at Babylon, he reported that
the Romans had fought thirty-two battles with the Greeks
without once conquering them, until they allied themselves
with Israel, on the stipulation that where Rome appointed
the commanding officers the Jews should appoint the gov-
ernors, and *vice versâ*.   *Avodah Zarah*, fol. 8, col. 2.

Manasseh did penance thirty-three years.
Sanhedrin, fol. 103, col. 1.

Balaam was thirty-three years of age when Phineas, the
robber, slew him.   *Ibid.*, fol. 106, col. 2.

For thirty-four years the kingdom of Persia lasted con-
temporaneously with the Temple.
Avodah Zarah, fol. 9, col. 1.

Abaii has said, "There are never fewer than thirty-six
righteous men in every generation who receive the presence
of the Shechinah; for it is said (Isa. xxx. 18), 'Blessed
are all those who wait upon Him.'" The numerical value
(by Gematria) of Him, is thirty-six.
Sanhedrin, fol. 97, col. 2.

The sons of Esau, of Ishmael, and of Keturah went on
purpose to dispute the burial (of Jacob); but when they
saw that Joseph had placed his crown upon the coffin, they
did the same with theirs. There were thirty-six crowns in
all, tradition says. "And they mourned with a great and
very sore lamentation." Even the very horses and asses
joined in it, we are told. On arriving at the Cave of
Machpelah, Esau once more protested, and said, "Adam and
Eve, Abraham and Sarah, Isaac and Rebekah, are all buried
here. Jacob disposed of his share when he buried Leah in
it, and the remaining one belongs to me." "But thou didst
sell thy share with thy birthright," remonstrated the sons
of Jacob. "Nay," rejoined Esau, "that did not include my

share in the burial-place." " Indeed it did," they argued,
" for our father, just before he died, said (Gen. 1. 5), ' In
my grave which I have bought for myself.' " " Where are
the title-deeds?" demanded Esau.   " In Egypt," was the
answer.   And   immediately   the   swift-footed Naphthali
started for the records.   ("So light of foot was he," says
the Book of Jasher, " that he could go upon the ears of
corn without crushing them.")   Hushim, the son of Dan,
being deaf, asked what was the cause of the commotion.
On being told what it was, he snatched up a club and
smote Esau so hard that his eyes dropped out and fell
upon the feet of Jacob; at which Jacob opened his eyes
and grimly smiled.   This is that which is written (Ps.
lviii. 10), " The righteous shall rejoice when he sees vengeance ; he shall wash his feet in the blood of the wicked."
Then Rebekah's prophecy came to pass (Gen. xxvii. 45),
" Why shall I be deprived also of you both in one day?"
For although they did not both die on the same day, they
were both buried on the same day.   *Soteh*, fol. 13, col. 1.

This story slightly varied, is repeated in the Book of Jasher and
in the Targum of Ben Uzziel.

The principal works of the hand are forty save one : —
To sow, to plow, to reap, to bind in sheaves, to thrash,
to winnow, to sift corn, to grind, to bolt meal, to knead,
to bake, to shear, to wash wool, to comb wool, to dye it,
to spin, to warp, to shoot two threads, to weave two
threads, to cut and tie two threads, to tie, to untie, to
sew two stitches, to tear two threads with intent to sew,
to hunt game, to slay, to skin, to salt a hide, to singe, to
tan, to cut up a skin, to write two letters, to scratch out
two letters with intent to write, to build, to pull down, to
put out a fire, to light a fire, to smite with a hammer, to
convey from one Reshuth* to another.

Shabbath, fol. 73, col. 1.

King Yanai had a single tree on the royal mound, whence
once a month they collected forty seahs (about fifteen
bushels) of young pigeons of three different breeds.

Berachoth, fol. 44, col. 1.

* A private property in opposition to a public.

Forty years before the destruction of the Temple the Sanhedrin were exiled, and they sat in the Halls of Commerce. *Shabbath*, fol. 15, col. 1.

Until one is forty eating is more advantageous than drinking. After that age the rule is reversed.

Ibid., fol. 152, col. 1.

The Rabbis have taught that during the forty years in which Simeon the Just officiated in the Temple the lot always fell on the right (see Lev. xvi. 8–10). After that time it sometimes fell on the right and sometimes on the left. The crimson band also, which in his time had always turned white, after that period sometimes turned white, and at others it did not change color at all.

Yoma, fol. 39, col. 1.

The Rabbis have taught :— Forty years before the destruction of the Temple the lot did not fall on the right, and the crimson band did not turn white ; the light in the west did not burn, and the gates of the Temple opened of themselves, so that Rabbi Yochanan ben Zacchai rebuked them, and said, "O Temple ! Temple ! why art thou dismayed ? I know thy end will be that thou shalt be destroyed, for Zachariah the son of Iddo has already predicted respecting thee (Zech. xi. 1), 'Open thy doors, O Lebanon, that the fire may devour thy cedars.'"

Ibid., fol. 39, col. 2.

During the forty years that Israel were in the wilderness there was not a midnight in which the north wind did not blow. *Yevamoth*, fol. 71, col. 1.

Rabbi Zadok fasted forty years that Jerusalem might not be destroyed, and so emaciated was he, that when he ate anything it might be seen going down his throat.

Gittin, fol. 56, col, 1.

Forty days before the formation of a child a Bath Kol proclaims, "The daughter of so-and-so shall marry the son of so-and-so ; the premises of so-and-so shall be the property of so-and-so." *Soteh*, fol. 2, col. 1.

Rav Hunna and Rav Chasda were so angry with one another that they did not meet for forty years. After that

Rav Chasda fasted forty days for having annoyed Rav Hunna, and Rav Hunna forty days for having suspected Rav Chasda.   *Bava Metzia*, fol. 33, col. 1.

A female who marries at forty will never have any children.

He who eats black cummin the weight of a denarius will have his heart torn out; so also will he who eats forty eggs or forty nuts, or a quarter of honey.

Tract Calah.

He that cooks in milk the nerve Nashe on a yearly festival, and then eats it, receives five times forty stripes save one, etc.   *Baitza*, fol. 12, col. 1.

He who passes forty consecutive days without suffering some affliction has received his good reward in his lifetime (*cf*. Luke xvi. 25).   *Erachin*, fol. 16, col. 2.

If a bath contain forty measures of water and some mud, people may, according to Rabbi Elazar, immerse themselves in the water of it, but not in the mud; while Rabbi Yehoshua says they may do so in both.

Mikvaoth, chap. ii. 10.

Rav Yehudah said in the name of Rav:—The Divine name, which consists of forty-two letters, is revealed only to him who is prudent and meek, who has reached the meridian of life, is not prone to wrath, not given to drink, and not revengeful. He that knows that name, and acts circumspectly in regard to it, and retains it sacredly, is beloved in heaven and esteemed on earth; He inspires men with reverence, and is heir both to the world that now is and that which is to come.

Kiddushin, fol. 71, col. 1.

A man should always devote himself to the study of the law and to the practice of good deeds, even if he does not do so for their own sake, as self-satisfied performance may follow in due course.   Thus, in recompense for the forty-two sacrifices he offered, Balak was accounted worthy to become the ancestor of Ruth. Rav Yossi bar Hunna has said, Ruth was the daughter of Eglon, the grandson of Balak, king of Moab.   *Sanhedrin*, fol. 105, col. 2.

These are the forty-five righteous men for whose sake the world is preserved. *Chullin*, fol. 92, col. 1.

Rabbi Meir had a disciple named Sumchus, who in every case assigned forty-eight reasons why one thing should be called clean and why another should be called unclean, though Scripture declared the contrary. (A striking illustration of Rabbinical ingenuity !)

Eiruvin, fol. 13, col. 2.

Forty-eight prophets and seven prophetesses prophesied unto Israel, and they have neither diminished nor added to that which is written in the law, except the reading of the Book of Esther. *Megillah*, fol. 14, col. 1.

The Rabbis teach that in future (in the days of the Messiah) all Scripture will be abolished except the Book of Esther, also all festivals except the feast of Purim. (See *Menorath Hamaor*, fol. 135, col. 1.)

By forty-eight things the law is acquired. These are study, attention, careful conversation, mental discernment, solicitude, reverential fear, meekness, geniality of soul, purity, attention to the wise, mutual discussion, debating, sedateness, learning in the Scripture and the Mishna, not dabbling in commerce, self-denial, moderation in sleep, aversion to gossip, etc., etc. *Avoth*, chap. 6.

When God gave the law to Moses, He assigned forty-nine reasons in every case for pronouncing one thing unclean and as many for pronouncing other things clean.

Sophrim, chap. 16, mish. 6.

He that has fifty zouzim, and trades therewith, may not glean what is left in the corner of the field (Lev. xix. 9). He that takes it, and has no right to it, will come to want before the day of his departure. And if one who is entitled to it leaves it to others more needy, before he dies he will not only be able to support himself, but be a stay to others. *Peah*, chap. 8, mish. 9.

Fifty measures of understanding were created in the world, and all except one were given to Moses; as it is said (Ps. viii. 5), "Thou hast made him a little lower than the angels." *Rosh Hashanah*, fol. 21, col. 2.

Poverty in a house is harder to bear than fifty plagues.

Bava Bathra, fol 116, col. 1.

The above saying is based on Job xix. 21, compared with Exod. viii. 19.

For fifty-two years no man traveled through the land of Judea. *Yoma*. fol. 54, col. 1.

Black cummin is one of the sixty deadly drugs.

Berachoth, fol. 40, col. 1.

Ulla and Rav Chasda were once traveling together, when they came up to the gate of the house of Rav Chena bar Chenelai. At sight of it Rav Chasda stooped and sighed. "Why sighest thou?" asked Ulla, "seeing, as Rav says, sighing breaks the body in halves; for it is said (Ezek. xxi. 6), 'sigh, therefore, O son of man, with the breaking of thy loins;' and Rabbi Yochanan says a sigh breaks up the whole constitution; for it is said (Ezek. xxi. 7), 'And it shall be when they say unto thee, Wherefore sighest thou? that thou shalt answer, For the tidings because it cometh, and the whole heart shall melt,'" etc. To this Rav Chasda replied, "How can I help sighing over this house, where sixty bakers used to be employed during the day, and sixty during the night, to make bread for the poor and needy; and Rav Chena had his hand always at his purse, for he thought the slightest hesitation might cause a poor but respectable man to blush; and besides he kept four doors open, one to each quarter of the heavens, so that all might enter and be satisfied? Over and above this, in time of famine he scattered wheat and barley abroad, so that they who were ashamed to gather by day might do so by night; but now this house has fallen into ruin, and ought I not to sigh?" *Ibid.*, fol. 58, col. 2.

Egypt is a sixtieth of Ethiopia, Ethiopia a sixtieth of the world, the world is a sixtieth part of the garden of Eden, the garden itself is but a sixtieth of Eden, and Eden a sixtieth of Gehenna. Hence the world in proportion to Gehenna is but as the lid to a caldron.

P'sachim, fol. 94, col. 1.

They led forth Metatron and struck him sixty bastinadoes with a cudgel of fire. *Chaggigah*, fol. 15, col. 1.

In the context of the foregoing quotation occurs an anecdote of Rabbi Elisha ben Abuyah which is too racy to let pass, and too characteristic to need note or comment. One day Elisha ben Abuyah was privileged to pry into Paradise, where he saw the recording angel Metatron on a seat registering the merits of the holy of Israel. Struck with astonishment at the sight, he exclaimed, "Is it not laid down that there is no sitting in heaven, no shortsightedness or fatigue?" Then Metatron, thus discovered, was ordered out and flogged with sixty lashes from a fiery scourge. Smarting with pain, the angel asked and obtained leave to cancel the merits of the prying Rabbi. One day — it chanced to be on Yom Kippur and Sabbath — as Elisha was riding along by the wall where the Holy of Holies once stood, he heard a Bath Kol proclaiming, "Return, ye backsliding children, but Acher abide thou in thy sin" (Acher was the Rabbi's nickname). A faithful disciple of his hearing this, and bent on reclaiming and reforming him, invited him to go and hear the lads of a school close by repeat their lessons. The Rabbi went, and from that to another and another, until he had gone the round of a dozen seminaries, in the last of which he called up a lad to repeat a verse who had an impediment in his speech. The verse happened to be Ps. 1. 16, "But unto the wicked, God saith, Why dost thou declare my law?" Acher fancied the boy said, and to Elisha (his own name), instead of and to Rasha, that is, the wicked. This roused the Rabbi into such fury of passion, that he sprang to his feet, exclaiming, "If I only had a knife at hand I would cut this boy into a dozen pieces, and send a piece to each school I have visited!"

A woman of sixty runs after music like a girl of six.
Moed Katon, fol. 9, col. 2.

Rabba, who only studied the law, lived forty years; Abaii, who both studied the law and exercised benevolence, lived sixty.   *Rosh Hashanah*, fol. 18, col. 1.

The manna which came down upon Israel was sixty ells deep.   *Yoma*, fol. 76, col. 1.

It is not right for a man to sleep in the daytime any longer than a horse sleeps. And how long is the sleep of a horse? Sixty respirations.   *Succah*, fol. 26, col. 2.

Abaii says, "When I left Rabbah, I was not at all hungry; but when I arrived at Meree, they served up before me sixty dishes, with as many sorts of viands, and I ate half of each, but as for hotch-potch, which the last dish contained, I ate up all of it, and would fain have eaten up the dish too." Abaii said, "This illustrates the proverb, current among the people, 'The poor man is hungry, and does not know when he has eaten enough; or, there is always room for a tit-bit.' "   *Meggillah*, fol. 7, col. 2.

There are sixty kinds of wine; the best of all is the red aromatic wine, and bad white wine is the worst.

Gittin, fol. 70, col. 1.

Samson's shoulders were sixty ells broad.

Soteh, fol. 10, col. 1.

Ebal and Gerizim were sixty miles from Jordan.

Ibid., fol. 36, col. 1.

One who makes a good breakfast can outstrip sixty runners in a race (who have not).

Bava Kama, fol. 92, col. 2.

A (hungry) person who looks on while another eats, experiences sixty unpleasant sensations in his teeth.   *Ibid.*

His wife made him daily sixty sorts of dainties, and these restored him again.   *Bava Metzia*, fol. 84, col. 2.

Rabbi Elazar, the son of Rabbi Shimon, once vindictively caused a man to be put to death, merely because he had spoken of him as Vinegar the son of Wine, a round-about way of reproaching him that he was the bad son of a good father, though it turned out afterward that the condemned man deserved death for a crime that he was not known to be guilty of at the time of his execution; yet the mind of the Rabbi was ill at ease, and he voluntarily did penance by subjecting himself in a peculiar fashion to great bodily suffering. Sixty woolen cloths were regularly spread under him every night, and these were found soaked in the morning with his profuse perspiration. The result of this was greater and greater bodily prostration, which his wife strove, as related above, day after day to repair, detaining him from college, lest the debates there should prove too much for his weakened frame. When his wife found that he persisted in courting these sufferings, and that her tender care, as well as her own patrimony, were being lavished on him in vain, she tired of her assiduity, and left him to his fate. And now, waited on by some sailors, who believed they owed to him deliverance from a watery grave, he was free to do as he liked. One day, being ministered to by them after a night's perspiration of the kind referred to, he went straight to college, and there decided sixty doubtful cases against the unanimous dissent of the assembly. Providential circumstances, which happened afterward, both proved that he was right in his judgment and that his wife was wrong in suffering her fondness for him to stand in the way of the performance of his public duties.

Elijah frequently attended the Rabbi's seat of instruction, and once, on the first of a month, he came in later than usual. Rabbi asked what had kept him so late. Elijah answered, "I have to wake up Abraham, Isaac, and Jacob one after the other, to wash the hands of each, and to wait until each has said his prayers and retired to rest again." "But," said Rabbi, "why do they not all get up at the same time?" The answer was, "Because if they prayed all at once, their united prayers would hurry on the coming of the Messiah before the time appointed." Then said Rabbi, "Are there any such praying people among us?" Elijah mentioned Rabbi Cheyah and his sons. Then Rabbi announced a fast, and the Rabbi Cheyah and his sons came to celebrate it. In the course of repeating the Shemoneh Esreh * they were about to say, "Thou restoreth life to the dead" when the world was convulsed, and the question was asked in heaven, "Who told them the secret?" So Elijah was bastinadoed sixty strokes with a cudgel of fire. Then he came down like a fiery bear, and dashing in among the people, scattered the congregation. *Bava Metzia,* fol. 85, col. 2.

When love was strong, we could lie, as it were, on the edge of a sword; but now, when love is diminished, a bed sixty ells wide is not broad enough for us.

Sanhedrin, fol. 7, col. 1.

The pig bears in sixty days. *Bechoroth,* fol. 8, col. 1.

Sixty iron mines are suspended in the sting of a gnat.

Chullin, fol. 58, col. 2.

An egg once dropped out of the nest of a bird called Bar-Yuchnei, which deluged sixty cities and swept away three hundred cedars. The question therefore arose, "Does the bird generally throw out its eggs?" Rav Ashi replied, "No; that was a rotten one."

Bechoroth, fol. 57, col. 2.

Everybody knows why a bride enters the nuptial chamber, but against him who sullies his lips by talking about it, the decree for good, though of seventy years' standing,

---

* A prayer consisting of eighteen Collects, which is repeated three times each day.

shall be reversed into a decree for evil. Rav Chasda says, "Whosoever disgraces his mouth (by evil communication), Gehenna shall be deepened for him; for it is said in Prov. xxii. 14, 'A deep pit for the mouth of strange words (immoral talk).'" Rav Nachman bar Yitzchak says, "The same punishment will be inflicted on him who listens to it and is silent; for it is said (Prov. xxii. 14), 'And he that is abhorred of the Lord shall fall therein.'"

Shabbath, fol. 33, col. 1.

(Jer. xxiii. 29), "Like a hammer that breaketh the rock in pieces," so is every utterance which proceedeth from the mouth of God, divided though it be into seventy languages.   Ibid., fol. 88, col. 2.

Rabbi Eliezer asked, "For whose benefit were those seventy bullocks intended?" See Num. xxix. 12–36. For the seventy nations into which the Gentile world is divided; and Rashi plainly asserts that the seventy bullocks were intended to atone for them, that rain might descend all over the world, for on the Feast of Tabernacles judgment is given respecting rain, etc. Woe to the Gentile nations for their loss, and they know not what they have lost! for as long as the Temple existed, the altar made atonement for them; but now, who is to atone for them?

Succah, fol. 55, col. 2.

Choni, the Maagol, once saw in his travels an old man planting a carob-tree, and he asked him when he thought the tree would bear fruit. "After seventy years," was the reply. "What!" said Choni, "dost thou expect to live seventy years and eat the fruit of thy labor?" "I did not find the world desolate when I entered it," said the old man; "and as my fathers planted for me before I was born, so I plant for those that will come after me."

Taanith, fol. 23, col. 1.

Mordecai was one of those who sat in the hall of the Temple, and he knew seventy languages.

Megillah, fol. 13, col. 2.

The Rabbis have taught:— During a prosperous year in Israel, a place that is sown with a single measure of seed produces five myriad cors of grain. In the tilled districts of Zoan, one measure of seed produces seventy cors; for we are told that Rabbi Meir said he himself had witnessed in the vale of Bethshean an instance of one measure of seed producing seventy cors. And there is no better land anywhere than the land of Egypt; for it is said, "As the garden of the Lord, like the land of Egypt." And there is no better land in all Egypt than Zoan, where several kings have resided; for it is written (Isa. xxx. 4), "His princes were in Zoan." In all Israel there was no more unsuitable soil than Hebron, for it was a burying-place, and yet Hebron was seven times more prolific than Zoan; for it is written (Num. xiii. 22), "Now Hebron was built seven years before Zoan in Egypt." For it is said (Gen. x. 6), "And the sons of Ham, Cush, Mizraim (that is, Egypt), Phut, and Canaan" (that is, Israel). It must, therefore, mean that it was seven times more prolific (the verb meaning both to build and to produce) than Zoan. This is only in the unsuitable soil of the land of Israel, Hebron, but in the suitable soil (the increase) is five hundred times. All this applies to a year of average return, but in one of special prosperity, it is written (Gen. xxvi. 12), "Then Isaac sowed in that land, and received in the same year an hundredfold, and the Lord blessed him." (The word years, is conveniently overlooked in working out the argument.) *Kethuboth*, fol. 112, col. 1.

The astrologers in Egypt said to Pharaoh, "What! shall a slave whose master bought him for twenty pieces of silver rule over us?" Pharaoh replied, "But I find him endowed with kingly qualities." "If that is the case," they answered, "he must know seventy languages." Then came the angel Gabriel, and taught him seventy languages.

Soteh, fol. 36, col. 2.

When the leviathan makes the deep boil, the sea does not recover its calm for seventy years; for it is said (Job xli. 32), "One would think the deep is to be hoary," and we cannot take the word "hoary" to imply a term of less than seventy years. *Bava Bathra*, fol. 75, col. 1.

Abba Chalepha Keruya once remarked to Rav Cheyah bar Abba, "The sum total of Jacob's family thou findest

11

reckoned at seventy, whereas the numbers added up make only sixty-nine. How is that?" Rav Cheyah made answer that the particle in verse 15, implies that Dinah must have been one of twin-sisters. "But," objected the other, "the same particle occurs also in connection with Benjamin, to say nothing of other instances." "Alas!" said Rav Cheyah, "I am possessed of a secret worth knowing, and thou art trying to worm it out of me." Then interposed Rav Chama bar Chanena, "The number may be made up by reckoning Jochebed in, for of her it is said (Num. xxvi. 59) 'that her mother bare her to Levi in Egypt;' her birth took place in Egypt, though she was conceived on the journey."

Bava Bathra, fol. 123, cols. 1, 2.

Rav Yehudah says in the name of Shemuel:—There is yet another festival in Rome, which is observed only once in seventy years, and this is the manner of its celebration. They take an able-bodied man, without physical defect, and cause him to ride upon the back of a lame one. They dress up the former in the garments of Adam (such as God made for him in Paradise), and cover his face with the skin of the face of Rabbi Ishmael, the high priest, and adorn his neck with a precious stone. They illuminate the streets, and then lead the two men through the city, a herald proclaiming before them, "The account of our Lord was false; it is the brother of our Lord that is the deceiver! He that sees this festival sees it, and he that does not see it now will never see it. What advantage to the deceiver is his deception, and to the crafty his craftiness?" The proclamation finishes up thus—"Woe to this one when the other shall rise again!" *Avodah Zarah*, fol. 11, col. 2.

The Targum Yarushalmi informs us that the Lord God wrought for Adam and his wife robes of honor from the cast-off skin of the serpent. We learn elsewhere that Nimrod came into possession of Adam's coat through Ham, who stole it from Noah while in the Ark. The glib tongue of tradition also tells how Esau slew Nimrod and appropriated the garment, and wore it for luck when hunting; but that on the day when he went to seek venison at the request of his dying parent, in his hurry he forgot the embroidered robe of Adam, and had bad luck in consequence. Then Jacob borrowed the left-off garment, and kept it for himself. The mask alluded to is accounted for thus : — The daughter of a Roman emperor took a fancy to have the skin of Rabbi Ishmael's face, and it accordingly, when he was dead, was taken off, and so embalmed as to retain its features, expression, and complexion, and the Jews say that it is still preserved among the relics at Rome. The able-bodied man in this prophetic mystery-play represents Esau, and the limping man is intended for Jacob. Rome (or Esau) is uppermost in that ceremonial, but the time is coming when Jacob will rise and invest himself in the blessings he so craftily obtained the reversion of.

Rabbi Yochanan said : — None were elected to sit in the High Council of the Sanhedrin except men of stature, of wisdom, of imposing appearance, and of mature age ; men who knew witchcraft and seventy languages, in order that the High Council of the Sanhedrin should have no need of an interpreter. *Sanhedrin*, fol. 17, col. 1.

Yehudah and Chiskiyah, the sons of Rabbi Cheyah, once sat down to a meal before Rabbi (the Holy) without speaking a word. "Give the boys some wine," said Rabbi, "that they may have boldness to speak." When they had partaken of the wine, they said, "The son of David will not come until the two patriarchal houses of Israel are no more," that is, the head of the Captivity in Babylon and the Prince in the land of Israel ; for it is written (Isa. viii. 14), "And he shall be for a sanctuary, and for a stone of stumbling and a rock of offense to both the houses of Israel." "Why, children," said Rabbi (who was patriarch of Tiberias), "you are thrusting thorns into my eyes." Rabbi Cheyah said, "Do not be offended at them. Wine is given with seventy, and so is a secret (the numerical value of each of these words is seventy) ; when wine enters the secret oozes out." *Ibid.*, fol. 38, col. 1.

A certain star appears once in seventy years and deceives the sailors (who guide their vessels by the position of the heavenly bodies ; and this star appears sometimes in the north and sometimes in the south.— *Rashi.*)

Horayoth, fol. 10, col. 1.

As eating olive berries causes one to forget things that he has known for seventy years, so olive oil brings back to the memory things which happened seventy years before.

Ibid., fol. 13, col. 2.

The outside of the shell of the purple mollusk resembles the sea in color; its bodily conformation is like that of a fish; it rises once in seventy years; its blood is used to dye wool purple, and therefore this color is dear.

Menachoth, fol. 44, col. 1.

The bearing-time of the flat-headed otter lasts seventy years; a parallel may be found in the carob-tree, from the planting to the ripening of the pods of which is seventy years. *Berachoth*, fol. 8, col. 1.

The Sanhedrin consisted of seventy-one members. It is recorded that Rabbi Yossi said, "Seldom was there contention in Israel, but the judicial court of seventy-one sat in the Lishkath-hagazith, *i. e.*, Paved Hall, and two (ordinary) courts of justice consisting of twenty-three, one of which sat at the entrance of the Temple-Mount, and the other at the entrance of the ante-court; and also (provincial) courts of justice, also comprising twenty-three members, which held their sessions in all the cities of Israel. When an Israelite had a question to propose, he asked it first of the court in his own city. If they understood the case, they settled the matter; but if not, they applied to the court of the next city. If the neighboring justices could not decide, they went together and laid the case in debate before the court which held its session at the entrance of the Temple-Mount. If these courts, in turn, failed to solve the problem, they appealed to the court that sat in the entrance of the ante-court, where a discussion was entered into upon the moot points of the case; if no decision could be arrived at, they all referred to the (supreme) court of seventy-one, where the matter was finally decided by the majority of votes."

As the disciples of Shammai and Hillel multiplied who had not studied the law thoroughly, contentions increased in Israel to such an extent that the law lost its unity and became as two. *Sanhedrin*, fol. 88, col. 2.

The Sanhedrin sat in a semicircle, in order that they might see one another; and two notaries stood before them, the one on the right and the other on the left, to record the pros and cons in the various processes. Rabbi Yehudah says there were three such notaries, one for the pros, one for the cons, and one to record both the pros and the cons. (*Sanhedrin*, fol. 36, col. 2.)

The witnesses (in capital cases) were questioned on seven points, as follows:—In what Shemitah (or septennial cycle) did it occur? In which year (of the cycle)? In what month? Upon what day? At what hour? In what place? . . . The more one questioned the more he was commended. (See Deut. xiii. 15; A. V., ver. 14.) (*Ibid.*, fol. 40, col. 1.)

In connection with the foregoing subject, let us string together some of the gems of forensic wisdom to be met with in the Talmud. A score or so of bona fide quotations, respecting judges, criminals and criminal punishment, and witnesses, will serve to illustrate this part of our subject.

JUDGES.

The judge, says the Scripture, who for but one hour administers justice according to true equity, is a partner, as it were, with God in His work of creation.

Shabbath, fol. 10, col. 1.

Despicable is the judge who judges for reward; yet his judgment is law, and must, as such, be respected.

Kethuboth, fol. 105, col. 1.

The judge who accepts a bribe, however perfectly righteous otherwise, will not leave this world with sane mind.

Ibid., fol. 105, col. 2.

A judge will establish the land if, like a king, he want nothing; but he will ruin it if, like a priest, he receive gifts from the threshing-floor.   *Ibid.*

Once when Shemuel was crossing a river in a ferryboat, a man lent a sustaining hand to prevent him from falling. "What," said the Rabbi, " have I done for thee, that thou art so attentive with thy services?" The man replied, "I have a lawsuit before thee." "In that case," said Shemuel, "thy attention has disqualified me from judging in thy lawsuit."

Ameimar was once sitting in judgment, when a man stepped forward and removed some feathers that were clinging to his hair. Upon this the judge asked, "What service have I done thee?" The man replied, "I have a case to bring up before thee, my lord." The Rabbi replied, "Thou hast disqualified me from being judge in the matter."

Mar Ukva once noticed a man politely step up and cover some saliva which lay on the ground before him. "What have I done for thee?" said the Rabbi. "I have a case to bring before thee," said the man. "Thou hast bribed me with thy kind attention," said the Rabbi; "I cannot be thy judge."

Rabbi Ishmael, son of Rabbi Yossi, had a gardener who regularly brought him a basket of grapes every Friday. Bringing it once on a Thursday, the Rabbi asked him the reason why he had come a day earlier. "My lord," said the gardener, "having a lawsuit to come off before thee to-day, I thought by so doing I might save myself the journey to-morrow." Upon this the Rabbi both refused to take the basket of grapes, though they were really his own, and declined to act as judge in the process. He, however, appointed two Rabbis to judge the case in his stead, and while they were investigating the evidence in the litigation he kept pacing up and down, and saying to himself, if the gardener were sharp he might say so-and-so in his own behalf. He was at one time on the point of speaking in defense of his gardener, when he checked himself and said, "The receivers of bribes may well look to their souls. If I feel partial who have not even taken a bribe of what was my own, how perverted must the disposition of those become who receive bribes at the hands of others!"

Kethuboth, fol. 105, col. 1.

The judge who takes a bribe only provokes wrath, instead of allaying it; for is it not said (Prov. xxi. 14), "A reward in the bosom bringeth strong wrath"?

Bava Bathra, fol. 9, col. 2.

Let judges know with whom and before whom they judge, and who it is that will one day exact account of their judgments; for it is said (Ps. lxxxii. 1), "God standeth in the assembly of God, and judgeth with the judges."

Sanhedrin, fol. 6, col. 2.

A judge who does not judge justly causeth the Shechinah to depart from Israel; for it is said (Ps. xii. 5), "For the oppression of the poor, the sighing of the needy, now will I depart, saith the Lord." *Sanhedrin*, fol. 7, col. 1.

The judge should ever regard himself as if he had a sword laid upon his thigh, and Gehenna were yawning near him ; as it is said (Solomon's Song, iii. 7, 8), "Behold the bed of Solomon (the judgment-seat of God), threescore valiant men are about it, of the valiant of Israel. They all hold swords, being expert in war (with injustice). Every one has his sword upon his thigh, for fear of the night" (the confusion that would follow).

Yevamoth, fol. 109, col. 2 ; *Sanhedrin*, fol. 7, col. 1.

Seven have, in the popular regard, no portion in the world to come : a notary, a schoolmaster, the best of doctors, a judge in his native place, a conjuror, a congregational reader, and a butcher.

Avoth d' Rabbi Nathan, chap. 36.

WITNESSES.

An ignoramus is ineligible for a witness.

The following are ineligible as witnesses of the appearance of the new moon : — Dice-players, usurers, pigeonfliers, sellers of the produce of the year of release, and slaves. This is the general rule ; in any case in which women are inadmissible as witnesses, they also are inadmissible here. *Rosh Hashanah*, fol. 22, col. 1.

Two disciples of the wise happened to be shipwrecked with Rabbi Yossi ben Simaii, and the Rabbi allowed their widows to re-marry on the testimony of women. Even the testimony of a hundred women is only equal to the evidence of one man (and that only in a case like the foregoing ; it is inadmissible in any other matter).

Yevamoth, fol. 115, col. 1.

"Whosoever is not instructed in Scripture, in the Mishna, and in good manners," says Rabbi Yochanan, "is not qualified to act as a witness." "He who eats in the street," say the Rabbis, "is like a dog ; " and some add that such a one is ineligible as a witness, and Rav Iddi bar Avin says the Halachah is as "some say." *Kiddushin*, fol. 40, col. 2.

Even when a witness is paid, his testimony is not thereby invalidated.   *Kiddushin*, fol. 58, col. 2.

Testimony that is invalidated in part is invalidated entirely.   *Bava Kama*, fol. 73, col. 1.

Let witnesses know with whom and before whom they bear testimony, and who will one day call them to account; for it is said (Deut. xix. 17), "Both the men between whom the controversy is shall stand before the Lord."
                    Sanhedrin, fol. 6, col. 2.

Those that eat another thing (*i. e.*, not pork, but those who receive charity from a Gentile.— Rashi and Tosefoth) are disqualified from being witnesses. When is this the case? When done publicly; but if in secret, not so.
                    Ibid., fol. 26, col. 2.

He who swears falsely in a capital case is unreliable as a witness in any other suit at law; but if he has perjured himself in a civil case only, his evidence may be relied upon in cases where life and death are concerned.
                    Ibid., fol. 27, col. 1.

He who disavows a loan is fit to be a witness; but he who disowns a deposit in trust is unfit.
                    Shevuoth, fol. 40, col. 2.

Shimon ben Shetach says, " Fully examine the witnesses; be careful with thy words, lest from them they learn to lie."   *Avoth*, chap. 1.

CRIMINALS AND CRIMINAL PUNISHMENTS.

Four kinds of capital punishment were decreed by the court of justice :— Stoning, burning, beheading, and strangling; or as Rabbi Shimon arranges them — Burning, stoning, strangling, and beheading. As soon as the sentence of death is pronounced, the criminal is led out to be stoned, the stoning-place being at a distance from the court of justice; for it is said (Lev. xxiv. 14), "Bring forth him that hath cursed without the camp." Then one official stands at the door of the court of justice with a flag in his hand, and another is stationed on horseback at such a distance as to be able to see the former. If, meanwhile, one comes and declares before the court, " I have something further to urge in defense of the prisoner," the man at the door waves his flag, and the mounted official rides forward and stops the procession. Even if the criminal himself says, " I have yet something to plead in my defense," he is to be brought back, even four or five times over, provided there is something of importance in his deposition. If the evidence is exculpatory, he is discharged ; if not, he is led out to be stoned. As he proceeds to the place of execution, a public crier goes before him and proclaims, " So-and-so, the son of So-and-so, goes out to be stoned because he has committed such-and-such a crime, and So-and-so and So-and-so are the witnesses. Let him who knows of anything that pleads in his defense come forward and state it." When about ten yards from the stoning-place, the condemned is called upon to confess his guilt. (All about to be executed were urged to confess, as by making confession every criminal made good a portion in the world to come ; for so we find it in the case of Achan, when Joshua said unto him (Josh. vii. 19), " My son, give, I pray thee, glory to the Lord God of Israel, and make confession unto him," etc. " And Achan answered Joshua and said, Indeed I have sinned." But where are we taught that his confession was his atonement? Where it is said (*ibid.*, v. 25), " And Joshua said, Why hast thou troubled us? The Lord shall trouble thee this day ; " as if to say, " This day thou shalt be troubled, but in the world to come thou shalt not be troubled.") About four yards from the stoning-place they stripped off the criminal's clothes, covering a male in front, but a female both before and behind. These are the words of Rabbi Yehudah ; but the sages say a man was stoned naked, but not a female.

The stoning-place was twice the height of a man, and this the criminal ascended. One of the witnesses then pushed him from behind, and he tumbled down upon his chest. He was then turned over upon his back : if he was killed, the execution was complete ; but if not quite dead, the second witness took a heavy stone and cast it upon his chest ; and if this did not prove effectual, then the stoning was completed by all present joining in the act; as it is said (Deut. xvii. 7), "The hands of the witnesses shall be first upon him to put him to death, and afterward the hands of all the people."

"Criminals who were stoned dead were afterward hanged." These are the words of Rabbi Eliezer; but the sages say none were hanged but the blasphemer and the idolator. "They hanged a man with his face toward the people, but a woman with her face toward the gallows." These are the words of Rabbi Eliezer; but the sages say a man is hanged, but no woman is hanged. . . . How then did they hang the man? A post was firmly fixed into the ground, from which an arm of wood projected, and they tied the hands of the corpse together and so suspended it. Rabbi Yossi says, "The beam simply leaned against a wall, and so they hung up the body as butchers do an ox or a sheep, and it was soon afterward taken down again, for if it remained over night a prohibition of the law would have been thereby transgressed." For it is said (Deut. xxi. 23), "His body shall not remain all night upon the tree, but thou shalt in any wise bury him that day; for he that is hanged is accursed of God," etc. That is to say, people would ask why this one was hanged; and as the reply would needs be, "Because he blasphemed God," this would lead to the use of God's name under circumstances in which it would be blasphemed.

The sentence of burning was carried out thus: — They fixed the criminal up to his knees in manure, and a hard cloth wrapped in a softer material was passed round his neck. One of the witnesses, taking hold of this, pulled it one way, and another the other, until the criminal was forced to open his mouth; then a wick of lead was lighted and thrust into his mouth, the molten lead running down into his bowels and burning them. Rabbi Yehudah asks, "If the criminal should die in their hands, how would that fulfill the commandment respecting burning?" But they forcibly open his mouth with a pair of tongues and the lighted wire (the molten lead) is thrust into his mouth, so that it goes down into his bowels and burns his inside.

The sentence of beheading was executed thus: — They sometimes cut off the criminal's head with a sword, as is done among the Romans. But Rabbi Yehudah says this was degrading, and in some cases they placed the culprit's head upon the block and struck it off with an ax. Some one remarked to him that such a death is more degrading still.

The sentence of strangling was carried out thus: — They fixed the criminal up to his knees in manure, and having twined a hard cloth within a soft one round his neck, one witness pulled one way and the other pulled in an opposite direction till life was extinct.

Sanhedrin, fol. 42, col. 2 ; fol. 49, col. 2 ; fol. 52, cols. 1, 2.

The above, which has been translated almost literally from the Talmud, may serve to remove many misconceptions now current as to the modes of capital punishment that obtained in Jewry.

In further illustration of this topic, we will append some of the legal decisions that are recorded in the Talmud, authenticating each by reference to folio and column. Examples might be multiplied by the score, but a sufficient number will be quoted to give a fair idea of Rabbinic jurisprudence.

If one who intends to kill a beast (accidentally) kill a man ; or if, purposing to kill a Gentile, he slay an Israelite ; or if he destroy a fœtus in mistake for an embryo, he shall be free ; *i. e.*, not guilty.

Ibid., fol. 78, col. 2.

He who has been flogged and exposes himself again to the same punishment is to be shut up in a narrow cell, in which he can only stand upright, and be fed with barley till he burst. *Ibid.*, fol. 81, col. 2.

If one commits murder, and there is not sufficient legal evidence, he is to be shut up in a narrow cell and fed with "the bread of adversity and the water of affliction" (Isa. xxx. 20). They give him this diet till his bowels shrink, and then he is fed with barley till (as it swells in his bowels) his intestines burst. *Ibid.*

A woman who is doomed, being *enceinte*, to suffer the extreme penalty of the law, is first beaten, about the womb, lest a mishap occur at the execution.

Erachin, fol. 7, col. 1.

If a woman who has vowed the vow of a Nazarite drink wine or defile herself by contact with a dead body (see

Num. vi. 2–6), she is to undergo the punishment of forty stripes.   *Nazir*, fol. 23, col. 1.

The Rabbis teach that when the woman has to be flogged, the man has only to bring a sacrifice; and that if she is not to be flogged, the man is not required to bring a sacrifice. (This is in reference to Lev. xix. 20, 21.)

                                   Kerithoth, fol. 11, col. 1.

Rav Yehudah says, "He that eats a certain aquatic insect, the swallowing of which while drinking would involve no penalty whatever — Tosefoth, receives forty stripes save one (the penalty for transgressing the negative precepts), for it belongs to the class of 'creeping things that do creep upon the earth' (Lev. xi. 29)." Rav Yehudah once gave a practical exemplification of this ruling of his.

Abaii says, "He that eats a particular animalcule found in stagnant water, receives four times forty stripes save one. For eating an ant this penalty is five times repeated, and for eating a wasp it is inflicted six times."

                                   Maccoth, fol. 16, col. 2.

When one is ordered to construct a booth, or to prepare a palm-branch for the Feast of Tabernacles, or to make fringes, and does not do so, he is to be flogged till his soul comes out of him.   *Chullin*, fol. 132, col. 2.

Once on a time, as the Rabbis relate, the wicked Government sent two officers to the wise men of Israel, saying, "Teach us your law." This being put into their hands, three times over they perused it; and when about to leave they returned it, remarking, "We have carefully studied your law, and find it equitable save in one particular. You say: When the ox of an Israelite gores to death the ox of an alien, its owner is not liable to make compensation; but if the ox of an alien gore to death the ox of an Israelite, its owner must make full amends for the loss of the animal; whether it be the first or second time that the ox has so killed another (in which case an Israelite would have to pay to another Israelite only half the value of the loss), or the third time (when he would be fined to the full extent of his neighbor's loss). Either 'neighbor' (in Exod. xxi. 35, for such the word signifies in the original Hebrew, though the Authorized Version has another) is taken strictly as referring to an Israelite only, and then an alien should be exempted as well; or if the word 'neighbor' is to be taken in its widest sense, why should not an Israelite be bound to pay when his ox gores to death the ox of an alien?" "This legal point," was the answer, "we do not tell the Government." As Rashi says in reference to the preceding Halacha, "an alien forfeits the right to his own property in favor of the Jews."

Bava Kama, fol. 38, col. 1.

Ptolemy, the king (of Egypt), assembled seventy-two elders of Israel and lodged them in seventy-two separate chambers, but did not tell them why he did so. Then he visited each one in turn and said, "Write out for me the law of Moses your Rabbi." The Holy One — blessed be He! — went and counseled the minds of every one of them, so that they all agreed, and wrote, "God created in the beginning," etc. *Megillah,* fol. 9, col. 1.

The Talmudic story of the origin of the Septuagint agrees in the main with the account of Aristeas and Josephus, but Philo gives the different version. Many of the Christian fathers believed it to be the work of inspiration.

Abraham was as tall as seventy-four people; what he ate and drank was enough to satisfy seventy-four ordinary men, and his strength was proportionate.

Sophrim, chap. 21, 9.

The venerable Hillel had eighty disciples, thirty of whom were worthy that the Shechinah should rest upon them, as it rested upon Moses our Rabbi; and thirty of them were worthy that the sun should stand still (for them), as it did for Joshua the son of Nun; and twenty of them stood midway in worth. The greatest of all of them was Jonathan ben Uzziel, and the least of all was Rabbi Yochanan ben Zacchai. It is said of Rabbi Yochanan ben Zacchai that he did not leave unstudied the Bible, the Mishna, the Gemara, the constitutions, the legends, the minutiæ of the law, the niceties of the scribes, the arguments *à fortiori* and from similar premises, the theory of the change of the moon, the Gematria, the parable of the unripe grapes and the foxes, the language of demons, of palm-trees, and of ministering angels.   *Bava Bathra*, fol. 134, col. 1.

A male criminal is to be hanged with his face toward the people, but a female with her face toward the gibbet. So says Rabbi Eliezer; but the sages say the man only is hanged, not the woman. Rabbi Eliezer retorted, "Did not Simeon the son of Shetach hang women in Askelon?" To this they replied, "He indeed caused eighty women to be hanged, though two criminals are not to be condemned in one day."   *Sanhedrin*, fol. 45, col. 2.

We may here repeat the story of the execution of the eighty women here alluded to, as that is told by Rashi on the preceding page of the Talmud. Once a publican, an Israelite but a sinner, and a great and good man of the same place, having died on the same day, were about to be buried. While the citizens were engaged with the funeral of the latter, the relations of the other crossed their path, bearing the corpse to the sepulchre. Of a sudden a troop of enemies came upon the scene and caused them all to take to flight, one faithful disciple alone remaining by the bier of his Rabbi. After a while the citizens returned to inter the remains they had so unceremoniously left, but by some mistake they took the wrong bier and buried the publican with honor, in spite of the remonstrance of the disciple, while the relatives of the publican buried the Rabbi ignominiously. The poor disciple felt inconsolably distressed, and was anxious to know for what sin the great man had been buried with contempt, and for what merit the wicked man had been buried with such honor. His Rabbi then appeared to him in a dream, and said, "Comfort thou thy heart, and come I will show thee the honor I hold in Paradise, and I will also show thee that man in Gehenna, the hinge of the door of which even now creaks in his ears.* But because once on a time I listened to contemptuous talk about the Rabbis and did not check it, I have suffered an ignoble burial, while the publican enjoyed the honor that was intended for me because he once distributed gratuitously among the poor of the city a banquet he had prepared for the governor, but of which the governor did not come to partake." The disciple having asked the Rabbi how long this publican was to be thus severely treated, he replied, "Until the death of Simeon the son of Shetach, who is to take the publican's place in Gehenna." "Why so?" "Because, though he knows there are several Jewish witches in Askelon, he idly suffers them to ply their infernal trade and does not take any steps to extirpate them." On the morrow the disciple reported this speech to Simeon the son of Shetach, who at once proceeded to take action against the obnoxious witches. He engaged eighty stalwart young men, and choosing a rainy

*Which were formed into sockets for the gates of hell to turn in.

day, supplied each with an extra garment folded up and stowed away in an earthern vessel. Thus provided, they were each at a given signal to snatch up one of the eighty witches and carry her away, a task they would find of easy execution, as, except in contact with the earth, these creatures were powerless. Then Simeon the son of Shetach, leaving his men in ambush, entered the rendezvous of the witches, who, accosting him, asked, "Who art thou?" He replied, "I am a wizard, and am come to experiment in magic." "What trick have you to show?" they said. He answered, "Even though the day is wet, I can produce eighty young men all in dry clothes." They smiled incredulously and said, "Let us see!" He went to the door, and at the signal the young men took the dry clothes out of the jars and put them on, then starting from their ambush, they rushed into the witches' den, and each seizing one, lifted her up and carried her off as directed. Thus overpowered, they were brought before the court, convicted of malpractices and led forth to execution.

Sanhedrin, fol. 44, col. 2.

(Exod. xxiii. 35), "And I will take away sickness from the midst of thee." It is taught that sickness (Machlah) means the bile. But why is it termed Machlah? Because eighty-three diseases are in it. Machlah by Gematria equals eighty-three; and all may be avoided by an early breakfast of bread and salt and a bottle of water.

Bava Kama, fol. 92, col. 2.

If in a book of the law the writing is obliterated all but eighty-five letters — as, for instance, in Num. x. 35, 36, "And it came to pass when the ark set forward," etc.,— it may be rescued on the Sabbath from a fire, but not otherwise. *Shabbath*, fol. 116, col. 1.

Elijah said to Rabbi Judah the brother of Rav Salla the Pious, "The world will not last less than eighty-five jubilees, and in the last jubilee the son of David will come."

Sanhedrin, fol. 97, col 2.

There was not a single individual in Israel who had not ninety Lybian donkeys laden with the gold and silver of Egypt.

Bechoroth, fol. 5, col. 2.

(2 Sam. xix. 35), "Can thy servant taste what I eat or what I drink?" From this we learn that in the aged the sense of taste is destroyed. . . . Rav says, "Barzillai the Gileadite reports falsely, for the cook at the house of

Rabbi (the Holy) was ninety-two years old, and yet could judge by taste of what was cooking in the pot."

Shabbath, fol. 152, col. 1.

Rava said, "Life, children, and competency do not depend on one's merit, but on luck; for instance, Rabbah and Rav Chasda were both righteous Rabbis; the one prayed for rain and it came, and the other did so likewise with the like result; yet Rav Chasda lived ninety-two years and Rabbah only forty. Rav Chasda, moreover, had sixty weddings in his family during his lifetime, whereas Rabbah had sixty serious illnesses in his during the short period of his life. At the house of the former even the dogs refused to eat bread made of the finest wheat flour, whereas the family of the latter were content to eat rough bread of barley and could not always obtain it." Rava also added, "For these three things I prayed to Heaven, two of which were and one was not granted unto me. I prayed for the wisdom of Rav Hunna and for the riches of Rav Chasda, and both these were granted unto me; but the humility and meekness of Rabbah, the son of Rav Hunna, for which I also prayed, was not granted."

Moed Katon, fol. 28, col. 1.

The judges who issued decrees at Jerusalem received for salary ninety-nine manahs from the contributions of the chamber. *Kethuboth*, fol. 105, col. 1.

Ninety-nine die from an evil eye for one who dies in the usual manner. *Bava Metzia*, fol. 107, col. 2.

The Rabbis have taught us who they are that are to be accounted rich. "Every one," says Rabbi Meir, "who enjoys his riches." But Rabbi Tarphon says, "Every one who has a hundred vineyards and a hundred fields, with a hundred slaves to labor in them." Rabbi Akiva pronounces him well off who has a wife that is becoming in all her ways. *Shabbath*, fol. 25, col. 2.

A light for one is a light for a hundred.

Ibid., fol. 122, col. 1.

When a Gentile lights a candle or a lamp on the Sabbath-eve for his own use, an Israelite is permitted to avail himself of its light, as a light for one is a light for a hundred; but it is unlawful for an Israelite to order a Gentile to kindle a light for his use.

A hundred Rav Papas and not one (like) Ravina!

A hundred zouzim employed in commerce will allow the merchant meat and wine at his table daily, but a hundred zouzim employed in farming will allow their owner only salt and vegetables. *Yevamoth*, fol. 63, col. 1.

A hundred women are equal to only one witness (compare Deut. xvii. 6 and xix. 15). *Ibid.*, fol. 88, col. 2.

If song should cease, a hundred geese or a hundred measures of wheat might be offered for one zouz, and even then the buyer would refuse paying such a sum for them.

Soteh, fol. 48, col. 1.

Rav says, "The ear that often listens to song shall be rooted out." Music, according to the idea here, raises the price of provisions. Do away with music and provisions will be so abundant that a goose would be considered dear at a penny. Theatres and music-halls are abominations to orthodox Jews, and the Talmud considers the voice of a woman to be immoral.

When Rabbi Zira returned to the land of Israel he fasted a hundred times in order that he might forget the Babylonian Talmud. *Bava Metzia*, fol. 85, col. 1.

This passage, as also that on another page, will appear surprising to many a reader, as we confess it does to ourselves. We must, however, give the Talmud great credit for recording such passages, and also the custodians of the Talmud for not having expunged them from its pages.

"Ye shall hear the small as well as the great" (Deut. i. 17). Resh Lakish said, "A lawsuit about a prutah (the smallest coin there is) should be esteemed of as much account as a suit of a hundred manahs."

Sanhedrin, fol. 8, col. 1.

Rav Yitzchak asks, "Why was Obadiah accounted worthy to be a prophet?" Because, he answers, he concealed a hundred prophets in a cave; as it is said (1 Kings xviii. 4), "When Jezebel cut off the prophets of the Lord, Obadiah took a hundred prophets and hid them by fifty in a cave." Why by fifties? Rabbi Eliezer explains, "He copied the plan from Jacob, who said, 'If Esau come to one company and smite it, then the other company which is left may escape.'" Rabbi Abuhu says, "It was because the caves would not hold any more."

Sanhedrin, fol. 39, col. 2.

"And it came to pass after these things that God did test Abraham" (Gen. xxii. 1). After what things? Rabbi Yochanan, in the name of Rabbi Yossi ben Zimra, replies, "After the words of Satan, who said, 'Lord of the Universe! Thou didst bestow a son upon that old man when he was a hundred years of age, and yet he spared not a single dove from the festival to sacrifice to Thee.' God replied, 'Did he not make this festival for the sake of his son? and yet I know he would not refuse to sacrifice that son at my command.' To prove this, God did put Abraham to the test, saying unto him, 'Take now thy son;' just as an earthly king might say to a veteran warrior who had conquered in many a hard-fought battle, 'Fight, I pray thee, this severest battle of all, lest it should be said that thy previous encounters were mere haphazard skirmishes.' Thus did the Holy One—blessed be He!—address Abraham, 'I have tried thee in various ways, and not in vain either; stand this test also, for fear it should be insinuated that the former trials were trivial and therefore easily overcome. Take thy son.' Abraham replied, 'I have two sons.' 'Take thine only son.' Abraham answered, 'Each is the only son of his mother.' 'Take him whom thou lovest.' 'I love both of them,' said Abraham. 'Take Isaac.' Thus Abraham's mind was gradually prepared for this trial. While on the way to carry out this Divine command Satan met him, and (parodying Job iv. 2–5) said, 'Why ought grievous trials to be inflicted upon thee? Behold thou hast instructed many, and thou hast strengthened the weak hands. Thy words have supported him that was falling, and now this sore burden is laid upon thee.' Abraham answered (anticipating Ps. xxvi. 11), 'I will walk in my integrity.' Then said Satan (see Job iv. 6), 'Is not the fear (of God) thy folly? Remember, I pray thee, who ever perished being innocent?' Then finding that he could not persuade him, he said (perverting Job iv. 12), 'Now a word came to me by stealth. I overheard it behind the

veil (in the Holy of Holies above). A lamb will be the sacrifice, and not Isaac.' Abraham said, 'It is the just desert of a liar not to be believed even when he speaks the truth.' "
Sanhedrin, fol. 89, col. 2.

It is better to have ten inches to stand upon than a hundred yards to fall. *Avoth d' Rab. Nathan*, chap. 1.

When Israel went up to Jerusalem to worship their Father who is in heaven, they sat so close together that no one could insert a finger between them, yet when they had to kneel and to prostrate themselves there was room enough for them all to do so. The greatest wonder of all was that even when a hundred prostrated themselves at the same time there was no need for the governor of the synagogue to request one to make room for another.
Ibid., chap. 35.

A man is bound to repeat a hundred blessings every day.
Menachoth, fol. 43, col. 2.

This duty, as Rashi tells us, is based upon Deut. x. 12, altering the word what into a hundred, by the addition of a letter.

This is what the so-called Pagan Goethe, intent on self-culture as the first if not the final duty of man, makes Serlo in his "Meister" lay down as a rule which one should observe daily. "One," he says, "ought every day to hear a little song, read a good poem, see a fine picture, and, if possible, speak a few reasonable words." The contrast between this advice and that of the Talmud here and elsewhere is suggestive of reflections.

He who possesses one manah may buy, in addition to his bread, a litra of vegetables; the owner of ten manahs may add to his bread a litra of fish; he that has fifty manahs may add a litra of meat; while the possessor of a hundred may have pottage every day.
Chullin, fol. 84, col. 1.

Ben Hey-Hey said to Hillel, "What does this mean that is written in Mal. iii. 18, 'Then shall ye return, and discern between the righteous and the wicked, between him that serveth God and him that serveth Him not'? Does the righteous here mean him that serveth God, and the wicked him that serveth Him not? Why this repetition?" To this Hillel replied, "The expressions, 'he that serveth God, and he that serveth Him not,' are both to be under-

stood as denoting 'perfectly righteous,' but he who repeats
his lesson a hundred times is not to be compared with one
who repeats it a hundred and one times." Then said Ben
Hey-Hey, "What! because he has repeated what he has
learned only one time less than the other, is he to be con-
considered as 'one who serveth Him not'?" "Yes!" was
the reply; "go and learn a lesson from the published
tariff of the donkey-drivers—ten miles for one zouz, eleven
for two." *Chaggigah*, fol. 9, col. 2.

Hillel was great and good and clever, but his exposition of Scripture, as we see from the above, is not always to be depended upon.
If, indeed, he was the teacher of Jesus, as some suppose him to have
been, then Jesus must, even from a Rabbinical stand-point, be regarded as greater than Hillel the Great, for He never handled the
Scriptures with such irreverence.

One hundred and three chapters (or psalms) were uttered
by David, and he did not pronounce the word Hallelujah
until he came to contemplate the downfall of the wicked;
as it is written (Ps. civ. 35), "Let the sinners be consumed out of the earth, and let the wicked be no more.
Bless the Lord, O my soul, Hallelujah!" Instead of one
hundred and three we ought to say a hundred and four,
but we infer from this that "Blessed is the man," etc., and
"Why do the heathen rage?" etc., are but one psalm.
Berachoth, fol. 9, col. 2.

One of the most charming women that we find figuring in the
Talmud was the wife of Rabbi Meir, Beruriah by name; and as we
meet with her in the immediate context of the above quotation, it
may be well to introduce her here to the attention of the reader. The
context speaks of a set of ignorant fellows (probably Greeks) who
sorely vexed the soul of Rabbi Meir, her husband, and he ar-
dently prayed God to take them away. Then Beruriah reasoned
with her husband thus :— "Is it, pray, because it is written (Ps. civ.
35), 'Let the sinners be consumed'? It is not written 'sinners,'
but 'sins.' Besides, a little farther on in the text it is said,
'And the wicked will be no more ;' that is to say, 'Let sins cease,
and the wicked will cease too.' Pray, therefore, on their behalf that
they may be led to repentance, and these wicked will be no more."
This he therefore did, and they repented and ceased to vex him. Of
this excellent and humane woman it may well be said, "She openeth her mouth with wisdom, and in her tongue is the law of kindness" (Prov. xxxi. 26). Her end was tragic. She was entrapped by

a disciple of her husband, and out of shame she committed suicide. See particulars by Rashi in Avodah Zarah, fol. 18, col. 2.

The Hasmoneans ruled over Israel during the time of the second Temple a hundred and three years; and for a hundred and three the government was in the hands of the family of Herod.   *Avodah Zarah*, fol. 9, col. 1.

Rabbi Yochanan the son of Zacchai lived a hundred and twenty years; forty he devoted to commerce, forty to study, and forty to teaching.
          Rosh Hashanah, fol. 30, col. 2.

One hundred and twenty elders, and among them several prophets, bore a part in composing the Eighteen Blessings (the Shemonah Esreh).   *Meggillah*, fol. 17, col. 2.

A similar tradition was current among the early Christians, with reference to the composition of the Creed. Its different sentences were ascribed to different apostles. However fitly this tradition may represent the community of faith with which the prophets on the one hand and the apostles on the other were inspired, it is not recommended by the critic as a proceeding calculated to ensure unity in a work of art.

Rabbi Shemuel says advantage may be taken of the mistakes of a Gentile. He once bought a gold plate as a copper one of a Gentile for four zouzim, and then cheated him out of one zouz into the bargain. Rav Cahana purchased a hundred and twenty vessels of wine from a Gentile for a hundred zouzim, and swindled him in the payment out of one of the hundred, and that while the Gentile assured him that he confidently trusted to his honesty. Rava once went shares with a Gentile and bought a tree, which was cut up into logs. This done, he bade his servant go to pick him out the largest logs, but to be sure to take no more than the proper number, because the Gentile knew how many there were. As Rav Ashi was walking abroad one day he saw some grapes growing in a roadside vineyard, and sent his servant to see whom they belonged to. "If they belong to a Gentile," he said, "bring some here to me; but if they belong to an Israelite, do not meddle with them." The owner, who happened to be in the vineyard, overheard the Rabbi's order and called out, "What! is it lawful to rob a Gentile?" "Oh, no," said

the Rabbi evasively; "a Gentile might sell, but an Israel
ite would not."   *Bava Kama*, fol. 113, col. 2.

This is given simply as a sample of the teaching of the Talmud
on the subject both by precept and example. There is no intention
to cast a slight on general Jewish integrity, or suggest distrust in
regard to their ethical creed.

Rabbon Gamliel, Rabbi Eliezer ben Azaryah, Rabbi
Yehoshua, and Rabbi Akiva once went on a journey to
Rome, and at Puteoli they already heard the noisy din of
the city, though at a distance of a hundred and twenty
miles. At the sound all shed tears except Akiva, who
began to laugh. "Why laughest thou?" they asked.
"Why do you cry?" he retorted. They answered, "These
Romans, who worship idols of wood and stone and offer
incense to stars and planets, abide in peace and quietness,
while our Temple, which was the footstool of our God, is
consumed by fire; how can we help weeping?" "That is
just the very reason," said he, "why I rejoice; for if such
be the lot of those who transgress His laws, what shall the
lot of those be who observe and do them?"
                                   Maccoth, fol. 24, col. 2.

When Adam observed that his sin was the cause of the
decree which made death universal he fasted one hundred
and thirty years, abstained all that space from intercourse
with his wife, and wore girdles of fig-leaves round his
loins. All these years he lived under divine displeasure,
and begat devils, demons, and spectres; as it is said
(Gen. v. 3), "And Adam lived a hundred and thirty
years, and begat in his own likeness, after his image,"
which implies that, until the close of those years, his offspring were not after his own image.
                                   Eiruvin, fol. 18, col. 2.

There is a tradition that there was once a disciple in
Yabneh who gave a hundred and fifty reasons to prove a
reptile to be clean (which the Scripture regards as unclean.—Compare Lev. xi. 29).   *Ibid.*, fol 13, col. 2.

The ablutionary tank made by Solomon was as large as
a hundred and fifty lavatories.   *Ibid.*, fol. 14, col. 1.

A hundred and eighty years before the destruction of the Temple, the empire of idolatry (Rome) began the conquest of Israel. *Shabbath*, fol. 15, col. 1.

The empire of Rome was, some think, so designated, because it strove with all its might to drag down the worship of God to the worship of man, and resolve the cause of God into the cause of the Empire.

During the time of the second Temple Persia domineered over Israel for thirty-four years and the Greeks held sway a hundred and eighty. *Avodah Zarah*, fol. 9, col. 1.

Foolish saints, crafty villains, sanctimonious women, and self-afflicting Pharisees are the destroyers of the world. What is it to be a foolish saint? To see a woman drowning in the river and refrain from trying to save her because of the look of the thing. Who is to be regarded as a crafty villain? Rabbi Yochanan says, " He who prejudices the magistrates by prepossessing them in favor of his cause before his opponent has had time to make his appearance." Rabbi Abhu says, " He who gives a denarius to a poor man to make up for him the sum total of two hundred zouzim; for it is enacted that he who possesses two hundred zouzim is not entitled to receive any gleanings, neither what is forgotten in the field, nor what is left in the corner of it (see Lev. xxiii. 22), nor poor relief either. But if he is only one short of the two hundred zouzim, and a thousand people give anything to him, he is still entitled to the poor man's perquisites." *Soteh*, fol. 21, col. 2.

The cup of David in the world to come will contain two hundred and twenty-one logs; as it is said (Ps. xxiii. 5), " My cup runneth over," the numerical value of the Hebrew word, " runneth over," being two hundred and twenty-one. *Yoma*, fol. 76, col. 1.

In the world to come the Holy One will make a grand banquet for the righteous from the flesh of the leviathan. *Bava Bathra*, fol. 75, col. 1. (See the Morning Service for the middle days of the Feast of Tabernacles.) God will make a banquet for the righteous on the day when He shows His mercy to the posterity of Isaac. After the meal the cup of blessing will be handed to Abraham, in order that he may pronounce the blessing, but he will plead excuse because he begat Ishmael. Then Isaac will be told to take the cup and speak the benediction of grace, but he also will plead his unworthiness because he begat Esau. Next Jacob also will refuse because he married two sisters. Then Moses, on the ground that he was unworthy to enter the land of promise, or even to be buried in it; and finally Joshua will plead unworthiness because he had no son. David will then be called upon to take the cup and bless, and he will respond, "Yea, I will bless, for I am worthy to bless, as it is said (Ps. cxvi. 13), 'I will take the cup of salvation, and call upon the name of the Lord.'" P'sachim, fol. 119, col. 2. This cup, as we are told above, will contain two hundred and twenty-one logs (which the Rabbis tell us, is the twenty-fourth part of a seah, therefore this cup will hold rather more than one-third of a hogshead of wine).

Beruriah once found a certain disciple who studied in silence. As soon as she saw him she spurned him and said, "Is it not thus written (2 Sam. xxiii. 5), 'Ordered in all and sure'? If ordered with all the two hundred and forty-eight members of thy body, it will be sure; if not, it will not be sure." It is recorded that Rabbi Eliezer had a disciple who also studied in silence, but that after three years he forgot all that he had learned.

Eiruvin, fol. 53, col. 2, and fol. 54, col. 1.

In continuation of the above we read that Shemuel said to Rav Yehudah, "Shrewd fellow, open thy mouth when thou readest, etc., so that thy reading may remain and thy life may be lengthened; as it is written in Prov. iv. 22, 'For they are life unto those that find them;' read not, 'that find them,' but read, 'that bring them forth by the mouth,' *i. e.*, that read them aloud." It was and is still a common custom in the East to study aloud.

As an anathema enters all the two hundred and forty-eight members of the body, so does it issue from them all. Of the entering-in of the anathema it is written (Josh. vi. 17), "And the city shall be accursed;" by Gematria amounting to two hundred and forty-eight. Of the coming-out of the anathema it is written (Hab. iii. 2), "In wrath remember mercy;" a transposition of the letters of the word for accursed, also amounting by Gematria to two hundred and forty-eight. Rabbi Joseph says, "Hang an anathema on the tail of a dog and he will still go on doing mischief."

Moed Katon, fol. 17, col. 1.

The human body has two hundred and forty-eight members :— Thirty in the foot — that is, six in each toe — ten in the ankle, two in the thigh, five in the knee, one in the

hip, three in the hip-ball, eleven ribs, thirty in the hand —
that is, six in each finger — two in the fore-arm, two in the
elbow, one in the upper arm, four in the shoulder. Thus
we have one hundred and one on each side ; to this add
eighteen vertebræ in the spine, nine in the head, eight in
the neck, six in the chest, and five in the loins.

Oholoth, chap. 1, mish. 8.

See also Eiruvin, fol. 53, col. 2, and the Musaph for the second
day of Pentecost. In the Musaph for the New Year there is a prayer
that runs thus, "Oh, deign to hear the voice of those who glorify
Thee with all their members, according to the number of the two
hundred and forty-eight affirmative precepts. In this month they
blow thirty sounds, according to the thirty members of the soles of
their feet ; the additional offerings of the day are ten, according to
the ten in their ankles ; they approach the altar twice, according to
their two legs ; five are called to the law, according to the five
joints in their knees ; they observe the appointed time to sound
the cornet on the first day of the month, according to the one
in their thigh ; they sound the horn thrice, according to the three in
their hips ; lo ! with the additional offering of the new moon they are
eleven, according to their eleven ribs ; they pour out the supplication
with nine blessings, according to the muscles in their arms, and which
contain thirty verses, according to the thirty in the palms of their
hands ; they daily repeat the prayer of eighteen blessings, according
to the eighteen vertebræ in the spine ; at the offering of the continual sacrifice they sound nine times, according to the nine muscles
in their head," etc., etc.

It is related of Rabbi Ishmael's disciples that they dis-
sected a low woman who had been condemned by the Government to be burned, and upon examination they found that
her body contained two hundred and fifty-two members.

Bechoroth, fol. 45, col. 1.

The regular period of gestation is either two hundred
and seventy-one, two hundred and seventy-two, or two
hundred and seventy-three days. *Niddah*, fol. 38, col. 1.

Revere the memory of Chananiah ben Chiskiyah, for had
it not been for him the Book of Ezekiel would have been
suppressed, because of the contradictions it offers to the
words of the law. By the help of three hundred bottles of
oil, which were brought up into an upper chamber, he prolonged his lucubrations, till he succeeded in reconciling all
the discrepancies. *Shabbath*, fol. 13, col. 2.

It is related of Johanan, the son of Narbai, that he used to eat three hundred calves, and to drink three hundred bottles of wine, and to consume forty measures of young pigeons by way of dessert. (Rashi says this was because he had to train many priests in his house.)

P'sachim, fol. 57, col. 1.

The keys of the treasury of Korah were so many that it required three hundred white mules to carry them. These, with the locks, were said to be made of white leather.

Ibid., fol. 119, col. 1.

The Midrash repeats the same story, and adds, "His wealth was his ruin." "He is as rich as Korah" is now a Jewish proverb.

Rav Chiya, the son of Adda, was tutor to the children of Resh Lakish, and once absented himself from his duties for three days. On his return he was questioned as to the reason of his conduct, and he gave the following reply: "My father bequeathed to me a vine, trained on high trellis-work as a bower, from which I gathered the first day three hundred bunches, each of which yielded a gerav of wine (a gerav is a measure containing as much as 288 egg-shells would contain). On the second day I again gathered three hundred bunches of smaller size, two only producing one gerav (one bunch yielding the quantity of wine 144 egg-shells would contain). The third day I also gathered three hundred bunches, but only three bunches to the gerav, and have yet left more than half of the grapes free for any one to gather them." Thereupon Resh Lakish observed to him, "If thou hadst not been so negligent (losing time in the instruction of my children), it would have yielded still more." *Kethuboth*, fol. 111, col. 2.

There were three hundred species of male demons in Sichin, but what the female demon herself was like is known to no one. *Gittin*, fol. 68, col. 1.

"Now, when Job's three friends heard of all this evil that was come upon him, they came each from his own place; Eliphaz the Temanite, Bildah the Shuhite, and Zophar the Naamathite: for they had made an appointment together to come and mourn with him, and to comfort him" (Job ii. 11). What is meant when it is said, "They had made an appointment together"? Rab. Yehudah says in the name of Rav, "This is to teach that they all came in by one gate." But there is a tradition that each lived three hundred miles away from the other. How then came they to know of Job's sad condition? Some say they had wreaths, others say trees (each representing an absent friend), and when any friend was in distress the one representing him straightway began to wither. Rava said, "Hence the proverb, 'Either a friend as the friends of Job, or death.'" *Bava Bathra*, fol. 16, col. 2.

Rashi tenders this explanation, that Job and his friends had each wreaths with their names engraved on them, and if affliction befell any one his name upon the wreath would change color.

Rabbi Yochanan says that Rabbi Meir knew three hundred fables about foxes, but we have only three of them, viz, "The fathers have eaten sour grapes, and the children's teeth are set on edge" (Ezek. xviii. 2); "Just balances and just weights" (Lev. xix. 36); "The righteous is delivered out of trouble, and the wicked cometh in his stead" (Prov. xi. 8).

Sanhedrin, fol. 38, col. 2, and fol. 39, col. 1.

Quite apropos to this we glean the following from Rashi:— A fox once induced a wolf to enter a Jewish dwelling to help the inmates to get ready the Sabbath meal. No sooner did he enter than the whole household set upon him, and so belabored him with cudgels that he was obliged to flee for his life. For this trick the wolf was indignant at the fox, and sought to kill him, but he pacified him with the remark, "They would not have beaten thee if thy father had not on a former occasion belied confidence, and eaten up the choicest pieces that were set aside for the meal." "What!" rejoined the wolf, "the fathers have eaten sour grapes, and shall the children's teeth be set on edge?" "Well," interrupted the fox, "come with me now and I will show thee a place where thou mayest eat and be satisfied." He thereupon took him to a well, across the top of which rested a transverse axle with a rope coiled round it, to each extremity of which a bucket was attached. The fox, entering the bucket, which happened to be at the top, soon descended by his own weight to the bottom of the well, and thereby raised the other bucket to the top. On the wolf inquiring at the fox why he had gone down there, he replied, because he knew there was meat and cheese to eat and be satisfied, in proof of which he pointed to a cheese, which happened to be the reflection of the moon on the water. Upon which the wolf inquired, "And how am I to get down beside you?" The fox replied, "By getting into the bucket at the top." He did as directed, and as he descended the bucket with the fox rose to the top. The wolf in this plight again appealed to the fox. "But how am I to get out?" The reply was, "The righteous is delivered out of trouble, and the wicked cometh in his stead;" and is it not written, "Just balances just weights?"

When Rabbi Eliezer, on his deathbed, taught Rabbi Akiva three hundred particulars to be observed in regard to the white spot covered with hair which was the sign of leprosy, the former lifted up his arms and placed them on his chest and exclaimed, "Woe is me, because of these my two arms, these two scrolls of the law, that are about to depart from this world; for if all the seas were ink, and all the reeds were quills, and all the men were scribes, they could not record all I have learned and all I have taught, and how much I have heard at the lips of sages in the schools. And what is more, I also taught three hundred laws based on the text, 'A witch shall not live.'"

Avoth d'Rab. Nathan, chap. 25.

This truly Oriental exaggeration, which Rabbi Eliezer ben Azariah so complacently applies to himself, was spoken also of Rabbi Yochanan before him (Bereshith Rabba); an acrostic poem in the Morning Service for Pentecost adopts the same hyperbole almost word for word, and turns it to very pious account. It is interesting to note how contemporary sacred literature abounds in similar hyperbolic expressions. In John xxi 25 it is said, "There are also many other things which Jesus did, the which, if they should be written every one, I suppose that even the world itself could not contain the books that should be written." Cicero, too, speaks of a glory of such a weight that even heaven itself is scarcely able to contain it; and Livy, on one occasion, describes the power of Rome as with difficulty restrained within the limits of the world.

Here it may not be out of place if we introduce a few of the many passages in the Talmud that treat of enchantment and witchcraft, as well as magic, charms, and omens. The list of quotations might be extended to a hundred, but we must confine ourselves to a score or so.

The daughters of Israel burn incense for (purposes of) sorcery.   *Berachoth,* fol. 53, col. 1.

Ben Azai (son of impudence), says, " . . . he who seats himself and then feels . . . (which must not be explained), the effects of witchcraft, even when practiced in Spain, will come upon him. What is the remedy when one forgets and first sits down and then feels? . . . When he rises let him say, 'Not these and not of these; not the witchcraft of sorcerers and not the sorcery of witches.'"

Berachoth, fol. 62, col. 1.

The daughters of Israel in later generations lapsed into the practice of witchcraft. *Eiruvin* fol. 64, col. 2.

Ameimar says, "The superior of the witches told me that when a person meets any of them he should mutter thus, 'May a potsherd of boiling dung be stuffed into your mouths, you ugly witches! may the hair with which you perform your sorcery be torn from your heads, so that ye become bald. May the wind scatter the crumbs wherewith ye do your divinations. May your spices be scattered and may the wind blow away the saffron you hold in your hands for the practicing of sorcery.'"

P'sachim, fol. 110, cols. 1, 2.

Yohanna, the daughter of Ratibi, was a widow, who bewitched women in their confinement.

See Rashi on *Soteh*, fol. 22, col. 1.

Rabbi Shimon ben Gamliel, in the name of Rabbi Yehoshua, says, "Since the destruction of the Temple a day has not passed without a curse; the dew does not come down with a blessing, and the fruits have lost their proper taste." Rabbi Yossi adds, "Also the lusciousness of the fruit is gone." Rabbi Shimon ben Elazar says, "With the decay of purity the taste and aroma (of the fruit) has disappeared, and with the tithes and richness of the corn." The sages say, "Lewdness and witchcraft ruin everything."

Soteh, fol. 48, col. 1.

A certain magician used to strip the dead of their shrouds. Once when he came to the tomb of Rav Tovi bar Mathna he was seized and held fast by the beard, but Abaii having interceded on behalf of his friend, the grip was let go and he was set at liberty. Next year he came again on the same errand, and again he was seized by the beard. This time Abaii's intercession was of no avail, and he was not liberated until they brought a pair of scissors and cut off his beard. *Bava Bathra*, fol. 58, col. 1

None were allowed to sit in the Sanhedrin unless they had a knowledge of magic.   *Sanhedrin*, fol. 17, col. 1.

Rabbi Shimon said, "An enchanter is one who passeth the exudation of seven different sorts of male creatures over the eye." The sages say he is one who practices and palms off optical illusions. Rabbi Akiva says, "He is one who calculates times and hours, and says To-day is good to start on a journey, To-morrow will be a lucky day for selling, The year before the Sabbatical year is generally good for growing wheat, The pulling up of pease will preserve them from being spoiled." According to the Rabbis, "An enchanter is he who augurs ill when his bread drops from his mouth, or if he drops the stick that supports him from his hand, or if his son calls after him, or a crow caws in his hearing, or a deer crosses his path, or he sees a serpent at his right hand or a fox on his left, or if he says to the tax-gatherer, 'Do not begin with me the first in the morning'; or, 'It is the first of the month'; or, 'It is the exit of the Sabbath,' *i. e.*, the commencement of a new week."

Ibid., fol. 65, col. 2.

"By the term witch," the Rabbis say, "we are to understand either male or female." "If so," it is asked, "why the term 'witch,' in Exod. xxii. 18, in the Hebrew verse 17, is in the feminine gender?" "Because," it is answered, "most women are witches."   *Ibid.*, fol. 67, col. 1.

If the proud (in Israel) were to cease, the magicians would also cease; as it is written (Isa. i. 25), "I will purge away thy dross and take away all thy tin."

Ibid., fol. 98, col. 1.

Among those who have no portion in the world to come is he who reads the books of the strangers, foreign books, books of outsiders. See also Sanhedrin, fol. 90, col. 1. Now Rav Yoseph says, "It is unlawful to read the Book of the Son of Sirach, . . . because it is written therein (Ecclesiasticus xlii. 9, etc., as quoted, or rather misquoted, in the Talmud), 'A daughter is a false treasure to her father: because of anxiety for her he cannot sleep at night; when she is young, for fear she should be seduced; in her virginity lest she play the harlot; in her marriageable age, lest she should not get married ; and when married, lest she should be childless ; and when grown old, lest she practice witchcraft.' " *Sanhedrin*, fol. 100, col. 2.

He who multiplieth wives multiplieth witchcraft.

Avoth, chap. 2.

Most donkey-drivers are wicked, but most sailors are pious. The best physicians are destined for hell, the most upright butcher is a partner of Amalek. Bastards are mostly cunning, and servants mostly handsome. Those who are well-descended are bashful, and children mostly resemble their mother's brother. Rabbi Shimon ben Yochai bids us "kill the best of Gentiles" (modern editions qualify this by adding, in time of war), "and smash the head of the best of serpents." "The best among women," he says, "is a witch." Blessed is he who does the will of God !

Sophrim, chap. 15, hal. 10.

On the Sabbath one may carry a grasshopper's egg as a charm against earache, the tooth of a living fox to promote sleep, the tooth of a dead fox to prevent sleep, and the nail of one crucified (as a remedy) for inflammation or swelling. For cutaneous disorders he is to repeat Baz Baziah, Mass Massiah, Cass Cassiah, Sharlaii, and Amarlaii (names of angels), etc. . . . As the mules do not increase and multiply, so may the skin disease not increase and spread upon the body of N., the son of the woman N., etc. *Shabbath*, fol. 67, col. 1.

"For night-blindness, let a man take a hair-rope and bind one end of it to his own leg and the other to a dog's, then let children clatter a potsherd after him, and call out, 'Old man ! dog ! fool ! cock !' Let him now collect seven pieces of meat from seven (different) houses; let him set them on the cross-bar of the threshold, then let him eat them on the town middens ; and after that let him undo the hair-rope, then let him say thus: 'Blindness of So-and-so, son of Mrs. So-and-so, leave So-and-so, son of Mrs. So-and-so, and be brushed into the pupil of the eye of the dog.' " (Quoted from "The Fragment," by Rev. W. H. Lowe of Cambridge.) *Gittin*, fol. 69, col. 1.

According to the Rabbis, a man should not drink water by night, for thus he exposes himself to the power of Shavriri, the demon of blindness. What then should he do if he is thirsty? If there be another man with him, let him rouse him up and say, "I am thirsty;" but if he be alone, let him tap upon the lid of the jug (to make the demon fancy there's some one with him), and addressing himself by his own name and the name of his mother, let him say, "Thy mother has bid thee beware of Shavriri, vriri, riri, iri, ri," in a white cup. Rashi says by this incantation the demon gradually contracts and vanishes as the sounds of the word Shavriri decrease.

Avodah Zarah, fol. 12, col. 2.

A python is a familiar spirit who speaks from his armpits; a wizard is one who speaks with the mouth. As the Rabbis have taught, a familiar spirit is one who speaks from his joints and his wrists; a wizard is one who, putting a certain bone into his mouth, causes it to speak.

Sanhedrin, fol. 65, cols. 1, 2.

He who says to a raven "Croak," and to a hen raven, "Droop thy tail and turn it this way as a lucky sign," is an imitator of the ways of the Amorites (Lev. xviii. 3).

Shabbath, fol. 67, col. 2.

Women going out on the Sabbath-day are allowed, as the Rabbis teach, to carry with them a certain stone believed to counteract abortion.

Abaii interrupts his exposition of this Halachah in order to enumerate certain antidotes to chronic fever which, he says, he had learned from his mother. Take a new zouz and then procure its weight in sea-salt; hang this round the neck, suspended by a papyrus fibre, so that it may rest just in the hollow in front. If this does not answer, go where two or more roads meet and watch for the first big ant that is going home loaded; lay hold of it and place it in a brass tube; stop up the end of the tube with lead, putting as many seals upon it as possible; then shake it, saying the while, "My load be upon thee, and thine upon me." To this Rav Acha, the son of Rav Hunna, objected to Rav Ashi, and asked, "Might not the ant have been already laden with another man's fever?" "True," observed the other; "nevertheless let him say, 'My load be upon thee as well as thine own.'" If this be not effective, then take a new earthenware pot, and going to the nearest stream, say, "Stream, stream, lend me a pot full of water for one who is on a visit to me." Wave it seven times round thy head and then throw the water back again, saying, "Stream, stream, take back thy borrowed water for my guest came and went the same day."

Rav Hunna then adds a prescription for a tertian fever, and Rabbi Yochanan gives the following as effective against a burning fever:—Take an iron knife, and having fastened a papyrus fibre to the nearest bramble, cut off a piece and say, "And the Angel of the Lord appeared to him in a flame of fire," etc., as in Exod. iii. 2. On the morrow cut off another piece and say, "The Lord saw that he (the fever) turned aside;" then upon the third day say, "Draw not hither," and stooping down, pray, "Bush, bush! the Holy One—blessed be He!—caused His Shechinah to lodge upon thee, not because thou art the loftiest, for thou art the lowest of all trees; and as when thou didst see the fire of Hananiah, Mishael, and Azariah, thou didst flee therefrom, so see the fire (fever) of this sufferer and flee from it."   *Shabbath*, fol. 66, col. 2, etc.

Rabba once created a man (out of dust) and sent him to Rabbi Zira, who having addressed the figure and received no answer, said, "Thou art (made) by witchcraft; return to thy native dust." Rav Chaneanah and Rav Oshayah sat together every Sabbath-eve studying the book Yetzirah (*i. e.*, the book of Creation), until they were able to create for themselves a calf (as large as a) three-year old, and they did eat thereof.   *Sanhedrin*, fol. 65, col, 2.

Yannai once turned in to a certain inn, and asked for water to drink, when they gave him (Shethitha, *i. e.*, water mixed with flour). He noticed that the lips of the woman who brought it moved (and so suspecting that something was wrong), he poured out a little of it and it became scorpions. He then said, "I have drunk of thine, now thou shalt drink of mine." The woman drank and

13

was transformed into an ass, which he mounted and rode to the market-place. One of her companions having come up, broke the spell, and the ass he had ridden was on the spot transformed back again into a woman. In reference to the above, Rashi naïvely remarks that "we are not to suppose that Yannai was a Rabbi, for he was not held in esteem, because he practiced witchcraft." But Rashi is mistaken ; see Sophrim, chap. 16, hal. 6.

Sanhedrin, fol. 67, col. 2.

Ten measures of witchcraft came into the world ; Egypt received nine measures, and the rest of the world one.

Kiddushin, fol. 49, col. 2.

The Rabbis say that on the Sabbath serpents and scorpions may be tamed by charming ; that a metal ring, such as may be carried on the Sabbath, may be applied as a remedy to a sore eye ; but that demons may not be consulted on that day about lost property. Rabbi Yossi has said, "This ought not to be done even on week-days." Rav Hunna says, "The Halachah does not enjoin as Rabbi Yossi says, and even he prohibits it only because of the risk there is in consulting demons. For instance, Rav Yitzchak bar Yoseph was once desperately delivered from the attacks of a vicious demon by a cedar-tree opening of its own accord and enclosing him in its trunk."

Sanhedrin, fol. 101, col. 1.

Rabbi Yochanan ben Zachai acquired a knowledge of the language of angels and demons for purposes of incantation.

Bava Bathra, fol. 134, col. 1.

"Neither shall ye use enchantments" . . . (Lev. xix. 26). Such, for instance, as those practiced with cats, fowls, and fishes.   *Sanhedrin*, fol. 66, col. 1.

Rav Ketina happened once, in his travels, to hear the noise of an earthquake just as he came opposite to the abode of one who was wont to conjure with human bones. Happening to mutter aloud to himself as he passed, "Does the conjurer really know what that noise is ?" a voice answered, "Ketina, Ketina, why shouldn't I know ? When the Holy One — blessed be He ! — thinks of His children who dwell in sorrowful circumstances among the nations of the earth, He lets fall two tears into the great sea, and His voice is heard from one end of the world to the other, and that is the rumbling noise we hear." Upon which Rav Ketina protested, "The conjurer is a liar, his words are not true; they might have been true, had there been two rumbling noises." The fact was, two such noises were heard, but Rav Ketina would not acknowledge it, lest, by so doing, he should increase the popularity of the conjurer. Rav Ketina is of the opinion that the rumbling noise is caused by God clapping His hands together, as it is said (Ezek. xxi. 22 ; A. V., ver. 17), "I will also smite My hands together, and I will cause My fury to rest."

Berachoth, fol. 59, col. 1.

Rabbi Elazar ben Azariah proclaimed this anathema with the blast of three hundred trumpets: — "Whoever shall take drink from the hand of a bride, no matter whether she be the daughter of a disciple of the wise or the daughter of an Amhaaretz, it is all one as if he drunk it from the hand of a harlot." Again, it is said, "He who receives a cup from the hands of a bride and drinks it therefrom, has no portion whatever in the world to come."

Tract Calah.

There was a place for collecting the ashes in the middle of the altar, and there were at times in it nearly as much as three hundred cors (equal to about 2830 bushels) of ashes. On Rava remarking that this must be an exaggeration, Rav Ammi said the law, the prophets, and the sages are wont to use hyperbolical language. Thus the law speaks of "Cities great and walled up to heaven" (Deut. i. 28) ; the prophets speak of "the earth rent with the sound of them" (1 Kings i. 40) ; the sages speak as above and also as follows. There was a golden vine at the entrance of the Temple, trailing on crystals, on which devotees who could used to suspend offerings of fruit and grape clusters. "It happened once," said Rabbi Elazer ben Rabbi Zadoc, "that three hundred priests were counted off to clear the vine of the offerings." *Chullin*, fol. 90, col. 2.

Three hundred priests were told off to draw the veil (of the Temple) aside; for it is taught that Rabbi Shimon ben Gamliel declared in the name of Rabbi Shimon the Sagan (or high priest's substitute), that the thickness of the veil was a handbreadth. It was woven of seventy-two cords, and each cord consisted of twenty-four strands. It was forty cubits long and twenty wide. Eighty-two myriads of damsels worked at it, and two such veils were made every year. When it became soiled, it took three hundred priests to immerse and cleanse it.   *Chullin.*

When Moses was about to enter Paradise he turned to Joshua and said, "If any doubtful matters remain, ask me now and I will explain them." To this Joshua replied, "Have I ever left thy side for an hour and gone away to any other? Hast thou not thyself written concerning me (Exod. xxxiii. 11), 'His servant Joshua, the son of Nun, a young man, departed not out of the Tabernacle?'" As a punishment for this pert reply, which must have distressed and confounded his master, Joshua's power of brain was immediately weakened, so that he forgot three hundred Halachahs, and seven hundred doubts sprang up to perplex him. All Israel then rose up to murder him, but the Holy One — blessed be He! — said unto him, "To teach thee the Halachahs and their explanation is impossible, but go and trouble them with work; as it is said (Josh. i. 1), 'Now after the death of Moses, the servant of the Lord, it came to pass that the Lord spake unto Joshua,'" etc.   *Temurah*, fol. 16, col. 1.

In the future God will assign to each righteous man three hundred and ten worlds as an inheritance; for it is said (Prov. viii. 21), "That I may cause those that love me to inherit substance, and I will fill their treasures." By Gematria equals three hundred and ten.

Sanhedrin, fol. 100, col. 1, and *Okitzin*, chap. 3, mish. 12.

An old woman once complained before Rav Nachman that the Head of the Captivity and certain Rabbis with him were enjoying themselves in her booth, which they had surreptitiously taken posession of and would not surrender, but Rav Nachman gave no heed to her remonstrance. Then she raised her voice and cried aloud, "A woman whose father had three hundred and eighteen slaves is now pleading before you, and you paying no heed to her!" Upon which Rav Nachman turned to his associates and said, "She is a bawling woman, but she has no right to claim the booth, only the value of its timber."

Succah, fol. 31, col. 1.

Elijah the Tishbite once said to Rav Yehudah, the brother of Rav Salla the Holy, "You ask why the Messiah does not come, even though it is just now the Day of Atonement." "And what," asked the Rabbi, "does the Holy One — blessed be He! — say to that?" "He says, 'Sin lieth at the door'" (Gen. iv. 7). "And what has Satan to say?" "He has no permission to accuse any one on the Day of Atonement." "How do we know this?" Ramma bar Chamma replied, "Satan by Gematria equals three hundred and sixty-four, therefore on that number of days only has he permission to accuse; but on the Day of Atonement (*i. e.*, the 365th day) he cannot accuse."

Yoma, fol. 20, col. 1.

Rav Yitzchak said, "What is the meaning of that which is written (Ps. cxl. 8), 'Grant not, O Lord, the desires of the wicked; further not his wicked device, lest they exalt themselves. Selah?'" It is the prayer of Jacob to the Lord of the universe that He would not grant to Esau, "the wicked, the desires of his heart." "Further not his wicked device," this refers to Germamia of Edom (*i. e.*, Rome), for if they (the Romans) were suffered to go forward they would destroy the whole world! Rav Chama bar Chanena said, "There are three hundred crowned heads in Germamia of Edom, and there are three hundred and sixty-five dukes in Babylon. These encounter each other daily, and one of them commits murder, and they strive to set up a king." *Meggillah*, fol. 6, col. 2.

In the great city (of Rome) there were three hundred and sixty-five streets, and in each street there were three hundred and sixty-five palaces, and in every one of these there were three hundred and sixty-five steps, each of which palaces contained sufficient store to maintain the whole world. *P'sachim*, fol. 118, col. 2.

There are three hundred and sixty-five negative precepts.

There were three hundred and ninety-four courts of law in Jerusalem, and as many synagogues; also the same number of high schools, colleges, and academies, and as many offices for public notaries.   *Kethuboth*, fol. 105, col. 1.

Rav Hunna had four hundred casks of wine which had turned into vinegar. On hearing of his misfortune, Rav Yehudah, the brother of Rav Salla the Holy, or, as some say, Rav Adda bar Ahavah, came and visited him, accompanied by the Rabbis. "Let the master," said they, "examine himself carefully." "What!" said he, "do you suppose me to have been guilty of wrong-doing?" "Shall we then," said they, "suspect the Holy One — blessed be He! — of executing judgment without justice?" "Well," said Rav Hunna, "if you have heard anything against me, don't conceal it." "It has been reported to us," said they, "that the master has withheld the gardener's share of the prunings." "What else, pray, did he leave me?" retorted Rav Hunna; "he has stolen all the produce of my vineyard." They replied, "There is a saying that whoever steals from a thief smells of theft." "Then," said he, "I hereby promise to give him his share." Thereupon, according to some, the vinegar turned to wine again; and, according to others, the price of vinegar rose to the price of wine.   *Berachoth*, fol. 5, col. 2.

Rav Adda bar Ahavah once saw a Gentile woman in the market-place wearing a red head-dress, and supposing that she was a daughter of Israel, he impatiently tore it off her head. For this outrage he was fined a fine of four hundred zouzim. He asked the woman what her name was, and she replied, "My name is Mathan." "Methun, Methun," he wittily rejoined, "is worth four hundred zouzim."

Ibid., fol. 20, col. 1.

Methun means patience and Mathan two hundred. The point lies either in the application of the term Methun, which means patience, as if to say, had he been so patient as to have first ascertained what the woman was, he would have saved his four hundred zouzim; or in the identity of the sound Mathan, *i. e.*, two hundred, which doubled, equals four hundred. This has long since passed into a proverb, and expresses the value of patience.

From the foregoing extract it would seem that it was not the fashion among Jewish females to wear head-dresses of a red color, as it was presumed to indicate a certain lightness on the part of the wearer; so Rav Adda in his pious zeal thought he was doing a good work in tearing it off from the head of the supposed Jewess. "Patience, patience is worth four hundred zouzim."

Custom among the Jews had then, as now, the force of religion. The Talmud says, "A man should never deviate from a settled custom. Moses ascended on high and did not eat bread (for there it is not the custom); angels came down to earth and did eat bread (for here it is the custom so to do)." Bava Metzia, fol. 86, col. 2.

In the olden time it was not the fashion for a Jew to wear black shoes (Taanith, fol. 22, col. 1). Even now, in Poland, a pious Jew, or a Chasid, would on no account wear polished boots or a short coat, or neglect to wear a girdle. He would at once lose caste and be subjected to persecution, direct or indirect, were he to depart from a custom. Custom is law, is an oft-quoted Jewish proverb, one among the most familiar of their household words, as "Custom is a tyrant," is among ours. Another saying we have is, "Custom is the plague of wise men, but is the idol of fools."

The following anecdotes are related by way of practically illustrating Ps. ii. 11, "Rejoice with trembling." Mar, the son of Ravina, made a grand marriage-feast for his son, and when the Rabbis were at the height of their merriment on the occasion, he brought in a very costly cup, worth four hundred zouzim, and broke it before them, and this occasioned them sorrow and trembling. Rav Ashi made a grand marriage-feast for his son, and when he noticed the Rabbis in high jubilation, he brought in a costly cup of white glass and broke it before them, and this made them sorrowful. The Rabbis challenged Rav Hamnunah on the wedding of his son Ravina, saying, "Give us a song, sir," and he sung, "Woe be to us, for we must die! Woe be to us, for we must die!" "And what shall we sing?" they asked in chorus by way of response. He replied, "Sing ye, 'Alas! where is the law we have studied? where the good works we have done? that they may protect us from the punishment of hell!'" Rabbi Yochanan, in the name of Rabbi Shimon ben Yochai, says, "It is unlawful for a man to fill his mouth with laughter in this world, for it is said in Ps. cxxvi., 'Then (but not now) will our mouth be filled with laughter,'" etc. It is related of Resh Lakish that he never

once laughed again all the rest of his life from the time
that he heard this from Rabbi Yochanan, his teacher.

Berachoth, fol. 30, col. 2, and fol. 31, col. 1.

A man once laid a wager with another that he would
put Hillel out of temper. If he succeeded he was to receive, but if he failed he was to forfeit, four hundred
zouzim. It was close upon Sabbath-eve, and Hillel was
washing himself, when the man passed by his door, shouting, "Where is Hillel? where is Hillel?" Hillel wrapped
his mantle round him and sallied forth to see what the
man wanted. "I want to ask thee a question," was the reply. "Ask on, my son," said Hillel. Whereupon the
man said, "I want to know why the Babylonians have
such round heads?" "A very important question, my son,"
said Hillel; "the reason is because their midwives are not
clever." The man went away, but after an hour he returned, calling out as before, "Where is Hillel? where is
Hillel?" Hillel again threw on his mantle and went out,
meekly asking, "What now, my son?" "I want to know,"
said he, "why the people of Tadmor are weak-eyed?"
Hillel replied, "This is an important question, my son,
and the reason is this, they live in a sandy country."
Away went the man, but in another hour's time he returned as before, crying out, "Where is Hillel? where is
Hillel?" Out came Hillel again, as gentle as ever, blandly
requesting to know what more he wanted. "I have a question to ask," said the man. "Ask on, my son," said
Hillel. "Well, why have the Africans such broad feet?"
said he. "Because they live in a marshy land," said
Hillel. "I have many more questions to ask," said the
man, "but I am afraid that I shall only try thy patience
and make thee angry." Hillel, drawing his mantle around
him, sat down and bade the man ask all the questions he
wished. "Art thou Hillel," said he, "whom they call a
prince in Israel?" "Yes," was the reply. "Well," said
the other, "I pray there may not be many more in Israel
like thee!" "Why," said Hillel, "how is that?" "Because," said the man, "I have betted four hundred zouzim
that I could put thee out of temper, and I have lost them
all through thee." "Be warned for the future," said

Hillel; "better it is that thou shouldst lose four hundred zouzim, and four hundred more after them, than it should be said of Hillel he lost his temper!"

Shabbath, fol. 31, col. 1.

Rabbi Perida had a pupil to whom he had to rehearse a lesson four hundred times before the latter comprehended it. One day the Rabbi was hurriedly called away to perform some charitable act, but before he went he repeated the lesson in hand the usual four hundred times, but this time his pupil failed to learn it. "What is the reason, my son," said he to his dull pupil, "that this time my repetitions have been thrown away?" "Because, master," naïvely replied the youth, "my mind was so pre-occupied with the summons you received to discharge another duty." "Well, then," said the Rabbi to his pupil, "let us begin again." And he repeated the lesson a second four hundred times. *Eiruvin*, fol. 54, col. 2.

Between Azel and Azel (1 Chron. viii. 38 and ix. 44), there are four hundred camel-loads of critical researches due to the presence of manifold contradictions.

P'sachim, fol. 62, col. 2.

Egypt has an area of four hundred square miles.

Ibid., fol. 94, col. 1.

The Targum of the Pentateuch was executed by Onkelos the proselyte at the dictation of Rabbi Eliezer and Rabbi Yehoshua, and the Targum of the prophets was executed by Jonathan ben Uzziel at the dictation of Haggai, Zachariah, and Malachi (!), at which time the land of Israel was convulsed over an area of four hundred square miles.

Meggillah, fol. 3, col. 1.

Mar Ukva was in the habit of sending on the Day of Atonement four hundred zouzim to a poor neighbor of his. Once he sent the money by his own son, who returned bringing it back with him, remarking, "There is no need to bestow charity upon a man who, as I myself have seen, is able to indulge himself in expensive old wine." "Well," said his father, "since he is so dainty in his taste, he must have seen better days. I will therefore double the amount

for the future." And this accordingly he at once remitted
to him.   *Kethuboth*, fol. 67, col. 2.

"And Joseph took an oath of the children of Israel,
. . . ye shall carry up my bones from hence" (Gen.
l. 25). Rabbi Chanena said, "There is a reason for this
oath. As Joseph knew that he was perfectly righteous,
why then, if the dead are to rise in other countries as well
as in the land of Israel, did he trouble his brethren to
carry his bones four hundred miles?" The reply is, "He
feared lest, if buried in Egypt, he might have to worm his
way through subterranean passages from his grave into the
land of Israel."   *Ibid.*, fol. 111, col. 1.

To this day among the Polish Jews the dead are provided for their
long subterranean journey with little wooden forks, with which, at the
sound of the great trumpet, they are to dig and burrow their way
from where they happen to be buried till they arrive in Palestine.
To avoid this inconvenience there are some among them who, on
the approach of old age, migrate to the Holy Land, that their bones
may rest there against the morning of the resurrection.

Rav Cahana was once selling ladies' baskets when he was
exposed to the trial of a sinful temptation. He pleaded
with his tempter to let him off and he promised to return,
but instead of doing so he went up to the roof of the house
and threw himself down headlong. Before he reached the
ground, however, Elijah came and caught him, and re-
proached him, as he caught him up, with having brought him
a distance of four hundred miles to save him from an act
of willful self-destruction. The Rabbi told him that it was
his poverty which had given to the temptation the power
of seduction. Thereupon Elijah gave him a vessel full of
gold denarii and departed.   *Kiddushin*, fol. 40, col. 1.

"Pashur, the son of Immer the priest" (Jer. xx. 1) had four
hundred servants, and every one of them rose to the rank of
the priesthood. One consequence was that an insolent priest
hardly ever appeared in Israel but his genealogy could be
traced to this base-born, low-bred ancestry. Rabbi Elazar
said, "If thou seest an impudent priest, do not think evil
of him, for it is said (Hos. iv. 4), 'Thy people are as
they that strive with the priest.'" *Ibid.*, fol. 70, col. 2.

David had four hundred young men, handsome in appearance and with their hair cut close upon their foreheads, but with long flowing curls behind, who used to ride in chariots of gold at the head of the army. These were men of power (men of the fist, in the original), the mighty men of the house of David, who went about to strike terror into the world. *Kiddushin*, fol. 76, col. 2.

Four hundred boys and as many girls were once kidnapped and torn from their relations. When they learned the purpose of their capture, they all exclaimed, "Better drown ourselves in the sea; then shall we have an inheritance in the world to come." The eldest then explained to them the text (Ps. lxviii. 22), "The Lord said, I will bring again from Bashan; I will bring again from the depths of of the sea." "From Bashan," *i. e.*, from the teeth of the lion; "from the depths of the sea," *i. e.*, those that drown themselves in the sea. When the girls heard this explanation they at once jumped all together into the sea, and the boys with alacrity followed their example. It is with reference to these that Scripture says (Ps. xliv. 22), "For thy sake we are killed all the day long; we are counted as sheep for the slaughter." *Gittin*, fol. 57, col. 2.

There were four hundred synagogues in the city of Byther, in each there were four hundred elementary teachers, and each had four hundred pupils. When the enemy entered the city they pierced him with their pointers; but when at last the enemy overpowered them, he wrapped them in their books and then set fire to them; and this is what is written (Lam. iii. 51), "Mine eye affecteth my heart because of all the daughters of my city." *Ibid.*, fol. 58, col 1.

The total population of Byther must have been something enormous when the children in it amounted to 64,000,000! The elementary teachers alone came to 160,000.

Once when the Hasmonean kings were engaged in civil war it happened that Hyrcanus was outside Jerusalem and Aristobulus within. Every day the besieged let down a box containing gold denarii, and received in return lambs for the daily sacrifices. There chanced to be an old man in the city who was familiar with the wisdom of the Greeks, and he hinted to the besiegers in the Greek language that so long as the Temple services were kept up the city could not be taken. The next day accordingly, when the money had been let down, they sent back a pig in return. When about half-way up the animal pushed with its feet against the stones of the wall, and thereupon an earthquake was felt throughout the land of Israel to the extent of four hundred miles. At that time it was the saying arose, "Cursed be he that rears swine, and he who shall teach his son the wisdom of the Greeks." (See Matt. viii. 30.)

Soteh, fol. 49, col. 2.

If one strikes his neighbor with his fist, he must pay him one sela ; if he slaps his face, he is to pay two hundred zouzim ; but for a back-handed slap the assailant is to pay four hundred zouzim. If he pulls the ear of another, or plucks his hair, or spits upon him, or pulls off his mantle, or tears a woman's head-dress off in the street, in each of these cases he is fined four hundred zouzim.

Bava Kama, fol. 90, col. 1.

There was once a dispute between Rabbi Eliezer and the Mishnic sages as to whether a baking-oven, constructed from certain materials and of a particular shape, was clean or unclean. The former decided that it was clean, but the latter were of a contrary opinion. Having replied to all the objections the sages had brought against his decision, and finding that they still refused to acquiesce, the Rabbi turned to them and said, "If the Halacha (the law) is according to my decision, let this carob-tree attest." Whereupon the carob-tree rooted itself up and transplanted itself to a distance of one hundred, some say four hundred, yards from the spot. But the sages demurred and said, "We cannot admit the evidence of a carob-tree." "Well, then," said Rabbi Eliezer, "let this running brook be a proof ; " and the brook at once reversed its natural course and flowed back. The sages refused to admit this proof also. "Then let the walls of the college bear witness that the law is according to my decision ; " upon which the walls began to bend, and were about to fall, when Rabbi Joshuah interposed and rebuked them, saying, "If the disciples of the sages wrangle with each other in the Halacha, what is that to you? Be ye quiet!" Therefore, out of respect to Rabbi Joshuah, they did not fall, and out of respect to Rabbi Eliezer they did not resume their former upright position, but remained toppling, which they continue to do to this day. Then said Rabbi Eliezer to the sages, "Let Heaven itself testify that the Halacha is according to my judgment." And a Bath Kol or voice from heaven was heard, saying, "What have ye to do with Rabbi Eliezer? for the Halacha is on every point according to his decision!" Rabbi Joshuah then stood up and proved from Scripture that even a voice from heaven was not to be regarded, "For Thou, O God, didst long ago write down in the law which Thou gavest on Sinai (Exod. xxiii. 2), 'Thou shalt follow the multitude.'" (See context.) We have it on the testimony of Elijah the prophet, given to Rabbi Nathan, on an oath, that it was with reference to this dispute about the oven God himself confessed and said, "My children have vanquished me! My children have vanquished me!"   *Bava Metzia*, fol. 59, col. 1.

In the sequel to the above we are told that all the legal documents of Rabbi Eliezer containing his decisions respecting things "clean" were publicly burned with fire, and he himself excommunicated. In consequence of this the whole world was smitten with blight, a third in the olives, a third in the barley, and a third in the wheat; and the Rabbi himself, though excommunicated, continued to be held in the highest regard in Israel.

The Rabbis said to Rabbi Hamnuna, "Rav Ami has written or copied four hundred copies of the law." He replied to them, "Perhaps only (Deut. xxxiii. 4) 'Moses commanded us a law.'" (He meant he did not imagine that any one man could possibly write out four hundred complete copies of the Pentateuch.)

Bava Bathra, fol. 14, col. 1.

Rabbi Chanena said, "If four hundred years after the destruction of the Temple one offers thee a field worth a thousand denarii for one denarius, don't buy it."

Avodah Zarah, fol. 9, col. 2.

We know by tradition that the treatise "Avodah Zarah," which our father Abraham possessed, contained four hundred chapters, but the treatise as we now have it contains only five.   *Avodah Zarah*, fol. 14, col. 2.

The camp of Sennacherib was four hundred miles in length.   *Sanhedrin*, fol. 95, col. 2.

"Curse ye Meroz," etc. (Judges v. 23). Barak excommunicated Meroz at the blast of four hundred trumpets (lit. horns or cornets).   *Shevuoth*, fol. 36, col. 1.

What is the meaning where it is written (Ps. x. 27), "The fear of the Lord prolongeth days, but the years of the wicked shall be shortened;" "The fear of the Lord prolongeth days" alludes to the four hundred and ten years the first Temple stood, during which period the succession of high priests numbered only eighteen. But "the years of the wicked shall be shortened" is illustrated by the fact that during the four hundred and twenty years that the second Temple stood the succession of high priests numbered more than three hundred. If we deduct the forty years during which Shimon the Righteous held office, and the eighty of Rabbi Yochanan, and the ten of Rabbi Ishmael ben Rabbi, it is evident that not one of the remaining high priests lived to hold office for a whole year.   *Yoma*, fol. 9, col. 1.

"The souls which they had gotten in Haran" (Gen. xii. 5). From this time to the giving of the law was four hundred and forty-eight years.
Avodah Zarah, fol. 9, col. 1.

A young girl and ten of her maid-servants were once kidnapped, when a certain Gentile bought them and brought them to his house. One day he gave a pitcher to the child and bade her fetch him water, but one of her servants took the pitcher from her, intending to go instead. The master, observing this, asked the maid why she did so. The servant replied, "By the life of thy head, my lord, I am one of no less than five hundred servants of this child's mother." The master was so touched that he granted them all their freedom.   *Avoth d'Rab. Nathan*, chap. 17.

Cæsar once said to Rabbi Yoshua ben Chananja, "This God of yours is compared to a lion, as it is written (Amos

iii. 8), 'The lion hath roared, who will not fear?' Wherein consists his excellency? A horseman kills a lion." The Rabbi replied, "He is not compared to an ordinary lion, but to a lion of the forest Ilaei." "Show me that lion at once," said the Emperor. "But thou canst not behold him," said the Rabbi. Still the Emperor insisted on seeing the lion; so the Rabbi prayed to God to help him in his perplexity. His prayer was heard; the lion came forth from his lair and roared, upon which, though it was four hundred miles away, all the walls of Rome trembled and fell to the ground. Approaching three hundred miles nearer, he roared again, and this time the teeth of the people dropped out of their mouths and the Emperor fell from his throne quaking. "Alas! Rabbi, pray to thy God that He order the lion back to his abode in the forest."

Chullin, fol. 59, col. 2.

All this is as nothing compared to the voice of Judah, which made all Egypt quake and tremble, and Pharaoh fall from his throne headlong, etc., etc. See Jasher, chap. 64, verses 46, 47.

The distance from the earth to the firmament is five hundred years' journey, and so it is from each successive firmament to the next, throughout the series of the seven heavens. *P'sachim*, fol. 94, col. 2.

"Now, as I beheld the living creatures, behold, one wheel upon the earth by the living creatures" (Ezek. i. 15). Rabbi Elazar says it was an angel who stood upon the earth, and his head reached to the living creatures. It is recorded in a Mishna that his name is Sandalphon, who towers above his fellow-angels to a height of five hundred years' journey; he stands behind the chariot and binds crowns on the head of his Creator. *Chaggigah*, fol. 13, col. 2.

In the Liturgy for the Feast of Tabernacles it is said that Sandalphon gathers in his hands the prayers of Israel, and, forming a wreath of them, he adjures it to ascend as an orb for the head of the supreme King of kings.

The mount of the Temple was five hundred yards square.
Middoth, chap. 2.

One Scripture text (1 Chron. xxi. 25) says, "So David gave to Ornan for the place six hundred shekels of gold by weight." And another Scripture (2 Sam. xxiv. 24) says, "So David bought the threshing-floor and the oxen for fifty shekels of silver." How is this? David took from each tribe fifty shekels, and they made together the total six hundred, *i. e.*, he took silver to the value of fifty shekels of gold.   *Zevachim*, fol. 116, col. 2.

Rabbi Samlai explains that six hundred and thirteen commandments were communicated to Moses; three hundred and sixty-five negative, according to the number of days in the year, and two hundred and forty-eight positive, according to the number of members in the human body. Rav Hamnunah asked what was the Scripture proof for this. The reply was (Deut. xxxiii. 4), "Moses commanded us a law" (Torah), which by Gematria answers to six hundred and eleven. "I am," and "Thou shalt have no other," which we heard from the Almighty Himself, together make up six hundred and thirteen.   *Maccoth*, fol. 23, col. 2.

David, we are told, reduced these commandments here reckoned at six hundred and thirteen, to eleven, and Isaiah still further to six, and then afterward to two. "Thus saith the Eternal, Observe justice and act righteously, for my salvation is near." Finally came Habakkuk, and he reduced the number to one all-comprehensive precept (chap. ii. 4), "The just shall live by faith." (See *Maccoth*, fol. 24, col. 1.)

The precept concerning fringes is as weighty as all the other precepts put together; for it is written, says Rashi (Num. xv. 39), "And remember all the commandments of the Lord." Now the numerical value of the word "fringes" is six hundred, and this with eight threads and five knots makes six hundred and thirteen.

Shevuoth, fol. 29, col. 1.

"For behold, the Lord, the Lord of hosts, doth take away from Jerusalem and from Judah the stay and the staff, the whole stay of bread and the whole stay of water, the mighty man and the man of war, the judge and the prophet," etc. (Isa. iii. 1, 2). By "the stay" is meant men mighty in the Scriptures, and by "the staff" men learned in the Mishna; such, for instance, as Rabbi Yehudah ben Tima and his associates. Rav Pappa and the Rabbis differed as to the Mishna; the former said there were six hundred orders of the Mishna, and the latter that there were seven hundred orders. "The whole stay of bread" means men distinguished in the Talmud; for it is said, "Come, eat of my bread, and drink of the wine which I have mingled" (Prov. ix. 5). And "the whole stay of water" means men skillful in the Haggadoth, who draw out the heart of man like water by means of a pretty story or legend, etc.

Chaggigah, fol. 14, col. 1.

There are seven hundred species of fish, eight hundred of locusts, twenty-four of birds that are unclean, while the species of birds that are clean cannot be numbered.

Chullin, fol. 63, col. 2.

"The same was Adino the Eznite," etc. (2 Sam. xxiii. 8). This mighty man when studying the law was as pliant as a worm; but when engaged in war he was as firm and unyielding as a tree; and when he discharged an arrow he killed eight hundred men at one shot.

Moed Katon, fol. 16, col. 2.

"Ye shall soon utterly perish from off the land" (Deut. iv. 26). The term soon uttered by the Lord of the Universe means eight hundred and fifty-two years.

Sanhedrin, fol. 38, col. 1.

There are nine hundred and three sorts of deaths in the world; for the expression occurs (Ps. lxviii. 20), "Issues of death." The numerical value of "issues" is nine hundred and three. The hardest of all deaths is by quinsy, and the easiest is the Divine kiss (of which Moses, Aaron, and Miriam died). Quinsy is like the forcible extraction of prickly thorns from wool, or like a thick rope drawn through a small aperture; the kiss referred to is like the extracting of a hair from milk.

Berachoth, fol. 8, col. 1.

When Moses went up on high, the ministering angels asked, "What has one born of a woman to do among us?" "He has come to receive the law," was the Divine answer. "What!" they remonstrated again, "that cherished treasure which has lain with Thee for nine hundred and seventy-four generations before the world was created, art Thou about to bestow it upon flesh and blood? What is mortal man

14

that Thou art mindful of him, and the son of earth that
Thou thus visitest him?   O Lord! our Lord! is not Thy
name already sufficiently exalted in the earth? Confer Thy
glory upon the heavens" (Ps. viii. 4, 6).   The Holy One
— blessed be He! — then called upon Moses to refute the
objection of the envious angels.   "I fear," pleaded he,
"lest they consume me with the fiery breath of their
mouth." Thereupon, by way of protection, he was bid approach and lay hold of the throne of God; as it is said
(Job xxvi. 9), "He lays hold of the face of His throne
and spreads His cloud over him."   Thus encouraged, Moses
went over the Decalogue, and demanded of the angels
whether they had suffered an Egyptian bondage and dwelt
among idolatrous nations, so as to require the first commandment; or were they so hardworked as to need a day
of rest, etc., etc.   Then the angels at once confessed that
they were wrong in seeking to withhold the law from
Israel, and they then repeated the words, "O Lord, how
excellent is Thy name in all the earth!" (Ps. viii. 9),
omitting the words, "Confer Thy glory upon the heavens."
And not only so, but they positively befriended Moses, and
each of them revealed to him some useful secret; as it is
said (Ps. lxviii. 18), "Thou hast ascended on high, thou
hast captured spoil, thou hast received gifts; because they
have contemptuously called thee man."

Shabbath, fol. 88, col. 2.

Nine hundred and seventy-four generations before the
world was created the law was written and deposited in
the bosom of the Holy One — blessed be He! — and sang
praises with the ministering angels.

Avoth d' Rab. Nathan, chap. 31.

If one is sick and at the point of death, he is expected
to confess, for all confess who are about to suffer the last
penalty of the law. When a man goes to the market
place, let him consider himself as handed over to the cus-
tody of the officers of judgment. If he has a headache,
let him deem himself fastened with a chain by the neck.
If confined to his bed, let him regard himself as mounting
the steps to be judged; for when this happens to him, he

is saved from death only if he have competent advocates, and these advocates are repentance and good works.
And if nine hundred and ninety-nine plead against him,
and only one for him, he is saved; as it is said (Job xxxiii.
23), "If there be an interceding angel, one among a thousand to declare for man his uprightness, then He is
gracious unto him and saith, Deliver him from going
down to the pit." *Shabbath*, fol. 32, col. 1.

Rav Hunna says, "A quarrel is like a breach in the
bank of a river; when it is once made it grows wider and
wider. . . . "A certain man used to go about and say,
"Blessed is he who submits to a reproach and is silent, for
a hundred evils depart from him." Shemuel said to Rav
Yehuda, "It is written in Scripture (Prov. xvii. 14), 'The
beginning of strife is as when one letteth out water.'"
Strife is the beginning of a hundred lawsuits.
Sanhedrin, fol. 7, col. 1.

When Solomon married the daughter of Pharaoh, she introduced to him a thousand different kinds of musical instruments, and taught him the chants to the various idols.
Shabbath, fol. 56, col. 2.

When Buneis, the son of Buneis, called on Rabbi (the
Holy), the latter exclaimed, "Make way for one worth a
hundred manahs!" Presently another visitor came, and
Rabbi said, "Make way for one worth two hundred manahs." Upon which Rabbi Ishmael, the son of Rabbi Yossi,
remonstrated, saying, "Rabbi, the father of the first-comer,
owns a thousand ships at sea and a thousand towns ashore!"
"Well," replied Rabbi, "when thou seest his father, tell
him to send his son better clad next time." Rabbi paid
great respect to those that were rich, and so did Rabbi
Akiva. *Eiruvin*, fol. 86, col. 1.

Rabbi Elazer ben Charsom inherited from his father a
thousand towns and a thousand ships, and yet he went
about with a leather sack of flour at his back, roaming from
town to town and from province to province in order to
study the law. This great Rabbi never once set eye on his
immense patrimony, for he was engaged in the study of the
law all day and all night long. And so strange was he to

his own servants, that they, on one occasion, not knowing
who he was, pressed him against his will to do a day's
work as a menial ; and though he pleaded with them as a
suppliant to be left alone to pursue his studies in the law,
they refused, and swore, saying, "By the life of Rabbi
Elazer ben Charsom, our master, we will not let thee go till
thy task is completed." He then let himself be enforced
rather than make himself known to them.

Yoma, fol. 35, col. 2.

The wife of Potiphar coaxed Joseph with loving words,
but in vain. She then threatened to immure him in prison,
but he replied (anticipating Ps. cxlvi. 7), "The Lord looseth
the prisoners." Then she said, "I will bow thee down with
distress ; I will blind thine eyes." He only answered (*ibid.*,
ver. 8), "The Lord openeth the eyes of the blind and
raiseth them that are bowed down." She then tried to
bribe him with a thousand talents of silver if he would
comply with her request, but in vain.   *Ibid.*

A Midrash tells us that Potiphar's wife not only falsely accused
Joseph herself, but that she also suborned several of her female friends
to do likewise. The Book of Jasher, which embodies the Talmudic
story quoted above, tells us that an infant in the cradle spoke up and
testified to Joseph's innocence, and that while Joseph was in prison
his inamorata daily visited him. More on this topic may be found in
the Koran, chap. xii. The amours of Joseph and Zulieka, as told by
the glib tongue of tradition, fitly find their consummation in marriage, and certain Moslems affect to see in all this an allegorical type
of Divine love, an allegory which some other divines find in the Song
of Solomon.

The thickness of the earth is a thousand paces or ells.

Succah, fol. 53, col. 2.

The crust of the earth as far as the abyss is a thousand ells, and
the abyss under the earth is fifteen thousand. There is an upper and a
lower abyss mentioned in Taanith, fol. 25, col. 2. Riddia, the angel
who has the command of the waters, and resides between the two
abysses, says to the upper, "disperse thy waters," and to the lower,
"let thy waters flow up."

Many may ask after thy peace, but tell thy secret only
to one of a thousand.   *Yevamoth*, fol. 63, col. 2.

The Rabbis have taught that if the value of stolen property is a thousand, and the thief is only worth, say, five

hundred, he is to be sold into slavery twice. But if the reverse, he is not to be sold at all.

Kiddushin, fol. 18, col. 2.

The Behemoth upon a thousand hills (Ps. l. 10), God created them male and female, but had they been allowed to propagate they would have destroyed the whole world. What did He do? He castrated the male and spayed the female, and then preserved them that they might serve for the righteous at the Messianic banquet; as it is said (Job xl. 16), "His strength is in his loins (*i. e.*, the male), and his force in the navel of his belly" (*i. e.*, the female).

Bava Bathra, fol. 74, col. 2.

This provision for the coming Messianic banquet is considered of sufficient importance to be mentioned year after year in the service for the Day of Atonement and also at the Feast of Tabernacles. The remark of D. Levi, that the feast here referred to is to be understood allegorically, involves rather sweeping consequences, as it is open to any one to annihilate many other expectations on the same principle.

The Holy One — blessed be He! — will add to Jerusalem gardens extending to a thousand times their numerical value, which equals one hundred and sixty-nine, etc.

Ibid., fol. 75, col. 2.

"Moreover Manasseh shed innocent blood very much" (2 Kings xxi. 16). Here (in Babylon) it is interpreted to mean that he murdered Isaiah, but in the West (*i. e.*, in Palestine) they say that he made an image of the weight of a thousand men, which was the number he massacred every day (as Rashi says, by the heaviness of its weight).

Sanhedrin, fol. 103, col. 2.

See Josephus, Antiq., Book X. chap. iii., sec. 1, for corroborative evidence. Tradition says that Manasseh caused Isaiah to be sawn asunder with a wooden saw. (See also Yevamoth, fol. 49, col. 2; Sanhedrin, fol. 103, col. 2.)

Nowhere in the Talmud do we find the name of the great image here referred to. What if we christen it the "Juggernaut of the Talmud"? May the tradition not be a prelusion or a reflex of that man-crushing monster? Anyhow, scholars are aware of a community of no inconsiderable extent between the conceptions and legends of the Hindoos and the Rabbis. One notable contrast, however, between this Juggernaut and that of the Hindoos is, that whereas in both cases the innocent suffered for the guilty, in the former the sacrifices were exacted to propitiate Satan, while in the latter they were freely offered in supposed propitiation of the gods.

The food consumed by Og, king of Bashan, consisted of a thousand oxen and as many of all sorts of other beasts, and his drink consisted of a thousand measures, etc.

Sophrim, chap. 21, mish. 9.

Solomon made ten candelabra for the Temple; for each he set aside a thousand talents of gold, which he refined in a crucible until they were reduced to the weight of one talent. *Menachoth*, fol. 29, col. 1.

There was an organ in the Temple which produced a thousand kinds of melody. *Eirchin*, fol. 11, col. 1.

The Magrepha, with its ten pipes and its ten-times-ten various notes (Eirchin, fol. 10, col. 2, and fol. 11, col. 1), which was said to have been used in the Temple service, must have been an instrument far superior to any organ in use at the time elsewhere.

If from a town numbering fifteen hundred footmen, such, for example, as the village of Accho, nine people be borne forth dead in the course of three successive days, it is a sure sign of the presence of the plague; but if this happen in one day or in four, then it is not the plague.

Taanith, fol. 21, col. 1.

Seventeen hundred of the arguments and minute rules of the Scribes were forgotten during the days of mourning for Moses. Othniel, the son of Kenaz, by his shrewd arguing restored them all as if they had never lapsed from the memory. *Temurah*, fol. 16, col. 1.

There was a great court at Jerusalem called Beth Yaazek, where all witnesses (who could testify to the time of the appearance of the new moon) used to assemble, and where they were examined by the authorities. Grand feasts were prepared for them as an inducement to them to come (and give in their testimony). Formerly they did not move from the place they happened to be in when overtaken by the Sabbath, but Rabbon Gamliel the elder ordained that they might in that case move two thousand cubits either way. *Rosh Hashanah*, fol. 21, col. 2.

He that is abroad (on the Sabbath) and does not know the limit of the Sabbath day's journey may walk two thousand moderate paces, and that is a Sabbath day's journey.   *Eiruvin*, fol. 42, col. 1.

Rabbon Gamliel had a hollow tube, through which, when he looked, he could distinguish a distance of two thousand cubits, whether by land or sea. By the same tube he could ascertain the depth of a valley or the height of a palm tree.   *Ibid.*, fol. 43, col. 2.

He who observes carefully the precepts respecting fringes will, as a reward, have two thousand eight hundred slaves to wait upon him ; for it is said (Zech. viii. 23), "Thus saith the Lord of hosts ; In those days it shall come to pass that ten men shall take hold out of all languages of the nations, even shall take hold of the skirt of him that is a Jew, saying, We will go with you, for we have heard that God is with you."   *Shabbath*, fol. 32, col. 2.

Rashi's explanation of this matter is very simple. The merit of the fringes lies in their being duly attached to "the four quarters" or skirts of the garments (Deut. xxii. 12). There are seventy nations in the whole world, and ten of each nation will take hold of each corner of the garment, which gives $70 \times 10 \times 4 = 2800$. Rabbi B'chai, commenting on Num. xv. 39, 40, repeats the same story almost word for word.

This passage (Zech. viii. 23) has lately been construed by some into a prophecy of the recent Berlin Congress, and the ten men mentioned are found in the representatives of the contracting parties, *i. e.*, England, France, Germany, Turkey, Russia, Austria, Italy, Greece, Roumania, and Servia.

Rav Hamnunah said, "What is it that is written (1 Kings iv. 32), 'And he spoke three thousand proverbs, and his songs were a thousand and five'?" It is intended to teach that Solomon uttered three thousand proverbs upon each and every word of the law, and for every word of the Scribes he assigned a thousand and five reasons.
                                Eiruvin, fol. 21, col. 2.

When Rabbi Eliezer was sick he was visited by Rabbi Akiva and his party. . . . "Wherefore have ye come?" he asked. "To learn the law," was the reply. "And why did you not come sooner?" "Because we had no leisure," said they. "I shall be much surprised," said he, "if you die a natural death." Then turning to Rabbi Akiva he said, "Thy death shall be the worst of all." Then folding his arms upon his breast, he exclaimed: "Woe unto my two arms! for they are like two scrolls of the law rolled up, so that their contents are hidden. Had they waited upon me, they might have added much to their knowledge of the law, but now that knowledge will perish with me. I have in my time learned much and taught much, and yet I have no more diminished the knowledge of my Rabbis by what I have derived from them than the waters of the sea are reduced by a dog lapping them. Over and above this I expounded three hundred," some allege he said three thousand, "Halachahs with reference to the growing of Egyptian cucumbers, and yet no one except Akiva ben Yoseph has ever proposed a single question to me respecting them. He and I were walking along the road one day when he asked me to instruct him regarding the cultivation of Egyptian cucumbers. I made but one remark, when the entire field became full of them. Then at his request I made a remark about cutting them, when lo! they all collected themselves together in one spot." Thus Rabbi Eliezer kept on talking, when all of a sudden he fell back and expired. *Sanhedrin*, fol. 68, col. 1.

The last words of this eminent Rabbi derive a tragic interest from the fact that he died while under sentence of excommunication.

Three thousand Halachoth were forgotten at the time of mourning for Moses, and among them the Halachah respecting an animal intended for a sin-offering the owner of which died before sacrificing it.

Temurah, fol. 16, col. 1.

All the prophets were rich men. This we infer from the account of Moses, Samuel, Amos, and Jonah. Of Moses, as it is written (Num. xvi. 15), "I have not taken one ass from them." Of Samuel, as it is written (1 Sam. xii. 3), "Behold, here I am; witness against me before the Lord, and before His anointed, whose ox have I taken? or whose ass have I taken?" Of Amos, as it is written (Amos vii. 14), "I was an herdsman and a gatherer of sycamore fruit," *i. e.*, I am proprietor of my herds and own sycamores in the valley. Of Jonah, as it is written (Jonah i. 3), "So he paid the fare thereof and went down into it." Rabbi Yochanan says he hired the whole ship. Rabbi Rumanus says the hire of the ship amounted to four thousand golden denarii. *Nedarim*, fol. 38, col. 1.

Four thousand two hundred and thirty-one years after the creation of the world, if any one offers thee for one single denarius a field worth a thousand denarii, do not buy it.
Avodah Zarah, fol. 9, col. 2.

Rashi gives this as the reason of the prohibition : For then the restoration of the Jews to their own land will take place, so that the denarius paid for a field in a foreign land would be money thrown away.

Four thousand two hundred and ninety-one years after the creation of the world the wars of the dragons and the wars of Gog and Magog will cease, and the rest of the time will be the days of the Messiah ; and the Holy One — blessed be He ! — will not renew His world till after seven thousand years. . . . Rabbi Jonathan said, "May the bones of those who compute the latter days (when the Messiah shall appear) be blown ; for some say, 'Because the time (of Messiah) has come and Himself has not, therefore He will never come !' But wait thou for Him, as it is said (Hab. ii. 3), 'Though He tarry, wait for Him.' Perhaps you will say, 'We wait, but He does not wait ;' learn rather to say (Isa. xxx. 18), 'And therefore will the Lord wait, that He may be gracious unto you ; and therefore will He be exalted, that He may have mercy upon you.'"
Sanhedrin, fol. 97, col. 2.

It is related of Rabbi Tarphon (probably the Tryphon of polemic fame) that he was very rich, but gave nothing to the poor. Once Rabbi Akiva met him and said, "Rabbi, dost thou wish me to purchase for thee a town or two?" "I do," said he, and at once gave him four thousand gold denarii. Rabbi Akiva took this sum and distributed it among the poor. Some time after Rabbi Tarphon met Rabbi Akiva and said, "Where are the towns thou purchasedst for me?" The latter seized hold of him by the arm and led him to the Beth Hamedrash, where, taking up a psalter, they read together till they came to this verse, "He hath dispersed, he hath given to the poor, his righteousness endureth forever" (Ps. cxii. 9). Here Rabbi Akiva paused and said, "This is the place I purchased for thee," and Rabbi Tarphon saluted him with a kiss.   *Tract. Callah.*

The Pentateuch contains five thousand eight hundred and eighty-eight verses. The Psalms have eight verses more than, and the Chronicles eight verses short of, that number.
                              Kiddushin, fol. 30, col. 1.

The number of verses in the Pentateuch is usually stated at 5845, the mnemonic sign of which is a word in Isaiah xxx. 26, the letters of which stand for 5845. The verse reads, "Moreover, the light of the moon shall be as the light of the sun." The Masorites tell us that the number of verses in the Psalms is 2527, and in the two Books of Chronicles 1656.

The world is to last six thousand years. Two thousand of these are termed the period of disorder, two thousand belong to the dispensation of the law, and two thousand are the days of the Messiah; but because of our iniquities a large fraction of the latter term is already passed and gone without the Messiah giving any sign of His appearing.   *Sanhedrin*, fol. 97, col. 1.

As the land of Canaan had one year of release in seven, so has the world one millennium of release in seven thousand years; for it is said (Isa. ii. 17), "And the Lord alone will be exalted in that day;" and again (Ps. xcii. 1), "A psalm or song for the Sabbath day," which means a long Sabbatic period; and again (Ps. xc. 4), "For a thousand years in Thy sight are but as the day of yesterday."   *Ibid.*

Tradition records that the ladder (mentioned Gen. xxviii. 12) was eight thousand miles wide, for it is written, "And behold the angels of God ascending and descending upon it." Angels ascending, being in the plural, cannot be fewer than two at a time, and so likewise must those descending, so that when they passed they were four abreast at least. In Daniel x. 6 it is said of the angel,

"His body was like Tarshish," and there is a story that
Tarshish extended two thousand miles.

Chullin, fol. 91, col. 2.

The tithes from the herds of Elazer ben Azaryah
amounted to twelve thousand calves annually.

Shabbath, fol. 54, col. 2.

It is said that Rabbi Akiva had twelve thousand pairs of
disciples dispersed about between Gabbath and Antipatris,
and all of them died within a short period because
they paid no honor to one another. The land was then
desolate until Rabbi Akiva came among our Rabbis of the
south and taught the law to Rabbis Meir, Yehudah, Yossi,
Shimon, and Elazer ben Shamua, who re-established its
authority. *Yevamoth*, fol. 26, col. 2.

After a lapse of twelve years, he returned accompanied
by twelve thousand disciples, etc.

Ravah bar Nachmaini was impeached for depriving the
revenue of the poll-tax on twelve thousand Jews, by detaining them annually at his academy for one month in
the spring, and for another month in the autumn; for great
multitudes from various parts of the country were wont, at
the two seasons of the Passover and the Feast of Tabernacles, to come to hear him preach, so that when the
king's officers came to collect the taxes they found none of
them at home. A royal messenger was accordingly despatched to apprehend him, but he failed to find him, for
the Rabbi fled to Pumbeditha, and from thence to Akra,
to Agmi, Sichin, Zeripha, Ein d'Maya, and back again to
Pumbeditha. Arrived at this place, both the royal messenger and the fugitive Rabbi happened to put up at the same
inn. Two cups were placed before the former on a table,
when, strange to say, after he had drunk and the table
was removed, his face was forcibly turned round to his
back. (This was done by evil spirits because he drank
even numbers — against which we are earnestly warned in
P'sachim, fol. 110, col. 1.) The inn-keeper, fearing the
consequences of such a misfortune happening to so high
an official at his inn, sought advice of the lurking Rabbi,
when the latter suggested that the table be placed again

before him with one cup only on it, and thus the even number would become odd, and his face would return to its natural position. They did so, and it was as the Rabbi had said. The official then remarked to his host, "I know the man I want is here," and he hastened and found him. "If I knew for certain," he said to the Rabbi, "that thy escape would cost my life only, I would let thee go, but I fear bodily torture, and therefore I must secure thee." And thereupon he locked him up. Upon this the Rabbi prayed, till the prison walls miraculously giving way he made his escape to Agma, where he seated himself at the root of a tree and gave himself up to meditation. While thus engaged he all at once heard a discussion in the academy of heaven on the subject of the hair mentioned in Lev. xiii. 25. The Holy One — blessed be He ! — declared the case to be " clean," but the whole academy were of a different opinion, and declared the case to be " unclean." The question then arose, " Who shall decide ? " " Ravah bar Nachmaini shall decide," was the unanimous reply, " for he said, 'I am one in matters of leprosy ; I am one in questions about tents ; and there is none to equal me.' " Then the angel of death was sent for to bring him up, but he was unable to approach him, because the Rabbi's lips never ceased repeating the law of the Lord. The angel of death thereupon assumed the appearance of a troop of cavalry, and the Rabbi, apprehesive of being seized and carried off, exclaimed, " I would rather die through that one (meaning the angel of death) than be delivered into the hands of the Government ! " At that very instant he was asked to decide the question in dispute, and just as the verdict " clean " issued from his lips his soul departed from his body, and a voice was heard from heaven proclaiming, " Blessed art thou, Ravah bar Nachmaini, for thy body is clean. 'Clean' was the word on thy lips when thy spirit departed." Then a scroll fell down from heaven into Pumbeditha announcing that Ravah bar Nachmaini was admitted into the academy of heaven. Apprised of this, Abaii, in company with many other Rabbis, went in search of the body to inter it, but not knowing the spot where he lay, they went to Agma, where they noticed a

great number of birds hovering in the air, and concluded
that the shadow of their wings shielded the body of the
departed.   There, accordingly, they found and buried him ;
and after mourning three days and three nights over his
grave, they arose to depart, when another scroll descended
threatening them with excommunication if they did so.
They therefore continued mourning for seven days and
seven nights, when, at the end of these, a third scroll descended and bade them go home in peace.   On the day of
the death of this Rabbi there arose, it is said, such a mighty
tempest in the air that an Arab merchant and the camel
on which he was riding were blown bodily over from one
side of the river Pappa to the other.   "What meaneth such
a storm as this?" cried the merchant, as he lay on the
ground.   A voice from heaven answered, "Ravah bar
Nachmaini is dead."   Then he prayed and fled, "Lord of
the universe, the whole world is Thine, and Ravah bar
Nachmaini is Thine !   Thou art Ravah's and Ravah is
Thine ;   but wherefore wilt Thou destroy the world?"   On
this the storm immediately abated, and there was a perfect
calm.   *Buva Metzia*, fol. 86, col. 1.

The above seems to be a Rabbinical satire on the Talmud itself
although the orthodox Jews believe that every word in it is historically
true.   Well, perhaps it is so ; and we outsiders are ignorant, and
without the means of judging.

Now we know what God does during the day, but how
does He occupy Himself in the night-time?   We may say
He does the same as at day-time ; or that during the
night He rides on a swift cherub over eighteen thousand
worlds; as it is said (Ps. lxviii. 17), "The chariots of
God are twenty thousand," less two thousand Shinan ; read
not Shinan but She-einan, *i.e.*, two thousand less than
twenty thousand, therefore eighteen thousand.
                    Avodah Zarah, fol. 3. col. 2.

Prince Contrukos asked Rabbon Yochanan ben Zacchai
how, when the detailed enumeration of the Levites amounted
to twenty-two thousand three hundred (the Gershonites,
7500 ; the Kohathites, 8600 ; the Merarites, 6200, making
in all 22,300), the sum total given is only twenty-two

thousand, omitting the three hundred. "Was Moses, your Rabbi," he asked, "a cheat or a bad calculator?" He answered, "They were first-borns, and therefore could not be substitutes for the first-born of Israel."

Bechoroth, fol. 5, col. 1.

"And the inhabitants of Jerusalem did him honor at his death" (2 Chron. xxxii. 33). This is Hezekiah, king of Judah, at whose funeral thirty-six thousand people attended bare-shouldered, . . . and upon his bier was laid a roll of the law, and it was said, "This man has fulfilled what is written in this book." *Bava Kama*, fol. 17, col. 1.

Sennacherib the wicked invaded Jewry with forty-five thousand princes in golden coronets, and they had with them their wives and odalisques; also eighty thousand mighty men clad in mail and sixty thousand swordsmen ran before him, and the rest were cavalry. With a similar army they came against Abraham, and a like force is to come up with Gog and Magog. A tradition teaches that the extent of his camp was four hundred parsaes or leagues, the extent of the horses' necks were forty parsaes. The total muster of his army was two hundred and sixty myriads of thousands, less one. Abaii asked, "Less one myriad, or one thousand, or one hundred? or more literally less one?" *Sanhedrin*, fol. 95, col. 2.

In the immediate context of the above extract we have the following legend concerning Sennacherib:—As Rabbi Abhu has said, "Were it not for this Scripture text it would be impossible to repeat what is written (Isa. vii. 20), 'In the same day shall the Lord shave with a razor that is hired, by them beyond the river, by the king of Assyria, the head and the hair of the feet; and it shall also consume the beard.'" The story is this:—The Holy One— blessed be He!—once disguised Himself as an elderly man and came to Sennacherib, and said, "When thou comest to the kings of the East and of the West, to force their sons into thine army, what wilt thou say unto them?" He replied, "On that very account I am in fear. What shall I do?" God answered him, "Go and disguise thyself." "How can I disguise myself?" said he. God replied, "Go and fetch me a pair of scissors and I will cut thy hair." Sennacherib asked, "Whence shall I fetch them?" "Go to yonder house and bring them." He went accordingly and observed a pair, but there he met the ministering angels disguised as men, grinding date-stones. He asked them for the scissors, but they said "Grind thou first a measure of date-stones, and then thou shalt have the scissors." He did as he was told, and so obtained the scissors. It was dark before he returned, and God said unto him, "Go and fetch some fire." This also he did, but while blowing the embers his beard was singed. Upon which God came and shaved his head and his beard, and said, "This is it which is written (Isa. vii. 20), 'It shall also consume the beard.'" Rav Pappa says this is the proverb current among the people, "Singe the face of a Syrian, and, if it pleases him, also set his beard in fire, and thou wilt not be able to laugh enough."

Sanhedrin, fol. 95, col. 2, and fol. 96, col. 1.

"He hath cut off in His fierce anger all the horn of Israel," etc. (Lam. ii. 3). These are the eighty thousand war-horns or battering-rams that entered the city of Byther, in which he massacred so many men, women, and children, that their blood ran like a river and flowed into the Mediterranean Sea, which was a mile away from the place.

Gittin, fol. 57, col. 1.

That mule had a label attached to his neck on which it was stated that its breeding cost a hundred thousand zouzim.

Bechoroth, fol. 8, col. 2.

Rabbi Yossi said, "I have seen Sepphoris (Cyprus) in the days of its prosperity, and there were in it a hundred and eighty thousand marts for sauces."

Bava Bathra, fol. 75, col. 2.

Rav Assi said three hundred thousand swordsmen went up to the Royal Mount and there slaughtered the people for three days and three nights, and yet while on the one side of the mount they were mourning, on the other they were merry; those on the one side did not know the affairs of those on the other. *Gittin*, fol. 57, col. 1.

A certain disciple prayed before Rabbi Chanina, and said, "O God! who art great, mighty, formidable, magnifi-

cent, strong, terrible, valiant, powerful, real and honored!"
He waited until he had finished, and then said to him,
"Hast thou ended all the praises of thy God? Need we
enumerate so many? As for us, even the three terms of
praise which we usually repeat, we should not dare to
utter had not Moses, our master, pronounced them in the
law (Deut. x. 17), and had not the men of the Great
Synagogue ordained them for prayer; and yet thou hast
repeated so many and still seemest inclined to go on. It
is as if one were to compliment a king because of his
silver, who is master of a thousand thousands of gold
denarii. Wouldst thou think that becoming?"

Berachoth, fol. 33, col. 2.

Rabbi Yossi ben Kisma relates, "I once met a man in
my travels and we saluted one another. In reply to a
question of his I said, 'I am from a great city of sages
and scribes.' Upon this he offered me a thousand thousand golden denarii, and precious stones and pearls, if I
would agree to go and dwell in his native place. But I
replied, saying, 'If thou wert to give me all the gold and
silver, all the precious stones and pearls in the world, I
would not reside anywhere else than in the place where the
law is studied.'" *Avoth*, chap. 6.

Thousands on thousands in Israel were named after
Aaron; for had it not been for Aaron these thousands of
thousands would not have been born. Aaron went about
making peace between quarreling couples, and those who
were born after the reconciliation were regularly named
after him. *Avoth d' Rab. Nathan*, chap. 12.

It is related by the Rabbis that Rabbon Yochanan ben
Zacchai was once riding out of Jerusalem accompanied by
his disciples, when he saw a young woman picking barley
out of the dung on the road. On his asking her name,
she told him that she was the daughter of Nikodemon ben
Gorion. "What has become of thy father's riches?" said
he, "and what has become of thy dowry?" "Dost thou
not remember," said she, "that charity is the salt of
riches?" (Her father had not been noted for this virtue.)
"Dost thou not remember signing my marriage contract?"

said the woman. "Yes," said the Rabbi, "I well remember it. It stipulated for a million gold denarii from thy father, besides the allowance from thy husband," etc.

Kethuboth, fol. 66, col. 2.

Abba Benjamin says, "If our eye were permitted to see the malignant sprites that beset us, we could not rest on account of them." Abaii has said, "They out-number us, they surround us as the earthed-up soil on our garden-beds." Rav Hunna says, "Every one has a thousand at his left side and ten thousand at his right" (Ps. xci. 7). Rava adds, "The crowding at the schools is caused by their pushing in ; they cause the weariness which the Rabbis experience in their knees, and even tear their clothes by hustling against them. If one would discover traces of their presence, let him sift some ashes upon the floor at his bedside, and next morning he will see, as it were, the footmarks of fowls on the surface. But if one would see the demons themselves, he must burn to ashes the after-birth of a first-born black kitten, the offspring of a first-born black cat, and then put a little of the ashes into his eyes, and he will not fail to see them," etc., etc.

Berachoth, fol. 6, col. 1.

In each camp there are suspended three hundred and sixty-five myriads of stars, etc.

Agrippa, being anxious to ascertain the number of the male population of Israel, instructed the priest to take accurate note of the Paschal lambs. On taking account of the kidneys, it was found that there were sixty myriad couples (which indicated) double the number of those that came up out of Egypt, not reckoning those that were ceremonially unclean and those that were out traveling. There was not a Paschal lamb in which less than ten had a share, so that the number represented over six hundred myriads of men. *P'sachim*, fol. 64, col. 2.

"It is unlawful to enumerate Israel even with a view to a meritorious deed" (*Yoma*, fol. 22, col. 2). From Rashi's comment on the former text it seems that the priest merely held up the duplicate kidneys, upon which the king's agent regularly laid aside a pea or a pebble into a small heap, which were afterwards counted up. See also Josephus, Book VI. chap. ix. sec. 3.

15

It might not be amiss to remind the reader in passing that if one were to reckon one hundred per minute for ten hours a day, it would take no less than sixteen days six hours forty minutes to count a million; and that it wonld take twenty men, reckoning at the same rate, to sum up the total number stated in the text in one day, so as to ascertain that there were 1,200,000 sacrifices at the Passover under notice, representing no less than 12,000,000 celebrants.

At the time when Israel in their eagerness first said, "We will do," and then, "We will hear" (Exod. xxix. 7), there came sixty myriads of ministering angels to crown each Israelite with two crowns, one for "we will do" and one for "we will hear." But when after this Israel sinned, there came down a hundred and twenty myriads of destroying angels and took the crowns away from them, as it is said (Exod. xxxiii. 6), "And the children of Israel stripped themselves of their ornaments by Mount Horeb." Resh Lakish says, "The Holy One — blessed be He! — will, in the future, return them to us; for it is said (Isa. xxxv. 10), 'The ransomed of the Lord shall return and come to Zion with songs and everlasting joy upon their heads,' i. e., the joy they had in days of yore, upon their heads."

Shabbath, fol. 88, col. 1.

Let no one venture out alone at night-time on Wednesdays and Saturdays, for Agrath, the daughter of Machloth, roams about accompanied by eighteen myriads of evil genii, each one of which has power to destroy.

P'sachim, fol. 112, col. 2.

It is related of Rabbi Elazar ben Charsom that his mother made him a shirt which cost two myriads of manahs, but his fellow-priests would not allow him to wear it, because he appeared in it as though he were naked.

Yoma, fol. 35, col. 2.

He who has not seen the double gallery of the Synagogue in Alexandria of Egypt, has not seen the glory of Israel. . . . There were seventy-one seats arranged in it according to the number of the seventy-one members of the greater Sanhedrin, each seat of no less value than twenty-one myriads of golden talents. A wooden pulpit was in the centre, upon which stood the reader holding a Sudarium (a kind of flag) in his hand, which he waved when the vast congregation were required to say Amen at the end of any benediction, which, of course, it was impossible for all to hear in so stupendous a synagogue. The congregation did not sit promiscuously, but in guilds; goldsmiths apart, silversmiths apart, blacksmiths, coppersmiths, embroiderers, weavers, etc., all apart from each other. When a poor craftsman came in, he took his seat among the people of his guild, who maintained him till he found employment. Abaii says all this immense population was massacred by Alexander of Macedon. Why were they thus punished? Because they transgressed the Scripture, which says (Deut. xvii. 16), "Ye shall henceforth return no more that way." *Succah*, fol. 51, col. 2.

The Rabbis teach that during a prosperous year in the land of Israel, a place sown with a measure of seed produces five myriad cors (a cor being equal to thirty measures). *Kethuboth*, fol. 112, col. 1.

Rav Ulla was once asked, "To what extent is one bound to honor his father and mother?" To which he replied, "See what a Gentile of Askelon once did, Dammah ben Nethina by name. The sages one day required goods to the value of sixty myriads, for which they were ready to pay the price, but the key of the store-room happened to be under the pillow of his father, who was fast asleep, and Dammah would not disturb him." Rabbi Eliezer was once asked the same question, and he gave the same answer, adding an interesting fact to the illustration: "The sages were seeking after precious stones for the high priest's breastplate, to the value of some sixty or eighty myriads of golden denarii, but the key of the jewel-chest happened to be under the pillow of his father, who was asleep at the time, and he would not wake him. In the following year, however, the Holy One — blessed be He! — rewarded him with the birth of a red heifer among his herds, for which the sages readily paid him such a sum as compensated him fully for the loss he sustained in honoring his parent." *Kiddushin*, fol. 31, col. 1.

"The Lord hath swallowed up all the habitations of Jacob" (Lam. ii. 2). Ravin came to Babylon and said in the name of Rabbi Yochanan, "These are the sixty myriads of cities which King Yannai (Jannæus) possessed on the royal mount. The population of each equalled the number that went up out of Egypt, except that of three cities in which that number was doubled. And these three cities were Caphar Bish (literally, the village of evil), so called because there was no hospice for the reception of strangers therein; Caphar Shichlaiim (village of water-cresses), so called because it was chiefly on that herb that the people subsisted; Caphar Dichraya (the village of male children), so called, says Rabbi Yochanan, because its women first gave birth to boys, and afterward to girls, and then left off bearing." Ulla said, "I have seen that place, and am sure that it could not hold sixty myriads of sticks." A Sadducee upon this said to Rabbi Chanina, "Ye do not speak the truth." The response was, "It is written (Jer. iii. 19), 'The inheritance of a deer,' as the skin of a deer, unoccupied by the body of the animal, shrinks, so also the land of Israel, unoccupied by its rightful owners, became contracted."

Gittin, fol. 57, col. 1.

Rabbi Yoshua, the son of Korcha, relates: "An aged inhabitant of Jerusalem once told me that in this valley two hundred and eleven thousand myriads were massacred by Nebuzaradan, captain of the guard, and in Jerusalem itself he slaughtered upon one stone ninety-four myriads, so that the blood flowed till it touched the blood of Zachariah, that it might be fulfilled which is said (Hos. ii. 4), 'And blood toucheth blood.' When he saw the blood of Zachariah, and noticed that it was boiling and agitated, he asked, 'What is this?' and he was told that it was the spilled blood of the sacrifices. Then he ordered blood from the sacrifices to be brought and compared it with the blood of the murdered prophet, when, finding the one unlike the other, he said, 'If ye tell me the truth, well and good; if not, I will comb your flesh with iron currycombs!' Upon this they confessed, 'He was a prophet, and because he rebuked us on matters of religion, we arose and killed him, and it is now some years since his blood has been in the restless condition in which thou seest it.' 'Well,' said he, 'I will pacify him.' He then brought the greater and lesser Sanhedrin and slaughtered them, but the blood of the prophet did not rest. He next slaughtered young men and maidens, but the blood continued restless as before. He finally brought school-children and slaughtered them, but the blood being still unpacified, he exclaimed, 'Zachariah! Zachariah! I have for thy sake killed the best among them; will it please thee if I kill them all?' As he said this the blood of the prophet stood still and quiescent. He then reasoned within himself thus, 'If the blood of one individual has brought about so great a punishment, how much greater will my punishment be for the slaughter of so many!' In short, he repented, fled from his house, and became a Jewish proselyte." *Gittin*, fol. 57, col. 2.

The same story is repeated in *Sanhedrin*, fol. 96, col. 2, with some variations; notably this, among others, that it was because the prophet prophesied the destruction of Jerusalem that they put him to death.

(Gen. xxvii. 2), "The voice is the voice of Jacob, but the hands are the hands of Esau." The first-named "voice" alludes to the voice of lamentation caused by Hadrian, who had at Alexandria in Egypt massacred twice the number of Jews that had come forth under Moses. The "voice of Jacob" refers to a similar lamentation occasioned by Vespasian, who put to death in the city of Byther four hundred myriads, or, as some say, four thousand myriads. "The hands are the hands of Esau," that is, the empire which destroyed our house, burned our Temple, and banished us from our country. Or the "voice of Jacob" means that there is no effectual prayer that is not offered up by the progeny of Jacob; and "the hands are the hands of Esau," that there is no victorious battle which is not fought by the descendants of Esau. *Ibid.*

Tamar and Zimri both committed fornication. The former (actuated by a good motive, see Gen. xxxviii. 26) became the ancestress of kings and prophets. The latter brought about the destruction of myriads in Israel. Rav Nachman bar Yitzchak says, "To do evil from a good motive is better than observing the law from a bad one" (*e. g.*, Tamar and Zimri, Lot and his daughters).

Nazir, fol. 23, col. 2.

The Rabbis have taught that the text, "And when it rested, he said, Return, O Lord, to the myriads and thousands of Israel" (Num. x. 36), intimates that the Shechinah does not rest upon less than two myriads and two thousands (two being the minimum plurality). Suppose one of the twenty-two thousand neglect the duty of procreation, is he not the cause of the Shechinah's departure from Israel?

Yevamoth, fol. 64, col. 1.

"And place over them to be rulers of thousands, and rulers of hundreds, and rulers of fifties, and rulers of tens" (Exod. xviii. 21). The rulers of thousands were six hundred in number, the rulers of hundreds six thousand, of fifties twelve thousand, and rulers of tens six myriads. The total number of rulers in Israel, therefore, was seven myriad eight thousand six hundred. *Sanhedrin*, fol. 18, col. 1.

Once upon a time the people of Egypt appeared before Alexander of Macedon to complain of Israel. "It is said (Exod. xii. 36), they argued, 'The Lord gave the people favor in the sight of the Egyptians, so that they lent unto them,' etc.;" and they prayed, "Give us now back the gold and the silver that ye took from us." Givia ben Pesisa said to the wise men (of Israel), "Give me permission to plead against them before Alexander. If they overcome me, say, 'You have overcome a plebeian only,' but if I overcome them, say, 'The law of Moses our master has triumphed over you.'" They accordingly gave him leave, and he went and argued thus, "Whence do ye produce your proof?" "From the law," said they. Then said he, "I will bring no other evidence but from the law. It is said (Exod. xii. 40), 'The sojourning of the children of Israel, who dwelt in Egypt, was four hundred and thirty years.' Pay us now the usufruct of the labor of the sixty myriads whom ye enslaved in Egypt for four hundred and thirty years." Alexander gave the Egyptians three days' grace to prepare a reply, but they never put in an appearance. In fact, they fled away and left both their fields and vineyards. *Ibid.*, fol. 91, col. 1.

"And Jethro said, Blessed be the Lord, who hath delivered you" (Exod. xviii. 10). A tradition says, in the name of Rabbi Papyes, "Shame upon Moses and upon the sixty myriads (of Israel), because they had not said, 'Blessed be the Lord,' till Jethro came and set the example."

Sanhedrin, fol. 94, col. 1.

"And let him dip his foot in oil" (Deut. xxxiii. 24), the Rabbis say, refers to the portion of Asher, which produces oil like a well. Once on a time, they relate, the Laodiceans sent an agent to Jerusalem with instructions to purchase a hundred myriads' worth of oil. He proceeded first to Tyre, and thence to Gush-halab, where he met with the oil merchant earthing up his olive trees, and asked him whether he could supply a hundred myriads' worth of oil. "Stop till I have finished my work," was the reply. The other, when he saw the business-like way in which he set to work, could not help incredulously exclaiming, "What! hast thou really a hundred myriads' worth of oil to sell? Surely the Jews have meant to make game of me." However he went to the house with the oil merchant, where a female slave brought hot water for him to wash his hands and feet, and a golden bowl of oil to dip them in afterward, thus fulfilling Deut. xxxiii. 24 to the very letter. After they had eaten together, the merchant measured out to him the hundred myriads' worth of oil, and then asked whether he would purchase more from him. "Yes," said the agent, "but I have no more money here with me." "Never mind," said the merchant; "buy it and I will go with thee to thy home for the money." Then he measured out eighteen myriads' worth more. It is said that he hired every horse, mule, camel, and ass he could find in all Israel to carry the oil, and that on nearing his city the people turned out to meet him and compliment him for the service he had done them. "Don't praise me," said the agent, "but this, my companion, to whom I owe eighteen myriads." This, says the narrator, illustrates what is said (Prov. xiii. 7), "There is that maketh himself (appear to be) rich, yet hath nothing; there is that maketh himself poor, yet hath great riches."

Menachoth, fol. 85, col. 2.

THE MIDRASHIM

« Precious in the sight of the Lord is the Aggadah, as explained
in the Midrashim »

INTRODUCTORY NOTE

THE Midrashim are ancient Rabbinical expositions of Holy Writ. The term Midrash (of which Midrashim is the plural form) occurs twice in the Hebrew Bible (2 Chron. xiii. 22, and xxiv. 27) ; and in both passages it is represented in the Anglican version by the word "story," while the more correct translation, "commentary," is relegated to the margin. "Legendary exposition" best expresses the full meaning of the word Midrash.

The Midrashim, for the most part, originated in a praiseworthy desire to familiarize the people with Holy Writ, which had, in consequence of changes in the vernacular, become to them, in the course of time, almost a dead letter. These Midrashim have little or nothing to do with the Halachoth or legal decisions of the Talmud, except in aim, which is that of illustration and explanation. They are not literal interpretations, but figurative and allegorical, and as such enigmatic. They are, however, to be received as utterances of the sages, and some even regard them of as binding obligation as the law of Moses itself. The following are fairly representative extracts.

(235)

THE MIDRASHIM

THE name of Abraham always precedes those of Isaac and Jacob except in one place (Lev. xxvi. 42), where it is said, "And I will remember my covenant with Jacob, and also my covenant with Isaac, and also my covenant with Abraham will I remember;" and thus we learn that all were of equal importance.

Midrash Rabbah, Gen. chap. 1.

In the Selichoth for the Day of Atonement the above reversal of the usual order of the names of Abraham, Isaac, and Jacob is thus referred to : "The first covenant Thou didst exalt, and the order of the contracting parties to it Thou hast reversed."

Abraham deserved to have been created before Adam, but the Holy One — blessed be He! — said, "Should he pervert things as I make them, then there will be no one to rectify them ; so behold I will create Adam first, and if he should make things crooked, then Abraham following him will make them straight again." *Ibid.*, chap. 14.

Abram was called Abraham, and Isaac was also called Abraham ; as it is written (Gen. xxv. 19), "Isaac, Abraham's son, Abraham." *Ibid.*, chap. 63.

"And he lay down in that place" (Gen. xxviii. 11). Rabbi Yuda said, "There he lay down, but he did not lie down during all the fourteen years he was hid in the house of Eber." Rabbi Nehemiah said, "There he lay down, but he did not lie down all the twenty years in which he stood in the house of Laban."

Ibid., chap. 68.

Vayash Kihu, "And kissed him" (Gen. xxxiii. 4), Rabbi Yanai asks, "Why is this word (in the original Hebrew) so pointed?" "It is to teach that Esau did not come to kiss him, but to bite him ; only the neck of Jacob our father became as hard as marble, and this blunted the teeth of the wicked one." "And what is taught by the expression 'And they wept'?" "The one wept for his neck and the other for his teeth."

Midrash Rabbah, chap. 78.

Rabbi Shimon ben Yochai in Sifri deliberately controverts this interpretation, and Aben Ezra says it is an "exposition fit only for children."

Esau said, "I will not kill my brother Jacob with bow and arrow, but with my mouth I will suck his blood," as it is said (Gen. xxxiii. 4), "And Esau ran to meet him, and embraced him, and kissed him, and they wept." Read not "and he kissed him," but read, "and he bit him." The neck of Jacob, however, became as hard as ivory, and it is respecting him that Scripture says (Cant. vii. 5), "Thy neck is as a tower of ivory," — so that the teeth of Esau became blunted; and when he saw that his desire could not be gratified, he began to be angry, and gnashed his teeth, as it is said (Ps. cxii. 10), "The wicked shall see it and be grieved; he shall gnash with his teeth."

Pirke d' Rab. Eliezer, chap. 36.

See also the previous quotation from the Midrash Rabbah. The Targum of Jonathan and also the Yerushalmi record the same fantastic tradition. In the latter it is given thus, "And Esau ran to meet him, and hugged him, and fell upon his neck and kissed him. Esau wept for the crushing of his teeth, and Jacob wept for the tenderness of his neck."

Abraham made a covenant with the people of the land, and when the angels presented themselves to him, he thought they were mere wayfarers, and he ran to meet them, purposing to make a banquet for them. This banquet he told Sarah to get prepared, just as she was kneading cakes. For this reason he did not offer them the cakes which she had made, but "ran to fetch a calf, tender and good." The calf in trepidation ran away from him and hid itself in the cave of Machpelah, into which he followed it. Here he found Adam and Eve fast asleep, with lamps burning over their couches, and the place pervaded with a sweet-smelling odor. Hence the fancy he took to the cave of Machpelah for a "possession of a burying-place."

Ibid.

Shechem, the son of Hamor, assembled girls together
playing on tambourines outside the tent of Dinah, and
when she "went out to see them," he carried her off, . . .
and she bare him Osenath. The sons of Jacob wished to
kill her, lest the people of the land should begin to talk
scandal of the house of their father. Jacob, however, engraved the holy Name on a metal plate, suspended it upon
her neck, and sent her away. All this being observed
before the Holy One — blessed be He ! — the angel Michael
was sent down, who led her to Egypt, into the house of
Potipherah ; for Osenath was worthy to become the wife
of Joseph.   *Pirke d'Rab. Eliezer*, chap. 48.

In Yalkut Yehoshua 9, Osenath is styled a proselyte ; and indeed
it might seem likely enough that Joseph induced her to worship the
true God. The Targum of Jonathan agrees with the version of the
Midrash above, while another tradition makes Joseph marry Zuleika,
the virgin widow of Potiphar, and says that she was the same woman
that is called Osenath (*Koran*, note to p. 193).

When Joseph's brethren recognized him, and were about
to kill him, an angel came down and dispersed them to
the four corners of the house. Then Judah screamed with
such a loud voice that all the walls of Egypt were leveled
with the dust, all the beasts were smitten to the ground,
and Joseph and Pharaoh, their teeth having fallen out,
were cast down from their thrones ; while all the men that
stood before Joseph had their heads twisted round with
their faces toward their backs, and so they remained till
the day of their death ; as it is said (Job iv. 10), "The
roaring of the lion (Judah), and the voice of the fierce
lion," etc.   *Vayegash*, chap. 5.

The tradition of a legend in our possession says that
Judah killed Esau. When? When Isaac died, Jacob and
(the chiefs of) the twelve clans went to bury him ; as it
is written (Gen. xxxv. 29), "And his sons Esau and
Jacob buried him." In the Midrash it is, "And Esau and
Jacob and his sons buried him," which fits the legend
better. Arrived at the cave, they entered it, and they
stood and wept. The (heads of the) tribes, out of respect
to Jacob, left the cave, that Jacob might not be put to
shame in their presence. Judah re-entered it, and finding

Esau risen up as if about to murder Jacob, he instantly went behind him and killed him. But why did he not kill him from the front? Because the physiognomy of Esau was exactly like that of Jacob, and it was out of respect to the latter that he slew Esau from behind.

Midrash Shochar Tov, chap. 18.

Tradition varies respecting the tragic end of Esau. The Book of Jasher (chap. 56, v. 64) and the Targum of Jonathan (in Vayechi) both say that Cushim the son of Dan slew Esau at the burial, not of Isaac, but of Jacob, because he sought to hinder the funeral obsequies, disputing the title to the sepulchre.

"Oh, that I had wings like a dove! for then I would fly away, and be at rest" (Ps. lv. 6). This is spoken of Abraham. But why like a dove? Rabbi Azariah, in the name of Rabbi Yudan, says, "Because all birds when tired rest on a rock or on a tree, but a dove, when tired of flying, draws in one wing to rest it, and continues her flight with the other." *Bereshith Rabbah*, chap. 39.

The Holy One — blessed be He! — said unto Abraham, "What should I tell thee? and with what shall I bless thee? Shall I tell thee to be perfectly righteous, or that thy wife Sarah be righteous before me? That ye both are already. Or shall I say that thy children shall be righteous? They are so already. But I will bless thee so that all thy children which shall in future ages come forth from thee shall be just like thee." Whence do we learn this? From Gen xv. 5: "And he said unto him, So (like thee) shall thy seed be." *Bamidbar Rabbah*, chap. 2.

"Every man . . . by his own standard" (Num. ii. 2). The several princes of Israel selected the colors for their banners from the color of the stones that were upon the breastplate of Aaron. From them other princes have learned to adorn their standards with different distinguishing colors. Reuben had his flag red, and leaves of mandrakes upon it. Issachar had his flag blue, and the sun and moon upon it. Naphtali had on his flag an olive tree, for this reason that (Gen. xlix. 20) "Out of Asher his bread shall be fat." *Ibid.*, chap. 7.

"And Abraham rose up early and saddled his ass" (Gen. xxii. 3). This is the ass on which Moses also rode when he came into Egypt; for it is said (Exod. iv. 20), "And Moses took his wife and his sons, and set them upon an ass." This is the ass on which the Son of David also shall ride; as it is said (Zech. ix. 9), "Poor, and riding upon an ass."   *Pirke d'Rab. Eliezer*, chap. 31.

In the morning service for Yom Kippur, there is an allusion to the Scripture passage with which our quotation opens. It is said that Abraham in "his great joy perverted the usual order," which a footnote explains thus—"In the greatness of his joy, that he had thus an opportunity of showing his obedience to God, he set aside the usual order of things, which was that the servant should saddle the ass, and saddled the ass himself, as mentioned Gen. xxii. 3." The animal referred to in the above remarks is spoken of in Sanhedrin, fol. 98, col. 1, as being of a hundred colors.

When Joseph saw the signs of Judah's anger, he began to tremble, and said (to himself), "Woe is me, for he may kill me!" And what were these signs? Tears of blood rolling down from Judah's right eye, and the hair that grew on his chest rising and penetrating through the five garments that he wore. Joseph then kicked the marble seat on which he was sitting, so that it was instantly shattered into fragments. Upon this Judah observed, "He is a mighty man, like one of us."   *Yalkut Vayegash.*

Abraham married three wives—Sarah, a daughter of Shem; Keturah, a daughter of Japheth; and Hagar, a daughter of Ham.   *Yalkut, Job*, chap. 8.

Rashi supposes that Keturah was one and the same with Hagar— so the Midrash, the Targum Yerushalmi, and that of Jonathan. The latter says, "Keturah, she is Hagar, who had been bound to him from the beginning," but Aben Ezra and most of the commentators contend that Keturah and Hagar are two distinct persons, and the use of the plural concubines, in verse 6, bears them out in this assertion.

The Holy One—blessed be He!—daily proclaims a new law in the heavenly court, and even all these were known to Abraham.   *Ibid.*, chap. 37.

A Gentile once asked Rabbi Yoshua ben Kapara, "Is it true that ye say your God sees the future?" "Yes," was

16

the reply. "Then how is it that it is written (Gen. vi.
6), 'And it grieved Him at His heart'?" "Hast thou,"
replied the Rabbi, "ever had a boy born to thee?" "Yes,"
said the Gentile; "and I rejoiced and made others rejoice
with me." "Didst thou not know that he would eventually
die?" asked the Rabbi. "Yes," answered the other; "but
at the time of joy is joy, and at the time of mourning,
mourning." "So it is before the Holy One — blessed be
He! — seven days He mourned before the deluge destroyed
the world." *Bereshith Rabbah*, chap. 27.

All the strength of the soul's mourning is from the third
to the thirtieth day, during which time she sits on the
grave, still thinking her beloved might yet return (to
the body whence she departed). When she notices that
the color of the face is changed, she leaves and goes away;
and this is what is written (Job. xiv. 22), "But his flesh
upon him shall have pain, and his soul shall mourn over
him." Then the mouth and the belly quarrel with one
another, the former saying to the latter, "All I have robbed
and taken by violence I deposited in thee;" and the latter,
having burst three days after its burial, saying to the
former, "There is all thou hast robbed and taken by violence! as it is written (Eccles. xii. 6), 'The pitcher is
broken at the fountain.'" *Ibid.*, chap. 100.

Job said, "Even the devil shall not dissuade me from
comforting those that mourn; for I would tell him that I
am not better than my Creator, who comforts Israel; as it
is said (Isa. li. 12), 'I, even I, am He that comforteth
you.'" *Psikta Nachmu.*

Once Rabbi Shimon ben Yehozedek addressed Rabbi
Sh'muel ben Nachman and said, "I hear that thou art a
Baal Aggadah; canst thou therefore tell me whence the
light was created?" "We learn," he replied in a whisper,
"that God wrapped Himself with light as with a garment,
and He has caused the splendor thereof to shine from one
end of the world to the other." The other said, "Why
whisperest thou, I wonder, since Scripture says so plainly
(Ps. civ. 2) 'Who covereth Himself with light as with a

garment ' ? " The reply was, " I heard it in a whisper, and in a whisper I have told it to thee."

Bereshith Rabbah, chap. 3.

" As the tents of Kedar " (Cant. i. 5). As the tents of the Ishmaelites are ugly without and comely within, so also the disciples of the wise, though apparently wanting in beauty, are nevertheless full of Scripture, and of the Mishnah and of the Talmud, of the Halacha and of the Aggadoth. *Shemoth Rabbah*, chap. 23.

" Write thou these words " (Exod. xxxiv. 37). That applies to the Law, the Prophets, and the Hagiographa, which were given in writing, but not to the Halachoth, the Midrashim, the Aggadoth, and the Talmud, which were given by the mouth. *Ibid.*, chap. 47.

Rabbi Samlai said to Rabbi Yonathan, " Instruct me in the Aggada." The latter replied, " We have a tradition from our forefathers not to instruct either a Babylonian or a Daromean in the Aggada, for though they are deficient in knowledge they are haughty in spirit."

Tal. Yerushalmi P' sachim, v. fol. 32, col. 1.

He who transcribes the Aggada has no portion in the world to come; he who expounds it is excommunicated; and he who listens to the exposition of it shall receive no reward.

Tal. Yerushalmi P'sachim, *Shabbath*, xvi. fol. 30, col. 2.

" Day unto day uttereth speech " (Ps. xix. 2, 3, 4) ; this means the Law, the Prophets, and the Hagiographa. " And night unto night showeth knowledge ; " this is the Mishnaioth. " There is no speech or langauge where their voice is not heard ; " these are the Halachoth. " Their line is gone out through all the earth ; " these are the Aggadoth, by which His great name is sanctified.

T. debei Aliahu, chap. 2.

Rabbi Yeremiah, the son of Elazar, said, " When the Holy One — blessed be He ! — created Adam, He created him an androgyne, for it is written (Gen. v. 2), ' Male and female created He them.' " Rabbi Sh'muel bar Nachman said, " When the Holy One — blessed be He ! — created Adam, He created him with two faces ; then He sawed him asunder, and split him (in two), making one back to the one-half, and another to the other."

Midrash Rabbah, chap. 8.

"And it repented the Lord that He had made man (Adam) on the earth, and it grieved Him at His heart" (Gen. vi. 6). Rabbi Berachiah says that when God was about to create Adam, He foresaw that both righteous people and wicked people would come forth from him. He reasoned therefore with Himself thus: "If I create him, then will the wicked proceed from him; but if I do not create him, how then shall the righteous come forth?" What then did God do? He separated the ways of the wicked from before Him, and assuming the attribute of mercy, so He created him. This explains what is written (Ps. i. 6), "For the Lord knoweth the way of the righteous, but the way of the wicked shall be lost." The way of the wicked was lost before Him, but assuming to Himself the attribute of mercy, He created him. Rabbi Chanina says, "It was not so! But when God was about to create Adam, He consulted the ministering angels and said unto them (Gen. i. 26), 'Shall we make man in our image after our likeness?' They replied, 'For what good wilt thou create him?' He responded, 'That the righteous may rise out of him.' This explains what is written, 'For the Lord knoweth the way of the righteous, but the way of the wicked shall be lost.' God informed them only about the righteous, but He said nothing about the wicked, otherwise the ministering angels would not have given their consent that man should be created." *Bereshith Rabbah*, chap. 8.

Rabbi Hoshaiah said, "When God created Adam the ministering angels mistook him for a divine being, and were about to say, 'Holy! holy! holy!' before him. But God caused a deep sleep to fall upon Adam, so that all knew he was only a man. This explains what is written (Isa. ii. 22), 'Cease ye from man, whose breath is in his nostrils; for wherein is he to be accounted of'?" *Ibid.*

Rabbi Yochanan saith, "Adam and Eve seemed as if they were about twenty years old when they were created."

Ibid., chap. 14.

Rav Acha said when God was about to create Adam He consulted the ministering angels, and asked them, saying, "Shall we make man?" They enquired, "Of what good will this man be?" He replied, "His wisdom will be greater than yours." One day, therefore, He brought together the cattle, the beasts, and the birds, and asked them the name of them severally, but they knew not. He then caused them to pass before Adam, and asked him, "What is the name of this and the other?" Then Adam replied, "This is an ox, this is an ass," and so on. "And thou, why is thy name Adam?" (*i. e.* in Hebrew, man). "I ought to be called Adam," was his reply, "for I was created from Adamah" (the ground). "And what is My name?" "It is meet Thou shouldst be called Lord, for Thou art Lord over all Thy creatures." Rav Acha says, "'I am the Lord, that is My name' (Isa. xlii. 8). 'That is My name which Adam called Me.'"

Bereshith Rabbah, chap. 17.

Rabba Eliezer says Adam was skilled in all manner of crafts. What proof is there of this? It is said (Isa. xliv. 11), "And the artisans, they are of Adam." *Ibid.*, chap. 24.

"And the Lord said, I will destroy man" (Gen. vi. 7). Rabbi Levi, in the name of Rabbi Yochanan, says that even millstones were destroyed. Rabbi Yuda, in the name of Rabbi Yochanan, declares even the very dust of Adam was destroyed. Rabbi Yuda, in the name of Rabbi Shimon, insists that even the (resurrection) bone of the spine, from which God will one day cause man to sprout forth again, was destroyed. *Ibid.*, chap. 28.

Concerning the bone, the *os coccygis*, there is an interesting story in Midrash Kohelet (fol. 114, 3), which may be appropriately inserted here. Hadrian (whose bones may they be ground, and his name blotted out) once asked Rabbi Joshua ben Chanania, "From what shall the human frame be reconstructed when it rises again?" "From Luz in the backbone," was the answer. "Prove this to me," said Hadrian. Then the Rabbi took Luz, a small bone of the spine, and immersed it in water, but it was not softened; he put it into the fire, but it was not consumed; he put it into a mill, but it could not be pounded; he placed it upon an anvil and struck it with a hammer, but the anvil split and the hammer was broken. (See also Zohar in "Genesis," 206, etc. etc.)

"A window shalt thou make to the ark" (Gen. vi. 16). Rabbi Amma says, "It was a real window." Rabbi Levi, on the other hand, maintained that it was a precious stone, and that during the twelve months Noah was in the ark he had no need of the light of the sun by day nor of the moon by night because of that stone, which he had kept suspended, and he knew that it was day when it was dim, and night when it sparkled. *Bereshith Rabbah*, chap. 31.

The transparency, ascribed to the ark, has given rise to various conjectures. The idea of Rabbi Levi, that it was a precious stone, has the sanction of the Targum of Jonathan; which volunteers the additional information that the gem was found in the river Pison.

Noah was deficient in faith, for he did not enter the ark till the water was up to his ankles. *Ibid.*, chap. 32.

"And he sent forth a raven" (Gen. viii. 7). The raven remonstrated, remarking, "From all the cattle, beasts, and fowls thou sendest none but me." "What need has the world for thee?" retorted Noah; "thou art good neither for food nor for sacrifice." Rabbi Eliezer says God ordered Noah to receive the raven, as the world would one day be in need of him. "When?" asked Noah. "When the waters are dried up from off the earth, there will in a time to come arise a certain righteous man who shall dry up the world, and then I shall want it." This explains what is written (1 Kings xvii. 6), "And the ravens brought him bread and flesh in the morning." *Ibid.*, chap. 33.

At the time God said to the serpent, "Upon thy belly thou shalt go" (Gen. iii. 14), the ministering angels descended and lopped off his hands and his feet. Then his voice was heard from one end of the world to the other.

Bereshith Midrash Rabbah, chap. 20.

When God said to the serpent, "And upon thy belly thou shalt go" (Gen. iii. 14), the serpent replied, "Lord of the universe! if this be Thy will, then I shall be as a fish of the sea without feet." But when God said to him, "And dust shalt thou eat," he replied, "If fish eat dust, then I also will eat it." Then God seized hold of the serpent and tore his tongue in two, and said, "O thou wicked one! thou hast commenced (to sin) with thy evil tongue;

thus I will proclaim it to all that come into the world that it was thy tongue that caused thee all this."

Letters of Rabbi Akiva.

"And Noah only remained" (Gen. vii. 23), except Og, king of Bashan, who sat on a beam of the ladders (which projected from the ark), and swore to Noah and his sons that he would be their slave forever. Noah made a hole in the ark through which he handed to Og his daily food. Thus he also remained, as it is said (Deut. iii. 11), "For only Og, king of Bashan, remained."

Pirke d'Rab. Eliezer, chap. 23.

"Unto Adam and his wife did the Lord God make coats of skins" (Gen. iii. 21), viz, to cover their nakedness; but with what? With fringes and phylacteries, "Coats of skins," viz, the leathern straps of the phylacteries; "and they sewed fig-leaves" (Gen. iii. 7), viz, fringes; "and made themselves aprons," this means the proclaiming of the Shema, "Hear, O Israel," etc.   *Yalkut Chadash.*

The aprons, which some (as Rashi, for instance) take to denote furs, the Targum of Jonathan says were made "from the skin of the serpent." The wardrobe of Adam afterward came into the possession of Esau and Jacob (see Targ. Yon. in Toledoth, and p. 199, No. 161, *ante*).

All the presents which our father Jacob gave to Esau will one day be returned by the nations of the world to the Messiah, and the proof of this is (Ps. lxxii. 10), "The kings of Tarshish and the isles shall return presents." It is not written here, "They shall bring," but they shall restore or return. *Midrash Rabbah Vayishlach,* chap. 78.

A philosopher once posed Rabbi Eliezer with the question, "Does not the prophet say (Mal. i. 4), 'They shall build, but I will throw down'? and do not buildings still exist?" To which the Rabbi answered, "The prophet does not speak of buildings, but of the schemes of designers. Ye all think to contrive and build up devices, to destroy and make an end of us, but He bringeth your counsels to nought. He throweth them down, so that your devices against us have no effect." "By thy life," said the philosopher, "it is even so; we meet annually for the purpose of compassing your ruin, but a certain old man comes and upsets all your projects" (namely, Elijah).

Yalkut Malachi.

When Israel came out of Egypt, Samael rose to accuse them, and thus he spoke: "Lord of the Universe! these have till now worshiped idols, and art Thou going to divide the sea for such as they?" What did the Holy One — blessed be He! — then do? Job, one of Pharaoh's high counselors, of whom it is written (Job i. 1), "That man was perfect and upright," He took and delivered to Samael, saying, as He did so, "Behold, he is in thy hand; do with him as thou pleasest." God thought to divert his evil designs by keeping him thus occupied with Job, that Israel meanwhile might cross the sea without any hindrance, after which He would return and rescue Job from his tender mercies. God then said to Moses, "Behold I have delivered Job to Satan; make haste. Speak unto the children of Israel that they go forward" (Exod. xiv. 15).

Midrash Rabbah Shemoth, chap. 21.

No man ever received a mite (in charity) from Job, and needed to receive such a second time (because of the good-luck it brought along with it). *Ibid.*

A superstitious belief prevails to some extent in Poland, among the Christian population as well as the Jews, that coins obtained in certain circumstances bring luck apart altogether from any virtue they may be supposed to convey from the giver. A penny obtained, for instance, the first thing in the morning, by stumbling on it in the street, by the sale of an article in the market, or by gift of charity, is considered to bode luck, and cherished as a pledge of good fortune by being slightly spat upon several times on receipt, and then carefully stowed away, for a longer or shorter period, in some safe sanctum. Job was the luckiest man that ever lived; his very goats even were so lucky as to kill the wolves that came to devour them; and a beggar, as we see, who received a mite from his hands, never needed afterward to beg an alms from him again. (See "Genesis according to the Talmud," p. 288, No. 16.)

"And Saul said unto the Kenites, Go, depart, etc.; for ye showed kindness to all the children of Israel" (1 Sam. xv. 6). And did they show kindness to all the children of Israel? No; but what is written is to teach that he who receives a disciple of the wise as a guest into his house, and gives him to eat and to drink, is as if he had shown kindness to all the children of Israel.

Midrash Sh'muel, chap. 18.

Rabbi Levi says, "When Solomon introduced the ark into the Temple, all the woodwork thereof freshened with sap and began to yield fruit, as it is said (Ps. xcii. 13), 'Those that be planted in the house of the Lord shall flourish in the courts of our God.' And thus it continued to bear fruit, which abundantly supplied the juveniles of the priestly caste till the time of Manasseh; but he, by introducing an image into the Temple, caused the Shechinah to depart and the fruit to wither; as it is said (Nah. i. 4), 'And the flower of Lebanon languisheth.'"

Midrash Tillin Terumah.

The land of Israel is situated in the centre of the world, and Jerusalem in the centre of the land of Israel, and the Temple in the centre of Jerusalem, and the Holy of holies in the centre of the Temple, and the foundation-stone on which the world was grounded, is situated in front of the ark. *Midrash Tillin Terumah, Kedoshim.*

In Ezek. v. 5 we read, "I have set Jerusalem in the midst of the nations and countries that are round about her." On the literal interpretation of these words it was asserted that Jerusalem was the very centre of the world, or, as Jerome quaintly called it, "the navel of the earth." In the Talmud we find a beautiful metaphor in illustration of this view. It is in the last six lines of the ninth chapter of Derech Eretz Zuta, which read thus: "Issi ben Yochanan, in the name of Shemuel Hakaton, says, 'The world is like the eyeball of man; the white is the ocean which surrounds the world, the black is the world itself, the pupil is Jerusalem, and the image in the pupil is the Temple. May it be built in our own days, and in the days of all Israel! Amen!'" The memory of this conceit is kept alive to this day among the Greek Christians, who still show the sacred stone in the Church of the Holy Sepulchre at Jerusalem. This notion is not confined to Jewry. Classic readers will at once call to mind the appellation Omphalos or navel applied to the temple at Delphi (Pindar, Pyth., iv. 131, vi. 3; Eurip. Ion., 461; Æsch. Chœph., 1034; Eum. 40, 167; Strabo, etc.).

Two sparks issued from between the two cherubim and destroyed the serpents and scorpions and burned the thorns in the wilderness. The smoke thereof, rising and spreading, perfumed the world, so that the nations said (Cant. iii. 6), "Who is this that cometh out of the wilderness like pillars of smoke, perfumed," etc.   *Ibid., Vayakhel.*

Better to lodge in the wilderness of the land of Israel than dwell in the palaces outside of it.

Midrash Rabbah, chap. 39.

"And give thee a pleasant land" (a coveted land) (Jer. iii. 19). Why is it called a coveted land? Because the Temple was in it. Another reason why it was so called is, because the fathers of the world have coveted it. Rabbi Shimon ben Levi says, "Because they (who are buried) there will be the first to be raised in the days of the Messiah."   *Shemoth Rabbah*, chap. 32.

"When the Lord thy God shall enlarge thy border, as He hath promised thee" (Deut. xii. 20). Rabbi Yitzchak said, "This scroll no man knows how long and how broad it is, but when unrolled it speaks for itself, and shows how large it is. It is so with the land of Israel, which, for the most part, consists of hills and mountains; but when the Holy One — blessed be He ! — shall level it, as it is said (Isa. xl. 4), 'Every valley shall be raised and every mountain and hill shall be made low, and the crooked shall be made straight, and the rough places smooth,' then shall that land speak, as it were, for herself, and its extent stand revealed."   *Devarim Rabbah*, chap. 4.

Blessed are they who dwell in the land of Israel, for they have no sin, no iniquity, either in their lives or in their deaths.   *Midrash Shochar Tov on Ps. lxxxv.*

"Better is a dry morsel and quietness therewith" (Prov. xvii. 1). This, saith Rabbi, means the land of Israel, for even if a man have nothing but bread and salt to eat, yet if he dwells in the land of Israel he is sure that he is a son of the world to come. "Than a house full of sacrifices with strife." This means the outside of the land, which is full of robbery and violence. Rabbi Y—— says, "He who walks but an hour in the land of Israel, and then dies within it may feel assured that he is a son of the world to come ; for it is written (Deut. xxxii. 43), 'And his earth shall atone for his people.'"   *Midrash Mishle.*

See also the Talmud, Kethuboth, fol. III, col. I. Dr. Benisch renders "and make expiation for His ground and His people." The Targums of Jonathan and the Yerushalmi have, "He will make atonement for His land and for His people;" and Onkelos puts it thus, "He will show mercy unto His land and His people." Our rendering, however, is in accordance with the sense given to it in the Talmud. There are Jews who travel about the world with bags of earth from the Holy Land, which they sell in small quantities for high prices to such as can afford it, and believe in its virtue as a protection against the worms of the grave.

Jerusalem is the light of the world; as it is said, "And the Gentiles shall come to Thy light" (Isa. lx. 3). And the light of Jerusalem is the Holy One — blessed be He! — as it is written, but "the Lord shall be unto thee an everlasting light" (Isa. lx. 19).

Bereshith Rabbah, chap. 59.

Ten portions of wisdom, ten portions of the law, and ten portions of hypocrisy are in the world; nine portions of each are in the land of Israel and one outside of it.

Midrash Rabbah Esther.

"And it shall come to pass that from one new moon to another, and from one Sabbath to another, shall all flesh come to worship before Me, saith the Lord" (Isa. lxvi. 23). But how is it possible that all flesh shall come every new moon and Sabbath to Jerusalem? Rabbi Levi saith, "In the future Jerusalem will be as the land of Israel, and the land of Israel will be as the whole world." But how will they come from the end of the world every new moon and Sabbath? "The clouds will come and carry them and bring them to Jerusalem, where they will perform their morning prayer, and will carry them back to their several homes; and this is the meaning of the prophet's saying (Isa. lx. 8), ' Who are these that fly as a cloud (in the morning), and as the doves to their windows (in the evening)?'"

Pesikta.

"He stood and measured the earth" (Hab. iii. 6). Rabbi Shimon ben Yochai expounded "He stood and measured" thus: "The Holy One — blessed be He! — measured all the nations, and He found none worthy to receive the law except the generation in the wilderness. He

measured all the mountains, and He found none on which
to give the law except Mount Sinai. He measured all
cities, and found none in which to build the Temple except
Jerusalem. He measured all lands, and found none worthy
to be given unto Israel except the one now called the land
of Israel. This it is that is written, "He stood up and
measured the earth." *Vayekra Rabbah*, chap. 13.

"I went down to the bottoms of the mountains" (Jonah
ii. 6). From this we learn that Jerusalem is situated on
seven hills. The world's "foundation-stone" sank to
"the depths" under the Temple of the Lord, and upon
this the sons of Korah stand and pray. (They) pointed
this out to Jonah. The fish said unto him, "Jonah, behold
thou art standing under the Temple of the Lord; therefore
pray, and thou shalt be answered."
Pirke d'Rab. Eliezer, chap. 10.

"And there went out fire from the Lord" (Lev. x. 2).
Abba Yossi saith, "Two threads of fire came out from the
Holy of holies, and these were disparted into four: two
entered the nostrils of the one (*i. e.*, Nadab), and two
entered the nostrils of the other (*i. e.*, Abihu), and thus
consumed them. Their souls were burned, but not their
garments; for it is said, 'So they went near, and carried
them in their coats'" (ver. 5).
Torath Cohanim, sec. *Shemini*.

Rabbi Jacob teaches that he who has no wife abideth
without good, without help, without joy, without blessing
or atonement, to which Rabbi Yehoshua ben Levi adds,
(yea) also without peace or life. Rabbi Cheya says that
he is not a perfect man, for it is said, "And blessed them
and called their name man" (Gen. v. 2), where both are
spoken of together as one man.
Midrash Rabbah Bereshith, chap. 17.

"My beloved is like a roe" (1 Cant. ii. 9). As a roe
leaps and skips from bush to bush, from covert to covert,
from hedge to hedge, so likewise does the Holy One —
blessed be He! — pass from synagogue to synagogue, and
from academy to academy, that He may bless Israel.
Pesikta.

(Cant. v. 1), "I came into My garden," the synagogues and academies; "My sister, My spouse," the congregation of Israel; "I have gathered My myrrh with My spice," the Bible (that is); "I have eaten My honeycomb with My honey" (this means) the Halachoth, Midrashoth, and Aggadoth; "I have drank My wine with My milk," this alludes to the good works which are reserved for the sages of Israel. After that, "Eat, O friends! drink, yea, drink freely, O beloved!"   *Yalkut Eliezer*, fol. 41, col. 2.

When Solomon brought the ark into the Temple and said, "Lift up your heads, O ye gates! and the King of glory shall come in," the gates were ready to fall upon him and crush his head, and they would have done so if he had not said at once, "The Lord of hosts, He is the King of glory" (Ps. xxiv. 9, 10). The Holy One — blessed be He! — then said to the gates, "Since ye have thus honored Me, by your lives! when I destroy My Temple, no man shall have dominion over you!" This was to inform us that while all the vessels of the Temple were carried into captivity, the gates of the Temple were stored away on the very spot where they were erected; for it is said (Lam. ii. 9), "Her gates are sunk into the ground."
                              Midrash Rabbah Devarim, chap. 15.

We are reminded of this tradition in the conclusion service for Yom Kippur, where we repeat, "Speedily thou shalt open the hidden gates to those who hold fast Thy law." The allusion is to "the gates of the Temple," which "are supposed to be sunk in the ground."

Rabbi Akiva once met on a journey a remarkably ugly man toiling along under a great load of wood. Rabbi Akiva said unto him, "I adjure thee to tell me whether thou art a man or a demon." "Rabbi," said he, "I was once a man, and it is now some time since I left the world. Day after day I have to carry a load like this, under which I am obliged to bow down, and submit three times a day to be burned," Then Rabbi Akiva asked him, "What was the reason of this punishment?" and the reply was, "I committed an immorality on the Day of Atonement." The Rabbi asked him if he knew of anything by which he might obtain for him a remission of his punishment. "I do," was the answer. "When a son whom I have left behind me is called up to the (public) reading of the law, and shall say, 'Blessed be the blessed Lord,' I shall be drawn out of hell and taken into Paradise." The Rabbi noted down the name of the man and his dwelling-place, whither he afterward went and made inquiries about him. The people of the place only replied, "The name of the wicked shall rot" (Prov. x. 7). Notwithstanding this, the Rabbi insisted, and said, "Bring his son to me." When they brought him, he taught the lad to repeat the blessing, which he did on the ensuing Sabbath at the public reading of the law; upon which his father was immediately removed from hell to Paradise. On the self-same night the father repaired direct to Rabbi Akiva, and gratefully expressed his hope that the Rabbi's mind might be as much at rest as his own was. *Midrash Assereth Hadibroht.*

There are three things which a man does not wish for: Grass to grow up among his grain-crops; to have a daughter among his children; or that his wine should turn to vinegar. Yet all these three are ordained to be, for the world stands in need of them. Therefore it is said, "O Lord, my God, Thou art very great! . . . He causeth the grass to grow for the cattle" (Ps. civ. 1, 14).

Midrash Tanchuma.

There are four cardinal points in the world, etc. The north point God created but left unfinished; for, said He, "Whoever claims to be God, let him come and finish this corner which I have left, and thus all will know that he is God." This unfinished corner is the dwelling-place of the harmful demons, ghosts, devils, and storms.

Pirke d'Rab. Eliezer, chap. 3.

A Min once asked Rabbi Akiva, "Who created this world?" "The Holy One—blessed be He!"—was the reply. "Give me positive proof of this," begged the other. "Come to-morrow," answered the Rabbi. On coming the next day, the Rabbi asked, "What are you dressed in?" "In a garment," was the reply. "Who made it?" asked the Rabbi. "A weaver," said the other. "I don't believe thee," said the Rabbi; "give me a positive proof of this."

"I need not demonstrate this," said the Min; "it stands to reason that a weaver made it." "And so thou mayest know that God created the world," observed the Rabbi. When the Min had departed, the Rabbi's disciples asked him, "What is proof positive?" He said, "My children, as a house implies a builder, and a garment a weaver, and a door a carpenter, so likewise the existence of the world implies that the Holy One — blessed be He! — created it."

Midrash Terumah.

When the Holy One — blessed be He! — created the world, it was a level expanse free from mountains; but when Cain slew Abel his brother, whose blood was trodden down on the earth, He cursed the ground, and immediately hills and mountains sprang into existence.

Midrash Vayosha.

"The Lord your God hath multiplied you, and behold ye are this day as the stars of heaven for multitude" (Deut. i. 10). Why did He bless them with stars? As there are degrees above degrees among these stars, so likewise are there degrees above degrees among Israel. Again, as these stars are without limit, without number, and of great power from one end of the world to the other, so likewise is Israel. (Cf. 1 Cor. xv. 41.)

Midrash Rabbah Devarim.

"Flee, my beloved" (A. V. "make haste," Cant. viii. 14). When Israel eat and drink, and bless and praise the Holy One — blessed be He! — He hearkeneth to their voice and is reconciled; but when the Gentiles eat and drink and blaspheme and provoke the Holy One — blessed be He! — He has a mind to destroy His world, until the Law enters and pleads in defense, "Lord of the universe! before Thou regardest those that blaspheme, look and behold Thy people Israel, who bless, and praise, and extol Thy great Name, with the Law, and with songs and with praises!" And the Holy Spirit shouts "Flee, my beloved! flee from the Gentiles, and hold fast to Israel!"

Midrash Rabbah Shir-Hashirim.

Rabbon Gamaliel called on Chilpa, the son of Caroyna, when the latter asked the Rabbi to pray on his behalf; and he prayed, "The Lord grant thee according to thine own heart" (Ps. xx. 4). Rabbi H——, son of Rabbi Isaac, said, "It was not so; he prayed thus, 'The Lord fulfill all thy petitions'; for a man often thinks in his heart to steal or commit some other transgression, and therefore 'The Lord grant thee according to thine own heart,' is a prayer not to be offered on behalf of every man." But the answer was, "His heart was perfect before his Creator, and therefore he did so pray on his behalf."

Midrash Shochar Tov, 20.

Thou wilt find that whithersoever the righteous go a blessing goes with them. Isaac went down to Gerar, and a blessing followed him. "Then Isaac sowed," etc. (Gen. xxvi. 12), Jacob went down to Laban (Gen. xxx. 27), and Laban said, "I have learned by experience that the Lord hath blessed me for thy sake." Joseph went down to Potiphar, and "the Lord blessed the Egyptian's house for Joseph's sake" (Gen. xxxix. 5). Thus also thou wilt find it was with the ark which came down to the house of Obed-edom, etc. (2 Sam. vi. 11). Our forefathers came into the land and a blessing followed at their heels, as it is said (Deut. vi. 11), "And houses full of good things," etc.

Yalkut Ekev.

"And the Lord put a word in Balaam's mouth" (Num. xxiii. 5). An angel took up his seat in Balaam's throat, so that when he wished to bless, the angel permitted him, but when he desired to curse, the angel tickled his throat and stopped him. "Word" in this place means simply an angel; as it is said (Ps. cvii. 20), "He sent His word and healed them." Rabbi Yochanan says, "There was an iron nail in his throat which permitted him when he wished to bless, but rasped his throat and prevented him when about to curse." "Word" in this place means only an iron nail; for it is said (Num. xxxi. 23), "Every thing (or word, for the original has both meanings) that may abide the fire."

Ibid.

Rabbi Avin said four kinds of excellency were created in the world: (1.) Man's excellency over the animal kingdom; (2.) the eagle's excellency over the feathered tribes;

(3.) the excellency of the ox over domestic cattle; and
(4.) the lion's excellency over the wild beasts. All were
fixed under the chariot of God; as it is said (Ezek. i. 10),
"As for the likeness of their faces, they four had the face
of a man, the face of a lion, the face of an ox, and the
face of an eagle." And why all this? In order that they
should not exalt themselves, but know that there is a
kingdom of heaven over them; and on this account it is
said (Eccles. v. 8), "He that is higher than the highest
regardeth, and there be higher than they." This is the
meaning of Exod. xv. 1 : "He hath triumphed gloriously."
                              Midrash Shemoth, chap. 23.

No man in Israel despised himself more than David when
the precepts of the Lord were concerned, and this is what
he said before God (Ps. cxxxi. 1, 2), "'Lord, my heart
was not haughty' when Samuel anointed me king. 'Nor
were mine eyes lofty' when I slew Goliath. 'Neither did
I exercise myself in matters too great and wonderful for
me' when I brought up the ark. 'Have I not behaved
myself, and hushed my soul, as a babe that is weaned of
his mother?' As a child which is not ashamed to uncover
himself before his mother, so have I likened myself before
Thee, in not being ashamed to depreciate myself before
Thee for Thy glory," etc. (See 2 Sam. vi. 20, 21.)
                              Bamidbar, chap. 4.

"I sleep, but my heart waketh" (Cant. v. 2). The Synagogue of Israel says "I sleep" with regard to the end
of days, "but my heart waketh" with regard to the redemption; "I sleep" with regard to redemption, but the
heart of the Holy One — blessed be He! — waketh to redeem me.   *Midrash Shir Hashirim.*

Rabbi Ishmael saith all the five fingers of the right hand
of the Holy One of Israel — blessed be He! — are severally
the efficient causes of redemptions. (1.) With His little
finger He pointed out to Noah how to construct the ark;
as it is said (Gen. vi. 15), "And thus thou shalt make it."
(2.) With the finger next to the little one He smote the
Egyptians; as it is said (Exod. viii. 19), "This is the finger of God." (3.) With the third finger from the little

17

one He wrote the tables; as it is said (Exod. xxxi. 18),
" Tables of stone written by the finger of God." (4.)
With the fourth finger, that which is next the thumb,
the Holy One — blessed be He ! — pointed out to Moses
how much the Israelites should give as a ransom for their
souls; as it is said (Exod. xxx. 13), "This shall they
give." (5.) With the thumb and the whole hand the
Holy One — blessed be He ! — will in the future destroy
the children of Esau, for they oppress the children of
Israel, as also the children of Ishmael, for they are their
enemies; as it is said (Micah v. 9), "Thine hand shall be
uplifted upon thy adversaries, and all thy enemies shall be
cut off."   *Pirke d' Rab. Eliezer*, chap. 48.

" For Mine own sake, for Mine own sake, will I do it "
(Isa. xlviii. 11). Why this repetition? The Holy One —
blessed be He ! — said, "As I redeemed you when you were
in Egypt for My name's sake " — (Ps. cvi. 8), "He saved
them for His name's sake," — " so in like manner will I do it
from Edom for My own name's sake. Again, as I redeemed
you in this world, so likewise will I redeem you in the
world to come ; " for thus He saith (Eccles. i. 9), " The
thing that hath been is that which shall be " (Isa. li. 11) ;
" The redeemed of the Lord shall return ; " not the redeemed of
Elijah, nor the redeemed of the Messiah, but " the redeemed
of the Lord."   *Midrash Shochar Tov Tehillim*, 107.

" Her children are gone into captivity before the enemy "
(Lam. i. 5). Rabbi Isaac saith, " Come and see how
greatly beloved are the children ! " The Sanhedrin were
exiled, but the Shechinah was not exiled with them. The
Temple guards were exiled, but the Shechinah was not
exiled with them. But with the children the Shechinah
also was exiled. This is that which is written (Lam. i.
5, 6), " Her children are gone, . . . and from the
daughter of Zion all her beauty (*i. e.*, the Shechinah) is
departed."   *Midrash Rabbah Eicha.*

" How doth the city sit solitary ! " (Lam. i. 1). Three
have, in prophesying, made use of this word " How " —
Moses, Isaiah, and Jeremiah. Moses said (Deut. i. 12),
" How can I myself bear your cumbrance ! " Isaiah said

(Isa. i. 21), "How is the faithful city become an harlot!" Jeremiah said (Lam. i. 1), "How doth the city sit solitary!" Rabbi Levi saith, "The thing is like to a matron who has three friends; one saw her in her prosperity, another saw her in her dissipation, and the third saw her in her pollution. So Moses saw Israel in their glory and prosperity, and he said, "How can I myself bear your cumbrance!" Isaiah saw them in their dissipation, and he said, "How is the faithful city," etc.; and Jeremiah saw them in their pollution, and he said, "How doth the city sit solitary!" *Midrash Rabbah Eicha.*

Hezekiah saith the judgment in Gehenna is six months' heat and six months' cold. *Midrash Reheh.*

Gehenna has sixteen mouths, four toward each cardinal point. The Gentiles say, "Hell is for Israel, but Paradise is for us." The Israelites say, "Ours is Paradise."
Midrash Aggadath Bereshith.

Rabbi Yochanan ben Zachai says, that coming once upon a man who was gathering wood, he addressed him, but at first he made no reply. Afterward, however, he came up and said, "Rabbi, I'm not a living man, but a dead one." "If thou art a dead man," said I, "what is this wood for?" He replied, "When I was alive upon earth, I and an associate of mine committed a certain sin in my shop, and when we were taken thence, we were sentenced to the punishment of mutual burning; so I gather wood to burn him, and he does the same to burn me." I then asked him, "How long are you to be punished thus?" He replied, "When I came here my wife was *enceinte*, and I know she gave birth to a boy. May I beg thee, therefore, to see that the child is instructed by a teacher, for as soon as he is able to repeat, 'Bless ye the blessed Lord!' I shall be brought up hence and be free from this punishment in hell." *Tanu d'by Eliyahu.*

Rabbi Berachia saith, "In order that the Minim, apostates, and wicked Israelites might not escape hell on account of their circumcision, the Holy One — blessed be He! — sends an angel to undo the effects of it, and they straightway descend to their doom. When Gehenna sees this, she opens her mouth and licks them." This is the purport of (Isa. v. 14), "And she opened her mouth to those without law" (*i. e.*, to those without the sign of the covenant).   *Midrash Rabbath Shemoth*, chap. 19.

"God hath also set the one over against the other" (Eccles. vii. 14), *i. e.*, the righteous and the wicked, in order that the one should atone for the other. God created the poor and the rich, in order that the one should be maintained by the other. He created Paradise and Gehenna, in order that those in the one should deliver those in the other. And what is the distance between them? Rabbi Chanina saith the width of the wall (between Paradise and Gehenna) is a handbreadth.

Yalkut Koheleth.

"Those passing through the valley of weeping make it a well; also blessings shall cover the teacher" (Ps. lxxxiv. 6, A. V.). "The valley of weeping" is Gehenna. "Make it a well," for their tears are like a well or spring. "Also blessings shall cover the teacher." Rabbi Yochanan saith, "The praises of God that ascend from Gehenna are more than those that ascend from Paradise, for each one that is a step higher than his neighbor praises God, and says, 'Happy am I that I am a step higher than the one below me.' 'Also blessings shall cover the teacher,' for they will acknowledge and say, 'Ye have taught well, and ye have instructed well, but we have not obeyed.'"

Yalkut Tehillim, 84.

Those of the house of Eliyahu have taught that Gehenna is above the sky, but some say it is behind the mountains of darkness.   *Tanu d' by Eliyahu.*

Gehenna was created before Paradise; the former on the second day and the latter on the third.   *Yalkut.*

In T. B. P'sachim, fol. 54, col. 1, it is said that the reason of the omission of the words, "And God saw that it was good," in respect to the second day of the creative week, was because hell-fire was then created; but see the context.

When Adam saw (through the Spirit) that his posterity would be condemned to Gehenna, he disobeyed the precept to procreate. But when he perceived that after twenty-six generations the Israelites would accept the law, he bestirred himself in compliance ; as it is said (Gen. iv. 1), *Adam vero cognovit uxorem suam Hevam.* *Yalkut.*

"And the souls they had gotten in Haran" (Gen. xii. 5). These are they who had been made proselytes. Whoever attracts a Gentile and proselytizes him is as much as if he had created him. Abraham did so to men and Sarah to women. *Bereshith Midrash Rabbah.*

"Sing and rejoice" (Zech. ii. 10). The Holy One — blessed be He ! — will in the future bring all the proselytes that were proselytized in this world, and judge all the nations of the world in their presence. He will say to them, "Why have ye left Me and served idols, which are nothing?" They will reply and say, "Had we applied at Thy door, Thou wouldst not have received us." Then will He say to them, "Let the proselytes that were made from among you come forward and testify against you." *P'sikta.*

These are the pious female proselytes — Hagar, Osenath, Zipporah, Shiphrah, Puah, the daughter of Pharaoh (Bathia), Rahab, Ruth, and Jael. *Yalkut Yehoshua,* 9.

"The Lord keepeth the proselytes" (Ps. cxlvi. 9). "I esteem it a great compliment on the part of the proselyte to leave his family and his father's house and come to Me. Therefore I on My part will command respecting him (Deut. x. 19), 'Love ye therefore the proselyte.'"
Midrash Shochar Tov, 146.

"I am a God near at hand" (Jer. xxiii. 23). "I am He who drew Jethro near, and did not keep him at a distance"; therefore thou also when a man comes to be proselytized in the name of Heaven, draw him near, do not repulse him or keep him at a distance. From this thou art to learn that while one repulses with the left hand he is to draw with the right, and not as Elisha did. (He repulsed Gehazi with both hands.) *Yalkut Jeremiah.*

Showers of rain are geater than the giving of the Law, for the giving of the Law was a gladsome event to Israel only, but rain is a cause of joy to the wide world, including cattle, beasts, and fowls. *Midrash Shochar Tov,* 117

David was a shepherd of Israel, and the Shepherd of David was the Holy One — blessed be He ! — as it is said (Ps. xxiii. 1), "The Lord is my Shepherd."

Midrash Rabbah, chap. 59.

Rav Pinchas says, "David in the Psalms calls five times upon the Holy One — blessed be He ! — to arise. (1.) 'Arise, O Lord ; save me, O my God !' (Ps. iii. 7). {2.) 'Arise, O Lord, in Thine anger !' (Ps. vii. 6). (3.) 'Arise, O Lord, let not man prevail !' (Ps. ix. 19). (4.) 'Arise, O Lord ; O God, lift up Thine hand : forget not the humble !' (Ps. x. 12). (5.) 'Arise, O Lord ; disappoint him !' But the Holy One — blessed be He ! — said unto David, 'My son, though thou call upon Me many a time to arise, I will not arise. But when do I arise? When thou seest the poor oppressed and the needy sighing, then will I arise.'" This explains what is written (Ps. xii. 5), "For the oppression of the poor, for the sighing of the needy, now will I arise, saith the Lord."

Bamidbar Rabbah, chap. 75.

"And Solomon's wisdom excelled" (1 Kings iv. 30). Thou findest that when Solomon desired to build the Temple he sent to Pharaoh Necho a request to send him artisans on hire. Pharaoh assembled his astrologers, who pointed out to him such artisans as were destined to die in the course of that year, and these he despatched to Solomon ; but he, through the Holy Ghost, seeing the fate that impended, provided each of them with a shroud and sent them back to Pharaoh with the message, "Hast thou no shrouds in which to bury thine own dead? Behold here I have provided them with them !" "For he was wiser than all men" (1 Kings iv. 31) ; "than all men," even than the first man, Adam.

Yalkut Eliezer, fol. 65, col. 2, n. 36.

"Ye are My witnesses, saith the Lord, that I am God" (Isa. xliii. 12). Rabbi Shimon ben Yochai expounds these words thus, "If ye are My witnesses, then I am God ; but if ye are not My witnesses, then I am not God."

Yalkut Jethro, n. 271.

" Let us hear the conclusion of the whole matter " (Eccles. xii. 13). Thou shalt ever hear the Law, even when thou dost not understand it. " Fear God," and give thy heart to Him. " And keep His commandments," for on account of the Law the whole world was created, that the world should study it.

Koheleth, as given in Tse-enah Ure-enah.

THE KABBALA

« The words of the wise and their dark sayings » (Prov. i. 6).

INTRODUCTORY NOTE

THE Hebrew word Kabbal means "to receive," and its derivative, Kabbalah, signifies, "a thing received," viz, "Tradition," which, together with the written law, Moses received on Mount Sinai, and we are told in the Talmud, Rosh Hashanah, fol. 19, col. 1, *i. e.*, "The words of the Kabbalah are just the same as the words of the law." In another part of this work we have seen that the Rabbis declare the Kabbalah to be above the law.

The Kabbalah is divided into two parts, viz, the symbolical and the real.

THE SYMBOLICAL KABBALAH

This teaches the secret of mystic sense of Scripture, and the thirteen rules by which the observance of the law is, not logically, but Kabbalistically expounded; viz, the rules of "Gematria," of "Notricon," of "Temurah," etc. To give some idea of this kind of exposition, we will explain each of these three rules in a manner which, though in the style of the Rabbis, will easily be understood by the Gentile reader.

1. "Gematria." This rule depends on the numerical value of each letter in the alphabet. The application of this rule in the solution of a disputed point is often such as to show quite as much absurdity as ingenuity. To make the subject still more clear, let us assume that a standard numerical value is attached to each letter in the English alphabet. *A* has the value of 1, *B* 2, *C* 3, *D* 4, *E* 5, *F* 6, *G* 7, *H* 8, *I* 9, *J* 10, *K* 20, *L* 30, *M* 40, *N* 50, *O* 60, *P* 70, *Q* 80, *R* 90, *S* 100, *T* 200, *U* 300, *V* 400, *W* 500, *X* 1000, *Y* 10,-000, *Z* 100,000. And let us now assume a point in dispute in order to illustrate how it is solved by Gematria. Suppose that the subject of discussion is the comparative superiority of the Hebrew and English languages, and Hugo and Baruch are the disputants. The former, being a Hebrew, holds that the Hebrew is superior to the English,

"because," says he, "the numerical value of the letters that form the word *Hebrew* is 610; whereas the numerical value of *English* is only 209." The latter, being an Englishman, holds, of course, exactly the contrary opinion, and argues as follows: "All the learned world must admit that the English is a living language, but not so the Hebrew; and as it is written (Eccles. ix. 4) that 'A living dog is better than a dead lion,' I therefore maintain that the English is superior to the Hebrew." The dispute was referred to an Oxford authority for decision, and a certain learned doctor decided it by —

2. "Notricon." This consists in forming a decisive sentence composed of words whose initial letters are in a given word; for instance, *Hebrew*: —"*H*ugo's *e*xcels *B*aruch's *r*easoning *e*very *w*ay." *English*: —"*E*nglish *n*o *g*ood *l*anguage, *i*s *s*carcely *h*armonious;" but *Hebrew*: — "*H*oly, *e*legant, *b*rilliant, *r*esonant, *e*liciting *w*onder!" This is a fair specimen of how to get at the secret sense of a word by the rule of "Notricon," and now we will proceed to explain —

3. "Temurah." This means permutation, or a change of the letters of the alphabet after a regularly adopted system. We know only five such permuted alphabets, but there may be more. The technical names of these five alphabets are: "Atbash," "Atbach," "Albam," "Aiakbechar," and "Tashrak." We will try to explain the first permuted alphabet only, as a mere specimen, for the general reader is not quite prepared to comprehend the rest, and a hint for the scholar is sufficient.

Here let the reader observe that as the letters of the English alphabet are more numerous and differently designated and arranged than those of the Hebrew, the "Atbash" of the Hebrew must necessarily become "Azby" in English. If now we write on one line and in regular order the first half of the alphabet, and the other half on the second line, but in reversed order, thus: —

$$a\ b\ c\ d\ e\ f\ g\ h\ i\ j\ k\ l\ m$$
$$z\ y\ x\ w\ v\ u\ t\ s\ r\ q\ p\ o\ n$$

we get thirteen couples of letters which exchange one with the other, viz, *a* and *z*, *b* and *y*, *c* and *x*, etc. These letters, when exchanged, give rise to a permuted alphabet, and this permuted alphabet takes its technical name from the first two couples of letters, *a* and *z*, *b* and *y*, or "Azby." Now if we wish to write, "Meddle not with them that are given to change," you have to change the letters of the couples and the following will be the result: "Nvwwov mlg drgs gsvn gszg ziv trem gl xszmtv." This is a specimen of the mysterious Temurah, and the "Azby" is the key to it. The other four permuted alphabets are of a similar nature and character, and are so highly esteemed among the sages and bards of Israel, that they often use them in their literary and poetical compositions. The Machzorim, or the Jewish Liturgies for the festivals, are full of compositions where the first letters of the sentences follow the order of either the "Atbash" or "Tashrak." The latter is simply a reversed order of the alphabet.

The Real Kabbalah

The "Real Kabbalah" consists of theoretical and practical mysteries.

1. The theoretical mysteries treat about the ten spheres, the four worlds, the essence and various names of God and of angels, also of the celestial hierarchy and its influences and effects on this lower world, of the mysteries of creation, of the mystical chariot described by the Prophet Ezekiel, of the different orders and offices of angels and demons, also of a great many other deep subjects, too deep for comprehension.

2. The practical Kabbalah is a branch of the theoretical, and treats of the practical use of the mysterious names of God and of angels. By uttering properly the Shem-ham-mephorash, *i. e.*, the ineffable name of Jehovah, or the names of certain angels, or by the mere repetition of certain Scripture texts, miracles and wonders were and still are performed in the Jewish world.

THE KABBALA

KNOW thou that the 613 Precepts of the Law form a compact with the Holy One — blessed be He ! — and with Israel, as it is often explained in the Zohar. It is written (Exod. iii. 15), " This is My name, and this is My memorial." " My name," in the Hebrew characters, together with " Yeho," amounts numerically to 365 ; " Vah," together with " My memorial," amounts to 248. Here we have the number 613 in the Holy One — blessed be He ! The soul is a portion of God from above, and this is mystically intimated by the degrees of " breath, spirit, soul," the initial and final letters of which amount to 613, while the middle letters of these amount to the number of " Lord, Almighty, God." The soul of Moses our Rabbi — peace be on him ! — embraced all the souls of Israel ; as it is said, Moses was equivalent to all Israel. " Moses our Rabbi" amounts to 613 ; and "Lord God of Israel" also amounts to 613.   *Kitsur Sh'lu*, p. 2, col. 2.

Now let us illustrate the subject of " fear and love." Fear proceedeth from love and love proceedeth from fear. And this you may demonstrate by writing their letters one over the other, and then dividing them by horizontal and perpendicular lines, thus Love perfecteth fear, and fear perfecteth love. This is to teach thee that both are united together.   *Ibid.*, p. 4, col. 2.

The Holy One — blessed be He ! — often brings affliction on the righteous though they have not sinned, in order that they may learn to keep aloof from the allurements of the world and eschew temptation to sin. From this it is plain that afflictions are good for man, and therefore our Rabbis, of blessed memory, have said, " As men bless with joy and a sincere heart for a benefit received, so likewise ought they joyfully to bless God when He afflicts them, as, though the special blessing be hidden from the children of

men, such affliction is surely intended for good. . . .
Or most souls being at present in a state of transmigration,
God requites a man now for what his soul merited in a
bypast time in another body, by having broken some of
the 613 precepts." *Kitzur Sh'lu*, p. 6, col. 1.

Thus we have the rule: No one is perfect unless he
has thoroughly observed all the 613 precepts. If this be
so, who is he and where is he that has observed all the
613 precepts? For even the lord of the prophets, Moses
our Rabbi — peace be on him! — had not observed them
all; for there are four obstacles which hinder one from observing all: (1.) There is the case of complete preven-
tion, such as the law of the priesthood, the precepts of
which only priests can observe, and yet these precepts are
included in the 613. Besides, there are among the number
precepts appertaining to the Levites which concern neither
priests nor Israelites, and also others which are binding on
Israelites with which priests and Levites have nothing whatever to do. (2.) Then there are impossible cases, as, for
instance, when one cannot observe the precept which enforces circumcision, because he has not a son to circumcise.
(3 and 4.) There are also conditional and exceptional cases,
as in the case of precepts having reference to the Temple
and to the land of Israel. *Ibid.*, p. 6, col. 2.

Therefore every Israelite is bound to observe only such
of the 613 precepts as are possible to him; and such as he
has not observed in consequence of hindrances arising from
unpreventable causes will be reckoned to him as if actually
performed. *Ibid.*

The Yalkut Shimeoni, in true Rabbinical style, amplifies still
farther the license conceded in the above quotations. Rabbi Eliezer
says that the Israelites bewailed thus before God, exclaiming, "We
would fain be occupied night and day in the law, but we have not
the necessary leisure." Then the Holy One — blessed be He! — said,
"Perform the commandment of the Phylacteries, and I will account
it as if you were occupied night and day in the study of the law."

Anyhow, all the precepts are being observed by all Israel
taken together, viz, the priests observe their part, the
Levites theirs, and the Israelites theirs; thus the whole
keep all. For the Holy One — blessed be He! — has writ-

ten a law for His faithful servants, the nation of Israel, and as a nation they keep the whole law. It is as once when a king wrote to his subjects thus, " Behold, I command you to prepare for war against the enemy ; raise the walls higher, collect arms, and store up victuals ; " and those that were builders looked after the walls, the armorers after the weapons, the farmers after the stores of food, etc., etc. Each, according to his ability, did all that was required of him, and all unitedly fulfilled the king's command.

Kitzur Sh'lu, p. 6, col. 2.

He who neglects to observe any of the 613 precepts, such as were possible for him to observe, is doomed to undergo transmigration (once or more than once) till he has actually observed all he had neglected to do in a former state of being. *Ibid.*

The sages of truth (the Kabbalists) remark that Adam contains the initial letters of Adam, David, and Messiah ; for after Adam sinned his soul passed into David, and the latter having also sinned, it passed into the Messiah. The full text is, " They shall serve the Lord their God, and David their king, whom I will raise up to them " (Jer. xxx. 9) ; and it is written, " My servant David shall be their king forever " (Ezek. xxxvii. 25) ; and thus " They shall seek the Lord their God, and David their king " (Hosea iii. 5).

Nishmath Chaim, fol. 152, col. 2.

Know thou that Cain's essential soul passed into Jethro, but his spirit into Korah, and his animal soul into the Egyptian. This is what Scripture saith, " Cain shall be avenged sevenfold " (Gen. iv. 24), *i. e.*, the initial letters of the Hebrew word rendered " shall be avenged," form the initials of Jethro, Korah, and Egyptian. . . . Samson the hero was possessed by the soul of Japhet, and Job by that of Terah. *Yalkut Reubeni*, Nos. 9, 18, 24.

Cain had robbed the twin sister of Abel, and therefore his soul passed into Jethro. Moses was possessed by the soul of Abel, and therefore Jethro gave his daughter to Moses. *Yalkut Chadash*, fol. 127, col. 3.

If a man be niggardly either in a financial or a spiritual regard, giving nothing of his money to the poor or not

18

imparting of his knowledge to the ignorant, he shall be
punished by transmigration into a woman. . . . Know
thou that Sarah, Hannah, the Shunammite (2 Kings iv. 8),
and the widow of Zarepta were each in turn possessed by
the soul of Eve. . . . The soul of Rahab transmigrated
into Heber the Kenite, and afterward into Hannah ; and this
is the mystery of her words, "I am a woman of a sorrowful spirit" (1 Sam. i. 15), for there still lingered in her
soul a sorrowful sense of inherited defilement. . . . Eli
possessed the soul of Jael, the wife of Heber the Kenite.
. . . Sometimes the souls of pious Jews pass by metempsychosis into Gentiles, in order that they may plead on
behalf of Israel and treat them kindly. For this reason have
our Rabbis of blessed memory said, "The pious of the nations of the world have a portion in the world to come."
Yalkut Reubeni, Nos. 1, 8, 61, 63.

We have it by tradition that when Moses our Rabbi —
peace be unto him ! — said in the law, "O God, the God
of the spirits of all flesh" (Num. xvi. 22), he meant mystically to intimate that metempsychosis takes place in all
flesh, in beasts, reptiles, and fowls. "Of all flesh" is, as
it were, "in all flesh." *Avodath Hakodesh*, fol. 49, col. 3.

It is also needful that thou shouldst know that the Kabbalists believe in metempsychosis from the body of one species
into the body of another species. Thou hast already been
informed of the mystery of clean and unclean animals ; and
some of the later sages of the Kabbalah say that the soul
of an unclean person will transmigrate into an unclean animal, or into abominable creeping things or reptiles. . . .
For one form of uncleanness the soul will be invested
with the body of a Gentile, who will (eventually) become
a proselyte ; for another, the soul will pass into the body
of a mule ; for others, it transmigrates into an ass, a woman
of Ashdod, a bat, a rabbit or a hare, a she-mule or a
camel. Ishmael transmigrated first into the she-ass of Balaam, and subsequently into the ass of Rabbi Pinchas ben
Yair.   *Nishmath Chaim*, chap. 13, No. 14.

The last paragraph may be illustrated by the well-known story
of the ass of R. Pinchas, which persistently objected to feed on

untithed provender. This is also said of the ass of Rabbi Chanina ben Dossa. See Avoth d'Rab. Nathan, chap. 8.

Sometimes the soul of a righteous man may be found in the body of a clean animal or fowl.

Caphtor Upherach, fol. 51, col. 2.

It sometimes happens that one sacrifices an animal with a human soul in it. And this is the mystic meaning of (Ps. xxxvi. 6), "O Lord, thou preservest man and beast." It is for this reason that we are commanded to have our slaughtering-knife without defect, for who knows if there be not a transmigrated soul in the animal? . . . Therefore the slaughter must needs be delicately done and the mode critically examined, on account of that which is written (Lev. xix. 18), "Thou shalt love thy neighbor as thyself." *Nishmath Chaim*, chap. 13, No. 4.

At each of the three meals of the Sabbath one should eat fish, for into them the souls of the righteous are transmigrated. And in relation to them it is written (Num. xi. 22), "All the fish of the sea shall be gathered together for them." *Yalkut Chadash*, fol. 20, col. 4, No. 9.

The soul of a slanderer is transmigrated into a silent stone. *Emeh Hamelech*, fol. 153, col. 2.

Rabbi Isaac Luria was once passing the great academy of Rabbi Yochanan in Tiberias, where he showed his disciples a stone in the wall, remarking, "In this stone there is a transmigrated soul, and it cries that I should pray on its behalf. And this is the mystic meaning of (Hab. ii. 11), 'The stone shall cry out of the wall.'"

Ibid., fol. 11, col. 2.

The murderer is transmigrated into water. The mystical sign of this is indicated in (Deut. xii. 16), "Ye shall pour it upon the earth as water;" and the meaning is, he is continually rolling on and on without any rest. Therefore let no man drink (direct) from a running tap or spout, but from the hollow of his hands, lest a soul pass into him, and that the soul of a wicked sinner.

Ibid., fol. 153, cols. 1, 2.

One who sins with a married woman is, after undergoing the penalty of wandering about as a fugitive and vagabond, transmigrated, together with his accomplice, into the mill-stone of a water-mill, according to the mystery of (Job xxxi. 10), " Let my wife grind unto another."

Emeh Hamelech, fol. 153, cols. 1, 2.

A butcher who kills an animal with a defective knife will die of the plague, and his soul will pass into a dog, whom he thus deprives of what belongs to him ; for it is said (Exod. xxii. 31), Ye shall cast it to the dogs."

Kitzur Sh'lh, fol. 17, col. 2.

An animal slaughtered with an improper knife is considered as if it had been "torn of beasts in the field," and the flesh of it, according ing to the law, belongs to the dogs. A careless butcher, selling the meat as food for man, deprives the dog of his due.

The sages of truth have written, " He who does not wash his hands before eating, as the Rabbis of blessed memory have ordained, will be transmigrated into a cata-ract, where he will have no rest, even as a murderer, who is also transmigrated into water." *Ibid.*, fol. 21, col. 2.

After washing his hands before a meal, he is to stretch out his fingers and turn the palms of his hands upward, as if in the act of receiving something from a friend, and then repeat (Ps. cxxxiv. 2), " Lift ye up your holy hands, and bless ye the Lord ! " *Ibid.*

The following are the usual blessings, " Blessed art Thou, O Lord, our God ! King of the universe ! who has sanctified us with His commandments, and has commanded us to wash the hands !" " Blessed art Thou, O Lord, our God ! King of the universe ! who bringeth forth bread from the earth !"

By means of combining the letters of the ineffable names, as recorded in " Book of Creation," Rava once created a man and sent him to Rav Zera. The man being unable to reply when spoken to, the Rabbi said to him, " Thou art a creation of the company (initiated in the mysteries of necromancy) ; return to thy dust."

Sanhedrin, fol. 65, col. 2.

In the Jerusalem Talmud, Sanhedrin, chap. 7, we read that, by the means above mentioned, a Rabbi created pumpkins, melons, and real deer and roes.

There is a living creature in heaven which by day has " Truth " upon its forehead, by which the angels know it is day; but in the evening it has "Faith" on its fore-head, whereby the angels know that night is near. Each time the living creature says, "Bless ye the blessed Lord," all the hosts above respond, "Blessed be the blessed Lord forever." *Kitzur Sh'lh*, fol. 42. col. 2.

Truth and faith are the essentials of religion, which are thirteen in number : —

1. God exists, and there is no period to His existence. The philosophers call it absolute existence, but the majority of Kabbalists term it "endless," which, by Gematria, is "light"; and again, by Gematria, is "Lord of the Universe." He is the cause of causes and the causing of causings, and from or by His existence all beings, spiritual and material, derive their existence.

2. He is one, and there is no unity like His, etc.

3. He has no bodily likeness, and is not corporeal.

4. He is first of everything, absolute beginning; as it is said, "I am the First and I am the Last" (Isa. xliv 6), and there is no beginning to His beginning.

5. None but Himself is to be worshiped and prayed to.

6. The gift of prophecy He has given to men esteemed and glorified by Him.

7. None arose like unto Moses, etc.

8. A law of truth He gave; this is the law from heaven, "In the beginning" unto "in the sight of all Israel." Also its comment received orally is likewise "a law (given) unto Moses from Sinai."

9. God will not change or alter His law forever. He will never change the law of Moses our Rabbi — peace be unto him! The law will suffer no addition or diminution (but it will abide even), as the prophet Malachi sealed it with the seal of the prophets in ending his words (Mal. iv. 4), "Remember ye the law of Moses My servant, which I commanded unto him in Horeb for all Israel." Formerly the law was in a garment of light, but in consequence of sin, the law became materialized in a garment of skin, in the same proportion as man became materialized in a body of flesh. In the future, after the redemption, however, the law will have the garment of light restored, and the Messiah will preach the law in terrible mysteries,

such as no ear has ever heard, and it will appear to us as a new law. But the law will not be altered, or made new, as the nations of the world say = Jer. xxxi. 30–33.

10. He observeth and knoweth all our secrets, etc.

11. There are rewards and punishments in the future, etc.

12. He will send at the end of days our Messiah from the seed of David to redeem His people Israel from among the nations, and restore to them the kingdom.

13. There will be a revival of the dead, etc.

Kitzur Sh'lh, fol. 7, col. 2.

Let a man believe that whatever occurs to him is from the Blessed One! For instance, when a wicked man meets him and abuses him, and puts him to shame, let him receive it with love, and say, " The Lord told him to curse, and he is the messenger of God on account of my sin."

Ibid., fol. 8, col. 1.

In every deed or transaction a man performs by his own free will, be it a matter of precept or of option, let the name of God be ready in his mouth. If, for instance, he erects a building, or buys a vessel, or makes a new garment, let him say with his mouth and utter with his lips, "This thing I do, for (the honor of) the union of the Shechinah with the Holy One — blessed be He!" *Ibid.*

Bismillahi Arrahmani Arraheemi," In the name of God, most merciful and compassionate," is the motto of every work undertaken by a Mohammedan.

A man should always desire that his neighbor may profit by him, and let him not strive to profit by his neighbor. Let his words be pleasant with the children of men if they shame him, and let him not shame them in return. If they deceive him, let him not deceive them in return, and let him take the yoke of the public upon his shoulders, and not impose it heavily on them in return. *Ibid.*

If — which God forbid! — thy neighbor has done thee an evil, pardon him at once ; for thou shouldst love him as thyself. If one hand is accidentally hurt by the other, should the wounded hand revenge its injury on the other? And, as urged before, thou shouldst rather say in thine heart, "It is from the Lord that it came to thee; it came as a messenger from the Holy One — blessed be He! — as a punishment for some sin." *Kitzur Sh'lh*, fol. 9. col. 2.

A sage who was very sorrowful was once comforted thus: "If thy sorrow relates to this world, may God decrease it; but if it relates to the world to come, may God increase it and add sorrow to sorrow." (See 2 Cor. vii. 10.)
Ibid., fol. 10, col. 1.

A man should not wade through water or traverse any dangerous place in company with an apostate, or even a wicked Jew, lest he be overtaken (in the same ruin) with him. (Comp. Eph. v. 7, 8; Rev. xviii. 4.)
Ibid., fol. 10, col. 2.

The influence of the son is relatively greater and more blessed than that of the father, for the merits of the father do not profit the son except in matters relating to this world (as by bequeathing him worldly inheritance); whereas the merits of the son do more than benefit the father in this world; they benefit him also in the world to come (by saying "Kadish"), which is enough to deliver his soul from purgatory. *Ibid.*, fol. 11, col. 2.

A common proverb says, "One father willingly maintains ten sons, but ten sons are not willing to support one father."
Ibid., fol. 12, col. 2.

The proper use of money is that thou learn the art of dealing honestly, so that thy No be no and thy Yes, yes; and as far as possible be benevolent with the money. "And the liberal by liberal things shall stand" (Isa. xxxii. 8).
Ibid.

The sage says, "The eye of a needle is not narrow enough for two friends, but the world in not wide enough for two enemies." *Ibid.*, fol. 14, col. 1.

"Create in me a clean heart, O God, and renew a right spirit within me" (Ps. li. 10). Know thou that the heart is the source of life, and is placed in the centre the body as the Holy of holies, as stated in the Book Zohar, is the central part of the world. Therefore one must have his heart cleansed from evil and all evil thoughts, otherwise he introduces an idol into the innermost part of the Temple, which ought to be a dwelling-place for the Shechinah. (See 1 Cor. iii, 16, 17, and vi. 19.)

Kitzur Sh'lh, fol. 14, col. 2.

He who gazes even on the little finger of a woman is as if he looked on her to lust after her. He should not give ear to a woman's voice, for the voice of a woman is lewdness. This sin is much discussed in the Zohar; it causes the husband to come to poverty, and deprives him and her sons of all respect. *Ibid.*, fol. 17, col. 1.

The sages of the Kabbalah were not singular in this view. The Talmud Yerush, Callah, fol. 58, col. 3, says, "He that looks upon a woman's heel is guilty of an act of lewdness."

Eating meat after cheese or cheese after meat is a very serious sin; and it is stated in the Zohar, section Mishpatim, that upon him who is without scruple in this regard, an evil spirit will rest for forty days, his soul will be from the spirit which has no holiness. *Ibid.*, fol. 18, col. 2.

The sages of the Kabbalah have written that it becomes him who has in him the fear of Heaven to have a vessel of water near his bed, in order that (on waking in the morning) he may not need to walk four ells without washing his hands, for he who walks four ells without washing his hands has forfeited his life as a divine punishment.

Ibid., fol. 43, col. 2.

When a man is dressing, he should first put on the right shoe and leave it unfastened till he has put on and fastened the left; then he should fasten the right, as it is explained in the Shulchan Aruch. *Ibid.*, fol. 44, col. 2.

The following are some of the many laws relating to the Shemonah-esreh, or the eighteen blessings which form the most devotional part of daily worship, and which are repeated three times on (ordinary) week-days, and four times on Sabbaths, new moons, and on appointed feasts : —

Before commencing the Shemonah-esreh one should step back three paces, in order to be able to advance three steps. The reason of this is that Moses our Rabbi — peace be on him ! — advanced before his prayer into the three

divisions, "darkness, clouds, and thick darkness" (Deut. iv.
11). And this is also the reason why after finishing the
Shemonah-esreh three steps backward are to be made, returning through these three parts or divisions.

This prayer is to be performed standing, and the feet so
joined together that they should seem as it were one foot
only, in order to be like the angels, of whom it is written
(Ezek. i. 7), "And their feet were (so in the original) a
straight foot," that is to say, their feet appeared as one
foot.

This attitude is a sign that the power of locomotion is
gone; he cannot pursue and attain any other object than
God. The Gentiles place their hands together, intending to
signify thereby that their hands are as it were bound; but
we, by placing our feet together, intend to signify that
they are as it were entirely bound, which is indicative of
greater humility; for with the hands bound one could still
run away in search of his own pleasure, which he cannot
do when the feet are bound.

Kitzur Sh'lh, fol. 48, col. 2, and fol. 49, col. 1.

It is lawful for him who rides upon an animal to pray
the eighteen benedictions, and when he comes to the point
when he should retrace three steps, he is to back the animal he is mounted on three steps. And so also it is lawful to pray the eighteen blessings when sitting and traveling in a wagon.   *Ibid.*, fol. 49, col. 1.

It is necessary to pay attention to the feet when the
worshiper repeats "Holy! holy! holy!" and he is to
lift up his eyes toward heaven. At the instant the Kid-
dushah is repeated he needs only lift up his heels, and
thereby his body from the earth toward heaven. . . .
According to Tanchuma it is necessary to lift up the feet
from the earth altogether, after the example of the angels,
of whom it is written (Isa. vi. 2), "And with two he did
fly." It is from this text that the sages have ordained
that a man should fly up (as it were) when he repeats
"Holy! holy! holy!" And let the chooser choose, *i. e.*,
it is optional either to lift up the heels only or to jump.
                                                  Ibid.

Any one who visits a synagogue may notice the observance of this practice. In the synagogues of the Chassidim, jumping is preferred to lifting up the heels.

It is written (Ps. cii. 17), "He will regard the prayer of the destitute," and it is not written, "He will hear." What else can the term "regard" mean than that there is a distinction between the prayer of an individual and the prayer of a community? For when a community prays, their prayer enters before the Holy One — blessed be He! — and He is not particular to regard and criticise their works and their intentions and thoughts, but receives their prayers immediately. But when an individual prays, the Holy One — blessed be He! — regards and scrutinizes his heart, whether it be devout and whether he be a righteous man. Therefore, one should always pray with the community, and this is why the text (Ps. cvii. 17) ends with the words, "And not despise their prayer." Although there are some of the community whose prayers, on account of their evil deeds, deserve to be despised, He, nevertheless, does not despise their prayer.

Kitzur Sh'lh, fol. 51, col. 1.

A man should study less on Friday, that he may occupy himself with the preparation for the Sabbath. And accordingly we find in the Gemara that some of the great and esteemed sages occupied themselves on that day in preparing what was needed for the Sabbath. Therefore, though one may have many servants to wait upon him, it is a great merit personally to prepare for the wants of the Sabbath in order thus to honor it; and let him not think it derogatory to his own honor to honor the Sabbath thus, for it is his honor to honor the Sabbath. It is written of H'A'ree of blessed memory, that he was in the habit of sweeping away the cobwebs in his house (in honor of the Sabbath), and it is well known to the initiated what a wonderful mystery it is to abolish the unclean spirits from the house, "And this is enough for him that understands." *Ibid.*, fol. 61, col. 1.

One should trim his finger-nails every Friday, never on Thursday, otherwise the nails will commence growing on the following Sabbath. He should pare the nails of the left hand first, beginning at the fourth finger and ending with the thumb; and then he should pare the nails of the right hand, beginning with the thumb and ending with the fourth finger; he should not vary the following order: 4th, 2d, 5th, 3d, 1st of the left hand; then the 1st, 3d, 5th, 2d, 4th of the right hand. Never pare two (contiguous) fingers one after the other, for it is dangerous, and it also impairs the memory. The reason and mystery about the order for paring the nails are well known to the expert.   *Kitzur Sh'lh.*

In the Zohar it is explained that the benefit of immersion on Friday amounts to the restoration of the soul to her proper place, for he who is bodily unclean has no soul.
                                   Ibid., fol. 61, col. 2.

Before entering the plunging-bath, he is to repeat (Gen. i. 10), "And God called the dry land earth, and the gathering together of the waters called He seas." When he stands in the water he is to repeat seven times (Ps. li. 10), "Create in me a clean heart, O God, and renew a right spirit within me," for the initials of "Create in me a clean heart," form the word "to dip," *i. e.*, to immerse. For it is through immersion that the unclean spirits and the "other side," are separated from him, and he becomes a new creature by examining and confessing his (evil) deeds, and forsaking them, and by engaging himself in repentance, and immersing himself, and meditating on elevating subjects, and especially so if he has immersed himself fourteen times.   *Ibid.*, fol. 61, col. 1.

When standing in the water he is to stoop four times, so that the water may reach his neck, answering to the four modes of legal execution. After that he is to repeat the form of confession, and while the water reaches up to his throat he is to repeat these three texts — Micah vii. 18–20, Jer. x. 24, and Ps. cxviii. 5, and then say, "As I cleanse my body here below, which is formed of clay, so may the ministering angels cleanse my soul, spirit, and ghost above in the river Dinor; and as I sanctify my body here below, so may the angels of the Most High, the mintering angels, sanctify my spirit, soul, and ghost in the river Dinor above! In the name of Jehovah, He is the God and in the name of Adonai, the Rock of all Ages. Blessed be the name of the glory of His kingdom forevermore!"   *Kitzur Sh'lh*, fol. 62, col. 1.

According to the Kabbalah, the thoroughgoing orthodox Jew has his hands full on Erev Shabbath, *i. e.*, Friday. We cannot here go over the entire proceeding prescribed, but we will briefly touch upon its salient features in the order as we find them.

After having prepared himself for immersion, as above described, he is to turn his face and bow first toward the west and then toward the east, repeating a certain formula, and then dip himself under the water. This over, he is to turn again east and west and repeat a different formula, and while meditating on certain given letters of certain mystical divine names and other known words, and their respective numerical values, he is to dip a second time under the water. Then turning and bowing again west and east, repeating the while a different formula, he proceeds to meditate on different letters of the divine names, and dips for the third and last time. As dipping fourteen times is the exception and not the rule, no farther directions are given about the matter, except a few additional formulæ and meditations.

When he comes out of the water he is to step backward in the same respectful manner as when he leaves the synagogue, and is to repeat Isa. iv. 3, 4, and Rabbi Akiva's commentary on the text Ezek. xxxvi. 25.

When he begins dressing he is to repeat Isa. liv. 17, and when he subsequently washes his face and hands and feet in warm water, to which is attached a great mystery, he is to say, "Behold, here I am, washing myself in honor of Sabbath the queen;" and add also Isa. iv. 4, and also, "I have washed my feet; how shall I defile them?" (Cant. v. 3.)

Happy is he who is able to provide himself with a complete suit of apparel down to the girdle, the shoes, and the hat for wearing on the Sabbath, different from those worn on week-days. Then he is to repeat the Book of Solomon's Song, and if unable to repeat the whole, he is, at all events, to repeat these four verses, the initials of the first word in each of which taken together form the word Jacob, Cant. i. 2, ii. 10, ii. 8, v. 1. After this he is to repeat certain portions of the Mishnah, and something of the Zohar or some other Kabbalistic work.

This over, the devout Israelite goes to the synagogue to meet his God as the bridegroom, and to receive the Sabbath as the bride. The service is well worthy of rehearsal, but we must refer for details to the Liturgy.

The Israelite returns home from the synagogue accompanied by two angels, one good and the other evil; and according to the condition of the domestic arrangements when he re-enters, he is blessed by the good angel or cursed by the evil one.

The Israelite is solemnly warned not to quarrel with his wife on Sabbath-eve, for the devils are very busy then to stir up more strife, as is illustrated by the story of Rabbi Meir.

Having repeated the usual hymn appointed for the Sabbath-eve, and pronounced the form of blessing over the cup of wine, he and his family commence their supper, which is carefully prepared of the very choicest viands, flesh and fish included. Hymns and a certain form of blessing after the meal complete the family duties of the day, and all retire to rest. The head of the family, if he be a pious Israelite, and especially a disciple of the wise, has a particular duty to perform—a duty which is based on Scripture and on the following text (Exod. xxxi. 16), "Wherefore the children of Israel shall keep the Sabbath." (*Kitzur Sh'lh*, fol. 64, col. 1.)

Of the laws relating to the Sabbath we can here only enumerate a few; we shall, however, take them in order as detailed in the book before us.

Jewish women, maid-servants and girls are warned not to order a Gentile woman on the Sabbath to do this or that, but they may instruct her on a work-day what she is to do on the Sabbath.

Geese, fowl, cats, dogs, etc., are not to be handled on the Sabbath. Neither are pocket-handkerchiefs, spectacles, etc., to be carried on the Sabbath in an unwalled town or village. Radishes are not to be salted in quantities, but each piece is to be dipped separately in salt and eaten. After dinner the Israelite is to take a siesta, for each letter forms the initial of a word, and the words thus formed are "Sleep on the Sabbath is a delight." (See Isa. lviii. 13.) Before he dozes off he is to repeat the last verse of the 90th and the whole of the 91st Psalm. The salutation should not be, as on working-days, "Good morning," but "Good Sabbath;" for respecting this it is said (Exod. xx. 8), "Remember the Sabbath-day to keep it holy." He is not to rise on the Sabbath as early as on the other days of the week, and this is based on Scripture. He is to be very careful with the fur garments that he may be wearing, lest he should pluck a hair therefrom, and for the same reason he is not to scratch his head or touch his beard on the Sabbath. He is not to wash his hands with salt or soap on the Sabbath, nor may he play at ball; he is not to knock with a rapper on a door, or ring the house-bell; nor, if he has married a widow, is he to co-habit with her on that day. *Kitzur Sh'lh*, fols. 65–67.

At the close of the Sabbath he is to pronounce over a cup of wine what is technically termed the " Separation," for the departure of the Sabbath, as given in the prayer-book. He is then to fold up his Tallith or veil and sing " Hamavdil," the first verse of which runs thus: —

" May He who maketh a distinction between the holy (Sabbath) and the profane (days of the week) pardon our sins and multiply our children and our money as the sand and as the stars in the night!"

Should he forget to fold his veil (Tallith), he is to shake it thoroughly the next morning, in order to get rid of the evil spirits that have harbored there during the night, and the reason is known to the lords of the Kab-balah. *Ibid.*, fol. 71, col. 1.

It is customary then to repeat a number of hymns and songs and legends wherein Elijah the Prophet is mentioned, because he it is that is to come and bring the tidings of redemption, for it is thus stated in Tosephta, that on the exit of the Sabbath Elijah of blessed memory sits under the " Tree of Life" and records in writing the merits of those that keep the Sabbath. Those that are particular repeat, and the very pious write, " Elijah the Prophet, Elijah the Prophet, Elijah the Prophet," a hundred and thirty times, for "Elijah the Prophet," by Gematria equals 120, to which add 10, the number of the letters, and the total is 130. *Ibid.*

The word Elijah is written a hundred and thirty times in tabular form, with the letters transposed. This can be understood better by forming a Kabbalistic table of the same word in English.

Elijah	Ehlija	Ejahli	Eijahl	Elhija
Elahij	Eljahi	Elhaji	Eljiah	Ealijh
Eahlij	Eajhli	Eaijhl	Ealhij	Ehalij
Ehlaij	Ehijla	Ehjial	Ehialj	Ehjail

and so on.

The last day of the month is called, "The little Day of Atonement," and it is fit and proper to do penance on that day. On the first day of the month it is a pious act to prepare an extra dish for dinner in honor of the day. God has given the first of the month (as a festival) more for women than for men, because the three annual festivals are according to the three patriarchs, Abraham, Isaac, and Jacob, and because the twelve months are according to the twelve tribes; and as the tribes sinned in the matter of the golden calf, and the women were unwilling to give up their golden earrings for that idolatrous purpose, therefore they deserved that God should give them as their reward the first days of the twelve months, according to the number of the tribes. *Kitzur Sh'lh*, fol. 72, col. 1.

It is a very pious act to bless the moon at the close of the Sabbath, when one is dressed in his best attire and perfumed. If the blessing is to be performed on the evening of an ordinary week-day the best dress is to be worn. According to the Kabbalists the blessings upon the moon are not to be said till seven full days after her birth, but, according to later authorities, this may be done after three days. The reason for not performing this monthly service under a roof, but in the open air, is because it is considered as a reception of the presence of the Shechinah, and it would not be respectful so to do anywhere but in the open air. It depends very much upon circumstances when and where the new moon is to be consecrated, and also upon one's own predisposition, for authorities differ. We will close these remarks with the conclusion of the Kitzur Sh'lu on the subject, which, at p. 72, col. 2, runs thus : —

" When about to sanctify the new moon, one should straighten his feet (as at the Shemonah-esreh) and give one glance at the moon before he begins to repeat the ritual blessing, and having commenced it he should not look at her at all. Thus should he begin — 'In the united name of the Holy and Blessed One and His Shechinah, through that Hidden and Concealed One! and in the name of all Israel ! ' Then he is to proceed with the 'Form of Prayer

for the New Moon ; ' word for word, without haste, but
with solemn deliberation, and when he repeats —

> 'Blessed is thy Former, blessed is thy Maker, blessed is thy Pos-
> sessor, blessed is thy Creator.'

He is to meditate on the initials of the four divine epithets
which form 'Jacob,' for the moon, which is called 'the
lesser light,' is his emblem or symbol, and he is also
called 'little' (see Amos vii. 2). This he is to repeat three
times. He is to skip three times while repeating thrice the
following sentence, and after repeating three times forward
and backward : thus (forward) —'Fear and dread shall fall
upon them by the greatness of Thine arm ; they shall be
as still as a stone ; ' thus (backward) — 'Still as a stone
may they be ; by the greatness of Thine arm may fear and
dread fall on them ; ' he then is to say to his neighbor
three times, 'Peace be unto you,' and the neighbor is to
respond three times, 'Unto you be peace.' Then he is to say
three times (very loudly), 'David, the king of Israel, liveth
and existeth ! ' and finally, he is to say three times —

> 'May a good omen and good luck be upon us and upon all Israel!
> Amen.' »

RABBINICAL ANA

RABBINICAL ANA

IT WAS said of Rabbi Tarphon, that though a very wealthy man, he was not charitable according to his means. One time Rabbi Akiba said to him, "Shall I invest some money for thee in real estate, in a manner which will be very profitable?" Rabbi Tarphon answered in the affirmative, and brought to Rabbi Akiba four thousand denars in gold, to be so applied. Rabbi Akiba immediately distributed the same among the poor. Some time after this Rabbi Tarphon met Rabbi Akiba, and asked him where the real estate which he had bought for him was situated. Akiba led his friend to the college, and showed him a little boy, who recited for them the 112th psalm. When he reached the ninth verse, "He distributeth, he giveth to the needy, his righteousness endureth forever : "

"There," said Akiba, "thy property is with David, the king of Israel, who said, 'he distributeth, he giveth to the needy.' "

"And wherefore hast thou done this?" asked Tarphon.

"Knowest thou not," answered Rabbi Akiba, "how Nakdimon, the son of Guryon, was punished because he gave not according to his means?"

"Well," returned the other, "why didst thou not tell me this ; could I not have distributed my means without thy aid?"

"Nay," said Akiba, "it is a greater virtue to cause another to give than to give one's self."

Rabbi Jochanan, the son of Lakkai, was once riding outside of Jerusalem, and his pupils had followed him. They saw a poor woman collecting the grain which dropped from the mouths and troughs of some feeding cattle, belonging to Arabs. When she saw the Rabbi, she addressed him in these brief words, "O Rabbi, assist me." He replied, "My daughter, whose daughter art thou?"

"I am the daughter of Nakdimon, the son of Guryon," she answered.

"Why, what has become of thy father's money?" asked the Rabbi; "the amount which thou didst receive as a dowry on thy wedding day?"

"Ah," she replied, "is there not a saying in Jerusalem, 'The salt was wanting to the money?'"

"And thy husband's money," continued the Rabbi; "what of that?"

"That followed the other," she answered; "I have lost them both."

The Rabbi turned to his scholars and said:—

"I remember, when I signed her marriage contract, her father gave her as a dowry one million golden denars, and her husband was wealthy in addition thereto."

The Rabbi sympathized with the woman, helped her, and wept for her.

"Happy are ye, oh sons of Israel," he said; "as long as ye perform the will of God naught can conquer ye; but if ye fail to fulfill His wishes, even the cattle are superior to ye."

Nachum, whatever occurred to him, was in the habit of saying, "This too is for the best." In his old age he became blind; both of his hands and both of his legs were amputated, and the trunk of his body was covered with a sore inflammation. His scholars said to him, "If thou art a righteous man, why art thou so sorely afflicted?"

"All this," he answered, "I brought upon myself. Once I was traveling to the house of my father-in-law, and I had with me thirty asses laden with provisions and all manner of precious articles. A man by the wayside called to me, 'O Rabbi, assist me.' I told him to wait until I unloaded my asses. When that time arrived and I had removed their burdens from my beasts, I found to my sorrow that the poor man had fallen and expired. I threw myself upon his body and wept bitterly. 'Let these eyes, which had no pity on thee, be blind,' I said; 'these hands that delayed to assist thee, let them be cut off, and also these feet, which did not run to aid thee.' And yet I was not satisfied until I prayed that my whole body might be stricken with a sore inflammation. Rabbi Akiba said to me, 'Woe to me that I find thee in this state! But I replied, 'Happy to thee that thou meetest me in this state, for through this I hope that my iniquity may be forgiven, and all my righteous deeds still remain recorded to gain me a reward of life eternal in the future world.'"

Rabbi Janay upon seeing a man bestowing alms in a public place, said, "Thou hadst better not have given at all, than to have bestowed alms so openly and put the poor man to shame.

"One should rather be thrown into a fiery furnace than be the means of bringing another to public shame."

Rabbi Juda said, "No one should sit down to his own meals, until seeing that all the animals dependent upon his care are provided for."

Rabbi Jochanan said that it is as pleasing in God's sight if we are kind and hospitable to strangers, as if we rise up early to study His law; because the former is in fact putting His law into practice. He also said, "He who is active in kindness toward his fellows is forgiven his sins."

Both this Rabbi and Abba say it is better to lend to the poor than to give to them, for it prevents them from feeling ashamed of their poverty, and is really a more charitable manner of aiding them. The Rabbis have always taught that kindness is more than the mere almsgiving of charity, for it includes pleasant words with the more substantial help.

Rabbi Hunnah said, "He who is proud in heart is as sinful as the idolater."

Rabbi Abira said, "He who is proud shall be humbled."

Heskaiah said, "The prayers of a proud-hearted man are never heard."

Rabbi Ashi said, "He who hardens his heart with pride, softens his brains with the same."

Rabbi Joshua said "Meekness is better than sacrifice"; for is it not written, "The sacrifices of God are a broken heart — a broken contrite spirit, Thou, oh Lord, will not despise?"

The son of Rabbi Hunnah said, "He who possesses a knowledge of God's law, without the fear of Him, is as one who has been intrusted with the inner keys of a treasury, but from whom the outer ones are withheld."

Rabbi Alexander said, "He who possesses worldly wisdom and fears not the Lord, is as one who designs building a house and completes only the door, for as David wrote in Psalm 111th, 'The beginning of wisdom is the fear of the Lord.'"

When Rabbi Jochanan was ill, his pupils visited him and asked him for a blessing. With his dying voice the Rabbi said, "I pray that you may fear God as you fear man." "What!" exclaimed his pupils, "should we not fear God more than man?"

"I should be well content," answered the sage, "if your actions proved that you feared Him as much. When you do wrong you first make sure that no human eyes see you; show the same fear of God, who sees everywhere, and everything, at all times."

Abba says we can show our fear of God in our intercourse with one another. "Speak pleasantly and kindly to everyone"; he says, "trying to pacify anger, seeking peace, and pursuing it with your brethren and with all the world, and by this means you will gain that 'favor and good understanding in the sight of God and man,' which Solomon so highly prized."

Rabbi Jochanan had heard Rabbi Simon, son of Jochay, illustrate by a parable that passage of Isaiah which reads as follows: "I, the Lord, love uprightness; but hate robbery (converted) into burnt-offering."

A king having imported certain goods upon which he laid a duty, bade his officers, as they passed the custom-house, to stop and pay the usual tariff.

Greatly astonished, his attendants addressed him thus: "Sire! all that is collected belongs to your majesty; why then give what must be eventually paid into thy treasury?"

"Because," answered the monarch, "I wish travelers to learn from the action I now order you to perform, how abhorrent dishonesty is in my eyes."

Rabbi Eleazer said: "He who is guided by righteousness and justice in all his doings, may justly be asserted to have copied God in His unbounded beneficence. For of Him (blessed be His name) we read, 'He loveth righteousness and justice'; that is, 'The earth is filled with the loving kindness of God.'" Might we think that to follow such a course is an easy task? No! The virtue of beneficence can be gained only by great efforts. Will it be difficult, however, for him that has the fear of God constantly before his eyes to acquire this attribute? No; he will easily attain it, whose every act is done in the fear of the Lord.

"A crown of grace is the hoary head; on the way of righteousness can it be found."

So taught Solomon in his Proverbs. Hence various Rabbis, who had attained an advanced age, were questioned by their pupils as to the probable cause that had secured them that mark of divine favor. Rabbi Nechumah answered that, in regard to himself, God had taken cognizance of three principles by which he had endeavored to guide his conduct.

First, he had never striven to exalt his own standing by lowering that of his neighbor. This was agreeable to the example set by Rabbi Hunna, for the latter, while bearing on his shoulders a heavy spade, was met by Rabbi Choana Ben Chanilai, who, considering the burden derogatory to the dignity of so great a man, insisted upon relieving him of the implement and carrying it himself. But Rabbi Hunna refused, saying, "Were this your habitual calling I might permit it, but I certainly shall not permit another to perform an office which, if done by myself, may be looked upon by some as menial."

Secondly, he had never gone to his night's rest with a heart harboring ill-will against his fellow-man, conformably with the practice of Mar Zutra, who, before sleeping, offered this prayer: "O Lord! forgive all those who have done me injury."

Thirdly, he was not penurious, following the example of the righteous Job, of whom the sages relate that he declined to receive the change due him after making a purchase.

Another Rabbi bearing also the name of Nechumah, replied to Rabbi Akiba, that he believed himself to have been blessed with long life because, in his official capacity, he had invariably set his face against accepting presents, mindful of what Solomon wrote, "He that hateth gifts will live." Another of his merits he conceived to be that of never resenting an offense; mindful of the words of Rabba, "He who is indulgent toward others' faults, will be mercifully dealt with by the Supreme Judge."

Rabbi Zera said that the merit of having reached an extreme age was in his case due, under Providence, to his conduct through life. He governed his household with mildness and forbearance. He refrained from advancing an opinion before his superiors in wisdom. He avoided rehearsing the word of God in places not entirely free from uncleanliness. He wore the phylacteries all day, that he might be reminded of his religious duties. He did not make the college where sacred knowledge is taught, a place of convenience, as, for instance, to sleep there, either occasionally or habitually. He never rejoiced over the downfall of a fellow-mortal, nor would he designate another by a name objectionable to the party personally, or to the family of which he was a member.

"Three friends," said the Rabbis, "has man. God, his father, and his mother. He who honors his parents honors God."

Rabbi Judah said, "Known and revealed are the ways of man. A mother coaxes a child with kind words and gentle ways, gaining honor and affection; therefore, the Bible says, 'Honor thy father,' before 'honor thy mother.' But in regard to fearing, as the father is the preceptor of the child, teaching it the law, the Bible says, 'Every man shall fear his mother,' before the word 'father.'"

Rabbi Ulah was once asked, "How extended should be this honor due to parents?"

He replied: —

"Listen, and I will tell ye how thoroughly it was observed by a heathen, Damah, the son of Nethina. He was a diamond merchant, and the sages desired to purchase from him a jewel for the ephod of the high priest. When they reached his house, they found that the key of the safe in which the diamond was kept was in the possession of Damah's father, who was sleeping. The son absolutely refused to wake his father, to obtain the key, even when the sages in their impatience offered him a much larger sum for the jewel than he had demanded. And further, when his father awoke, and he delivered the diamond to the purchasers, and they offered him the larger sum which they had named, he took from it his first price, returning the balance to them, with the words, 'I will not profit by the honor of my father.'"

Man cannot always judge of man, and in the respect paid to parents by their children, earthly eyes cannot always see the truth. For instance, a child may feed his parents on dainties, and yet deserve the punishment of a disrespectful son; while another may send his father to labor, and yet deserve reward. How may this be?

A certain man placed dainty food before his father, and bade him eat thereof. When the father had finished his meal, he said : —

"My son, thou hast prepared for me a most delicious meal. Wherefrom didst thou obtain these delicacies?"

And the son replied, insultingly : —

"Eat as the dogs do, old man, without asking questions."

That son inherited the punishment of disrespect.

A certain man, a miller, had a father living with him, at the time when all people not working for themselves were obliged to labor a certain number of days for the government. When it came near the time when this service would be required of the old man, his son said to him, "Go thou and labor for me in the mill, and I will go and work for the government."

He said this because they who labored for the government were beaten if their work proved unsatisfactory, and he thought "it is better for me to run the chance of being beaten than to allow my father to risk it." Therefore, he deserved the reward of the son who "honors his father."

Rabbi Chiyah asserted that God preferred honor shown to parents, to that displayed toward Himself. "It is written," said he, "'Honor the Lord from thy wealth.' How? Through charity, good deeds, putting the mezuzah upon thy doorposts, making a tabernacle for thyself during Succoth, etc.; all this if thou art able. If thou art poor the omission is not counted a sin or a neglect. But it is written, 'Honor thy father and thy mother,' and the duty is demanded alike of rich and poor; aye, even shouldst thou be obliged to beg for them from door to door."

Rabbi Abahu said, "Abini, my son, hath obeyed this precept even as it should be observed."

Abini had five children, but he would not allow any of them to open the door for their grandfather, or attend to his wants when he himself was at home. Even as he desired them in their lives to honor him, so he paid respect to his father. Upon one occasion his father asked him for a glass of water. While he was procuring it the old man fell asleep, and Abini, re-entering the room, stood by his father's side with the glass in his hand until the latter awoke.

"What is fear?" and "What is honor?" ask the Rabbis.

Fear thy mother, and thy father by sitting not in their seats and standing not in their places; by paying strict attention to their words and interrupting not their speech. Be doubly careful not to criticise or judge their arguments or controversies.

Honor thy father and thy mother, by attending to their wants; giving them to eat and to drink; put their raiment upon them, and tie their shoes if they are not able to perform these services for themselves.

Rabbi Eleazer was asked how far honor toward parents should be extended, and he replied: "Cast all thy wealth into the sea; but trouble not thy father and thy mother."

Simon, the son of Jochai, said: "As the reward to those who honor their parents is great, so is the punishment equally great for those who neglect the precept."

———

Rabbi Jochanan said, "It is best to study by night, when all is quiet; as it is written, 'Shout forth praises in the night.'"

Reshbi Lakish said, "Study by day and by night; as it is written, 'Thou shalt meditate therein day and night.'"

Rabbi Chonan, of Zepora said, "The study of the law may be compared to a huge heap of dust that is to be cleared away. The foolish man says, 'It is impossible that I should be able to remove this immense heap, I will not attempt it;' but the wise man says, 'I will remove a little to-day, some more to-morrow, and more the day after, and thus in time I shall have removed it all.'

"It is the same with studying the law. The indolent pupil says, 'It is impossible for me to study the Bible. Just think of it, fifty chapters in Genesis; sixty-six in Isaiah, one hundred and fifty Psalms, etc. I cannot do it;' but the industrious student says, 'I will study six chapters every day, and so in time I shall acquire the whole.'"

In Proverbs 24: 7, we find this sentence: "Wisdom is too high for a fool."

"Rabbi Jochanan illustrates this verse with an apple depending from the ceiling. The foolish man says, 'I cannot reach the fruit, it is too high;' but the wise man says, 'It may be readily obtained by placing one step upon another until thy arm is brought within reach of it.' The foolish man says, 'Only a wise man can study the entire law,' but the wise man replies, 'It is not incumbent upon thee to acquire the whole.'"

Rabbi Levi illustrates this by a parable.

A man once hired two servants to fill a basket with water. One of them said, "Why should I continue this useless labor? I put the water in one side and it immediately leaks out of the other; what profit is it?"

The other workman, who was wise, replied, "We have the profit of the reward which we receive for our labor."

It is the same in studying the law. One man says, "What does it profit me to study the law when I must ever continue it or else forget what I have learned." But the other man replies, "God will reward us for the will which we display even though we do forget."

Rabbi Ze-irah has said that even a single letter in the law which we might deem of no importance, if wanting, would neutralize the whole law. In Deuteronomy 22 : 17, we read, " Neither shall he take to himself many wives, that his heart may turn away." Solomon transgressed this precept, and it is said by Rabbi Simon that the angels took note of his ill-doing and addressed the Deity : " Sovereign of the world, Solomon has made Thy law even as a law liable to change and diminution. Three precepts he has disregarded, namely, ' He shall not acquire for himself many horses'; ' neither shall he take to himself many wives ' ; ' nor shall he acquire to himself too much silver and gold.' " Then the Lord replied, " Solomon will perish from the earth ; aye, and a hundred Solomons after him, and yet the smallest letter of the law shall not be dispensed with."

———

The Rabbis have often applied in a figurative sense, various passages of Holy Writ, among others the opening verse of the 55th chapter of Isaiah. " Ho, every one of ye that thirsteth, come ye to the water, and he, too, that hath no money ; come ye, buy and eat ; yea, come, buy without money and without price, wine and milk."

The three liquids which men are thus urged to procure are considered by the sages of Israel as typical of the law.

One Rabbi asked, " Why is the word of God compared to water ? "

To this question the following answer was returned : " As water runs down from an eminence (the mountains), and rests in a low place (the sea), so the law, emanating from Heaven, can remain in the possession of those only who are humble in spirit."

Another Rabbi inquired, " Wherefore has the Word of God been likened to wine and milk ? " The reply made was, " As these fluids cannot be preserved in golden vessels, but only in those of earthenware, so those minds will be the best receptacles of learning which are found in homely bodies."

Rabbi Joshua ben Chaninah, who was very homely in appearance, possessed great wisdom and erudition ; and one of his favorite sayings was, that " though many have exhibited a vast amount of knowledge, notwithstanding their personal attractions, yet had they been less handsome, their acquirements might have been more extensive."

The precepts are compared to a lamp; the law of God to a light. The lamp gives light only so long as it contains oil. So he who observes the precepts receives his reward while performing them. The law, however, is a light perpetual; it is a protection forever to the one who studies it, as it is written : —

"When thou walkest, it (the law) will guide thee; when thou liest down, it will watch over thee; and when thou awakenest, it will converse with thee."

When thou walkest it will guide thee — in this world; when thou liest down, it will watch over thee — in the grave; when thou awakenest, it will converse with thee — in the life to come.

A traveler upon his journey passed through the forest upon a dark and gloomy night. He journeyed in dread; he feared the robbers who infested the route he was traversing; he feared that he might slip and fall into some unseen ditch or pitfall on the way, and he feared, too, the wild beasts, which he knew were about him. By chance he discovered a pine torch, and lighted it, and its gleams afforded him great relief. He no longer feared brambles or pitfalls, for he could see his way before him. But the dread of robbers and wild beasts was still upon him, nor left him till the morning's dawn, the coming of the sun. Still he was uncertain of his way, until he emerged from the forest, and reached the cross-roads, when peace returned unto his heart.

The darkness in which the man walked was the lack of religious knowledge. The torch he discovered typifies God's precepts, which aided him on the way until he obtained the blessed sunlight, compared to God's holy word, the Bible. Still, while man is in the forest (the world), he is not entirely at peace; his heart is weak, and he may lose the right path; but when he reaches the cross-roads (death), then may we proclaim him truly righteous, and exclaim : —

"A good name is more fragrant than rich perfume, and the day of death is better than the day of one's birth."

Rabbi Jochanan, the son of Broka, and Rabbi Eleazer, the son of Chismah, visited their teacher, Rabbi Josah, and he said to them : —

"What is the news at the college ; what is going on?"

"Nay," they answered, "we are thy scholars ; it is for thee to speak, for us to listen."

"Nevertheless," replied Rabbi Josah, "no day passes without some occurrence of note at the college. Who lectured to-day?"

"Rabbi Eleazer, the son of Azaryah."

"And what was his subject?"

"He chose this verse from Deuteronomy," replied the scholar : —

"'Assemble the people together, the men, the women, and the children ;' and thus he expounded it : —

"'The men came to learn, the women to listen ; but wherefore the children? In order that those who brought them might receive a reward for training their children in the fear of the Lord.'

"He also expounded the verse from Ecclesiastes : —

"'The words of the wise are like goads, and like nails fastened (are the words of) the men of the assemblies, which are given by one shepherd.'

"'Why is the law of God compared to a goad?' he said. 'Because the goad causes the ox to draw the furrow straight, and the straight furrow brings forth a plenty of good food for the life of man. So does the law of God keep man's heart straight, that it may produce good food to provide for the life eternal. But lest thou shouldst say, "The goad is movable, so therefore must the law be," it is also written, "as nails," and likewise, as "nails fastened," lest thou shouldst argue that nails pounded into wood diminish from sight with each stroke, and that therefore by this comparison God's law would be liable to diminution also. No ; as a nail fastened or planted, as a tree is planted to bring forth fruit and multiply.

"'The men of assemblies are those who gather in numbers to study the law. Frequently controversies arise among them, and thou mightest say, "With so many differing opinions how can I settle to a study of the law?" Thy answer is written in the words which are given by one shepherd. From one God have all the laws proceeded. Therefore make thy ears as a sieve, and incline thy heart to possess all these words.'"

Then said Rabbi Josah, "Happy the generation which Rabbi Eleazer teaches."

The Rabbis of Jabnah expressed their regard for all human beings, learned and unlearned, in this manner: —

"I am a creature of God and so is my neighbor. He may prefer to labor in the country; I prefer a calling in the city. I rise early for my personal benefit; he rises early to advance his own interests. As he does not seek to supplant me, I should be careful to do naught to injure his business. Shall I imagine that I am nearer to God because my profession advances the cause of learning and his does not? No. Whether we accomplish much good or little good, the Almighty will reward us in accordance with our righteous intentions."

Abaygeh offered the following as his best advice: —

" . . . Let him be also affable and disposed to foster kindly feelings between all people; by so doing he will gain for himself the love both of the Creator and His creatures."

Rabba always said that the possession of wisdom and a knowledge of the law necessarily led to penitence and good deeds. "For," said he, "it would be useless to acquire great learning and the mastery of biblical and traditional law and act irreverently toward one's parents, or toward those superior on account of age or more extensive learning."

"The fear of the Lord is the beginning of wisdom; a good understanding have all those who do God's commands."

Rabba said, "Holy Writ does not tell us that to study God's commands shows a good understanding, but to do them. We must learn, however, before we can be able to perform; and he who acts contrary through life to the teachings of the Most High had better never have been born."

"The wise man is in his smallest actions great: the fool is in his greatest actions small."

A pupil once inquired of his teacher, "What is real wisdom?" The teacher replied, "To judge liberally, to think purely, and to love thy neighbor." Another teacher answered, "The greatest wisdom is to know thyself."

"Beware of conceit and pride of learning; learn thy tongue to utter, 'I do not know.'"

If a man devotes himself to study, and becomes learned, to the delight and gratification of his teachers, and yet is modest in conversation with less intelligent people, honest in his dealings, truthful in his daily walks, the people say, "Happy is the father who allowed him to study God's law; happy the teachers who instructed him in the ways of truth; how beautiful are his ways; how meritorious his deeds! Of such an one the Bible says, ' He said to me, Thou art my servant; oh, Israel, through thee am I glorified.'"

But when a man devotes himself to study, and becomes learned, yet is disdainful with those less educated than himself, and is not particular in his dealings with his fellows, then the people say of him, "Woe to the father who allowed him to study God's law; woe to those who instructed him; how censurable is his conduct; how loathsome are his ways! 'Tis of such an one the Bible says, 'And from his country the people of the Lord departed.'"

———

When souls stand at the judgment-seat of God, the poor, the rich, and the wicked each are severally asked what excuse they can offer for not having studied the law. If the poor man pleads his poverty he is reminded of Hillel. Though Hillel's earnings were small he gave half each day to gain admittance to the college.

When the rich man is questioned, and answers that the care of his fortune occupied his time, he is told that Rabbi Eleazer possessed a thousand forests and a thousand ships, and yet abandoned all the luxuries of wealth and journeyed from town to town searching and expounding the law.

When the wicked man pleads temptation as an excuse for his evil course, he is asked if he has been more tempted than Joseph, more cruelly tried than he was, with good or evil fortune.

Yet though we are commanded to study God's law, we are not to make of it a burden; neither are we to neglect for the sake of study any other duty or reasonable recreation. "Why," once asked a pupil, "is 'thou shalt gather in thy corn in its season' a Scriptural command? Would not the people gather their corn when ripe as a matter of course? The command is superfluous."

"Not so," replied the Rabbis; "the corn might belong to a man who for the sake of study would neglect work. Work is holy and honorable in God's sight, and He would not have men fail to perform their daily duties even for the study of His law."

———

Bless God for the good as well as for the evil. When you hear of a death say, "Blessed is the righteous Judge."

Prayer is Israel's only weapon, a weapon inherited from its fathers, a weapon proved in a thousand battles. Even when the gates of prayer are shut in heaven, those of tears are open.

We read that in the contest with Amalek, when Moses lifted up his arms Israel prevailed. Did Moses's hands affect the war, to make it or to break it? No; but while the ones of Israel look upward with humble heart to the Great Father in Heaven, no evil can prevail against them.

"And Moses made a serpent of brass and put it upon a pole; and it came to pass that if a serpent had bitten any man, when he beheld the serpent of brass he lived."

Had the brazen serpent the power of killing or of giving life? No; but while Israel looks upward to the Great Father in Heaven, He will grant life.

"Has God pleasure in the meat and blood of sacrifices?" ask the prophets.

No. He has not so much ordained as permitted them. "It is for yourselves," He says; "not for me, that ye offer."

A king had a son whom he daily discovered carousing with dissolute companions, eating and drinking.

20

"Eat at my table," said the king; "eat and drink, my son, even as pleaseth thee; but let it be at my table, and not with dissolute companions."

The people loved sacrificing, and they made offerings to strange gods; therefore, God said to them: "If ye will sacrifice, bring your offerings at least to me."

Scripture ordains that the Hebrew slave who loves his bondage shall have his ears pierced against the doorpost. Why?

Because that ear heard from Sinai's heights these words: "They are my servants; they shall not be sold as bondsmen." My servants, and not my servant's servants; therefore, pierce the ear of the one who loves his bondage and rejects the freedom offered him.

He who sacrifices a whole offering shall be rewarded for a whole offering; he who offers a burnt-offering shall have the reward of a burnt-offering; but he who offers humility to God and man shall receive as great a reward as though he had offered all the sacrifices in the world.

The God of Abraham will help the one who appoints a certain place to pray to the Lord.

Rabbi Henah said, "When such a man dies they will say of him, 'A pious man, a meek man, hath died; he followed the example of our father Abraham.'"

How do we know that Abraham appointed a certain place to pray?

"Abraham rose early in the morning and went to the place where he stood before the Lord."

Rabbi Chelboh said, "We should not hurry when we leave a place of worship."

"This," said Abayyeh, "is in reference to leaving a place of worship; but we should certainly hasten on our way thither, as it is written, 'Let us know and hasten to serve the Lord.'"

Rabbi Zabid said, "When I used to see the Rabbis hurrying to a lecture in their desire to obtain good seats, I thought to myself, 'they are violating the Sabbath.' When, however, I heard Rabbi Tarphon say, 'One should always hasten to perform a commandment even on the Sabbath,' as it is written, 'They shall follow after the Lord when He roareth like a lion,' I hurried also, in order to be early in attendance."

That place wherein we can best pray to God is His house; as it is written : —

"To listen to the praises and prayers which Thy servant prays before Thee." Alluding to the service in the house of God.

Said Rabin, the son of Ada, "Whence do we derive the tradition, that when ten men are praying in the house of God the Divine Presence rests among them?

"It is written, 'God stands in the assembly of the mighty.' That an assembly or congregation consists of not less than ten, we learn from God's words to Moses in regard to the spies who were sent out to view the land of Canaan. 'How long,' said he, 'shall indulgence be given to this evil congregation?' Now the spies numbered twelve men; but Joshua and Caleb being true and faithful, there remained but ten to form the 'evil congregation.'"

"Whence do we derive the tradition that when even one studies the law, the Divine Presence rests with him?"

"It is written, 'In every place where I shall permit my name to be mentioned, I will come unto thee and I will bless thee.'"

Four biblical characters offered up their prayers in a careless, unthinking manner; three of them God prospered; the other met with sorrow. They were, Eleazer, the servant of Abraham; Caleb, the son of Ye Phunneh; Saul, the son of Kish; and Jephtah the Giladite.

Eleazer prayed, "Let it come to pass that the maiden to whom I shall say, 'Let down thy pitcher, I pray thee, that I may drink'; and she shall say, 'Drink, and to thy camels also will I give drink'; shall be the one Thou hast appointed for Thy servant Isaac."

Suppose a slave had appeared and answered all the requirement which Eleazer proposed, would Abraham and Isaac have been satisfied? But God prospered his mission, and "Rebecca came out."

Caleb said, "He that will smite Kiryath-sepher, and cap-ture it, to him will I give 'Achsah, my daughter, for wife."

Would he have given his daughter to a slave or a heathen?

But God prospered him, and "Othniel, the son of Kenaz, Caleb's younger brother, conquered it, and he gave him 'Achsah, his daughter, for wife."

Saul said, "And it shall be that the man who killeth him (Goliath) will the king enrich with great riches, and his daughter will he give him."

He ran the same risk as Caleb, and God was good to him also ; and David, the son of Jesse, accomplished that for which he had prayed.

Jephtah expressed himself thus: "If thou wilt indeed de-liver the children of Amon into my hand, then shall it be that whatsoever cometh forth out of the doors of my house to meet me when I return in peace from the children of Amon, shall belong to the Lord, and I will offer it up for a burnt-offering."

Supposing an ass, or a dog, or a cat, had first met him upon his return, would he have sacrificed it for a burnt-offering? God did not prosper this risk, and the Bible says, "And Jephtah came to Mizpah unto his house, and behold his daughter came out to meet him."

Said Rabbi Simon ben Jochai, "The requests of three persons were granted before they had finished their prayers — Eleazer, Moses, and Solomon.

"In regard to Eleazer we learn, ' And before he had yet finished speaking that, behold Rebecca came out.'

"In regard to Moses, we find, ' And it came to pass when he had made an end of speaking all these words, that the ground that was under them was cloven asunder, and the earth opened her mouth and swallowed them.' " (Korach and his company.)

"In regard to Solomon, we find, ' And just when Solo-mon had made an end of praying, a fire came down,' " etc.

Rabbi Jochanan said in the name of Rabbi Joseh, "To those who delight in the Sabbath shall God give inherit-ance without end. As it is written, ' Then shalt thou find delight in the Lord,' etc. ' And I will cause thee to enjoy the inheritance of Jacob, thy father.' Not as it was promised to Abraham, 'Arise and walk through the land to its length and breadth.' Not as it was promised to Isaac, 'I will give thee all that this land contains'; but as it was promised to Jacob, 'And thou shalt spread abroad, to the West, and to the East, to the North, and to the South.'"

Rabbi Jehudah said that if the Israelites had strictly observed the first Sabbath, after the command to sanctify the seventh day had been given, they would have been spared captivity; as it is written, "And it came to pass on the seventh day, that there went out some of the people to gather (the Mannah), but they found nothing." And in the next chapter we find, "Then came Amalek, and fought with Israel in Rephidim."

One Joseph, a Jew, who honored the Sabbath, had a very rich neighbor, who was a firm believer in astrology. He was told by one of the professional astrologers that his wealth would become Joseph's. He therefore sold his estate, and bought with the proceeds a large diamond, which he sewed in his turban, saying, "Joseph can never obtain this." It so happened, however, that while standing one day upon the deck of a ship in which he was crossing the sea, a heavy wind arose and carried the turban from his head. A fish swallowed the diamond, and being caught and exposed for sale in the market, was purchased by Joseph to supply his table on the Sabbath eve. Of course, upon opening it he discovered the diamond.

Rabbi Ishmael, the son of Joshua, was asked, "How did the rich people of the land of Israel become so wealthy?" He answered, "They gave their tithes in due season, as it is written, 'Thou shalt give tithes, in order that thou mayest become rich.'" "But," answered his questioner, "tithes were given to the Levites, only while the holy temple existed. What merit did they possess while they dwelt in Babel, that they became wealthy there also?" "Because," replied the Rabbi, "they honored the Holy Law by expounding it." "But in other countries, where they did not expound the Law, how did they deserve wealth?" "By honoring the Sabbath," was the answer.

Rabbi Achiya, the son of Abah, said, "I sojourned once in Ludik, and was entertained by a certain wealthy man on the Sabbath day. The table was spread with a sumptuous repast, and the dishes were of silver and gold. Before making a blessing over the meal the master of the house said, 'Unto the Lord belongeth the earth, with all that it contains.' After the blessing he said, 'The heavens are the heavens of the Lord, but the earth hath He given to the children of men.' I said to my host, 'I trust you will excuse me, my dear sir, if I take the liberty of asking you how you have merited this prosperity?' He answered, 'I was formerly a butcher, and I always selected the finest cattle to be killed for the Sabbath, in order that the people might have the best meat on that day. To this, I believe firmly, I owe my prosperity.' I replied, 'Blessed be the Lord, that He hath given thee all this.'"

The Governor Turnusrupis once asked Rabbi Akiba, "What is this day you call the Sabbath more than any other day?" The Rabbi responded, "What art thou more than any other person?" "I am superior to others," he replied, "because the emperor has appointed me governor over them."

Then said Akiba, "The Lord our God, who is greater than your emperor, has appointed the Sabbath day to be holier than the other days."

When man leaves the synagogue for his home an angel of good and an angel of evil accompany him. If he finds the table spread in his house, the Sabbath lamps lighted, and his wife and chidren in festive garments ready to bless the holy day of rest, then the good angel says: —

"May the next Sabbath and all thy Sabbaths be like this. Peace unto this dwelling, peace;" and the angel of evil is forced to say, "Amen!"

But if the house is not ready, if no preparations have been made to greet the Sabbath, if no heart within the dwelling has sung, "Come, my beloved, to meet the bride; the presence of the Sabbath let us receive;" then the angel of evil speaks and says: —

"May all thy Sabbaths be like this;" and the weeping angel of goodness, responds, "Amen!"

Samson sinned against the Lord through his eyes, as it is written, "I have seen a woman of the daughters of the Philistines. . . . This one take for me, for she pleaseth in my eyes." Therefore through his eyes was he punished, as it is written, "And the Philistines seized him, and put out his eyes."

Abshalom was proud of his hair. "And like Abshalom there was no man as handsome in all Israel, so that he was greatly praised; from the sole of his foot up to the crown of his head there was no blemish on him. And when he shaved off the hair of his head, and it was at the end of every year that he shaved it off, because it was too heavy on him so that he had to shave it off, he weighed the hair of his head at two hundred shekels by the king's weight." Therefore by his hair was he hanged.

Miriam waited for Moses one hour (when he was in the box of bulrushes). Therefore the Israelites waited for Miriam seven days, when she became leprous. "And the people did not set forward until Miriam was brought in again."

Joseph buried his father. "And Joseph went up to bury his father." There was none greater among the children of Israel than Joseph. Moses excelled him afterward, however; therefore we find, "And Moses took the bones of Joseph with him." But the world has seen none greater than Moses, therefore 'tis written, "And He (God) buried him in the valley."

———

When trouble and sorrow become the portion of Israel, and the fainthearted separate from their people, two angels lay their hands upon the head of him who withdraws, saying, "This one shall not see the comfort of the congregation."

When trouble comes to the congregation it is not right for a man to say, "I will go home; I will eat and drink; and things shall be peaceful to me;" 'tis of such a one that the holy book speaks, saying, "And behold there is gladness and joy; slaying of oxen, and killing of sheep; eating of flesh, and drinking of wine. 'Let us eat and drink, for to-morrow we must die.' And it was revealed in my ears by the Lord of Hosts; surely the iniquity shall not be forgiven ye until ye die."

Our teacher, Moses, always bore his share in the troubles of the congregation, as it is written, "They took a stone and put it under him." Could they not have given him a chair or a cushion? But then he said, "Since the Israelites are in trouble (during the war with Amalek) lo, I will bear my part with them, for he who bears his portion of the burden will live to enjoy the hour of consolation. Woe to the one who thinks, 'Ah, well, I will neglect my duty; who can know whether I bear my part or not;' even the stones of his house, aye, the limbs of the trees, shall testify against him, as it is written, 'For the stones will cry from the wall, and the limbs of the trees will testify.'"

———

Rabbi Meir said, "When a man teaches his son a trade, he should pray to the Possessor of the world, the Dispenser of wealth and poverty; for in every trade and pursuit of life both the rich and the poor are to be found. It is folly for one to say, 'This is a bad trade, it will not afford me a living;' because he will find many well to do in the same occupation. Neither should a successful man boast and say, 'This is a great trade, a glorious art, it has made me wealthy;' because many working in the same line as himself have found but poverty. Let all remember that everything is through the infinite mercy and wisdom of God."

Rabbi Simon, the son of Eleazer, said, "Hast thou ever noted the fowls of the air and beasts of the field how easily their maintenance is provided for them; and yet they were only created to serve me. Now should not I find a livelihood with even less trouble, for I was made to serve my fellow-creatures? But, alas! I sinned against my Creator, therefore am I punished with poverty and obliged to labor."

Rabbi Judah said, "Most mule-drivers are cruel. They beat their poor beasts unmercifully. Most camel-drivers are upright. They travel through deserts and dangerous places, and have time for meditation and thoughts of God.

The majority of seamen are religious. Their daily peril makes them so. The best doctors are deserving of punishment. In the pursuit of knowledge they experiment on their patients, and often with fatal results. The best of butchers deserve to be rated with the Amalekites, they are accustomed to blood and cruelty; as it is written of the Amalekites, 'How he met thee by the way and smote the hindmost of thee, and that were feeble behind thee, when thou wast faint and weary.' "

Man is born with his hands clenched; he dies with his hands wide open. Entering life he desires to grasp everything; leaving the world, all that he possessed has slipped away.

Even as a fox is man; as a fox which seeing a fine vineyard lusted after its grapes. But the palings were placed at narrow distances, and the fox was too bulky to creep between them. For three days he fasted, and when he had grown thin he entered into the vineyard. He feasted upon the grapes, forgetful of the morrow, of all things but his enjoyment; and lo, he had again grown stout and was unable to leave the scene of his feast. So for three days more he fasted, and when he had again grown thin, he passed through the palings and stood outside the vineyard, meagre as when he entered.

So with man; poor and naked he enters the world, poor and naked does he leave.

Alexander wandered to the gates of Paradise and knocked for entrance.

"Who knocks?" demanded the guardian angel.

"Alexander."

"Who is Alexander?"

"Alexander — the Alexander — Alexander the Great — the conqueror of the world."

"We know him not," replied the angel; "this is the Lord's gate, only the righteous enter here."

Alexander begged for something to prove that he had reached the gates of Paradise, and a small piece of a skull was given to him. He showed it to his wise men, who placed it in one scale of a balance. Alexander poured gold and silver into the other scale, but the small bone weighed heavier; he poured in more, adding his crown jewels, his diadem; but still the bone outweighed them all. Then one of the wise men, taking a grain of dust from the ground placed that upon the bone, and lo, the scale flew up.

The bone was that which surrounds the eye of man; the eye of man which naught can satisfy save the dust which covers it in the grave.

———

When the righteous dies, 'tis earth that meets with loss. The jewel will ever be a jewel, but it has passed from the possession of its former owner. Well may the loser weep.

Life is a passing shadow, say the Scriptures. The shadow of a tower or a tree; the shadow which prevails for a time? No; even as the shadow of a bird in its flight, it passeth from our sight, and neither bird nor shadow remains.

"My lover goes down into his garden, to the beds of spices, to wander about in the garden and pluck roses" (Song of Songs).

The world is the garden of my lover, and he my lover is the King of kings. Like a bed of fragrant spices is Israel, the sweet savour of piety ascends on high, the perfume of learning lingers on the passing breeze, and the bed of beauty is fenced round by gentle peace. The plants flourish and put forth leaves, leaves giving grateful shelter to those who suffer from the heats and disappointment of life, and my lover seeking the most beautiful blossom, plucks the roses, the students of the law, whose belief is their delight.

When the devouring flames seize upon the cedar, shall not the lowly hyssop fear and tremble? When anglers draw the great leviathan from his mighty deeps, what hope have the fish of the shallow pond? When the fishing-line is dropped into the dashing torrent, can they feel secure, the waters of the purling brook?

Mourn for those who are left; mourn not for the one taken by God from earth. He has entered into the eternal rest, while we are bowed with sorrow.

Rabbi Akiba was once traveling through the country, and he had with him an ass, a rooster, and a lamp.

At nightfall he reached a village where he sought shelter for the night without success.

"All that God does is done well," said the Rabbi, and proceeding toward the forest he resolved to pass the night there. He lit his lamp, but the wind extinguished it. "All that God does is done well," he said. The ass and the rooster were devoured by wild beasts; yet still he said no more than "All that God does is done well."

Next day he learned that a troop of the enemy's soldiers had passed through the forest that night. If the ass had brayed, if the rooster had crowed, or if the soldiers had seen his light he would surely have met with death, therefore he said again, "All that God does is done well."

Once when Rabbi Gamliel, Rabbi Eleazer, the son of Azaria, Rabbi Judah, and Rabbi Akiba were walking together, they heard the shouts and laughter and joyous tones of a multitude of people at a distance. Four of the Rabbis wept; but Akiba laughed aloud.

"Akiba," said the others to him, "wherefore laugh? These heathens who worship idols live in peace, and are merry, while our holy city lies in ruins; weep, do not laugh."

"For that very reason I laugh, and am glad," answered Rabbi Akiba. "If God allows those who transgress His will to live happily on earth, how infinitely great must be the happiness which He has stored up in the world to come for those who observe His commands."

Upon another occasion these same Rabbis went up to Jerusalem. When they reached Mount Zophim and saw the desolation about them they rent their garments, and when they reached the spot where the Temple had stood and saw a fox run out from the very site of the holy of holies four of them wept bitterly; but again Rabbi Akiba appeared merry. His comrades again rebuked him for this, to them, unseemly state of feeling.

"Ye ask me why I am merry," said he; "come now, tell me why ye weep?"

" Because the Bible tells us that a stranger (one not descended from Aaron) who approaches the holy of holies shall be put to death, and now behold the foxes make of it a dwelling-place. Why should we not weep?"

" Ye weep," returned Akiba, " from the very reason which causes my heart to be glad. Is it not written, 'And testify to me, ye faithful witnesses, Uriah, the priest, and Zachariah, the son of Berachiahu?' Now what hath Uriah to do with Zachariah? Uriah lived during the existence of the first Temple, and Zachariah during the second. Know ye not that the prophecy of Uriah is compared to the prophecy of Zachariah. From Uriah's prophecy we find, 'Therefore for your sake Zion will be plowed as is a field, and Jerusalem will be a desolation, and the mount of Zion shall be as a forest;' and in Zachariah we find, 'They will sit, the old men and women, in the streets of Jerusalem.' Before the prophecy of Uriah was accomplished I might have doubted the truth of Zachariah's comforting words; but now that one has been accomplished, I feel assured that the promises to Zachariah will also come to pass, therefore am I glad."

" Thy words comfort us, Akiba," answered his companions. " May God ever provide us comfort."

Still another time, when Rabbi Eleazer was very sick and his friends and scholars were weeping for him, Rabbi Akiba appeared happy, and asked them why they wept. " Because," they replied, " our beloved Rabbi is lying between life and death." " Weep not, on the contrary be glad therefor," he answered. " If his wine did not grow sour, if his flag was not stricken down, I might think that on earth he received the reward of his righteousness; but now that I see my teacher suffering for what evil he may have committed in this world, I rejoice. He hath taught us that the most righteous among us commit some sin, therefore in the world to come he will have peace."

———

While Rabbi Eleazer was sick, the four elders, Rabbi Tarphon, Rabbi Joshua, Rabbi Eleazer, the son of Azoria, and Rabbi Akiba, called upon him.

"Thou art better to Israel than the raindrops to earth, or the raindrops are for this world only, while thou, my teacher, have helped the ripening of fruit for this world and the next," said Rabbi Tarphon.

"Thou art better to Israel than the sun, for the sun is for this world alone; thou hast given light for this world and the next," said Rabbi Joshua.

Then spoke Rabbi Eleazer, the son of Azoria: —

"Thou art better to Israel," said he, "than father and mother to man. They bring him into the world, but thou, my teacher, showest him the way into the world of immortality."

Then said Rabbi Akiba: —

"It is well that man should be afflicted, for his distresses atone for his sins."

"Does the Bible make such an assertion, Akiba?" asked his teacher.

"Yes," answered Akiba. "'Twelve years old was Manassah when he became king, and fifty-and-five years did he reign in Jerusalem, and he did what was evil in the eyes of the Lord' (Kings). Now, how was this? Did Hezekiah teach the law to the whole world and not to his son Manassah? Assuredly not; but Manassah paid no attention to his precepts, and neglected the word of God until he was afflicted with bodily pain, as it is written, 'And the Lord spoke to Manassah and to his people, but they listened not, wherefore the Lord brought over them the captains of the armies belonging to the king of Assyria, and they took Manassah prisoner with chains, and bound him with fetters, and led him off to Babylon; and when he was in distress he besought the Lord his God, and humbled himself greatly before the God of his fathers. And he prayed to Him, and He permitted Himself to be entreated by him and heard his supplication, and brought him back to Jerusalem unto his kingdom. Then did Manassah feel conscious that the Lord is indeed the (true) God.'

"Now, what did the king of Assyria to Manassah? He placed him in a copper barrel and had a fire kindled beneath it, and while enduring great torture of his body, Manassah was further tortured in his mind. 'Shall I call upon the Almighty?' he thought. 'Alas! His anger burns against me. To call upon my idols is to call in vain,— alas, alas, what hope remains to me!'

"He prayed to the greatest of his idols, and waited in vain for a reply. He called to the lesser gods, and remained unanswered. Then with trembling heart he addressed the great Eternal.

"'O Eternal! God of Abraham, Isaac, and Jacob, and their descendants, the heavens and the earth are the works of Thy hand. Thou didst give to the sea a shore, controlling with a word the power of the mighty deep. Thou art merciful as Thou art great, and Thou hast promised to accept the repentance of those who return to Thee with upright hearts. As numerous are my sins as the sands which cover the seashore. I have done evil before Thee, committing abominations in Thy presence and acting wickedly. Bound with fetters I come before Thee, and on my knees I entreat Thee, in the name of Thy great attributes of mercy, to compassionate my suffering and my distress. Pardon me, O Lord, forgive me. Do not utterly destroy me because of my transgressions. Let not my punishment eternally continue. Though I am unworthy of Thy goodness, O Lord, yet save me in Thy mercy. Henceforth will I praise Thy name all the days of my life, for all Thy creatures delight in praising Thee, and unto Thee is the greatness and the goodness forever and ever, Selah!'"

"God heard this prayer, even as it is written, 'And He permitted Himself to be entreated by him, and brought him back to Jerusalem unto his kingdom.'"

"From which we may learn," continued Akiba, "that affliction is an atonement for sin."

Said Rabbi Eleazer, the great, "It is commanded 'thou shalt love the Lord thy God with all thy soul and with all that is loved by thee.'

"Does not 'with all thy soul' include 'with all that is loved by thee?'

"Some people love themselves more than they love their money; to them 'tis said, 'with all thy soul;' while for those

who love their money more than themselves the commandment reads, 'with all that is loved by thee.'"

But Rabbi Akiba always expounded the words, "with all thy
soul," to mean "even though thy life be demanded of thee."

When the decree was issued forbidding the Israelities to
study the law, what did Rabbi Akiba?

He installed many congregations secretly, and in secret
lectured before them.

Then Papus, the son of Juda said to him : —

"Art not afraid, Akiba? Thy doings may be discovered,
and thou wilt be punished for disobeying the decree."

"Listen, and I will relate to thee a parable," answered
Akiba. "A fox, walking by the river side, noticed the
fishes therein swimming and swimming to and fro, never
ceasing ; so he said to them, 'Why are ye hurrying, what
do ye fear?'

" 'The nets of the angler,' they replied.

" 'Come, then,' said the fox, 'and live with me on dry
land.'

"But the fishes laughed.

" 'And art thou called the wisest of the beasts?' they
exclaimed ; 'verily thou art the most foolish. If we are
in danger even in our element, how much greater would be
our risk in leaving it.'

"It is the same with us. We are told of the law that it
is 'our life and the prolongation of our days.' This is it
when things are peaceful with us ; how much greater is our
need of it then in times like these?"

It is said that it was but shortly after this when Rabbi
Akiba was imprisoned for teaching the law, and in the
prison in which he was incarcerated he found Papus, who
had been condemned for some other offense.

Rabbi Akiba said to him : —

"Papus, what brought thee here?"

And Papus replied : —

"Joy, joy, to thee, that thou art imprisoned for studying
God's law ; but woe, woe is mine that I am here through
vanity."

When Rabbi Akiba was led forth to execution, it was
just at the time of the morning service.

" ' Hear, O Israel! the Lord our God, the Lord is one,' "
he exclaimed in a loud and firm voice.

The torturers tore his flesh with pointed cards, yet still
he repeated, " The Lord is one."

" Always did I say," he continued, "that ' with all thy
soul,' meant even though life should be demanded of thee,
and I wondered whether I should ever be able to so
observe it. Now see, to-day, I do so; ' the Lord is one. ' "

With these word he died.

Elishah ben Abuyah, a most learned man, became in
after-life an apostate. Rabbi Meir had been one of his pupils, and he never failed in the great love which he bore
for his teacher.

It happened upon one occasion when Rabbi Meir was
lecturing in the college, that some students entered and
said to him : —

" Thy teacher, Elishah, is riding by on horseback on
this holy Sabbath day."

Rabbi Meir left the college, and overtaking Elishah
walked along by his horse's side.

The latter saluted him, and asked : —

" What passage of Scripture hast thou been expounding? "

" From the book of Job," replied Rabbi Meir. " ' The
Lord blessed the latter days of Job more than the beginning.' "

" And how didst thou explain the verse? " said Elishah.

" That the Lord increased his wealth twofold."

" But thy teacher, Akiba, said not so," returned Elishah.
" He said that the Lord blessed the latter days of Job with
twofold of penitence and good deeds."

" How," inquired Rabbi Meir, " wouldst thou explain the
verse, ' Better is the end of a thing than the beginning
thereof.' If a man buys merchandise in his youth and
meets with losses, is it likely that he will recover his substance in old age? Or, if a person studies God's law in
his youth and forgets it, is it probable that it will return
to his memory in his latter days? "

" Thy teacher, Akiba, said not so," replied Elishah; " he
explained the verse, ' Better is the end of a thing when

the beginning was good.' My own life proves the sound-
ness of this explanation. On the day when I was admitted into the covenant of Abraham, my father made a
great feast. Some of his visitors sang, some of them
danced, but the Rabbis conversed upon God's wisdom and
His laws. This latter pleased my father, Abuyah, and he
said, 'When my son grows up ye shall teach him and he
shall become like ye; he did not cause me to study for
God's sake but only to make his name famous through
me. Therefore, in my latter days have I become wicked
and an apostate; and now, return home."

" And wherefore? "

" Because, on the Sabbath day, thou art allowed to go so
far and no farther, and I have reckoned the distance thou
hast traveled with me by the footsteps of my horse."

" If thou art so wise," said Rabbi Meir, " as to reckon
the distance I may travel by the footsteps of thy horse,
and so particular for my sake, why not return to God and
repent of thy apostacy?"

Elishah answered : —

" It is not in my power. I rode upon horseback once on
the Day of Atonement; yea, when it fell upon the Sabbath, and when I passed the synagogue I heard a voice
crying, 'Return, oh backsliding children, return to me and
I will return to ye; except Elishah, the son of Abuyah,
he knew his Master and yet rebelled against Him.' "

What caused such a learned man as Elishah to turn to
evil ways?

It is reported that once while studying the law in the
vale of Genusan, he saw a man climbing a tree. The man
found a bird's-nest in the tree, and taking the mother with
the young ones he still departed in peace. He saw another
man who finding a bird's-nest followed the Bible's command
and took the young only, allowing the mother to fly away;
and yet a serpent stung him as he descended, and he died.
" Now," thought he, " where is the Bible's truth and promises? Is it not written, 'And the young thou mayest
take to thyself, but the mother thou shalt surely let go,
that it may be well with thee and that thou mayest live
many days.' Now, where is the long life to this man who

21

followed the precept, while the one who transgressed it is unhurt?"

He had not heard how Rabbi Akiba expounded this verse, that the days would be long in the future world where all is happiness.

There is also another reason given as the cause for Elishah's backsliding and apostacy.

During the fearful period of religious persecution, the learned Rabbi Judah, whose life had been passed in the study of the law and the practice of God's precepts, was delivered into the power of the cruel torturer. His tongue was placed in a dog's mouth and the dog bit it off.

So Elishah said, "If a tongue which uttered naught but truth be so used, and a learned, wise man be so treated, of what use is it to avoid having a lying tongue and being ignorant. Lo, if these things are allowed, there is surely no reward for the righteous, and no resurrection for the dead."

When Elishah waxed old he was taken sick, and Rabbi Meir, learning of the illness of his aged teacher, called upon him.

"Oh return, return unto thy God." entreated Rabbi Meir.

"What!" exclaimed Elishah, "return! and could He receive my penitence, the penitence of an apostate who has so rebelled against Him?"

"Is it not written," said Meir, "'Thou turnest man to contrition?' No matter how the soul of man may be crushed, he can still turn to his God and find relief."

Elishah listened to these words, wept bitterly and died. Not many years after his death his daughters came, poverty stricken, asking relief from the colleges. "Remember," said they, "the merit of our father's learning, not his conduct."

The colleges listened to the appeal and supported the daughters of Elishah.

———

Rabbi Judah, Rabbi Joseh, and Rabbi Simon were conversing one day, when Judah ben Gerim entered the apartment and sat down with the three. Rabbi Judah was speaking in a complimentary strain of the Gentiles (Romans). "See," said he, "how they have improved their cities, how beautiful they have made them, and how much they have done for the comfort and convenience of the citizens; bath-houses, bridges, fine broad streets, surely much credit is due them."

"Nay," answered Rabbi Simon, "all that they have done has been from a selfish motive. The bridges bring them in a revenue, for all who use them are taxed; the bath-houses are for their personal adornment —'tis all selfishness, not patriotism."

Judah ben Gerim repeated these remarks to his friends, and finally they reached the ears of the emperor. He would not allow them to pass unnoticed. He ordered that Judah, who had spoken well of the nation, should be advanced in honor; that Joseh, who had remained silent instead of seconding the assertions, should be banished to Zipore; and that Simon, who had disputed the compliment, should be put to death.

The latter with his son fled and concealed himself in the college when this fiat became known to him. For some time he remained there comparatively safe, his wife bringing his meals daily. But when the officers were directed to make diligent search he became afraid, lest through the indiscretion of his wife his place of concealment might be discovered.

"The mind of woman is weak and unsteady," said he, "perhaps they may question and confuse her, and thus may death come upon me."

So leaving the city, Simon and his son took refuge in a lonely cave. Near its mouth some fruit trees grew, supplying them with food, and a spring of pure water bubbled from rocks in the immediate vicinity. For thirteen years Rabbi Simon lived here, until the emperor died and his decrees were repealed. He then returned to the city.

When Rabbi Phineas, his son-in-law, heard of his return, he called upon him at once, and noticing an apparent neglect in the mental and physical condition of his relative, he exclaimed, "Woe, woe! that I meet thee in so sad a condition!"

But Rabbi Simon answered : —

"Not so ; happy is it that thou findest me in this condition, for thou findest me no less righteous than before. God has preserved me, and my faith in Him, and thus hereafter shall I explain the verse of Scripture, 'And Jacob came perfect.' Perfect in his physical condition, perfect in his temporal condition, and perfect in his knowledge of God."

Antoninus, in conversing with Rabbi Judah, said to him :

"In the future world, when the soul comes before the Almighty Creator for judgment, may it not find a plea of excuse for worldly wickedness in saying, 'Lo, the sin is the body's ; I am now free from the body ; the sins were not mine'?"

Rabbi Judah answered, "Let me relate to thee a parable. A king had an orchard of fine figs, which he prized most highly. That the fruit might not be stolen or abused, he placed two watchers in the orchard, and that they themselves might not be tempted to partake of the fruit, he chose one of them a blind man, and the other one lame. But lo, when they were in the orchard, the lame man said to his companion, 'I see very fine figs ; they are luscious and tempting ; carry me to the tree, that we may both partake of them.'

"So the blind man carried the lame man, and they ate of the figs.

"When the king entered the orchard he noticed at once that his finest figs were missing, and he asked the watchers what had become of them.

"The blind man answered : —

"'I know not. I could not steal them ; I am blind ; I cannot even see them.'

"And the lame man answered : —

"'Neither could I steal them ; I could not approach the tree.'

"But the king was wise, and he answered : —

"'Lo, the blind carried the lame,' and he punished them accordingly.

"So it is with us. The world is the orchard in which the Eternal King has placed us, to keep watch and ward, to till its soil and care for its fruit. But the soul and body are the man; if one violates the precepts, so does the other, and after death the soul may not say, 'It is the fault of the body to which I was tied that I committed sins;' no, God will do as did the owner of the orchard, as it is written:—

"'He shall call from the heaven above, and to the earth to judge his people.'

"He shall call from the 'heaven above,' which is the soul, and to the 'earth below,' which is the body, mixing with the dust from whence it sprung."

A heathen said to Rabbi Joshua, "Thou believest that God knows the future?"

"Yes," replied the Rabbi.

"Then," said the questioner, "wherefore is it written, 'The Lord said, I will destroy everything which I have made, because it repenteth me that I have made them'? Did not the Lord foresee that man would become corrupt?"

Then said Rabbi Joshua, "Hast thou children?"

"Yes," was the answer.

"When a child was born, what didst thou?"

"I made a great rejoicing."

"What cause hadst thou to rejoice? Dost thou not know that they must die?"

"Yes, that is true; but in the time of enjoyment I do not think of the future."

"So was it with God," said Rabbi Joshua. "He knew that men would sin; still that knowledge did not prevent the execution of his beneficent purpose to create them."

One of the emperors said to Rabon Gamliel:—

"Your God is a thief, as it is written, 'And the Lord God caused a deep sleep to fall upon Adam, and he slept. And He took a rib from Adam.'"

The Rabbi's daughter said, "Let me answer this aspersion. Last night robbers broke into my room, and stole therefrom a silver vessel: but they left a golden one in its stead."

The emperor replied, "I wish that such thieves would come every night."

Thus was it with Adam; God took a rib from him, but placed a woman instead of it.

Rabbi Joshua, of Saknin, said in the name of Rabbi Levi, "The Lord considered from what part of the man he should form woman; not from the head, lest she should be proud; not from the eyes, lest she should wish to see everything; not from the mouth, lest she might be talkative; nor from the ear, lest she should wish to hear everything; nor from the heart, lest she should be jealous; nor from the hand, lest she should wish to find out everything; nor from the feet in order that she might not be a wanderer; only from the most hidden place, that is covered even when a man is naked — namely, the rib."

The scholars of Rabbi Simon ben Jochai once asked him : —

"Why did not the Lord give to Israel enough manna to suffice them for a year, at one time, instead of meting it out daily?"

The Rabbi replied : —

"I will answer ye with a parable. There was once a king who had a son to whom he gave a certain yearly allowance, paying the entire sum for his year's support on one appointed day. It soon happened that this day on which the allowance was due, was the only day in the year when the father saw his son. So the king changed his plan, and gave his son each day his maintenance for that day only, and then the son visited his father with the return of each day's sun.

"So was it with Israel; each father of a family, dependent upon the manna provided each day by God's bounty, for his support and the support of his family, naturally had his mind devoted to the Great Giver and Sustainer of life."

When Rabbi Eleazer was sick his scholars visited him, and said, "Rabbi, teach us the way of life, that we may inherit eternity."

The Rabbi answered, "Give honor to your comrades. Know to whom you pray. Restrain your children from frivolous conversation, and place them among the learned men, in order that they may acquire wisdom. So may you merit life in the future world."

When Rabbi Jochanan was sick his scholars also called upon him. When he beheld them he burst into tears.

"Rabbi!" they exclaimed, "Light of Israel! The chief pillar! Why weep?"

The Rabbi answered, "Were I to be brought before a king of flesh and blood, who is here to-day and to-morrow in the grave; who may be angry with me, but not forever; who may imprison me, but not forever; who may kill me, but only for this world; whom I may sometimes bribe; even then I would fear. But now, I am to appear before the King of kings, the Most Holy One, blessed be He, who lives through all eternity. If He is wroth, it is forever. If He imprisons me, it is forever; if He slays me, it is for the future world; and I can bribe Him neither with words nor money. Not only this, two paths are before me, one leading to punishment, the other to reward, and I know not which one I must travel. Should I not weep?"

The scholars of Rabbi Johanan, the son of Zakai, asked of their teacher this question: —

"Wherefore is it, that according to the law, the punishment of a highwayman is not as severe as the punishment of a sneak thief? According to the Mosaic law, if a man steals an ox or a sheep, and kills it or sells it, he is required to restore five oxen for the one ox, and four sheep for the one sheep; but for the highwayman we find, 'When he hath sinned and is conscious of his guilt, he shall restore that he hath taken violently away; he shall restore it and its principal, and the fifth part thereof he shall add thereto.' Therefore, he who commits a highway robbery pays as punishment one-fifth of the same, while a sneak thief is obliged to return five oxen for one ox, and four sheep for one sheep. Wherefore is this?"

"Because," replied the teacher, "the highway robber treats the servant as the master. He takes away violently in the presence of the servant, the despoiled man, and the master — God. But the sneak thief imagines that God's eye is not upon him. He acts secretly, thinking, as the Psalmist says, 'The Lord doth not see, neither will the God of Jacob regard it.' Listen to a parable. Two men made a feast. One invited all the inhabitants of the city, and omitted inviting the king. The other invited neither the king nor his subjects. Which one deserves condemnation? Certainly the one who invited the subjects and not the king. The people of the earth are God's subjects. The sneak thief fears their eyes, yet he does not honor the eye of the king, the eye of God, which watches all his actions."

Rabbi Meir says, "This law teaches us how God regards industry. If a person steals an ox he must return five in its place, because while the animal was in his unlawful possession it could not work for its rightful owner. A lamb, however, does no labor, and is not profitable that way; therefore he is only obliged to replace it fourfold."

Rabbi Nachman dined with his teacher, Rabbi Yitzchak, and upon departing after the meal, he said, "Teacher, bless me!"

"Listen," replied Rabbi Yitzchak. "A traveler was once journeying through the desert, and when weary, hungry, and thirsty, he happened upon an oasis, where grew a fruitful tree, wide-branched, and at the foot of which there gushed a spring of clear, cool water.

"The stranger ate of the luscious fruit, enjoying and resting in the grateful shade, and quenching his thirst in the sparkling water which bubbled merrily at his feet.

"When about to resume his journey, he addressed the tree and spoke as follows: —

"'Oh, gracious tree, with what words can I bless thee, and what good can I wish thee? I cannot wish thee good fruit, for it is already thine; the blessing of water is also thine; and the gracious shade thrown by thy beauteous branches the Eternal has already granted thee, for my good and the good of those who travel by this way. Let me pray to God, then, that all thy offspring may be goodly as thyself.'

"So it is with thee, my pupil. How shall I bless thee? Thou art perfect in the law, eminent in the land, respected, and blessed with means. May God grant that all thy offspring may prove goodly as thyself."

A wise man, say the Rabbis, was Gebiah ben Pesisah. When the children of Canaan accused the Israelites of stealing their land, saying, "The land of Canaan is ours, as it is written, 'The land of Canaan and its boundaries belong to the Canaanites,'" and demanded restitution, Gebiah offered to argue the case before the ruler.

Said Gebiah to the Africans, "Ye bring your proof from the Pentateuch, and by the Pentateuch will I refute it. 'Cursed be Canaan; a servant of servants shall he be unto his brethren.' To whom does the property of a slave belong? To his master. Even though the land belonged to ye, through your servitude it became Israel's."

"Answer him," said the ruler.

The accusers asked for three days' time to prepare their reply, but at the end of the three days they had vanished.

Then came the Egyptians, saying, "'God gave the Israelites favor in the eyes of the Egyptians, and they lent them gold and silver.' Now return us the gold and silver which our ancestors lent ye."

Again Gebiah appeared for the sages of Israel.

"Four hundred and thirty years," said he, "did the children of Israel dwell in Egypt. Come, now, pay us the wages of six hundred thousand men who worked for ye for naught, and we will return the gold and silver."

Then came the children of Ishmael and Ketura, before Alexander of Mukdon, saying, "The land of Canaan is ours, as it is written, 'These are the generations of Ishmael, the son of Abraham;' even as it is written, 'These are the generations of Isaac, the son of Abraham.' One son is equal to the other; come, give us our share."

Again Gebiah appeared as counsel for the sages.

"From the Pentateuch, which is your proof, will I confound ye" said he. "Is it not written 'Abraham gave all that he had to Isaac, but unto the sons of the concubines that Abraham had, Abraham gave gifts?' The man who gives his children their inheritance during his life does not design to give it to them again after his death. To Isaac Abraham left all that he had; to his other children he gave gifts, and sent them away."

PROVERBIAL SAYINGS AND TRADITIONS

Do not to others what you would not have others do to you.

The ass complains of the cold even in July (Tamuz.)

First learn and then teach.

Few are they who see their own faults.

A single light answers as well for a hundred men as for one.

Victuals prepared by many cooks will be neither hot nor cold.

Truth lasts forever, but falsehood must vanish.

This is the punishment of the liar, that when he tells the truth nobody believes him.

Use thy best vase to-day, for to-morrow it may, perchance, be broken.

When Satan cannot come himself he sends wine as a messenger.

Woe to the children banished from their father's table.

A handful of food will not satisfy the lion, neither can a pit be filled again with its own dust.

Pray to God for mercy until the last shovelful of earth is cast upon thy grave.

Cease not to pray even when the knife is laid upon thy neck.

Open not thy mouth to speak evil.

To be patient is sometimes better than to have much wealth.

The horse fed too liberally with oats becomes unruly.

Happy the pupil whose teacher approves his words.

When the cucumbers are young we may tell whether they will become good for food.

Poverty cometh from God, but not dirt.

Our kindly deeds and our generous gifts go to heaven as messengers, and plead for us before our Heavenly Father.

The noblest of all charities is in enabling the poor to earn a livelihood.

The camel wanted to have horns and they took away his ears.

The egg of to-day is better than the hen of to-morrow.

The world is a wedding.

Youth is a wreath of roses.

A myrtle even in the desert remains a myrtle.

Teach thy tongue to say, " I do not know."

The house which opens not to the poor will open to the physician.

The birds of the air despise a miser.

Hospitality is an expression of Divine worship.

Thy friend has a friend, and thy friend's friend has a friend ; be discreet.

Do not place a blemish on thine own flesh.

Attend no auctions if thou hast no money.

Rather skin a carcass for pay, in the public streets, than lie idly dependent on charity.

Deal with those who are fortunate.

What is intended for thy neighbor will never be thine.

The weakness of thy walls invites the burglar.

The place honors not the man, 'tis the man who gives honor to the place.

The humblest man is ruler in his own house.

If the fox is king bow before him.

If a word spoken in its time is worth one piece of money, silence in its time is worth two.

Tobias committed the sins and his neighbor received the punishment.

Poverty sits as gracefully upon some people as a red saddle upon a white horse.

Drain not the waters of thy well while other people may desire them.

The doctor who prescribes gratuitously gives a worthless prescription.

The rose grows among thorns.

The wine belongs to the master but the waiter receives the thanks.

He who mixes with unclean things becomes unclean himself; he whose associations are pure becomes more holy with each day.

No man is impatient with his creditors.

Make but one sale, and thou art called a merchant.

Mention not a blemish which is thy own, in detraction of thy neighbor.

If certain goods sell not in one city, try another place.

He who reads the letter should execute the message.

A vessel used for holy purposes should not be put to uses less sacred.

Ornament thyself first, then magnify others.

Two pieces of coin in one bag make more noise than a hundred.

Man sees the mote in his neighbor's eye, but knows not of the beam in his own.

The rivalry of scholars advances science.

If thou tellest thy secret to three persons, ten know of it.

When love is intense both find room enough upon one board of the bench; afterward they may find themselves cramped in a space of sixty cubits.

When wine enters the head the secret flies out.

When a liar speaks the truth he finds his punishment in the general disbelief.

Sorrow for those who disappear never to be found.

The officer of the king is also a recipient of honors.

He who studies cannot follow a commercial life; neither can the merchant devote his time to study.

There is no occasion to light thy lamp at noontide.

If thy friends agree in calling thee an ass, go and get a halter around thee.

At the gate of abundance there are many brothers and friends; at the gate of misery there is neither brother nor friend.

The consciousness of God's presence is the first principle of religion.

A man's home means his wife.

He who divorces his wife is hated before God.

If thy wife is small, bend down to take her counsel.

The daughter is as the mother was.

Do not confine your children to your own learning, for they were born in another time.

What the child says out of doors he has learned indoors.

This world is an ante-chamber to the next.

The just of all nations have a portion in the future reward.

Every nation has its special guardian angel, its horoscopes, its ruling planets and stars. But there is no planet for Israel. Israel shall look but to God. There is no mediator between those who are called His children and their Father which is in heaven.

From the very spoon that the carver carved, he has to swallow hot mustard.

The laborer is allowed to shorten his prayers.

He who teaches his son to trade is as if he taught him to steal.

The laborer at his work need not rise before the greatest doctor.

Life is a passing shadow, says the Scripture. Is it the shadow of a tower or a tree? A shadow which prevails for a while? No. It is the shadow of a bird in its flight —away flies the bird, and there is neither bird nor shadow.

Man's passions at first are like a cobweb's thread, at last become like the thickest cable.

Were it not for the existence of passions no one would build a house, marry a wife, beget children, or do any work.

There is not a single bird more persecuted than the dove, yet God has chosen her to be offered upon the altar. The bull is hunted by the lion, the sheep by the wolf, the goat by the tiger. And God said: "Bring me a sacrifice, not from those that persecute, but from them that are persecuted."

Prayer is Israel's only weapon, a weapon inherited from his fathers, a weapon tried in a thousand battles.

When the righteous die, they live; for their example lives.

Let the fruit pray for the welfare of the leaf.

Meat without salt is fit only for the dogs.

Trust not thyself until the day of thy death.

Woe to the country which hath lost its leader; woe to the ship when its captain is no more.

He who increaseth his flesh but multiplieth food for the worms.

The day is short, the labor great, and the workman slothful.

Be yielding to thy superior; be affable toward the young; be friendly with all mankind.

Silence is the fence round wisdom.

Without law, civilization perishes.

Every man will surely have his hour.

Rather be the tail among lions than the head among foxes.

Into the well which supplies thee with water cast no stones.

Many a colt's skin is fashioned to the saddle which its mother bears.

Truth is heavy, therefore few care to carry it.

Say little and do much.

He who multiplieth words will likely come to sin.

Sacrifice thy will for others, that they may be disposed to sacrifice their wills for thee.

Study to-day, delay not.

Look not upon thy prayers as on a task; let thy supplications be sincere.

He who is loved by man is loved by God.

Honor the sons of the poor; they give to science its splendor.

Do not live near a pious fool.

A small coin in a large jar makes a great noise.

Use thy noble vase to-day; to-morrow it may break.

The cat and the rat make peace over a carcass.

He who walks each day over his estate finds a coin daily.

The dog follows thee for the crumbs in thy pocket.

The soldiers fight, and the kings are heroes.

When the ox is down many are the butchers.

Descend a step in choosing thy wife; ascend a step in choosing thy friend.

Beat the gods and their priests will tremble.

The sun will set without thy assistance.

Hold no man responsible for his utterances in times of grief.

One man eats, another says grace.

He who curbs his wrath merits forgiveness for his sins.

Commit a sin twice and it will not seem to thee a crime.

While our love was strong we lay on the edge of a sword, now a couch sixty yards wide is too narrow for us.

Study is more meritorious than sacrifice.

Jerusalem was destroyed because the instruction of the young was neglected.

The world is saved by the breath of school children. Even to rebuild the Temple, the schools must not be closed.

Blessed is the son who has studied with his father, and blessed the father who has instructed his son.

Avoid wrath and thou wilt avoid sin; avoid intemperance and thou wilt not provoke Providence.

When others gather, do thou disperse; when others disperse, gather.

When thou art the only purchaser, then buy; when other buyers are present, be thou nobody.

The foolish man knows not an insult, neither does a dead man feel the cutting of a knife.

Three shall not enter Paradise — the scoffer, the hypocrite, and the slanderer.

Rabbi Gamaliel ordered his servant Tobi to bring something good from the market, and he brought a tongue. At another time he told him to bring something bad, and he also returned with a tongue. "Why did you on both occasions fetch a tongue?" the Rabbi asked. "It is the source of good and evil," Tobi replied. "If it is good, there is nothing better; if it is bad, there is nothing worse."

The forest trees once asked the fruit trees: "Why is the rustling of your leaves not heard in the distance?" The fruit trees replied: "We can dispense with the rustling to manifest our presence; our fruits testify for us." The fruit trees then inquired of the forest trees:

"Why do your leaves rustle almost continually?" "We are forced to call the attention of man to our existence."

Too many Captains sink the ship.

An old man is a trouble in the house; an old woman is a treasure in the house.

Two pieces of coin in one bag make more noise than a hundred.

When the flood came over the earth and everything was threatened with destruction, and every kind of beast came in pairs to Noah, the Lie, too, asked admittance into the ark. Noah, however, refused. "Only pairs may enter here," he said. The Lie went in search of a companion, and at last met Vice, whom it invited to go to the ark. "I am willing to keep company with thee, if thou wilt promise to give me all thy earnings," said Vice. The Lie agreed, and they were both admitted into the ark. After they left the ark, the Lie regretted her agreement, and wished to dissolve partnership with Vice, but it was too late, and thus it is current that "what Lie earneth, Vice consumeth."

Support the aged without reference to religion; respect the learned without reference to age.

Repent the day before thy death.

Ten measures of wisdom came into the world; the law of Israel received nine measures, and the balance of the world one. Ten measures of beauty came into the world; Jerusalem received nine measures, and the rest of the world one.

The world stands on three pillars: law, worship, and charity.

When he who attends the synagogue regularly is prevented from being present, God asks for him.

His enemies will humble themselves before the one who builds a place of worship.

He who is able to attend synagogue, and neglects to do so, is a bad neighbor.

One need not stand upon a high place to pray, for it is written, "Out of the depths have I called unto Thee, oh Lord." The same Rabbi prohibits moving about or talking during the progress of prayers, enlarging on Solomon's

22

advice, "Keep thy foot when thou goest into the house of the Lord, and be more ready to hear than to offer the sacrifice of fools."

The cock and the owl both await daylight. "The light," says the cock, "brings me delight; but what in the world art thou waiting for?"

The thief who finds no opportunity to steal, considers himself an honest man.

A Galilean said, "When the shepherd is angry with his flock, he appoints for its leader a blind bellwether."

Though it is not incumbent upon thee to complete the work, thou must not therefore cease from pursuing it. If the work is great, great will be thy reward, and thy Master is faithful in His payments.

There are three crowns: of the law, the priesthood, and the kingship; but the crown of a good name is greater than them all.

Who gains wisdom? He who is willing to receive instruction from all sources. Who is the mighty man? He who subdueth his temper. Who is rich? He who is content with his lot. Who is deserving of honor? He who honoreth mankind.

Despise no man and deem nothing impossible; every man hath his hour and everything its place.

Iron breaks stone; fire melts iron; water extinguishes fire; the clouds consume water; the storm dispels clouds; man withstands the storm; fear conquers man; wine banishes fear; sleep overcomes wine, and death is the master of sleep; but "charity," says Solomon, "saves even from death."

How canst thou escape sin? Think of three things: whence thou comest, whither thou goest, and before whom thou must appear. The scoffer, the liar, the hypocrite, and the slanderer can have no share in the future world of bliss. To slander is to commit murder.

Cold water morning and evening is better than all the cosmetics.

The question is asked, "Why is man born with hands clinched, but has his hands wide open in death?" And the answer is: "On entering the world, man desires to grasp everything; but when leaving it he takes nothing away."

Two dry logs and one wet; the dry ones kindle the wet.

He who seeks for a faultless brother will have to remain brotherless.

A town which has no school should be abolished.

Jerusalem was destroyed because the instruction of the young was neglected.

He who instructs a child is as if he had created it.

The teachers are the guardians of the State.

Learn first and philosophize afterward.

To what may he be compared who teaches a child? To one who writes on clean paper; and to what may he be compared who teaches an old man? To one who writes on blotted paper.

Be eager to acquire knowledge; it does not come to thee by inheritance.

Four dispositions are found among those who sit for instruction, before the wise, and they may be respectively compared to a sponge, a funnel, a strainer, and a sieve; the sponge imbibes all, the funnel receives at one end and discharges at the other, the strainer suffers the wine to pass through, but retains the lees, and the sieve recovers the bran, but retains the fine flour.

To pray loudly is not a necessity of devotion; when we pray we must direct our hearts toward heaven.

Charity is greater than all.

Who gives charity in secret is greater than Moses.

He finds authority for this saying in the words of Moses, " For I was afraid of the anger," and the words of Solomon which he presents as an answer, " A gift given in secret pacifieth anger."

A miser is as wicked as an idolater.

Charity is more than sacrifices.

" He who gives (charity) becomes rich," or as it is written, " A beneficent soul will be abundantly gratified."

One day a philosopher inquired of Rabbi Akiba, "If your God loves the poor, why does He not support them?"

"God allows the poor to be with us ever," responded Akiba, "that the opportunities for doing good may never fail."

"But," returned the philosopher, "how do you know that this virtue of charity pleases God? If a master punishes his slaves by depriving them of food and clothing, does he feel pleased when others feed and clothe them?"

"But suppose, on the other hand," said the Rabbi, "that the children of a tender father, children whom he could no longer justly assist, had fallen into poverty, would he be displeased if kind souls pitied and aided them? We are not the slaves of a hard master. God calls us His children, and Himself we call our Father."

When one stands at the judgment-seat of God these questions are asked: —

"Hast thou been honest in all thy dealings?"

"Hast thou set aside a portion of thy time for the study of the law?"

"Hast thou observed the first commandment?"

"Hast thou, in trouble, still hoped and believed in God?"

"Hast thou spoken wisely?"

All the blessings of a household come through the wife, therefore should her husband honor her.

Men should be careful lest they cause women to weep, for God counts their tears.

In cases of charity, where both men and women claim relief, the latter should be first assisted. If there should not be enough for both, the men should cheerfully relinquish their claims.

A woman's death is felt by nobody as by her husband.

Tears are shed on God's altar for the one who forsakes his first love.

He who loves his wife as himself, and honors her more than himself, will train his children properly; he will meet, too, the fulfillment of the verse, "And thou shalt know that there is peace in thy tent, and thou wilt look over thy habitation and shall miss nothing."

I never call my wife "wife," but "home," for she, indeed, makes my home.

He who possesses a knowledge of God, and a knowledge of man, will not easily commit sin.

The Bible was given us to establish peace.

He who wrongs his fellow-man, even in so small a coin as a penny, is as wicked as if he should take life.

He who raises his hand against his fellow in passion is a sinner.

Be not the friend of one who wears the cloak of a saint to cover the deformities of a fool.

One who gives way to passion is as bad as an idolater.

Hospitality is as great a virtue as studying the law.

"Never put thyself in the way of temptation," advised Rabbi Judah; "even David could not resist it."

Rabbi Tyra, on being asked by his pupils to tell them the secret which gained him a happy, peaceful old age, replied, "I have never cherished anger with my family; I have never envied those greater than myself, and I have never rejoiced in the downfall of any one."

Unhappy is he who mistakes the branch for the tree, the shadow for the substance.

Thy yesterday is thy past; thy to-day thy future; thy to-morrow is a secret.

The best preacher is the heart; the best teacher is time; the best book is the world; the best friend is God.

Life is but a loan to man; death is the creditor who will one day claim it.

Understand a man by his own deeds and words. The impressions of others lead to false judgment.

He through whose agency another has been falsely punished stands outside of heaven's gates.

The sins of the bad-tempered are greater than his merits.

The man who sins is foolish as well as wicked.

The good actions which we perform in this world take form and meet us in the world to come.

Better to bear a false accusation in silence, than by speaking to bring the guilty to public shame.

He who can feel ashamed will not readily do wrong.

There is a great difference between one who can feel ashamed before his own soul and one who is only ashamed before his fellow-man.

God's covenant with us included work; for the command, "Six days shalt thou work and the seventh shalt thou rest," made the "rest" conditional upon the "work."

God first told Adam to dress the Garden of Eden, and to keep it, and then permitted him to eat of the fruit of his labor.

God did not dwell in the midst of Israel till they had worked to deserve His presence, for he commanded, "They shall make me a sanctuary, and then I will dwell in the midst of them."

When Jerusalem was in the hands of the Romans, one of their philosophers asked of the Rabbis : —

"If your God dislikes idolatry, why does He not destroy the idols and so put temptation out of the way?"

The wise men answered : —

"Would you have the sun and the moon destroyed because of the foolish ones who worship them? To change the course of nature to punish sinners, would bring suffering to the innocent also."

Rabbi Judah said : —

"He who refuses to teach a precept to his pupil is guilty of theft, just as one who steals from the inheritance of his father; as it is written, 'The law which Moses commanded us is the inheritance of the congregation of Jacob.' But if he teaches him, what is his reward?"

Raba says, "He will obtain the blessing of Joseph."

Rabbi Eleazer said : —

"That house where the law is not studied by night should be destroyed.

"The wealthy man who aids not the scholar desirous of studying God's law will not prosper.

"He who changes his word, saying one thing and doing another, is even as he who serveth idols."

Rabbi Chamah, the son of Pappa, said : —

"He who eats or drinks and blesses not the Lord, is even as he who stealeth, for it is said, 'The heavens are the heavens of the Lord, and the earth hath He given to the children of men.' "

Rabbi Simon, the son of Lakish, said : —

"They who perform one precept in this world will find it recorded for their benefit in the world to come ; as it is written, 'Thy righteousness will go before thee, the glory of the Lord will gather thee in.' And the same will be the case, in contrast, with those who sin. For the Bible says, 'Which I commanded thee this day to do them,' to 'do them,' the precepts, to-day, though the reward is not promised to-day ; but in the future, ordinances obeyed, will testify in thy favor, for 'thy righteousness will go before thee.' "

The Rabbis pronounced those the " friends of God," who being offended thought not of revenge ; who practiced good through love for God, and who were cheerful under suffering and difficulties. Of such Isaiah wrote, " They shall shine forth like the sun at noonday."

Love thy wife as thyself ; honor her more than thyself. He who lives unmarried, lives without joy. If thy wife is small, bend down to her and whisper in her ear. He who sees his wife die, has, as it were, been present at the destruction of the sanctuary itself. The children of a man who marries for money will prove a curse to him.

He who has more learning than good deeds is like a tree with many branches but weak roots ; the first great storm will throw it to the ground. He whose good works are greater than his knowledge is like a tree with fewer branches but with strong and spreading roots, a tree which all the winds of heaven cannot uproot.

Better is the curse of the righteous man than the blessing of the wicked. Better the curse of Achia, the Shelonite, than the blessing of Bil'am, the son of Beor. Thus did Achia curse the Israelites, " And the Lord will smite Israel as the reed is shaken in the water." The reed bends but it breaks not, for it groweth by the water, and its roots are strong. Thus did Bil'am bless Israel, " As cedar trees beside the waters." Cedars do not grow beside the waters ;

their roots are weak, and when strong winds blow they
break in pieces.

———

A very wealthy man, who was of a kind, benevolent disposition, desired to make his slave happy. He gave him,
therefore, his freedom, and presented him with a shipload
of merchandise.

"Go," said he, "sail to different countries, dispose of
these goods, and that which thou mayest receive for them
shall be thy own."

The slave sailed away upon the broad ocean, but before
he had been long upon his voyage a storm overtook him;
his ship was driven on a rock and went to pieces; all on
board were lost, all save this slave, who swam to an island
shore near by. Sad, despondent, with naught in the world,
he traversed this island, until he approached a large and
beautiful city; and many people approached him joyously,
shouting, "Welcome! welcome! Long live the king!"
They brought a rich carriage, and placing him therein,
escorted him to a magnificent palace, where many servants
gathered about him, clothing him in royal garments, addressing him as their sovereign, and expressing their obedience
to his will.

The slave was amazed and dazzled, believing that he was
dreaming, and all that he saw, heard, and experienced
was mere passing fantasy. Becoming convinced of the reality of his condition, he said to some men about him for
whom he experienced a friendly feeling:—

"How is this? I cannot understand it. That you should
thus elevate and honor a man whom you know not, a poor,
naked wanderer, whom you have never seen before, making
him your ruler, causes me more wonder than I can readily
express."

"Sire," they replied, "this island is inhabited by spirits.
Long since they prayed to God to send them yearly a son
of man to reign over them, and He has answered their
prayers. Yearly He sends them a son of man, whom they
receive with honor and elevate to the throne; but his dignity and power ends with the year. With its close his
royal garments are taken from him, he is placed on board

a ship and carried to a vast and desolate island, where, unless he has previously been wise and prepared for this day, he will find neither friend nor subject, and be obliged to pass a weary, lonely, miserable life. Then a new king is selected, and so year follows year. The kings who preceded thee were careless and indifferent, enjoying their power to the full, and thinking not of the day when it should end. Be wiser thou ; let our words find rest within thy heart."

The newly-made king listened attentively to all this, and felt grieved that he should have lost even the time he had already missed for making preparations for his loss of power.

He addressed the wise man who had spoken, saying, " Advise me, oh, spirit of wisdom, how I may prepare for the days which will come upon me in the future."

" Naked thou camest to us and naked thou wilt be sent to the desolate island of which I have told thee," replied the other. " At present thou art king, and may do as pleaseth thee ; therefore send workmen to this island ; let them build houses, till the ground, and beautify the surroundings. The barren soil will be changed into fruitful fields, people will journey there to live, and thou wilt have established a new kingdom for thyself, with subjects to welcome thee in gladness when thou shalt have lost thy power here. The year is short, the work is long : therefore be earnest and energetic."

The king followed this advice. He sent workmen and materials to the desolate island, and before the close of his temporary power it had become a blooming, pleasant, and attractive spot. The rulers who had preceded him had anticipated the day of their power's close with dread, or smothered all thought of it in revelry ; but he looked forward to it as a day of joy, when he should enter upon a career of permanent peace and happiness.

The day came ; the freed slave, who had been made king, was deprived of his authority ; with his power he lost his royal garments ; naked he was placed upon a ship, and its sails set for the desolate isle.

When he approached its shores, however, the people whom he had sent there came to meet him with music, song, and great joy. They made him a prince among them, and he lived with them ever after in pleasantness and peace.

The wealthy man of kindly disposition is God, and the slave to whom He gave freedom is the soul which He gives to man. The island at which the slave arrives is the world; naked and weeping he appears to his parents, who are inhabitants that greet him warmly and make him their king. The friends who tell him of the ways of the country are his "good inclinations." The year of his reign is his span of life, and the desolate island is the future world, which he must beautify by good deeds, "the workmen and material," or else live lonely and desolate forever.

The Emperor Adrian, passing through the streets of Tiberias, noticed a very old man planting a fig tree, and pausing, said to him : —

"Wherefore plant that tree? If thou didst labor in thy youth, thou shouldst now have a store for thy old age, and surely of the fruit of this tree thou canst not hope to eat."

The old man answered : —

"In my youth I worked, and I still work. With God's good pleasure I may e'en partake of the fruit of this tree I plant. I am in His hands."

"Tell me thy age," said the emperor.

"I have lived for a hundred years."

"A hundred years old, and still expect to eat from the fruit of this tree?"

"If such be God's pleasure," replied the old man; "if not, I will leave it for my son, as my father left the fruit of his labor for me."

"Well," said the emperor, "if thou dost live until the figs from this tree are ripe, I pray thee let me know of it."

The aged man lived to partake of that very fruit, and remembering the emperor's words, he resolved to visit him. So, taking a small basket, he filled it with the choicest figs from the tree, and proceeded on his errand. Telling the palace guard his purpose, he was admitted to the sovereign's presence.

"Well," asked the emperor, "what is thy wish?"

The old man replied : —

"Lo, I am the old man to whom thou didst say, on the day thou sawest him planting a fig tree, 'If thou livest to eat of its fruit, I pray thee let me know;' and behold I have come and brought thee of the fruit, that thou mayest partake of it likewise."

The emperor was very much pleased, and emptying the man's basket of its figs, he ordered it to be filled with gold coins.

When the old man had departed, the courtiers said to the emperor : —

"Why didst thou so honor this old Jew?"

"The Lord hath honored him, and why not I?" replied the emperor.

Now next door to this old man there lived a woman, who, when she heard of her neighbor's good fortune, desired her husband to try his luck in the same quarter. She filled for him an immense basket with figs, and bidding him put it on his shoulder, said, "Now carry it to the emperor; he loves figs and will fill thy basket with golden coin."

When her husband approached the gates of the palace, he told his errand to the guards, saying, "I brought these figs to the emperor; empty my basket I pray, and fill it up again with gold."

When this was told to the emperor, he ordered the old man to stand in the hallway of the palace, and all who passed pelted him with his figs. He returned home wounded and crestfallen to his disappointed wife.

"Never mind, thou hast one consolation," said she; "had they been cocoanuts instead of figs thou mightest have suffered harder raps."

———

A citizen of Jerusalem traveling through the country was taken very sick at an inn. Feeling that he would not recover, he sent for the landlord and said to him, "I am going the way of all flesh. If after my death any party should come from Jerusalem and claim my effects, do not deliver them until he shall prove to thee by three wise acts that he is entitled to them ; for I charged my son before starting upon my way, that if death befell me he would be obliged to prove his wisdom before obtaining my possessions."

The man died and was buried according to Jewish rites, and his death was made public that his heirs might appear. When his son learned of his father's decease he started from Jerusalem for the place where he had died. Near the gates of the city he met a man who had a load of wood for sale. This he purchased and ordered it to be delivered at the inn toward which he was traveling. The man from whom he bought it went at once to the inn, and said, "Here is the wood."

"What wood?" returned the proprietor; "I ordered no wood."

"No," answered the woodcutter, "but the man who follows me did; I will enter and wait for him."

Thus the son had provided for himself a welcome when he should reach the inn, which was his first wise act.

The landlord said to him, "Who art thou?"

"The son of the merchant who died in thy house," he replied.

They prepared for him a dinner, and placed upon the table five pigeons and a chicken. The master of the house, his wife, two sons, and two daughters sat with him at the table.

"Serve the food," said the landlord.

"Nay," answered the young man; "thou art master, it is thy privilege."

"I desire thee to do this thing ; thou art my guest, the merchant's son ; pray help the food."

The young man thus entreated divided one pigeon between the two sons, another between the two daughters, gave the third to the man and his wife, and kept the other two for himself. This was his second wise act.

The landlord looked somewhat perplexed at this mode of distribution, but said nothing.

Then the merchant's son divided the chicken. He gave to the landlord and his wife the head, to the two sons the legs, to the two daughters the wings, and took the body for himself. This was his third wise act.

The landlord said : —

"Is this the way they do things in thy country? I no-ticed the manner in which thou didst apportion the pigeons, but said nothing; but the chicken, my dear sir! I must really ask thee thy meaning."

Then the young man answered : —

"I told thee that it was not my place to serve the food, nevertheless when thou didst insist I did the best I could, and I think I have succeeded. Thyself, thy wife, and one pigeon make three; thy two sons and one pigeon make three; thy two daughters and one pigeon make three; and myself and two pigeons make three also, therefore is it fairly done. As regards the chicken, I gave to thee and thy wife the head, because ye are the heads of the family; I gave to each of thy sons a leg, because they are the pil-lars of the family, preserving always the family name; I gave to each of thy daughters a wing, because in the nat-ural course of events they will marry, take wing, and fly away from the home-nest. I took the body of the chicken because it looks like a ship, and in a ship I came here and in a ship I hope to return. I am the son of the merchant who died in thy house; give me the property of my dead father."

"Take it and go," said the landlord. And giving him his father's possessions the young man departed in peace.

A certain man, a native of Athina (a city near Jerusa-lem), visited the city of Jerusalem, and after leaving it, ridiculed the place and its inhabitants. The Jerusalemites were very wroth at being made the subjects of his sport, and they induced one of their citizens to travel to Athina, to induce the man to return to Jerusalem, which would give them an opportunity to punish his insolence.

The citizen thus commissioned reached Athina, and very shortly fell in with the man whom he had come to meet. Walking through the streets together one day, the man from Jerusalem said, "See, the string of my shoe is broken; take me, I pray, to the shoemaker."

The shoemaker repaired the string, and the man paid him a coin more in value than the worth of the shoes.

Next day, when walking with the same man, he broke the string of his other shoe, and going to the shoemaker, he paid him the same large sum for repairing that.

"Why," said the man of Athina, "shoes must be very dear in Jerusalem, when thou payest such a price but for repairing a string."

"Yes," answered the other; "they bring nine ducats, and even in the cheapest times from seven to eight."

"Then it would be a profitable employment for me to take shoes from my city and sell them in thine."

"Yes, indeed; and if thou wilt but let me know of thy coming I will put thee in the way of customers."

So the man of Athina, who had made merry over the Jerusalemites, bought a large stock of shoes and set out for Jerusalem, informing his friend of his coming. The latter started to meet him, and greeting him before he came to the gates of the city, said to him : —

"Before a stranger may enter and sell goods in Jerusalem, he must shave his head and blacken his face. Art thou ready to do this?"

"And why not," replied the other, "as long as I have a prospect of large profits; why should I falter or hesitate at so slight a thing as that?"

So the stranger, shaving the hair from his head and blackening his face (by which all Jerusalem knew him as the man who had ridiculed the city), took up his place in the market, with his wares spread before him.

Buyers paused before his stall, and asked him : —

"How much for the shoes?"

"Ten ducats a pair," he answered; "or I may sell for nine; but certainly for not less than eight."

This caused a great laugh and uproar in the market, and the stranger was driven from it in derision and his shoes thrown after him.

Seeking the Jerusalemite who had deceived him, he said : —

"Why hast thou so treated me? did I so to thee in Athina?"

"Let this be a lesson to thee," answered the Jerusalemite. "I do not think thou wilt be so ready to make sport of us in the future."

A young man, upon his journeys through the country, fell in with a young woman, and they became mutually attached. When the young man was obliged to leave the neighborhood of the damsel's residence, they met to say " good-by." During the parting they pledged a mutual faith, and each promised to wait until, in the course of time, they might be able to marry. "Who will be the witness of our betrothal?" said the young man. Just then they saw a weasel run past them and disappear in the wood. " See," he continued, " this weasel and this well of water by which we are standing shall be the witnesses of our betrothal; " and so they parted. Years passed, the maiden remained true, but the youth married. A son was born to him, and grew up the delight of his parents. One day while the child was playing he became tired, and lying upon the ground fell asleep. A weasel bit him in the neck, and he bled to death. The parents were consumed with grief by this calamity, and it was not until another son was given them that they forgot their sorrow. But when this second child was able to walk alone it wandered without the house, and bending over the well, looking at its shadow in the water, lost its balance and was drowned. Then the father recollected his perjured vow, and his witnesses, the weasel and the well. He told his wife of the circumstance, and she agreed to a divorce. He then sought the maiden to whom he had promised marriage, and found her still awaiting his return. He told her how, through God's agency, he had been punished for his wrongdoing, after which they married and lived in peace.

————

A wise Israelite, dwelling some distance from Jerusalem, sent his son to the Holy City to complete his education. During his son's absence the father was taken ill, and feeling that death was upon him he made a will, leaving all his property to one of his slaves, on condition that he should allow the son to select any one article which pleased him for an inheritance.

As soon as his master died, the slave, elated with his good fortune, hastened to Jerusalem, informed his late master's son of what had taken place, and showed him the will.

The young man was surprised and grieved at the intelli-gence, and after the alloted time of mourning had expired, he began to seriously consider his situation. He went to his teacher, explained the circumstances to him, read him his father's will, and expressed himself bitterly on account of the disappointment of his reasonable hopes and expec-tations. He could think of nothing that he had done to offend his father, and was loud in his complaints of in-justice.

"Stop," said his teacher; "thy father was a man of wisdom and a loving relative. This will is a living monu-ment to his good sense and far-sightedness. May his son prove as wise in his day."

"What!" exclaimed the young man. "I see no wisdom in his bestowal of his property upon a slave; no affection in this slight upon his only son."

"Listen," returned the teacher. "By his action thy father hath but secured thy inheritance to thee, if thou art wise enough to avail thyself of his understanding. Thus thought he when he felt the hand of death approaching. 'My son is away; when I am dead he will not be here to take charge of my affairs; my slaves will plunder my estate, and to gain time will even conceal my death from my son, and deprive me of the sweet savour of mourning.' To prevent these things he bequeated his property to his slave, well knowing that the slave, believing in his appar-ent right, would give thee speedy information, and take care of the effects, even as he has done."

"Well, well, and how does this benefit me?" impatiently interrupted the pupil.

"Ah!" replied the teacher, "wisdom I see rests not with the young. Dost thou not know that what a slave pos-sesses belongs but to his master? Has not thy father left thee the right to select one article of all his property for thy own? Choose the slave as thy portion, and by possess-ing him thou wilt recover all that was thy father's. Such was his wise and loving intention."

The young man did as he was advised, and gave the slave his freedom afterward. But ever after he was wont to exclaim:—

"Wisdom resides with the aged, and understanding in length of days."

David, King of Israel, was once lying upon his couch and many thoughts were passing through his mind.

"Of what use in this world is the spider?" thought he; "it but increases the dust and dirt of the world, making places unsightly and causing great annoyance."

Then he thought of an insane man: —

"How unfortunate is such a being. I know that all things are ordained by God with reason and purpose, yet this is beyond my comprehension; why should men be born idiots, or grow insane?"

Then the mosquitoes annoyed him, and the king thought: —

"What can the mosquito be good for? why was it created in the world? It but disturbs our comfort, and the world profits not by its existence."

Yet King David lived to discover that these very insects, and the very condition of life, the being of which he deplored, were ordained even to his own benefit.

When he fled from before Saul, David was captured in the land of the Philistines by the brothers of Goliath, who carried him before the King of Gath, and it was only by pretending idiocy that he escaped death, the king deeming it impossible that such a man could be the kingly David; as it is written, "And he disguised his reason before their eyes, and played the madman in their hands, and scribbled on the doors of the gate, and let his spittle run down upon his beard."

Upon another occasion David hid himself in the cave of Adullam, and after he had entered the cave it chanced that a spider spun a web over the opening thereto. His pursuers passed that way, but thinking that no one could have entered the cave protected by the spider's web without destroying it, they continued on their way.

The mosquito also was of service to David when he entered the camp of Saul to secure the latter's weapon. While stooping near Abner, the sleeping man moved and placed his leg upon David's body. If he moved, he would

23

awake Abner and meet with death, if he remained in that position morning would dawn and bring him death; he knew not what to do, when a mosquito alighted upon Abner's leg; he moved it quickly, and David escaped.

Therefore sang David:—

"All my bones shall say, O Lord, who is like unto Thee."

———

The Israelites were commanded to visit Jerusalem on three festivals. It happened upon one occasion that there was a scarcity of water in the city. One of the people called upon a certain nobleman who was the owner of three wells, and asked him for the use of the water which they contained, promising that they should be refilled by a stated date, and contracting in default of this to pay a certain large amount in silver as forfeit. The day came, there had been no rain, and the three wells were dry. In the morning the owner of the wells sent for the promised money. Nakdemon, the son of Gurion, the man who had undertaken this burden for his people's sake, replied, "The day is but begun; there is yet time."

He entered the Temple and prayed that God might send rain and save him all his fortune which he had ventured. His prayer was answered. The clouds gathered and the rain fell. As he passed out of the Temple with a grateful heart, he was met by his creditor, who said:—

"True, the rain has refilled my wells, but it is dark; the day has gone, and according to our agreement thou must still pay me the promised sum."

Once more Nakdemon prayed, and lo, the clouds lifted and the sinking sun smiled brightly on the spot where the men stood, showing that the sunlight of day was still there, though the rain-clouds had temporarily obscured its gleams.

———

There was a certain family, the family of Abtinoss, the members of which were learned in the art of preparing the incense used in the service. Their knowledge they refused to impart to others, and the directors of the Temple, fearing that the art might die with them, discharged them from the service, and brought other parties from Alexandria, in Egypt, to prepare the sweet perfume. These latter were unable to afford satisfaction, however, and the directors were obliged to give the service back into the hands of the family of Abtinoss, who on their part refused to accept it again, unless the remuneration for their services was doubled. When asked why they so persistently refused to impart their skill to others, they replied that they feared they might teach some unworthy persons, who would afterward use their knowledge in an idolatrous worship. The members of this family were very particular not to use perfume of any kind themselves, lest the people should imagine that they put the sweet spices used in the manufacture of the incense to a baser use.

An exactly similar case to the above occurred with the family of Garmah, which had the monopoly of the knowledge of preparing the show-bread used in the services of the Temple.

It was in reference to these cases that the son of Azai said, " In thy name they shall call thee, and in thy city they shall cause thee to live, and from thy own they will give thee," meaning that trustful persons should not fear that others might steal their occupations ; " for in thy name they will call thee," as with the families of Abtinoss and Garmah ; "and from thy own they will give thee," meaning that what a man earns is his own, and cannot be taken away.

Rabbi Jochanan, the son of Levi, fasted and prayed to the Lord that he might be permitted to gaze on the angel Elijah, he who had ascended alive to heaven. God granted his prayer, and in the semblance of a man Elijah appeared before him.

"Let me journey with thee in thy travels through the world," prayed the Rabbi to Elijah ; "let me observe thy doings, and gain in wisdom and understanding."

"Nay," answered Elijah ; "my actions thou couldst not understand ; my doings would trouble thee, being beyond thy comprehension."

But still the Rabbi entreated : —

"I will neither trouble nor question thee," he said; "only let me accompany thee on thy way."

"Come, then," said Elijah; "but let thy tongue be mute. With thy first question, thy first expression of astonishment, we must part company."

So the two journeyed through the world together. They approached the house of a poor man, whose only treasure and means of support was a cow. As they came near, the man and his wife hastened to meet them, begged them to enter their cot, and eat and drink of the best they could afford, and to pass the night under their roof. This they did, receiving every attention from their poor but hospitable host and hostess. In the morning Elijah rose up early and prayed to God, and when he had finished his prayer, behold the cow belonging to the poor people dropped dead. Then the travelers continued on their journey.

Much was Rabbi Jochanan perplexed. "Not only did we neglect to pay them for their hospitality and generous services, but his cow we have killed;" and he said to Elijah, "Why didst thou kill the cow of this good man, who —— "

"Peace," interrupted Elijah; "hear, see, and be silent. If I answer thy questions we must part."

And they continued on their way together.

Toward evening they arrived at a large and imposing mansion, the residence of a haughty and wealthy man. They were coldly received; a piece of bread and a glass of water were placed before them, but the master of the house did not welcome or speak to them, and they remained there during the night unnoticed. In the morning Elijah remarked that a wall of the house required repairing, and sending for a carpenter, he himself paid the money for the repair, as a return, he said, for the hospitality they had received.

Again was Rabbi Jochanan filled with wonder, but he said naught, and they proceeded on their journey.

As the shades of night were falling they entered a city which contained a large and imposing synagogue. As it was the time of the evening service they entered and were much pleased with the rich adornments, the velvet cushions,

and gilded carvings of the interior. After the completion
of the service, Elijah arose and called out aloud, "Who is
here willing to feed and lodge two poor men this night?"
none answered, and no respect was shown to the traveling
strangers. In the morning, however, Elijah re-entered the
synagogue, and shaking its members by the hands, he said,
"I hope that you may all become presidents."

Next evening the two entered another city, when the
Shamas (sexton) of the synagogue, came to meet them, and
notifying the members of his congregation of the coming of two strangers, the best hotel of the place was
opened to them, and all vied in showing them attention
and honor.

In the morning, on parting with them, Elijah said,
"May the Lord appoint over you but one president."

Jochanan could resist his curiosity no longer. "Tell
me," said he to Elijah, "tell me the meaning of all these
actions which I have witnessed. To those who have treated
us coldly thou hast uttered good wishes; to those who have
been gracious to us thou hast made no suitable return.
Even though we must part, I pray thee explain to me the
meaning of thy acts."

"Listen," said Elijah, "and learn to trust in God, even
though thou canst not understand His ways. We first
entered the house of the poor man, who treated us so
kindly. Know that it had been decreed that on that very
day his wife should die. I prayed unto the Lord that the
cow might prove a redemption for her; God granted my
prayers, and the woman was preserved unto her husband.
The rich man, whom next we called up, treated us coldly,
and I repaired his wall. I repaired it without a new foundation, without digging to the old one. Had he repaired it
himself he would have dug, and thus discovered a treasure
which lies there buried, but which is now forever lost to
him. To the members of the synagogue who were inhos-
pitable I said, 'May you all be presidents,' and where many
rule there can be no peace; but to the others I said, 'May
you have but one president;' with one leader no misunder-
standing may arise. Now, if thou seest the wicked prosper-
ing, be not envious; if thou seest the righteous in poverty

and trouble, be not provoked or doubtful of God's justice. The Lord is righteous, His judgments all are true ; His eyes note all mankind, and none can say, 'What dost thou?'"

With these words Elijah disappeared, and Jochanan was left alone.

There was once a man who pledged his dearest faith to a maiden, beautiful and true. For a time all passed pleasantly, and the maiden lived in happiness. But then the man was called from her side, he left her ; long she waited, but he did not return. Friends pitied her and rivals mocked her ; tauntingly they pointed at her, and said, "He has left thee ; he will never come back." The maiden sought her chamber, and read in secret the letters which her lover had written to her, the letters in which he promised to be ever faithful, ever true. Weeping she read them, but they brought comfort to her heart ; she dried her eyes and doubted not.

A joyous day dawned for her ; the man she loved returned, and when he learned that others had doubted and asked her how she had preserved her faith, she showed his letters to him, declaring her eternal trust.

Israel, in misery and captivity, was mocked by the nations ; her hopes of redemption were made a laughing-stock ; her sages scoffed at ; her holy men derided. Into her synagogues, into her schools went Israel ; she read the letters which her God had written, and believed in the holy promises which they contained.

God will in time redeem her ; and when He says : —

"How could you alone be faithful of all the mocking nations?"

She will point to the law and answer : —

"Had not Thy law been my delight, I should long since have perished in my affliction."

When God was about to created man the angels gathered about him. Some of them opening their lips exclaimed, "Create, O God, a being who shall praise Thee from earth even as we in heaven sing Thy glory."

But others said : —

" Hear us, Almighty King, create no more! The glorious harmony of the heavens which Thou hast sent to earth will be by man disturbed, destroyed."

Then silence fell upon the contesting hosts as the Angel of Mercy appeared before the throne of grace on bended knees.

Sweet was the voice which said entreatingly : —

" O, Father, create Thou man ; make him Thine own noble image. With heavenly pity will I fill his heart, with sympathy toward every living thing impress his being ; through him will they find cause to praise Thee."

Then the Angel of Mercy ceased, and the Angel of Peace with tearful eyes spoke thus : —

" O God, create him not ! Thy peace he will disturb, the flow of blood, will follow sure his coming. Confusion, horror, war, will blot the earth, and Thou wilt no longer find a pleasant place among Thy works on earth."

Then spoke in stern tones the Angel of Justice : —

" And Thou wilt judge him, God ; he shall be subject to my sway."

The Angel of Truth approached, saying : —

" Cease ! O God of truth, with man Thou sendest falsehood to the earth."

Then all were silent, and out of the deep quietness the Divine words came : —

" Thou, O Truth, shall go to earth with him, and yet remain a denizen of heaven ; 'twixt heaven and earth to float, connecting link between the two."

It was customary in Bithar when a child was born for the parents to plant a young cedar tree, to grow up with the infant. It happened upon one occasion when the daughter of the emperor was riding through the city, that her chariot broke down, and her attendants pulled up a young cedar tree to use in repairing it. The man who had planted the tree, seeing this, attacked the servants and beat them severely. This action incensed the emperor, who immediately dispatched an army of eighty thousand men against the city. These captured it and killed the inhabitants, men, women, and children. The rivers ran red with

blood, and 'tis said that the ground was rich and prolific
to the farmers for seven years, from the bodies of those
who perished, said to be four hundred thousand Israelites.

———

When the guilt of the Israelites grew too great for the
forbearance of the Most High, and they refused to listen to
the words and warnings of Jeremiah, the prophet left Jerusalem and traveled to the land of Benjamin. While he was
in the holy city, and prayed for mercy on it, it was spared ;
but while he sojourned in the land of Benjamin, Nebuchadnezzar laid waste the land of Israel, plundered the holy
Temple, robbed it of its ornaments, and gave it a prey to
the devouring flames. By the hands of Nebuzaradan did
Nebuchadnezzar send (while he himself remained in Riblah)
to destroy Jerusalem.

Before he ordered the expedition he endeavored by means
of signs, in accordance with the superstition of his age, to
ascertain the result of the attempt. He shot an arrow from
his bow, pointing to the west, and the arrow turned toward
Jerusalem. Then he shot again, pointing toward the east,
and the arrow sped toward Jerusalem. Then he shot once
more, desiring to know in which direction lay the guilty
city which should be blotted from the world, and for the
third time his arrow pointed toward Jerusalem.

When the city had been captured, he marched with his
princes and officers into the Temple, and called out mock-
ingly to the God of Israel, " And art thou the great God
before whom the world trembles, and we here in thy city
and thy Temple ! "

On one of the walls he found the mark of an arrow's
head, as though somebody had been killed or hit near by,
and he asked, " Who was killed here ? "

" Zachariah, the son of Yehoyadah, the high priest," answered the people ; " he rebuked us incessantly on account
of our transgressions, and we tired of his words, and put
him to death."

The followers of Nebuchadnezzar massacred the inhabitants of Jerusalem, the priests and the people, old and
young, women, and children who were attending school,
even babies in the cradle. The feast of blood at last

shocked even the leader of the hostile heathens, who ordered a stay of this wholesale murder. He then removed all the vessels of gold and silver from the Temple, and sent them by his ships, to Babel, after which he set the Temple on fire.

The high priest donned his robe and ephod, and saying, " Now that the Temple is destroyed, no priest is needed to officiate," threw himself into the flames and was consumed. When the other priests who were still alive witnessed this action, they took their harps and musical instruments and followed the example of the high priest. Those of the people whom the soldiers had not killed were bound in iron chains, burdened with the spoils of the victors, and carried into captivity. Jeremiah the prophet returned to Jerusalem and accompanied his unfortunate brethren, who went out almost naked. When they reached a place called Bet Kuro, Jeremiah obtained better clothing for them. And he spoke to Nebuchadnezzar and the Chaldeans, and said, " Think not that of your own strength you were able to overcome the people chosen of the Lord ; 'tis their iniquities which have condemned them to this sorrow."

Thus the people journeyed on with crying and moaning until they reached the rivers of Babylon. Then Nebuchad-nezzar said to them, " Sing, ye people,— play for me,— sing the songs ye were wont to sing before your great Lord in Jerusalem."

In answer to this command, the Levites hung their harps upon the willow trees near the banks of the river, as it is written, " Upon the willows in her midst had we hung up our harps." Then they said, " If we had but performed the will of God and sung His praises devoutly, we should not have been delivered into thy hands. Now, how can we sing before thee the prayers and hymns that belong only to the One Eternal God ? " as it is said, " How should we sing the song of the Lord on the soil of the stranger ? "

Then said the officers of the captors, " These men are men of death ; they refuse to obey the order of the king ; let them die."

But forth stepped Pelatya, the son of Yehoyadah, and thus he addressed Nebuchadnezzar : —

"Behold, if a flock is delivered into the hands of a shepherd, and a wolf steals a lamb from the flock, tell me, who is responsible to the owner of the lost animal?"

"Surely the shepherd," replied Nebuchadnezzar.

"Then listen to thine own words," replied Pelatya. "God has given Israel into thy hands; to Him art thou responsible for those who are slain."

The king ordered the chains to be removed from the captives, and they were not put to death.

———

Through Kamtzah and Bar Kamtzah was Jerusalem destroyed; and thus it happened.

A certain man made a feast; he was a friend of Kamtzah, but Bar Kamtzah he hated. He sent a messenger to Kamtzah with an invitation to his banquet, but this messenger making a mistake, delivered the invitation to his master's enemy, Bar Kamtzah.

Bar Kamtzah accepted the invitation, and was on hand at the appointed time, but when the host saw his enemy enter his house, he ordered him to leave at once.

"Nay," said Bar Kamtzah, "now that I am here, do not so insult me as to send me forth. I will pay thee for all that I may eat and drink."

"I want not thy money," returned the other, "neither do I desire thy presence; get thee gone at once."

But Bar Kamtzah persisted.

"I will pay the entire expense of thy feast," he said; "do not let me be degraded in the eyes of thy guests."

The host was determined, and Bar Kamtzah withdrew from the banquet-room in anger.

"Many Rabbis were present," said he in his heart, "and not one of them interfered in my behalf, therefore this insult which they saw put upon me must have pleased them."

So Bar Kamtzah spoke treacherously of the Jews unto the king, saying, "The Jews have rebelled against thee."

"How can I know this?" inquired the king.

"Send a sacrifice to their Temple and it will be rejected," replied Bar Kamtzah.

The ruler then sent a well-conditioned calf to be sacrificed for him in the Temple, but through the machinations of Bar Kamtzah the messenger inflicted a blemish upon it, and, of course, not being fit for the sacrifice it was not accepted.

Through this cause was Cæsar sent to capture Jerusalem, and for two years he besieged the city. Four wealthy citizens of Jerusalem had stored up enough food to last the inhabitants a much longer time than this, but the people being anxious to fight with the Romans, destroyed the storehouses and brought dire famine upon the city.

A certain noble lady, Miriam, the daughter of Baythus, sent her servant to purchase some flour for household use. The servant found that all the flour had been sold, but there was still some meal which he might have purchased. Hurrying home, however, to learn his mistress's wishes in regard to this, he discovered on his return that this too had been sold, and he could obtain nothing save some coarse barley meal. Not wishing to purchase this without orders he returned home again, but when he returned to the storehouse to secure the barley meal, that was gone also. Then his mistress started out herself to purchase food, but she could find nothing. Suffering from the pangs of hunger she picked from the street the skin of a fig and ate it; this sickened her and she died. But previous to her death she cast all her gold and silver into the street, saying, "What use is this wealth to me when I can obtain no food for it?" Thus were the words of Ezekiel fulfilled: —

"Their silver shall they cast into the streets."

After the destruction of the storehouses, Rabbi Jochanan in walking through the city saw the populace boiling straw in water and drinking of the same for sustenance. "Ah, woe is me for this calamity!" he exclaimed; "how can such a people strive against a mighty host?" He applied to Ben Batiach, his nephew, one of the chiefs of the city, for permission to leave Jerusalem. But Ben Batiach replied, "It may not be; no living body may leave the city." "Take me out then as a corpse," entreated Jochanan. Ben Batiach assented to this, and Jochanan was placed in a coffin and carried through the gates of the

city ; Rabbi Eleazer, Rabbi Joshua, and Ben Batiach acting as pall-bearers. The coffin was placed in a cave, and
after they had all returned to their homes Jochanan arose
from the coffin and made his way to the enemy's camp.
He obtained from the commander permission to establish
an academy in Jabna with Rabbon Gamliel as the principal.

Titus soon captured the city, killed many of the people,
and sent the others into exile. He entered the Temple,
even in the Most Holy, and cut down the veil which separated it from the less sacred precincts. He seized the
holy vessels, and sent them to Rome.

From this history of Kamtzah and Bar Kamtzah we
should learn to be careful of offending our neighbors, when
in so slight a cause such great results may originate. Our
Rabbis have said that he who causes his neighbor to blush
through an insult, should be compared to the one who
sheds blood.

———

During the terrible times which followed the fall of
the Holy City, Hannah and her seven sons were cast into
prison.

According to their ages they were brought before the
tyrant conqueror, and commanded to pay homage to him
and his gods.

"God forbid," exclaimed the eldest lad, "that I should
bow to thy image. Our commandments say to us, 'I am
the Lord thy God;' to no other will I bow."

He was immediately led out to execution, and the same
demand made of his brother, the second son.

"My brother bowed not," he answered, "and no more
will I."

"Wherefore not?" asked the tyrant.

"Because," replied the lad, "the second commandment of the
Decalogue tells us, 'Thou shalt have no other God but me.'"

His death followed immediately his brave words.

"My religion teaches me, 'Thou shalt worship no other
God," said the third son, "and I welcome the fate accorded
to my brothers rather than bow to thee or thy images."

The same homage was demanded of the fourth son, but
brave and faithful as his brethren, he replied, "'He that

sacrificeth unto any God save unto the Lord only,'" and was slain pitilessly.

"'Hear, O Israel! the Lord our God, the Lord is One,'" exclaimed the fifth lad, yielding up his young life with the watchword of Israel's hosts.

"Why art thou so obstinate?" was asked of the sixth brother, when he, too, was brought before the tyrant and scorned the propositions made him.

"'The Lord thy God is in the midst of thee, a mighty and terrible God,'" he said; and died for the principles he proclaimed.

Then the seventh and youngest boy was brought before the murderer of his relatives, who addressed him kindly, saying : —

"My son, come bow before my gods."

And the child answered : —

"God forbid! Our holy religion teaches us 'Know therefore this day, and reflect in thy heart that the Lord he is God, in the heavens above and on the earth beneath there is none else.' Never will we exchange our God for any other, neither will He exchange us for any other nation, for as it is written, 'Thou hast this day acknowledged the Lord,' so is it also written, 'And the Lord hath acknowledged thee this day, that thou art unto him a peculiar people!'"

Still the tyrant spoke smoothly, and with kind words.

"Thou art young," he said; "thou hast seen but little of the pleasures and joys of life, not as much as has fallen to the portion of thy brethren. Do as I wish thee and thy future shall be bright and happy."

"The Lord will reign forever and ever," said the lad; "thy nation and thy kingdom will be destroyed; thou art here to-day, to-morrow in the grave; to-day elevated, to-morrow lowly; but the most Holy One endures forever."

"See," continued the other, "thy brothers lie slain before thee; their fate will be thine if thou refusest to do as I desire. See, I will cast my ring to the ground, stoop thou and pick it up; that I will consider allegiance to my gods."

"Thinkest thou that I fear thy threats?" returned the unterrified lad; "why should I fear a human being more than the great God, the King of kings?"

"Where and what is thy God?" asked the oppressor. "Is there a God in the world?"

"Can there be a world without a Creator?" replied the youth. "Of thy gods 'tis said, 'mouths they have, but speak not.' Of our God the Psalmist says, 'By the word of the Lord were the heavens made.' Thy gods have 'eyes but see not,' but 'the eyes of the Lord run to and fro in the whole earth!' Thy gods have 'ears but hear not,' but of our God 'tis written, 'The Lord hearkened and heard.' Of thy gods 'tis said, 'a nose they have but smell not,' while our God 'smelled the sweet savor.' 'Hands have thy gods but they touch not,' while our God says, 'My hand hath also founded the earth.' Of thy gods 'tis written, 'feet they have but walk not,' while Zachariah tells us of our God, 'His feet will stand that day upon the mount of Olives.'"

Then said the cruel one : —

"If thy God hath all these attributes, why does He not deliver thee from my power?"

The lad replied : —

"He delivered Chananyah and his companions from the power of Nebuchadnezzar, but they were righteous men, and Nebuchadnezzar was a king deserving of seeing a miracle performed, but for me, alas, I am not worthy of redemption, neither art thou worthy of a demonstration of God's power."

"Let the lad be slain as were his brothers," commanded the tyrant.

Then spoke Hannah, the mother of the boys : —

"Give me my child," she cried, "oh, cruel king, let me fold him in my arms ere thou destroyest his innocent young life."

She threw her arms around the lad, clasping him tightly to her bosom, and pressing her lips to his. "Take my life," she cried; "kill me first before my child."

"Nay," he answered, scoffingly, "I cannot do it, for thy own laws forbid ; 'Whether it be ox or sheep ye shall not kill it and its young in one day.'"

"Oh, woe to thee," replied the mother, "thou who art so particular to regard the laws." Then pressing her boy to her heart, "Go, my dear one," she said, "say to Abraham that my sacrifice hath exceeded his. He built one altar whereon to sacrifice Isaac; thy mother hath built seven altars and sacrificed seven Isaacs in one day. He was but tempted; thy mother hath performed."

After the execution of her last son, Hannah became insane, and threw herself from her house-top. Where she fell, she expired.

Happy are ye, ye seven sons of Hannah; your portion in the future world was waiting for you. In faithfulness ye served your God, and with her children shall your mother rejoice forever in the eternal world.

Moses Maimonides, one of the greatest of Jewish commentators, and a descendant of Rabbi Judah, the compiler of the Mishna, was born in the city of Cordova, Spain, March 30, 1135. His father was somewhat advanced in life when he married, and it is said that he entered into the conjugal state through having dreamed several successive times that he was wedded to the daughter of a butcher in his neighborhood; the lady whom he did actually marry.

Moses was the only child of this lady, who died shortly after his birth. His father lamented her demise for about a year, and then married again, several children being the result of this second union.

Moses displayed no love for study in his youth; a fact which grieved his father much. All efforts to induce him to become more studious failed; his brothers called him "the butcher's boy," as a term of reproach for his dullness; and finally, in anger, his father drove him from his home.

While traveling, entirely friendless, Moses fell in with a learned Rabbi, and admired his wisdom and knowledge so much that he resolved to study zealously and emulate such attainments.

Many years after this a new preacher was announced to lecture in the synagogue, at Cordova, upon a designated Sabbath. Numerous rumors of his wonderful learning and eloquence were rife, and all were anxious to hear him. In matter, delivery, earnestness, and effect, the sermon excelled all that the people had before listened to, and to the amazement of Maimonides the elder, and his sons, they recognized in the man all were eager to honor, their outcast relative.

The first commentary of Maimonides is upon the Mishna, and it concludes with these words : —

" I, Moses, the son of Maymon, commenced this commentary when twenty-three years of age. I have finished it at the age of thirty in the land of Egypt."

Maimonides fled from Spain to Cairo, in Egypt, from fanaticism and persecution. There he studied the Greek and Chaldaic languages, becoming master of both after seven years' attention. His fame spread through the country. His scientific standing and his general knowledge were universally recognized, and his books were not only valued by his brethren in faith, but by all the cultured and enlightened of his day.

It is said that the king of Egypt appointed him as one of his staff of physicians. The enlightened men of the kingdom were divided into seven grades, each grade occupying a corresponding position near the throne of the king on state occasions. The monarch considered Maimonides so much superior to the others that he made for him a special position. This, Moses, a modest man, declined. The other physicians, however, were jealous of his high standing, and being unable to injure him openly, they endeavored to accomplish his ruin in a secret manner.

The king was taken very sick, and Maimonides attended him. Taking advantage of this, the physicians put poison in the draught which Moses had prepared for him, and then informed the king that the latter designed his death. To prove their words, they gave some of the mixture to a dog, and the animal died.

The king was grieved and surprised, and Maimonides, struck dumb with amazement, was unable to say a word.

" Death is the penalty for one who attempts to assassinate his ruler," said the king. "Choose now the mode of thy punishment."

Moses asked for three days for consideration, which the king granted. During this time he prepared a certain mixture, and instructed his pupils to have it ready and apply it according to his directions, when he should be brought home senseless. He then appeared before the king, and desired to have his veins opened. The vital artery was missed, as he had anticipated, and the result was as he had foreseen. After his recovery, he fled from Egypt, taking refuge in a cave, where he wrote his *Yad Hazakah* (the "Strong Hand"), consisting of fourteen divisions, typified by the word *Yad*. which also means fourteen.

Maimonides simplified the Talmudical rules and traditions, making them clear to the comprehension of all. He was the author of an exhaustive work, entitled, *Mishne Torah*, the "Second Law, which was eagerly copied and extensively disseminated. He also wrote many philosophical treatises leveled against atheism, and designed to prove that God produced the world from naught, and at the age of fifty gave to the world his great work, *Moreh Nebuchim* ("Guide of the Perplexed"), to which Rabbi Judah Charizi added an appendix.

Maimonides died at the age of seventy years, and his remains were interred at Cairo, Egypt. Both Jews and Gentiles mourned his loss. The lamentation in Jerusalem was intense, a fast was declared, the synagogues were opened, and a portion of the law (Levit. 25 : 12 to end), and the fifth chapter of Samuel 1, were made parts of the service of the day.

———

During the reign of one of the bishops in Metz, there lived a Jew in that city, who was called Rabbi Amnon. He was of illustrious family, of great personal merit, rich and respected by the Bishop and the people. The Bishop frequently pressed him to abjure Judaism and embrace Christianity, but without the slightest avail. It happened, however, upon a certain day, being more closely pressed than usual, and somewhat anxious to be rid of the Bishop's importunities, he said hastily, " I will consider the subject, and give thee an answer in three days."

24

As soon as he had left the Bishop's presence, however, his heart smote him, and an unquiet conscience blamed him for admitting, even in this manner, a doubt of the true faith.   He reached home overwhelmed with grief; meat was set before him, but he refused to eat; and when his friends visited him and ascertained the cause of his low spirits, he refused their proffered consolation, saying, "I shall go down mourning to the grave for these words." On the third day, while he was still lamenting his imprudent concession, the Bishop sent for him, but he refused to answer the call.

Having refused several of the Bishop's messengers, they were finally ordered to seize him, and bring him by force before the prelate.

"Amnon," said the Bishop, "why didst thou not come to me, according to thy promise, to inform me of thy decision in regard to my request?"

"Let me," answered Amnon, "pronounce my own doom for this neglect.   Let my tongue, which uttered those hasty, doubting words, be cut out; a lie I uttered, for I never intended to consider the proposition."

"Nay," said the Bishop, "I will not cut out thy tongue, but thy feet which refused to come to me, shall be cut off, and the other parts of thy obstinate body shall be also punished and tormented."

Under the Bishop's eye and order, the toes and thumbs of Rabbi Amnon were then cut off, and after having been severely tortured, he was sent home in a carriage, his mangled members beside him.

Rabbi Amnon bore all this with the greatest resignation, firmly hoping and trusting that this earthly torment would plead his pardon with God.

His life after this was of course to be measured only by days.   The Feast of the New Year came round, while he was living, and he desired to be carried to the synagogue. He was conveyed to the house of God, and during the service he requested to be allowed to utter a prayer.   The words which proved to be his last were as follows:—

"I will declare the mighty holiness of this day, for it is awful and tremendous.   Thy kingdom is exalted thereon;

Thy throne is established in mercy, and upon it Thou dost rest in truth. Thou art the Judge, who chastiseth, and from Thee naught may be concealed. Thou bearest witness, writest, sealest, recordest, and rememberest all things, aye, those which we imagine long buried in the past. The Book of Records thou openest; the great *shophar* (cornet) is sounded; even the angels are terrified, and they cry aloud, 'The Day of Judgment dawns upon us,' for in judgment they, the angels, are not faultless.

"All who have entered the world pass before Thee, Even as the shepherd causes the flock he numbers to pass under his crook, so Thou, O Lord, causest every living soul to pass before Thee. Thou numberest, Thou visitest; appointing the limitations of every creature, Thy judgment and Thy sentence.

"On the New Year it is written, on the Day of Atonement it is sealed. Aye, all Thy decrees are recorded. Who is to live and who to die. The names of those to meet death by fire, by water, or by the sword; through hunger, through thirst, and with the pestilence. All is recorded. Those who are to have tranquillity, those who are to be disturbed. Those who are to be troubled, those who are to be blessed with repose. Those who are to be prosperous, those for whom affliction is in store. Those who are to become rich, who poor; who exalted, who cast down; but penitence, prayer, and charity, O Lord, may avert all evil decrees."

When he had finished this declaration, in which he designed to acknowledge his sin and the justice of his punishment, Rabbi Amnon expired, dying fitiy in God's house, among the assembled sons of Israel.

FASTS AND FESTIVALS

PASSOVER

THE feast of unleavened bread, or "Passover," begins
upon the evening of the 14th day of *Nissan* (April),
and was instituted in commemoration of our ancestors' redemption from Egypt, a memorial forever. During
its continuance we are strictly forbidden the use of any
leavened thing.

Moses said to the Israelites in the name of the Lord : —
"Draw out and take for yourselves a lamb," etc.

By the observance of this precept they would deserve well
of God and He would redeem them, for when He spoke
they were "naked and bare" of good deeds and meritorious acts.

"Draw out and take for yourselves a lamb."

Draw yourselves away from the idols which ye are wor-
shiping with the Egyptians, the calves and lambs of stone
and metal, and with one of the same animals through which
ye sin, prepare to fulfill the commandments of your God.

The planet sign of the month *Nissan* is a lamb; therefore, that the Egyptians might not think that through the
powers of the lamb they had thrown off the yoke of slavery, God commanded His people to take a lamb and eat it.

They were commanded to roast it whole and to break no
bone of it, so that the Egyptians might know that it was
indeed a lamb which they had consumed.

The Lord said to Moses, "Tell the children of Israel that
they shall borrow of the Egyptians gold and silver vessels,"
in order that it might not be afterward said, "The words
'they will make them serve, and they will afflict them,' were
fulfilled: but the words 'they shall go out with great substance,' did not come to pass."

When Moses told the Israelites that they should go up out of Egypt with great substance, they answered, "Would that we could go even empty-handed," like to the servant confined in prison.

"To-morrow," said the jailer to him, "I will release thee from prison, and give thee much money."

"Let me go to-day, and give me nothing," replied the prisoner.

On the seventh day of the Passover the children of Israel passed through the Red Sea on dry land.

A man was once traveling along the road and his son preceded him on the way. A robber appeared in the path, and the man put his son behind him. Then lo, a wolf came after the lad, and his father lifted him up and carried him within his arms.

The sea was before the Israelites, the Egyptians were behind them, so God lifted up His child and carried it within His arms.

When Israel suffered from the hot rays of the sun God "spread the cloud for a covering;" when they were hungry He sent them bread from heaven; and when they thirsted "He brought forth floods from a rock."

PENTECOST

The Feast of Weeks, or "Pentecost," occurs upon the sixth day of the third month, *Sivan* (June). It is called the Feast of Weeks because forty-nine days, or seven weeks, duly numbered, elapse between the second day of Passover, when (during the existence of the Temple) a sheaf of green barley was offered, and this festival, when two loaves made of the first flour of the wheat harvest were "brought before the Lord." It is also the anniversary of the delivery of the commandment from Mount Sinai.

Why does not the Bible particularize in this as on other occasions, and say directly, "On the sixth day of the third month was the law given?"

Because in ancient times the men called "wise" placed their faith and dependence upon the planets. They divided these into seven, apportioning one to each day of the week. Some nations selected for their greatest god the sun, other nations the moon, and so on, and prayed to them and worshiped them. They knew not that the planets moved and changed according to the course of nature, established by the Most High, a course which He might change according to His will, and into their ignorant ideas many of the Israelites had entered. Therefore, as they considered the planets as seven, God made many other things depending on that number, to show that as He made them, so had He made the planets.

The seventh day of the week He made the Sabbath; the seventh year he made the year of rest; after seven times seven years, or after seven Sabbatical years, He ordained the Jubilee, or year of release. Seven days He gave to the Passover festival, and seven days to the Feast of Tabernacles. Seven days was Jericho surrounded, and seven priests took seven trumpets and marched round its walls seven times upon the seventh day.

Therefore, after numbering seven weeks during the ripening time of the grain, the Israelites were to hold a holy convocation, to praise the One who can prevent all things, but who cannot be prevented; who can change all things, but is unchangeable.

The first day the Israelites were redeemed from slavery and superstition; the fiftieth day a law was given them for their guide through life; therefore they are commanded to number these days and remember them.

The children of Ishmael, says the legend, were asked to accept the law. "What does it contain?" they asked. "Thou shalt not steal," was the answer. "How can we then accept it," they returned, "when thus was our forefather blessed, 'Thy hand shall be against every man?'"

The children of Esau were asked to accept the law, and they also inquired, "What does it contain?" "Thou shalt not kill," was the answer. "We cannot accept it, then," said they, "for thus did our father Isaac bless us, 'By the sword shalt thou live.'"

When Israel was asked to accept the law, the people answered, "We will do and obey."

New Year, or the Day of Memorial

On the first day of the seventh month, *Tishri* (October), is the commemoration of the creation of the world. Then the cornet is blown to announce to the people that a new year has begun its course, and to warn them to examine strictly their conduct and make amends therein where amends are needed.

Would not any person of sense, knowing that he must appear before a Court of Judgment, prepare himself therefor? Either in a civil or a criminal case would he not seek for counsel? How much more, then, is it incumbent upon him to prepare for a meeting with the King of kings, before whom all things are revealed. No counsel can help him in his case; repentance, devotion, charity, these are the arguments which must plead in his favor. Therefore, a person should search his actions and repent his transgressions previous to the day of judgment. In the month of *Elul* (September) he should arouse himself to a consciousness of the dread justice awaiting all mankind.

This is the season when the Lord pardoned the Israelites who had worshiped the molten calf. He commanded Moses to reascend the mount for a second tablet, after he had destroyed the first. Thus say the sages, "The Lord said unto Moses in the month *Elul*, 'Go up unto me on the mountain,' and Moses went up and received the second tablet at the end of forty days. Before he ascended he caused the trumpet to be sounded through the camp." Since that time it is customary to sound the *shophar* (cornet) in the synagogues, to give warning to the people that the day of judgment, New Year, is rapidly approaching, and with it the Day of Atonement. Therefore, propitiatory prayers are said twice every day, morning and evening, from the second day of *Elul* until the eve of the Day of Atonement, which period comprises the last forty days which Moses passed on Sinai, when God was reconciled to Israel and pardoned their transgressions with the molten calf.

Rabbi Eleazer said, "Abraham and Jacob were born in *Tishri*, and in *Tishri* they died. On the first of *Tishri* the universe was created, and during the Passover was Isaac born. On the first of *Tishri* (New Year), Sarah, Rachel, and Hannah, three barren women, were visited. On the first day of *Tishri* our ancestors discontinued their rigorous labor in Egypt. On the first of *Tishri* Adam was created; from his existence we count our years, that is the sixth day of the creation. On that day, too, did he eat of the forbidden fruit, therefore is the season appointed for one of penitence, for the Lord said to Adam, 'This shall be for a sign in future generations; thy descendants shall be judged upon these days, and they shall be appointed as days of pardon and forgiveness.'"

Four times in the year the Lord pronounces His decrees.

First, New Year, the first of *Tishri*. Then the judgments of all human beings for the coming year are ordained.

Second, The first day of Passover. Then the scarcity or fullness of the crops is determined.

Third, Pentecost. Then the Lord blesses the fruit of the trees, or bids them bear not in plenty.

Fourth, The Feast of Tabernacles. Then the Lord determines whether the rain shall bless the earth in its due season or not.

Man is judged on New Year's and the decree is made final on the Day of Atonement.

Rabbi Nathan has said that man is judged at all times.

Thus taught Rabbi Akiba. "Why does the law command the bringing of a sheaf of barley on the Passover? Because the Passover is the season of the harvest of the grain. The Lord says, 'Offer for me a sheaf of barley on Passover, that I may bless the grain which is in the field.'

"Why does the Bible say, 'Bring two loaves of the new wheat on Pentecost?' Because at Pentecost time the fruit ripens, and God says, 'Offer for me two loaves of the new wheat, in order that I may bless the fruit which is on the trees.'

"Why were we commanded to bring a drink-offering of water into the Temple on the Feast of Tabernacles? Because then is the season of rain, and the Lord says, 'Bring the drink-offering of water to me, in order that I may bless the rain of the year.'

"Why do they make the cornet which they blow of a ram's horn? In order that the Lord may remember the ram which was sacrificed instead of Isaac, and allow the merits of the patriarchs to weigh in favor of their descendants, as it is written in the Decalogue, 'Showing mercy to thousands of those who love me and keep my commandments.'"

On New Year's day they recite in the synagogues the record of the binding of Isaac for the same purpose. While God has mercy upon His creatures He gives them a season for repentance, that they may not perish in their wickedness, therefore as it is written in Lamentations 3 : 40, we should "search through and investigate our ways and return unto the Lord."

During the year man is apt to grow callous as to his transgressions, therefore the cornet is sounded to arouse him to the consciousness of the time which is passing so rapidly away. "Rouse thee from thy sleep," it says to him; "the hour of thy visitation approaches." The Eternal wishes not to destroy His children, merely to arouse them to repentance and good resolves.

Three classes of people are arraigned for judgment: the righteous, the wicked, and the indifferent. To the righteous the Lord awards a happy life; the wicked He condemns, and to the indifferent ones He grants a respite. From New Year's day until the Day of Atonement His judgment He holds in abeyance; if they repent truly they are classed with the righteous for a happy life, and if they remain untouched, they are counted with the wicked.

Three sounds for the cornet are commanded in the Bible. A pure sound (*T'kiah*), a sound of alarm or trembling (*T'ruah*), and, thirdly, a pure sound again (*T'kiah*).

The first sound typifies man's first awakening to penitence; he must search well his heart, desert his evil ways, and purify his thoughts, as it is written, "Let the wicked forsake his ways and the man of unrighteousness his thoughts, and let him return unto the Lord."

The alarm sound typifies the sorrow which a repentant man feels for his misconduct and his earnest determination to reform.

The last sound is the pure sound again, which typifies a sincere resolve to keep the repentant heart incorrupt.

The Bible says to us:—

"The word is very nigh unto thee, in thy mouth and in thy heart, that thou mayest do it." This verse teaches us that repentance is nearer to those who believe in God and His book than fanatics would make it. Difficult penances are ordained for the sinner among them. He must fast many days, or travel barefoot through rugged ways, or sleep in the open air. But we are not required to travel to the nether end of the ocean or to climb to mountain tops, for our Holy Word says to us, "It is not in heaven, neither is it beyond the sea, but the Word is very nigh."

In three ways may we repent:—

First, By words of mouth, finding birth in an honest heart.

Secondly, With our feelings, sorrow for sins committed.

Thirdly, By good deeds in the future.

Rabbi Saadiah declared that God commanded us to sound the cornet on New Year's day for ten reasons.

First, Because this day is the beginning of the creation, when God began to reign over the world, and as it is customary to sound the trumpets at the coronation of a king, we should in like manner proclaim by the sound of the cornet that the Creator is our king,— as David said, "With trumpets and the sound of the cornet, shout ye before the Lord."

Secondly, As the New Year day is the first of the ten penitential days, we sound the cornet as a proclamation to admonish all to return to God and repent. If they do not so, they at least have been informed, and cannot plead ignorance. Thus we find that earthly kings publish their decrees with such concomitant, that none may say, "We heard not this."

Thirdly, To remind us of the law given on Mount Sinai, where it is said, "The voice of the cornet was exceeding loud." To remind us also that we should bind ourselves anew to the performance of its precepts, as did our ancestors, when they said, "All that the Lord hath said will we do and obey."

Fourthly, To remind us of the prophets, who were compared to watchmen blowing the trumpet of alarm, as we find in Ezekiel, "Whosoever heareth the sound of the cornet and taketh not warning, and the sound cometh and taketh him away, his blood shall be upon his own head; but he that taketh warning shall save his life."

Fifthly, To remind us of the destruction of the Temple and the fearsome sound of the battle-cry of our enemies. "Because thou hast heard, oh my soul, the sound of the trumpet, the alarm of war." Therefore when we hear the sound of the cornet we should implore God to rebuild the Temple.

Sixthly, To remind us of the binding of Isaac, who willingly offered himself for immolation, in order to sanctify the Holy Name.

Seventhly, That when we hear the terrifying sound, we may, through dread, humble ourselves before the Supreme Being, for it is the nature of these martial instruments to produce a sensation of terror, as the prophet Amos observes, "Shall a trumpet be blown in a city, and the people not to be terrified?"

Eightly, To remind us of the great and terrible Day of Judgment, on which the trumpet is to be sounded, as we find in Zeph., "The great day of the Lord is near, and hasteneth much, a day of the trumpet and of shouting."

Ninthly, To remind us to pray for the time when the outcasts of Israel are to be gathered together, as promised in Isaiah, "And it shall come to pass in that day, the great trumpet shall be sounded, and those shall come who were perishing in the land of Assyria."

Tenthly, To remind us of the resurrection of the dead, and our firm belief therein. "Yea, all ye that inhabit the world, and that dwell on the earth, when the standard is lifted upon the mountain, behold, and when the trumpet is sounded, hear!" says the prophet Isaiah.

Therefore should we set our hearts to these seasons, and fulfill the precept that the Bible commands us, as it is written : —

"And the Lord commanded us to do all the statutes . . . that it might be well with us at all times."

The Day of Atonement

The hearts of all who fear God should tremble with the reflection that all the deeds of the creature are known to the Creator, and will be by Him accounted to them for good or evil. God is ready at all times to acknowledge true penitence ; and of repentance there are seven degrees :

First, the righteous man, who repents his misconduct as soon as he becomes aware of his sin. This is the best and most complete.

Secondly, Of the man who has for some time led a life of sin, yet who, in the vigor of his days, gives over his evil ways and conquers his wrong inclinations. As Solomon has said, "Remember thy Creator in the days of thy youthful vigor." While in the prime of life abandon thy evil ways.

Thirdly, Of the one who was prevented by some cause from the commission of a contemplated sin, and who truly repents his evil intention. "Happy is the man who fears the Lord," said the Psalmist. The man, not the woman? Aye, all mankind. The word is used to denote strength ; those who repent while still in their youth.

Fourthly, of the one who repents when his sin is pointed out to him, and he is rebuked for the same, as in the instance of the inhabitants of Nineveh. They repented not until Jonah proclaimed to them, "Yet forty days more, and Nineveh shall be overthrown." The men of Nineveh believed in God's mercy, and though the decree had been pronounced against them, yet they repented. "And God saw their work, that they had returned from their evil ways, and God bethought Himself of the evil which He had spoken that He would do to them, and He did it not." Therefore say the Rabbis, "Our brethren, neither sackcloth nor fasting will gain forgiveness for sins; but repentance of the heart and good deeds; for it is not said of the men of Nineveh, "God saw their fasting and sackcloth," but "God saw their work, that they had turned from their evil ways."

Fifthly, Of those who repent when trouble befalls them. How much nobler is this than human nature! Instance Jephtah: "Did ye not hate me . . . and why are ye come unto me now when you are in distress?" But the infinite mercy of our God accepts even such repentance; as it is written, "When thou art in tribulation, and all these things have overtaken thee . . . then wilt thou return unto the Lord thy God." Founded upon this is the proverb of the fathers, "Repentance and good deeds form a shield against punishment."

Sixthly, The repentance of age. Even when man grows old and feeble, if he repents truly, his atonement will be received. As the Psalmist says, "Thou turnest man to contrition, and sayest, 'Return, ye children of men.'" Meaning, man can return at any time or any age, "Return, ye children of men."

Say the Rabbis, "Although a man has been righteous in his youth and vigor, yet if he rebels against the will of God in his old age, the merit of his former goodness shall be lost to him, as it is written, 'When a righteous man turns away from his righteousness and doeth wrong, and dieth therefor; through his wrong which he hath done must he die.' But a man who has been wicked in his early days, and feels true sorrow and pentinence in his old age, shall not be called 'wicked' any more. This, however, is not gracious penitence when it is so long delayed."

Seventhly, Is the last degree of penitence. Of the one who is rebellious against his Creator during all the days of his life; turns to Him only when the hand of death is laid upon him.

Say the Rabbis, if a person is sick, and the hour of his decease approaches, they who are by his deathbed should say to him, "Confess thy sins to thy Creator."

They who are near the point of death should confess their shortcomings. The sick man is as the man who is before a court of justice. The latter may have advocates to defend him or laud his case, but the only advocates of the former must be penitence and good deeds. As is written in the Book of Job, "If there be now about him one single angel as defender, one out of a thousand, to tell for man his uprightness; then is he gracious unto him, and saith, 'Release him from going down to the pit; I have found an atonement.'"

Thus we have seven different degrees of penitence, and he who neglects them all must suffer in the world to come. Therefore fulfill the duties laid upon you; repent as long as you are able to amend. As the Rabbis say, "Repent in the antechamber, that thou mayest enter the room of state."

"Turn ye, turn ye from your evil ways; wherefore will ye die, O house of Israel!" exclaimed the prophet Ezekiel; and what does this warning mean? without repentance ye shall die.

Penitence is thus illustrated by a parable: —

There was once a great ship which had been sailing for many days upon the ocean. Before it reached its destination, a high wind arose, which drove it from its course; until, finally, becalmed close to a pleasant-appearing island, the anchor was dropped. There grew upon this island beautiful flowers and luscious fruits in "great profusion"; tall trees lent a pleasing, cooling shade to the place, which appeared to the ship's passengers most desirable and inviting. They divided themselves into five parties; the first party determined not to leave the ship, for said they, "A fair wind may arise, the anchor may be raised, and the ship sail on, leaving us behind; we will not risk the chance of missing our destination for the temporary pleasure which this island offers." The second party went on shore for a short time, enjoyed the perfume of the flowers, tasted of the fruit, and returned to the ship happy and refreshed, finding their places as they had left them; losing nothing, but rather gaining in health and good spirits by the recreation of their visit on shore. The third party also visited the island, but they stayed so long that the fair wind did arise, and hurrying back they just reached the ship as the sailors were lifting the anchor, and in the haste and confusion many lost their places, and were not as comfortable during the balance of their voyage as at the outset. They were wiser, however, than the fourth party; these latter stayed so long upon the island and tasted so deeply of its pleasures, that they allowed the ship's bell of warning to sound unheeded. Said they, "The sails are still to be set; we may enjoy ourselves a few minutes more." Again the bell sounded, and still they lingered, thinking, "The captain will not sail without us." So they remained on shore until they saw the ship moving; then in wild haste they swam after it and scrambled up the sides, but the bruises and injuries which they encountered in so doing were not healed during the remainder of the voyage. But, alas, for the fifth party. They ate and drank so deeply that they did not even hear the bell, and when the ship started they were left behind. Then the wild beasts hid in the thickets made of them a prey, and they who escaped this evil, perished from the poison of surfeit.

The "ship" is our good deeds, which bear us to our destination, heaven. The "island" typifies the pleasures of the world, which the first set of passengers refused to taste or look upon, but which when enjoyed temperately, as by the second party, make our lives pleasant, without causing us to neglect our duties. These pleasures must not be allowed, however, to gain too strong a hold upon our senses. True, we may return, as the third party, while there is yet time and but little bad effect, or even as the fourth party at the eleventh hour, saved, but with bruises and injuries which cannot be entirely healed; but we are in danger of becoming as the last party, spending a lifetime in the pursuit of vanity, forgetting the future, and perishing even of the poison concealed in the sweets which attracted us.

Who hath sorrow? Who hath woe?

He who leaves much wealth to his heirs, and takes with him to the grave a burden of sins. He who gathers wealth without justice. "He that gathereth riches and not by

right in the midst of his days shall he leave them." To
the portals of eternity his gold and his silver cannot accompany the soul of man ; good deeds and trust in God
must be his directing spirits.

Although God is merciful and pardons the sins of man
against Himself, he who has wronged his neighbor must
gain that neighbor's forgiveness before he can claim the
mercy of the Lord. "This must ye do," said Rabbi
Eleazer, " that ye may be clean from all your sins before
the Lord. The Day of Atonement may gain pardon for
the sins of man against his Maker, but not for those
against his fellow-man, till every wrong done is satisfied."

If a man is called upon to pardon his fellow, freely he
must do it ; else how can he dare, on the Day of Atonement, to ask pardon for his sins against the Eternal? It is
customary on this day for a man to thoroughly cleanse
himself bodily and spiritually, and to array himself in
white fresh clothing, to typify the words of Isaiah, "Though
your sins should be as scarlet, they shall become white as
snow."

It happened that the mayor of a city once sent his servant to the market to purchase some fish. When he reached
the place of sale he found that all the fish save one had
been sold, and this one a Jewish tailor was about purchas-
ing. Said the mayor's servant, " I will give one gold piece
for it ; " said the tailor, " I will give two." The mayor's
messenger then expressed his willingness to pay three gold
pieces for it, but the tailor claimed the fish, and said he
would not lose it though he should be obliged to pay ten
gold pieces for it. The mayor's servant then returned
home, and in anger related the circumstance to his master.
The mayor sent for his subject, and when the latter appeared before him asked : —

" What is thy occupation?"

" A tailor, sir," replied the man.

" Then how canst thou afford to pay so great a price for
a fish, and how dare degrade my dignity by offering for it
a larger sum than that offered by my servant?"

25

" I fast to-morrow," replied the tailor, " and I wished the fish to eat to-day, that I might have strength to do so. I would not have lost it even for ten pieces of gold."

" What is to-morrow more than any other day? " asked the mayor.

" Why art thou more than any other man? " returned the other.

" Because the king hath appointed me to this office."

" Well," replied the tailor, " the King of kings hath appointed this day to be holier than all other days, for on this day we hope that God will pardon our transgressions."

" If this be the case thou wert right," answered the mayor, and the Israelite departed in peace.

Thus if a person's intention is to obey God, nothing can hinder its accomplishment. On this day God commanded His children to fast, but they must strengthen their bodies to obey Him by eating on the day before. It is a person's duty to sanctify himself, bodily and spiritually, for the approach of this great day. He should be ready to enter at any moment into the Fearful Presence with repentance and good deeds as his companions.

A certain man had three friends. One of these he loved dearly ; the second he loved also, but not as intensely as the first ; but toward the third one he was quite indifferently disposed.

Now the king of the country sent an officer to this man, commanding his immediate appearance before the throne. Greatly terrified was the man at this summons. He thought that somebody had been speaking evil of him, or probably accusing him falsely before his sovereign, and being afraid to appear unaccompanied before the royal presence, he resolved to ask one of his friends to go with him. First he naturally applied to his dearest friend, but he at once declined to go, giving no reason and no excuse for his lack of friendliness. So the man applied to his second friend, who said to him : —

" I will go with thee as far as the palace gates, but I will not enter with thee before the king."

In desperation the man applied to his third friend, the one whom he had neglected, but who replied to him at once : —

"Fear not; I will go with thee, and I will speak in thy defense. I will not leave thee until thou art delivered from thy trouble."

The "first friend" is a man's wealth, which he must leave behind him when he dies. The "second friend" is typified by the relatives who follow him to the grave and leave him when the earth has covered his remains. The "third friend," he who entered with him into the presence of the king, is as the good deeds of a man's life, which never desert, but accompany him to plead his cause before the King of kings, who regardeth not person nor taketh bribery.

Thus taught Rabbi Eleazer : —

"On this great and tearful day the angel Samal finds no blots, no sins on Israel." Thus he addresses the Most High : —

"'O Sovereign Lord, upon the earth this day one nation pure and innocent exists. Even as the angels is Israel on this Atonement Day. As peace exists in heaven, so rests it now upon this people, praying to Thy Holy Name.'

"God hears this testimony of His angel, and pardon's all His people's sins."

But though the Almighty thus forgives our sins, we may not repeat them with impunity, for "to such a one as saith, 'I will commit a sin and repent,' there can be no forgiveness, no repentance."

FEAST OF TABERNACLES

The Feast of Tabernacles begins on the fifteenth day of the seventh month, *Tishri* (October), and during its continuance, seven days, the Israelites are commanded to dwell in tabernacles or booths. This is designed to keep fresh in their memory the tents with formed their homes during their forty years' sojourn in the wilderness. The symbols of the festival are branches of the palm, bound with sprigs of myrtle and willow, and a citron.

The Lord said, "This is not to be to you a fast as the Day of Atonement; eat, drink, be merry, and sacrifice peace-offerings thereon." The Bible says, "Seven days unto the Lord"; therefore we should in all our merriment devote a few serious thoughts to Him.

The Feast of Tabernacles is held in the autumn, after the fruits of the field have been garnered in the storehouses, according to the words of the Bible, "The Feast of Tabernacles shalt thou hold for thyself seven days when thou hast gathered in the produce of thy thesh-floor and thy wine-press."

This dwelling in booths is also to bring to mind the manner in which the Israelites lived for forty years after they left Egypt. With merely temporary walls to protect them from summer's heat and winter's cold, from wind and storm. God was with them through all their generations, and they were protected from all evil.

According to the opinion of some of the Rabbis, the Israelites did not really dwell in booths in the wilderness, but were surrounded by clouds — by seven clouds. Four clouds, one at each of the four sides; a fifth, a shadow, to protect them from the hot rays of the sun; the sixth, a pillar of fire to give them light by night (they being able to see as clearly by night as by day); and the seventh, to precede their journeying and direct their way.

The children of Isael departed from Egypt in *Nissan* (April), and obtained immediately these booths, which they made use of for forty years. Thus they were in booths during the entire cycle of the year, and we could as easily commemorate this fact in the spring as in the fall, in the summer as in the winter. Why, then, has God made autumn, and neither spring nor summer, the season of observance? Because if we dwelt in booths in the summer, it would be a question whether we did so in obedience to God's behest or for our own gratification; for many people seek airy retreats during this season; but in the fall, when the trees lose their leaves, and the air grows cold and chilling, and it is the time to fix our houses for the winter, then by inhabiting these temporary residences, we display our desire to do as our Creator has bidden us.

The Feast of Tabernacles is also the Feast of Ingathering, when we should thank God for the kindness shown us, and the treasure with which He has blessed us. When the Eternal has provided man with his sustenance, in the long evenings which follow he should meditate and study his Bible, and make this indeed a " feast to the Lord," and not entirely for personal gratification.

The four species belonging to the vegetable kingdom which we use in this festival, are designed to remind us of the four elements of nature, which work under the direction and approval of the Most High, and without which all things would cease to exist. Therefore the Bible commands us on this " feast of the Lord," to give thanks, and bring before Him these four species, each typifying one of the elements.

" Ye shall take for yourselves the fruit of the tree *hadar* " (the citron). Its color is high yellow and resembles fire. The second species is the palm branch (Heb. *Lulab*). The palm is a high tree, growing up straight in the air, and its fruit is sweet and delicious to the taste; this then represents the second element, air. The third is the bough of the myrtle, one of the lowliest of trees, growing close to the ground; its nature, cold and dry as earth, fits it to represent that element. The fourth is " the willow of the brook," which grows in perfection close beside the water, dropping its branches into the stream, and symbolizing thus the last element, water.

The Bible teaches us that for each of these four elements we owe special thanks to God.

The citron we hold in the left hand, and the other three we grasp together in the right. This we do because the citron contains in itself all that the others represent. The outside skin is yellow, fire; the inside skin is white and damp, air; the pulp is watery, water; and the seeds are dry, earth. It is taken into the left hand, because the right hand is strongest, and the citron is but one, while the other emblems are three.

These four emblems represent likewise the four principal members of the human body. The citron is shaped somewhat like a heart, without which we could not live, and with which man should serve his fellows; the palm branch represents the spine, which is the foundation of the human

frame, in front of which the heart lies; this signifies that
we should serve God with our entire body.   The branches
of the myrtle resemble a human eye, with which man recognizes the deeds of his fellows, and with which he may
obtain a knowledge of the law.   The leaves of the willow
represent the lips, with which man may serve the Eternal
and thank Him.   The myrtle is mentioned in the Bible before the willow, because we are able to see and know a
thing before we can call its name with our lips; man
is able to look into the Bible before he can study the
same.   Therefore, with these four principal parts of the
human frame should we praise the Creator, as David
said, " All my bones shall say, O Lord, who is like unto
Thee?"

Maimonides, in his work called *Moreh Nebuchim* (" The
Guide of the Perplexed "), explains that God commanded
the Israelites to take these four emblems during this festival to remind them that they were brought out from the
wilderness, where no fruit grew, and no people lived, into
a land of brooklets, waters, a land flowing with milk and
honey.   For this reason did God command us to hold in
our hands the precious fruit of this land while singing
praises to Him, the One who wrought miracles in our behalf, who feeds and supports us from the productiveness
of the earth.

The four emblems are different in taste, appearance, and
odor, even as the sons of men are different in conduct and
habits.

The citron is a valuable fruit; it is good for food and
has a most pleasant odor.   It is compared to the intelligent
man, who is righteous in his conduct toward God and his
fellow-man.   The odor of the fruit is his good deeds; its
substance is his learning, on which others may feed.
This is perfect among the emblems, and is, therefore,
always mentioned first, and taken by itself in one
hand.

The palm branch brings forth fruit, but is without odor.
It is compared to those people who are learned, but who
are wanting in good deeds; they who know the law, but
transgress its mandates.

The myrtle is compared to those people who are naturally good, who act correctly toward God and man, but who are uneducated.

The willow of the brook has neither fruit nor odor; it is, therefore, compared to the people who have no knowledge and who perform no good deeds.

The Rabbis have said that he who has failed to participate in the keeping of the Tabernacle Festival in Jerusalem has failed to taste real enjoyment in his life. The first day of the feast was kept with great solemnity, and the middle days with joy and gladness in various methods of public amusement.

The Temple in Jerusalem was provided with a gallery for the women, which was called the apartment of the women, and the men sat below, as is still the custom of the synagogue. Thither all repaired. The young priests filled the lamps of the large chandeliers with oil, and lighted them all, even that the place was so bright that its reflection lighted the streets of the city. Hymns and praises were chanted by the pious ones, and the Levites praised the Lord with harps, cornets, trumpets, flutes, and other instruments of harmony. They stood upon fifteen broad steps, reaching from the lower floor to the gallery, the court of the women. And they sang fifteen psalms as they ascended, beginning with "A song of Degrees," and the large choir joined voices with them. The ancient Hillel was accustomed to address the assemblages on these occasions.

"If God's presence dwells here," he was used to say, "then are ye here, each one of you, the souls of each; but if God should be removed from your midst through disobedience then which of you could be here?" For the Lord has said. "If thou wilt come to My house, then will I come to thy house, but if thou refusest to visit My dwelling, I will also neglect to enter yours;" as it is written, "In every place where I shall permit My name to be mentioned I will come unto thee and I will bless thee."

Then some of the people answered: —

"Happy were the days of our youth, for they have not set to blush the days of our old age." These were men of piety.

Others answered : —

"Happy is our old age, for therein have we atoned for the sins of our youth." These were repentants.

Then joining together, both parties said : —

"Happy is the one who is free from sin ; but ye who have sinned, repent, return to God, and ye will be forgiven."

The festival was continued during the entire night ; for when the religious exercises concluded the people gave themselves up to innocent but thorough enjoyment.

This festival was also called the "Festival of Drawing Water."

Because, during the existence of the Temple, wine was offered during the year for a burnt-offering, but on the Feast of Tabernacles they offered two drink-offerings, one of wine and one of water. Of the other they made a special festival on the second day of the Tabernacle assemblage, calling it the Feast of Drawing the Water. It was founded upon the words of the prophet : —

"And ye shall draw water with joy from the fountains of salvation."

HANNUKAH

This festival is observed for eight days during the ninth month *Kislev* (December), and commemorates the dedication of the Temple after it had been defiled by Antiochus Epiphanes, whose armies were overthrown by the valiant Maccabees, Hashmoneans.

The Most Holy One has frequently wrought wonders in behalf of his children in their hour of need, and thereby displayed His supreme power to the nations of the world. These should prevent man from growing infidel and ascribing all happiness to the course of nature. The God who created the world from naught, may change at His will the nature which He established. When the Hashmoneans gained, with the aid of God, their great victory, and restored peace and harmony to their land, their first act was to cleanse and dedicate the Temple, which had been defiled, and on the twenty-fifth day of *Kislev*, in obedience to the teachings of the Rabbis, we inaugurate the "Dedi-

cation Feast" by lighting the lamps or candles prepared
expressly for this occasion. The first night we light one,
and then an additional one each succeeding night of its
continuance. We also celebrate it by hymns of thanksgiv-
ing and hallelujahs.

This feast is foreshadowed in the Book of Numbers.
When Aaron observed the offerings of the princes of each
of the tribes and their great liberality, he was conscious of
a feeling of regret, because he and his tribe were unable to
join with them. But these words were spoken to comfort
him, "Aaron, thy merit is greater than theirs, for thou
lightest and fixest the holy lamps."

When were these words spoken?

When he was charged with the blessing to be found in
Numbers 6 : 23, as will be found in the Book of Maccabees
in the Apocrypha.

The Lord said unto Moses, "Thus say unto Aaron. In
the generations to come, there will be another dedication
and lighting of the lamps, and through thy descendants
shall the service be performed. Miracles and wonders will
accompany this dedication. Fear not for the greatness of
the princes of thy tribe ; during the existence of the Temple thou shalt sacrifice, but the lighting of the lamps shall
be forever, and the blessing with which I have charged
thee to bless the people shall also exist forever. Through
the destruction of the Temple the sacrifices will be abolished,
but the lighting of the dedication of the Hashmoneans will
never cease."

The Rabbis have ordained this celebration by lighting of
lamps, to make God's miracle known to all coming generations, and it is our duty to light the same in the synagogues and in our homes.

Although the Lord afflicted Israel on account of iniquities, He still showed mercy, and allowed not a complete
destruction, and to this festival do the Rabbis again apply
the verse in Leviticus 26 : 44 : —

"And yet for all that, though they be in the land of
their enemies, will I not cast them away, neither will I
loathe them to destroy them utterly, to break my covenant
with them, for I am the Lord their God."

And thus do the Rabbis explain the same : —

"Will I not cast them away." In the time of the Chaldeans I appointed Daniel and his companions to deliver them.

"Neither will I loathe them." In the time of the Assyrians I gave them Matthias, his sons and their comrades, to serve them.

"To destroy them." In the time of Haman I sent Mordecai and Esther to rescue them.

"To break my covenant with them." In the time of the Romans I appointed Rabbi Judah and his associates to work their salvation.

"For I am the Eternal, your God." In the future no nation shall rule over Israel, and the descendants of Abraham shall be restored to their independent state.

The dedication commemorated by Hannukah occurred in the year 3632 — 129 B. C. E.

PURIM

This festival, occurring on the fourteenth day of the twelfth month, *Adar* (March), is to commemorate the deliverance of the Hebrews from the wiles of Haman, through the God-aided means of Mordecai and Esther.

Although the Holy One threatens the Israelites, in order that they may repent of their sins, He has also tempted them, in order to increase their reward.

For instance, a father who loves his son, and desires him to improve his conduct, must punish him for his misdeeds; but it is a punishment induced by affection which he bestows.

A certain apostate once said to Rabbi Saphra : —

"It is written, 'Because I know you more than all the nations of the earth, therefore I visit upon you your iniquities;' how is this? If a person has a wild horse, is it likely that he would put his dearest friend upon it, that he might be thrown and hurt?"

Rabbi Saphra answered : —

"Suppose a man lends money to two persons; one of these is his friend, the other his enemy. He will allow his friend to repay him in installments, that the discharge of the debt may not prove onerous; but from his enemy he will require the amount in full. The verse you quote will apply in the same manner, 'I love you, therefore will I visit upon you your iniquities;' meaning, 'I will punish you for them as they occur, little by little, by which means you may have quittance and happiness in the world to come.'"

The action of the king in delivering his signet ring to Haman had more effect upon the Jews than the precepts and warnings of forty-eight prophets who lectured to them early and late. They clothed themselves in sackcloth, and repented truly with tears and fasting, and God had compassion upon them and destroyed Haman.

Although the reading of the Book of Esther (*Megilah*) on Purim is not a precept of the Pentateuch, 'tis nevertheless binding upon us and our descendants. Therefore the day is appointed as one of feasting and gladness, and interchange of presents, and also of gifts to the poor, that they too may rejoice. As in the decree of Haman, no distinction was made between rich and poor, as all alike were doomed to destruction, it is proper that all should have equal cause to feel joyful, and therefore in all generations the poor should be liberally remembered on this day.